AF707478

Engineering the Metaverse

Other related titles:

You may also like

- PBTE112 | Imoize | Advanced Metaverse Wireless Communication Systems | Contracted May 2023
- PBCE135 | Ganesh | Cognitive Sensors for Computer Vision, in production | Published Aug 2023
- PBPC073 – PBPC074 – PBPC075 | Zhou | Computer Vision: Fundamentals, technologies and applications | Contracted Nov 2023
- PBPC021 | Lafruit | Virtual Reality and Light Field Immersive Video Technologies for Real-World Applications | Published Dec 2021
- PBHE042 | Chowdhary | Computer Vision and Recognition Systems Using Machine and Deep Learning Approaches: Fundamentals, technologies and applications | Published Oct 2021

We also publish a wide range of books on the following topics:
Computing and Networks
Control, Robotics and Sensors
Electrical Regulations
Electromagnetics and Radar
Energy Engineering
Healthcare Technologies
History and Management of Technology
IET Codes and Guidance
Materials, Circuits and Devices
Model Forms
Nanomaterials and Nanotechnologies
Optics, Photonics and Lasers
Production, Design and Manufacturing
Security
Telecommunications
Transportation

All books are available in print via https://shop.theiet.org or as eBooks via our Digital Library https://digital-library.theiet.org.

IET COMPUTING SERIES 070

Engineering the Metaverse

Enabling technologies, platforms and use cases

Edited by
Pethuru Raj
Prasanna Kumar, D. P. Sharma, Kavita Saini,
B. Narendra Kumar Rao, Harshavardhan Kosuri,
Nagendra Panini Challa and R. Ranjana

The Institution of Engineering and Technology

About the IET

This book is published by the Institution of Engineering and Technology (The IET).

We inspire, inform and influence the global engineering community to engineer a better world. As a diverse home across engineering and technology, we share knowledge that helps make better sense of the world, to accelerate innovation and solve the global challenges that matter.

The IET is a not-for-profit organisation. The surplus we make from our books is used to support activities and products for the engineering community and promote the positive role of science, engineering and technology in the world. This includes education resources and outreach, scholarships and awards, events and courses, publications, professional development and mentoring, and advocacy to governments.

To discover more about the IET please visit https://www.theiet.org/.

About IET books

The IET publishes books across many engineering and technology disciplines. Our authors and editors offer fresh perspectives from universities and industry. Within our subject areas, we have several book series steered by editorial boards made up of leading subject experts.

We peer review each book at the proposal stage to ensure the quality and relevance of our publications.

Get involved

If you are interested in becoming an author, editor, series advisor, or peer reviewer please visit https://www.theiet.org/publishing/publishing-with-iet-books/ or contact author_support@theiet.org.

Discovering our electronic content

All of our books are available online via the IET's Digital Library. Our Digital Library is the home of technical documents, eBooks, conference publications, real-life case studies and journal articles. To find out more, please visit https://digital-library.theiet.org.

In collaboration with the United Nations and the International Publishers Association, the IET is a Signatory member of the SDG Publishers Compact. The Compact aims to accelerate progress to achieve the Sustainable Development Goals (SDGs) by 2030. Signatories aspire to develop sustainable practices and act as champions of the SDGs during the Decade of Action (2020–30), publishing books and journals that will help inform, develop, and inspire action in that direction.

In line with our sustainable goals, our UK printing partner has FSC accreditation, which is reducing our environmental impact to the planet. We use a print-on-demand model to further reduce our carbon footprint.

Published by The Institution of Engineering and Technology, London, United Kingdom

The Institution of Engineering and Technology (the "**Publisher**") is registered as a Charity in England & Wales (no. 211014) and Scotland (no. SC038698).

Copyright © The Institution of Engineering and Technology and its licensors 2024

First published 2024

All intellectual property rights (including copyright) in and to this publication are owned by the Publisher and/or its licensors. All such rights are hereby reserved by their owners and are protected under the Copyright, Designs and Patents Act 1988 ("**CDPA**"), the Berne Convention and the Universal Copyright Convention.

With the exception of:

(i) any use of the publication solely to the extent as permitted under:

a. the CDPA (including fair dealing for the purposes of research, private study, criticism or review); or
b. the terms of a licence granted by the Copyright Licensing Agency ("**CLA**") (only applicable where the publication is represented by the CLA); and/or

(ii) any use of those parts of the publication which are identified within this publication as being reproduced by the Publisher under a Creative Commons licence, Open Government Licence or other open source licence (if any) in accordance with the terms of such licence, no part of this publication, including any article, illustration, trade mark or other content whatsoever, may be used, reproduced, stored in a retrieval system, distributed or transmitted in any form or by any means (including electronically) without the prior permission in writing of the Publisher and/or its licensors (as applicable).

The commission of any unauthorised activity may give rise to civil or criminal liability.

Please visit https://digital-library.theiet.org/copyrights-and-permissions for information regarding seeking permission to reuse material from this and/or other publications published by the Publisher. Enquiries relating to the use, including any distribution, of this publication (or any part thereof) should be sent to the Publisher at the address below:

The Institution of Engineering and Technology
Futures Place
Kings Way
Stevenage
Herts, SG1 2UA, United Kingdom

www.theiet.org

Whilst the Publisher and/or its licensors believe that the information and guidance given in this publication is correct, an individual must rely upon their own skill and judgement when performing any action or omitting to perform any action as a result of any statement, opinion or view expressed in the publication and neither the Publisher nor its licensors assume and hereby expressly disclaim any and all liability to anyone for any loss or damage caused by any action or omission of an action made in reliance on the publication and/or any error or omission in the publication, whether or not such an error or omission is the result of negligence or any other cause. Without limiting or otherwise affecting the generality of this statement and the disclaimer, whilst all URLs cited in the publication are correct at the time of press, the Publisher has no responsibility for the persistence or accuracy of URLs for external or third-party internet websites and does not guarantee that any content on such websites is, or will remain, accurate or appropriate.

Whilst every reasonable effort has been undertaken by the Publisher and its licensors to acknowledge copyright on material reproduced, if there has been an oversight, please contact the Publisher and we will endeavour to correct this upon a reprint.

Trade mark notice: Product or corporate names referred to within this publication may be trade marks or registered trade marks and are used only for identification and explanation without intent to infringe.

Where an author and/or contributor is identified in this publication by name, such author and/or contributor asserts their moral right under the CPDA to be identified as the author and/or contributor of this work.

British Library Cataloguing in Publication Data
A catalogue record for this product is available from the British Library

ISBN 978-1-83953-880-3 (hardback)
ISBN 978-1-83953-881-0 (PDF)

Typeset in India by MPS Limited

Cover image: FatCamera/E+ via Getty Images

Contents

About the editor

Pethuru Raj is chief architect in the Edge AI division of Reliance Jio Platforms Ltd., Bangalore, India. He focuses on emerging technologies such as the metaverse, Internet of Things (IoT), artificial intelligence (AI) model optimization, big and streaming data analytics, blockchain, digital twins, cloud-native and edge computing, and 5G/6G. He has authored and edited 40+ books and contributed 40+ book chapters. He is a professional member of ACM.

Prasanna Kumar is senior VP (cloud ops) and chief data scientist (AI & data platform) at Business Optima, USA. His AI & ML technology solutions have been deployed in companies such as Apple, Tesla, Microsoft, Amazon and Johnson & Johnson. He is the co-creator of the Pulse Engine and was the first to introduce multi-sentiment classification more than a decade ago, which is now prevalent in the industry. He is a member of the IET.

D. P. Sharma is a computer scientist and research adviser at the Department of Computer Science of MAISM, Rajasthan Technical University Kota, India. He has been on lien leave to serve foreign assignments since 2008. He is a disability rights activist involved in designing policies for inclusive internet access. He has actively participated in the United Nations Internet Governance Forum (IGF) and presided over the sessions of Govt of India's IGF.

Kavita Saini is an associate professor at the School of Computing Science and Engineering, Galgotias University, India. Her research interests include web-based instructional system (WBIs), software engineering, blockchain and database. She has published several academic books. She is a member of the IEEE. She holds a PhD in web-based instructional systems from Banasthali Vidyapeeth, Rajasthan, India.

B. Narendra Kumar Rao is a professor in the School of Computing, Mohan Babu University, Tirupat, India. His research interests include software testing, embedded systems and machine learning. He was the convener for the *International Conference on Data Analytics, and Intelligent Computing and Cyber Security*. He has edited two conference proceedings. He received his PhD degree in CSE from Jawarharlal Nehru Technological University, Hyderabad, India.

Harshavardhan Kosuri is CTO and co-founder of Aautiverse, Hyderabad, India. He is a metaverse, AI & ML leader who has created Deep Tech platforms with metaverse and AI technologies for Metaverse Real-estate, Edutech, eSports, digital payments, recruitment platforms and eCommerce industries. He is a research schooler in Metaverse. He is skilled in software development life cycle (SDLC), requirements analysis, agile methodologies, software development, infrastructure and software project management.

Nagendra Panini Challa is an associate professor in the School of Computer Science and Engineering (SCOPE) at VIT-AP University, India. His research interests include Computer Vision, Ontology and Machine Learning. He is the IET Hyderabad Region Young Professional Chair in India. He has initiated the IET student chapter at VIT-AP with 150+ student and professional members in this region. He is an active reviewer for several SCI-indexed journals and conferences.

R. Ranjana is an associate professor in the Department of Artificial Intelligence and Data Science, Dr. Mahalingam College of Engineering and Technology. Her research interests include deep learning and its applications. She is actively involved in organizing IEEE conferences. She has served as a journal editorial member and reviewer. She is a member of the IEEE and a life member of CSI. She received her PhD on energy aware resource management in cloud data centers from Anna University, India.

Chapter 1
Demystifying metaverse system engineering

Pethuru Raj[1]

Abstract

Physical reality (PR) refers to the real world around us. Conversely, we hear and read a lot about virtual reality (VR), augmented reality (AR), and other innovations. In VR, reality is generated entirely by a computer. Interestingly, new applications are emerging for VR. It all started with games, entertainment, and education. VR evangelists and exponents now list that VR can benefit field worker training, which is vital for intelligent manufacturing. For example, crane operators are taught the nitty-gritty of operating heavy-load cranes efficiently in adverse conditions.

Augmented reality (AR) is the captivating idea of technologically enhancing real-world objects through computer-generated perceptual information. The perception can be through different sensory modalities (text, image, video, audio, etc.). Mixed Reality (MR) merges real and virtual worlds to produce new experiences and environments. Herein, physical and digital objects co-exist and interact in real time. Mixed reality is a hybrid of reality and virtual reality. This can be visualized as a reality–virtuality continuum spanning 100% physical reality at one end of the spectrum and 100% virtual reality at the other. Besides VR, AR, and MR technologies, other contributing technologies exist to set up and sustain business-critical and people-centric metaverse systems. In this chapter, we will write about the growing significance of the fast-emerging and evolving metaverse paradigm. Also, this chapter will throw light on the prominent metaverse modeling, designing, development, and deployment technologies.

Keywords: Metaverse Engineering; Web 3.0; Blockchain; Virtual Reality; Augmented Reality; Mixed Reality; eXtended Reality; Edge Computing

1.1 Introduction

Digital twins—Let us start the chapter with a short description of the exciting concept of digital twins (DTs). A DT is typically a virtual representation of any physical system. DTs are the real-time digital counterparts of a physical asset,

[1]Edge AI Division, Reliance Jio Platforms Ltd., Bangalore, India

process, people, and system. DTs represent knowledge workers and field forces. DTs are the virtual worlds in which service providers, product designers, and knowledge workers communicate, collaborate, and share through a virtual presence on any device. For example, automotive and aerospace companies will build immersive virtual spaces (metaverses). This arrangement empowers workers and experts to interact virtually through chats, emails, video calls, and face-to-face meetings. DTs are the core and central system that enables such knowledge sharing.

As discussed above, DTs, produced based on modeling and simulation, play a critical role. Simulation allows automotive and aerospace design teams to make DTs of their creations and then run simulations. This helps them to pinpoint all possible optimization opportunities. Trying to find the same in the physical environment alone complicates the matter. In a nutshell, the power of simulation will be a game-changer for enterprising businesses. Therefore, the paradigm of the metaverse is being explored across various industries. Experts point out several innovations, disruptions, and transformations, such as optimizing production planning and accelerating design in the automotive and aerospace sectors. Other widely reported improvisations brought in through the metaverse significantly increase the productivity of industry 4.0 and 5.0 systems and accuracy for consumer-packaged goods companies. Businesses with a decisive understanding of the power of the metaverse conundrum can elegantly make forward-looking business decisions to considerably increase return on investment (ROI) and reduce the total cost of ownership (TCO). The metaverse's thriving and the trendsetting idea has laid a stimulating and sparkling foundation for worldwide enterprises to confidently explore new avenues toward making additional revenues.

The Mesmerizing Metaverse—Metaverse pioneers and proponents also point out that optimum immersive reality systems are essential for producing ultra-realistic and high-fidelity DT visuals, which immensely contribute to modeling and simulation. Metaverse applications are being realized at the intersection of virtual and real worlds. The enabling technologies are described below.

- **Advanced communication infrastructure**—Basic metaverse applications are produced and delivered with a 5G cellular communication network. With the 6G network, advanced metaverse systems can be engineered and deployed for public usage. Low latency is highly critical to providing an immersive experience in a metaverse.
- **Cloud-native computing infrastructure**—Enterprise-scale applications are designed, developed, deployed, and improved using proven and potential cloud-native principles. Metaverse applications can significantly benefit if metaverse system engineers methodically follow the precepts of cloud-native computing.
- **Blockchain-enabled secure access of metaverse data**—As explained below, blockchain databases are critical for ensuring the tightest data security. The distributed and decentralized architectural style being proposed by blockchain remarkably improves data availability.
- **Development & management platforms**—The metaverse consumes many precious resources, such as computing, power, and energy. Therefore, a platform-based resource management and optimization approach is the way forward.

- **Digitization and digitalization technologies**—Edge technologies such as the Internet of Things (IoT) digitize all physical, mechanical, electrical, and electronic systems. When purposefully interacting, digitized objects produce a massive quantity of multi-structured data. AI is the most fundamental and futuristic technology for making sense of metaverse data.
- **High-precision 3D AI-based spatial mapping**—As mentioned above, AI plays a crucial role in shaping the metaverse. By cognitively leveraging deep learning (DL) algorithms and models for computer vision, it is possible to perform high-fidelity 3D scene reconstruction, scene segmentation, and 3D object recognition. AI provides the precise fusion of the natural and virtual worlds.
- **Edge computing, analytics, and AI**—With the accumulation of resources-intensive edge devices in our every environment (homes, hospitals, retail stores, manufacturing floors, warehouses, defense zones, eating joints, entertainment plazas, sports stadiums, educational campuses, tunnels, expressways, airports, railway stations, etc.), different parts of the metaverse are bound to happen in traditional clouds and hugely popular edge environments. Edge computing facilitates data security, lower latency, and real-time data collection, cleansing, and crunching. Several business and technology advantages are being derived from edge analytics.

AR/VR facilitates establishing 3D virtual environments by leveraging the ultra-low latency capability offered by 5G. In the 6G era, the network latency is expected to go down to 1 or 2 μs. Cloud-native infrastructures (off-premise, on-premise, and edge), in conjunction with head-mounted displays, smartphones, handhelds, and laptops, enable an authentic and mesmerizing experience of much-trumpeted metaverse systems. In short, sophisticated technologies such as computing, communication, storage, and cybersecurity simplify the complex process of metaverse system engineering. Further on, multiple reality-enabling technologies help build and release industrial enterprise metaverses.

The Internet is a growing network of networked smartphones, laptops, tablets, and server machines. In the future, IoT sensors, devices, and microservices will join the bulging Internet. With the ready availability of AR/VR devices, the dream of immersive mixed reality is to be elegantly fulfilled. The current Internet is going through a series of stunning and scintillating transformations.

The metaverse is a virtual space that allows users to socialize and work outside the real world. This technology aims to next-generation systems that blur the line between reality and the virtual. Metaverse uses proven and potential technologies such as blockchain, virtual reality, augmented reality, Web 3.0 infrastructure, advanced communication technologies, the IoT, artificial intelligence, cybersecurity, etc., to set up and enrich virtual environments for many emerging requirements.

Metaverse blockchain offers access to a 3D digital space that represents a simulated physical environment. By leveraging VR and AR devices, the metaverse can mimic many real-world scenarios and provide additional functionalities and facilities. Users can use Metaverse wallet solutions to store their digital assets when making financial transactions in the virtual setup.

In the metaverse world, users are typically represented as digital avatars who can purposely interact with the different digital objects and applications in a metaverse. Using avatars, users can go shopping, eat in restaurants, deal in real estate, play games in stadiums, visit exotic monuments, learn in an industrialized environment, etc. Users must use VR/AR gizmos and gadgets such as headsets, handles, remote controls, etc., to connect and interact within a virtual setup.

1.2 A bit on digital transformation

Experts agree that digital technologies' faster maturity and stability have laid a stimulating foundation for the metaverse. In this section, we illustrate promising and potential technologies. Here is a list of popular digital technologies.

- Artificial Intelligence (AI) Model Engineering, Evaluation, Optimization, and Deployment
- Integrated Analytics (Big and Streaming Data)
- Data Processing Architectures (Lambda and Kappa)
- Cybersecurity and Blockchain Technologies
- The Internet of Things (IoT) Sensors and Devices
- AI-centric Processing Units (GPU, TPU, NPU, VPU, etc.)
- Advanced Communication Technologies and Network Topologies
- Intelligent Digital Twins and Cyber-Physical Systems
- Enterprise-grade Application Architecture Patterns (MSA, EDA, etc.)
- Metaverse Technologies (AR/VR/MR, Web 3.0, etc.)
- Data Mesh and Fabric for integrating data from different and distributed sources
- Cloud-native Computing for Next-Generation Software Engineering
- Edge Intelligence
- DevOps, Site Reliability Engineering, Value Stream Management, Platform Engineering

With the broader adoption and adaptation of digital technologies, innovations and disruptions will occur in all kinds of business workloads, IT services, and personal and social applications.

- Digital technologies and tools are the most significant business automation and transformation enablers.
- Digital infrastructures and platforms are growing in stature and contributions.
- Digital services and applications are quickly built and delivered through configuration, customization, and composition.
- Digital products, solutions, and middleware are experiencing unprecedented adoption and adaptation.
- All physical assets and mechanical, electrical, and electronic systems in everyday environments are digitized.

As a result, a few noteworthy implications are indicated below.

1. Millions of digital services,
2. Billions of connected devices
3. Trillions of digitized entities.
4. Zettabytes of digital data (1,000,000,000,000,000,000,000 (10^{21}) bytes)

New buzzwords such as digital living, governance, economy, enterprises, currencies, etc., emerge and evolve fast. Metaverse is to represent the next generation of the digital era.

1.3 The emergence of the metaverse

A metaverse expert and exponent has come out with an exciting description of what differentiates the metaverse era from the digital era. The overwhelmingly accepted gist of the metaverse is to create a universe wherein the delectable goal of merging physical reality with digital virtuality is getting extemporarily fulfilled. Such convergence creates and sustains a stimulating environment for thought leaders and pioneers to envisage unforeseen use cases for business and people transformation. A multitude of multifaceted sensors and actuators can cooperate reasonably to support multisensory interactions with virtual environments, digital objects, and people, such as virtual reality (VR), augmented reality (AR), mixed reality (MR), and extended reality (XR) products and systems. Advanced headgear and head-mounted displays are well-known VR and AR devices playing the prominent and pulsating role of intermediaries for establishing a seamless and spontaneous linkage between IoT sensors/devices, digitized objects (all kinds of physical, mechanical, and electrical systems are digitized through edge technologies), and scores of virtual applications running in edge devices and cloud servers. The physical world is purposefully integrated with the virtual world to create sophisticated use cases for businesses and ordinary people in everyday engagements and assignments.

Hence, the metaverse is a networked immersive environment on multi-user platforms. This facilitates seamless embodied user communication in real-time and dynamic interactions with digital artifacts. It started with virtual worlds where avatars were able to teleport among them. The metaverse will feature social and immersive VR platforms compatible with multiplayer online video games and AR collaborative spaces. The global user-created game platform Roblox represents nine fundamental features of the metaverse: identity, friends, immersion, low friction/latency, variety/diversity, anytime (temporal persistence), anywhere (spatial persistence), economic system, and civilization. With a suite of enabling technologies and tools, the paradigm of the metaverse is becoming a severe affair. In the subsequent sections, we will discuss breakthrough metaverse engineering technologies. There is an insistence on competent products, platforms, processes, practices, and patterns for smoothening the journey of metaverse system engineering.

1.4 Metaverse engineering technologies

The metaverse is a 3D virtual space that combines physical and virtual worlds. This convergence has unleashed a steady stream of innovations, disruptions, and transformations. Education and training can be insightful and immersive for learners and education service providers. In the metaverse, retail will become an immersive shopping experience. Virtual events will be more integrated rather than physical events. Moreover, every local and remote interaction will become stunningly resilient and versatile with the metaverse.

The six salient features of metaverse technology are:

- **Digital identity**—Metaverse allows users to present themselves as digital avatars. That means users can socialize and interact at their own will without any hindrance from the outside world.
- **Multiple device support**—Users can access the metaverse anywhere on any device.
- **Economy**—The surging popularity of blockchain as the metaverse's infrastructure has established its economic model. Cryptocurrencies and NFTs allow users to trade, exchange, and earn securely. Blockchain empowers the metaverse to be highly secure, transparent, and immutable for trading functions.
- **Digital community**—In the metaverse, users can connect, socialize, and interact with each other freely. Knowledge sharing is an essential contribution of the metaverse. Users (digital avatars) can play games with their friends, share their expertise and experiences with others, join virtual sessions, etc., within the virtual world.
- **Real-time experience**—With 5G and 6G (in the future), users in the metaverse can enjoy real-time interactions without any perceptible delay.

The emergence of several ground-breaking information and communication technologies (ICT) is a boosting factor towards the metaverse era. This section will shed some light on these technologies and how they merge to achieve bigger and better metaverse systems.

Blockchain—Blockchain started its arduous and lengthy innings as a viable method of storing and securing digital data. Blockchain is a public ledger that multiple parties may view simultaneously. Any data collected and stocked in blockchain ledgers cannot be modified without the people's consent. Each new record is converted into a block with a unique and distinguishing hash. Blockchain is a digital ledger that records all kinds of transactions in a transparent, immutable, and decentralized manner. A block is formed to store a record of transactions, and each block is then interconnected to form a chain. Blockchain ensures the unbreakable and impenetrable security for data. The decentralization aspect is projected as the single most differentiator of the blockchain concept. That is, no single entity has control over the entire chain. Thereby, data is highly secure and tamper-resistant.

The peer-to-peer (P2P) networking enshrined in blockchain eliminates the need for expensive intermediaries. The trust being ensured by intermediaries and mediators is being accomplished through P2P networking. Cryptography is another exciting technique propelling the paradigm of blockchain. There are several other enablers of blockchain. There are open-source and commercial-grade platforms, frameworks, and accelerators that simplify the onset of blockchain applications. The blockchain landscape is fast evolving, with many researchers contributing immensely to making blockchain penetrative, pervasive, and persuasive.

Blockchain guarantees the authentication of complex transactions and also provides the traceability factor. Experts write that blockchain ensures safer transactions, lowers compliance expenses, and accelerates data transfer processes. Blockchain aids in contract administration and product auditing. Blockchain can manage land titles and deeds. E-voting can get a boost with blockchain. Here is how blockchain works.

- An authorized participant enters a transaction, and the technology must verify it.
- This operation generates a block that reflects the particular transaction or data.
- The block is distributed to each computer node in the network.
- Authorized nodes verify the transaction; the blockchain includes the block.
- The transaction ends when the update is delivered across the network.

In the beginning, cryptocurrencies like Bitcoin were the most popular application of blockchain technology. With a deeper understanding of the blockchain concept, many newer use cases came into the picture and prominence across industry domains. Industries such as IoT device and data security, supply chain management, healthcare, land record management, financial services, and even art are keenly exploring and experimenting with blockchain to guarantee transparency, traceability, and optimization.

On another dimension, blockchain technology's core contribution enables integration **between the real and the digital economy. Blockchain intrinsically supports transparency, decentralization, trust, and immutability. Peer-to-peer networking eliminates costly intermediaries, which is the cornerstone of blockchain.** By employing multiple database servers in distributed places, the typical problems of data centralization are eliminated. Through decentralization, the requirements, such as universal and simplified accessibility of distributed and digital data and software services, are elegantly fulfilled. In short, data in transit and rest are tightly secured. For the metaverse era, the role and responsibility of blockchain databases are termed as higher. Blockchain is essential for the digital economy. The widely articulated use cases of blockchain include smart contracts, decentralized applications (dApps), and **Non-Fungible Tokens (NFTs). Data security, sharing, integrity, and interoperability are also accomplished through the intelligent leverage of blockchain. All these are mandatory for metaverse system engineering.**

Blockchain technology is ideally suited to fulfill the varying needs of the metaverse. As stated, blockchain can fulfill non-functional enterprise-scale and production-grade software systems requirements. Blockchain and metaverse are touted as two fascinating concepts capable of redefining how we interact with digital spaces and assets. Experts envisage fresh possibilities and opportunities with these two widely celebrated technologies clubbing together. In this section, we are to discuss how blockchain technology empowers the metaverse landscape. Blockchain has become the pivotal and pertinent technology that simplifies how we interact with digital assets at the ground level, social platforms, and cloud-hosted applications.

As articulated above, the metaverse is a digital universe where users can interact with each other and digital objects in real time. It is like attending a meeting, exploring an art gallery, or playing a game in an immersive digital environment. Besides entertainment, the metaverse is seen as a powerful technology for fresh exploration, education, etc. Metaverse has the strength to bring about a series of evolutions, revolutions, and inventions. The way we work, interact, socialize, and live is to change radically with the step-in of the metaverse. Path-breaking applications will occur when the physical world synchronizes and synergizes with the digital world.

Blockchain's distinguished capabilities of decentralization and transparency come in handy in sufficiently enriching the metaverse. With close alignment with blockchain, creating an innovative and secure 3D digital environment is possible. The interoperability property, succulently strengthened by blockchain, lessens the workload associated with setting up and sustaining metaverse environments. Blockchain facilitates smooth communication among various metaverse components. The complex and critical aspect of data exchange amongst participating assets, avatars, and applications is hugely simplified by blockchain.

Digital Ownership and Asset Management—Digital assets are essential in the metaverse. People get represented as digital avatars. Establishing the ownership of virtual real estate, goods, and artworks is paramount to ensure the much-trumpeted immersive experience. Blockchain gives verifiable ownership and provenance. Individuals' digital possessions are incredibly secure, tradable, and genuinely unique. Smart contracts are another offshoot of blockchain. Smart contracts are typically self-executing code safely secured on the blockchain database. When some routine or unexpected events happen, smart contracts do the corresponding actions in an automated manner. Therefore, human interpretation, involvement, and instruction must be improved. Smart contracts provide a trusted framework for buying, selling, and trading digital assets within the metaverse. Digital assets can be tracked, traced, and traded to get better value for assets. Thus, ownership and management of digital assets are entirely done at the behest of blockchain.

Seamless Interoperability—Multiple virtual spaces, platforms, and assets should interact to produce and improve metaverse applications. Blockchain's unique decentralized nature guarantees interoperability. This empowers different and distributed metaverse systems to find and share data dynamically. Blockchain ensures much-needed trust in an untrustworthy situation. Boundaryless information flow, as promoted by the Open Group (https://www.opengroup.org/) a long time back, is being provided by blockchain. This interoperability facet opens the door for boundless collaboration. Users can enjoy and experience the unique characteristics of different metaverse environments.

Identity and Privacy Protection—In the ensuing digital era, user identity must be thoroughly protected. Blockchain-inspired identity management systems are being seen as a critical advancement. Users can maintain control over their personal information. In the metaverse, interactions occur predominantly, and hence, user identity and privacy must be safeguarded to foster a safe and secure environment.

Empowering Creators and Artists — Without a doubt, the metaverse is a canvas for creativity. Artists, music directors, product designers, and developers can leverage the advancements in the metaverse to be generative and creative. They can earn big money through their digital creations. However, it is neither simple nor straightforward. Blockchain comes to the rescue. Blockchain has introduced decentralized marketplaces and royalty mechanisms. With these in place, creators can get the correct compensation for their work. That is, creators can monetize their creations. Blockchain-enabled metaverse is to spur innovation.

In a nutshell, blockchain will be an indispensable technology for the domain of the metaverse to flourish in the years to unfold. Blockchain can help in finding any virtual object without any centralized system. The capability of identifying and tracking digital assets in a decentralized manner goes a long way in strengthening the metaverse. As with blockchain, finding any virtual object without any centralized system is possible. The ability to identify and track their digital assets in a decentralized manner is an integral part of the metaverse.

1.4.1 Interactive technologies

Metaverse empowers social interaction, entertainment, education, and business. Multiple industries, including healthcare, manufacturing, education, and retail, are to benefit significantly from metaverse technologies. Metaverse can be used to create virtual reality environments for training or education purposes. Metaverse can also be used to create virtual storefronts for businesses or virtual spaces for social interaction. Metaverse will be a multifaceted platform (can be deployed as a service in public, private, hybrid, and edge clouds) for business behemoths and start-ups, institutions, governments, healthcare and hospitality service providers, etc. Metaverse can train new employees to gain skills or provide a safe environment for product testing. The other fields, such as real estate, supply chain, transport, sports, music, and entertainment, are being sufficiently empowered through the metaverse.

As inscribed above, VR, AR, MR, and XR products enable the much-needed interactive technologies for the metaverse. Augmented reality (AR), virtual reality (VR), mixed reality (MR), and extended reality (XR) solutions are the primary interactive technologies shaping the metaverse. These devices and displays contribute immensely to gaming, entertainment, education, exploration, and experimentation.

Augmented reality (AR) guarantees an interactive experience by enhancing the real world with computer-generated information to enable real-time learning and understanding. Using software, mobile apps, and hardware such as AR glasses, AR overlays digital content onto real-life environments and objects. This facilitates interactive learning of the environment. There are street view services to get to know a neighborhood before we visit. Similarly, there are interior decoration applications to see what furniture looks like in our living room. These are typical use cases of AR. In entertainment, AR is in the form of filtering that alters a person's appearance in a photo. There are AR games that blend real and virtual spaces. Generally, AR is for integrating virtual 3D objects into a 3D natural environment in real time. AR is being leveraged across multiple industry domains such as manufacturing, healthcare, national security, path planning, etc. IoT networks can be augmented and optimized with human ingenuity and creativity.

AR superimposes digital information onto real-world objects to create a 3D experience. Such superimposition empowers users to interact with both the physical and digital worlds. An AR-enabled device with a camera, such as smart glasses, a tablet, or a smartphone, can parse a video feed to identify a physical object or the environment around the user. Locating a piece of machinery, visualizing the layout of a warehouse, etc., are AR-inspired use cases. DTs represent the digital version of any physical system or process. DTs are used to synchronize physical objects with their digital versions, which are primarily made to run on cloud environments. All kinds of log, operational, health condition, performance, and behavioral data of physical systems get captured meticulously and fed into their DTs to extract many actionable insights in time. The AR device then downloads information about the physical object from the cloud. It superimposes digital information over the object using markers or trackers like GPS, accelerometers, orientation, and barometric sensors.

Towards Industry 4.0 and 5.0 systems, AR is to play a critical contributory role. Many operational inefficiencies are getting surmounted, production downtime come down considerably, production identification and resolution are quickened, etc. Thus, AR extends its helping hand to intelligent manufacturing and factory automation. AR is extensively used for asset identification in industrial environments or multi-specialty hospitals. AR is to teach field workers during training how to operate sophisticated industrial machinery optimally. The AR-induced training enriches newly joined employees with all the correct and relevant details, such as how to use complex machinery and the risks involved while operating powerful machines. In conjunction with scores of IoT sensors and devices, DTs, cybersecurity, etc., AR can prototype, test, and finetune a virtual object for features-rich and complex products to be built. Such a capability helps product designers to deeply and decisively understand the nitty-gritty of the product to be developed. Such acquired knowledge helps product engineers to artistically design and develop competent and cognitive products that can substantially enhance user experience and ecstasy.

AR ensures maintenance, operational control, and safety in any industrial environment. Workers can get all the details about any machine in their work spots and instantly get the expert's help in resolving any issues with the machine. With AR, employees can continuously hone their skills to achieve enhanced productivity. By incorporating AR into the quality control and assurance process, it is possible to prevent product defects proactively and pre-emptively. Production processes can be investigated, rationalized, and optimized to quickly reach the market with quality products. In short, AR will help identify fresh avenues to increase revenues.

Statistics show that businesses can achieve a productivity improvement of 32% by adopting AR. Businesses use AR-powered applications to provide step-by-step procedures, user manuals, and operational guides to appropriately train and prepare newly joined workers for the battle ahead. This partially or even entirely removes human trainers. Thus, industrial operations are being automated, accelerated, and augmented through the intelligent usage of distinct advancements in the AR space.

In summary, AR glasses allow users to overlay digital information in the real world. AR simulations typically provide users with an immersive environment where they can interact beneficially with objects and other people. Many AR applications are being accessed through our mobile devices. Virtual try-on is one prominent use case.

Snap Inc. is adapting AR behind its popular filters and lenses, which are the tools that can add glittery makeup or cartoon eyes to someone's video selfie. This is to help retailers use AR on their websites and apps. This helps online shoppers try clothing, footwear, and accessories on a retailer's site. Using AR, a virtual try-on may extend to accommodate shoes, bags, dresses, eyeglasses, waist belts, and other accessories. In short, AR is helping B2C e-commerce applications increase their sales using 3D animation. AR lets you experience virtual objects in a real-world environment. In short, AR does not create an individual digital setup; rather, it enhances the real-world experience by adding special features such as objects, images, and sounds.

Virtual Reality (VR) technology helps create digital 3D interactive environments and experiences for users with the help of a wearable device (a specially designed device called a VR headset or helmet). The VR headset provides a much-insisted aspect of user immersion in the virtual world. Simply speaking, VR leads in realizing realistic simulated environments by leveraging many pivotal technologies cogently and collaboratively. The VR technology puts users in a 3D world where they can immerse and interact with other participants. Such 3D virtual spaces bridge the gap between actual and digital. The settings allow users to delve deeply into the digital surroundings, creating engrossing experiences for themselves.

VR is to create and render immersive experiences for users. VR gives wings to users to thrive on their curiosity and allows users to traverse beyond their physical world to explore new things mentally. In short, VR constructs an immersive simulated environment for users to do many things. The 3D experience involves images, videos, and audio to create a realistic digital environment.

VR head-mounted displays (headgear) are essential for enjoying all that is being provided by the metaverse. VR is being seen as a vital infrastructure module for the metaverse era. VR is to strengthen the metaverse, which promises to initiate a grandiose shift from reality to a dynamic virtual world. Robust VR software solutions are required to design the online space. Precisely speaking, VR software and hardware solutions are the two vitals that support the design, development, and usage of metaverse environments.

VR technologies primarily provide the means for interacting with the more expansive multiverse platforms. Within that access role, VR can support a variety of metaverse use cases. For example, VR can be combined with the DT technology. As stated elsewhere, DTs are the virtual representations of complex and critical physical systems on the ground, machines on a manufacturing floor, supply chains, industrial processes, etc. Technologists can use the VR extension of a DT to simulate various issues.

VR and DTs (https://www.techtarget.com/whatis/feature/The-metaverse-explained-Everything-you-need-to-know) synchronize and synergize towards building and using industrial metaverse systems. This strategically sound combination has streamlined and smoothened the path toward industry 4.0 and 5.0 applications. Smart manufacturing and factory automation goals are being elegantly fulfilled through the convergence of VR and DTs. Organizations can employ VR to consider the effects of different design decisions. They can also build simulated prototypes to avoid the cost of creating physical ones. VR is also being used for employee safety training. Assembly line workers can train virtually before working on the physical factory floor. Emergency responders can use VR disaster training to practice in a virtual environment.

In healthcare, VR training would let surgeons "repeat a specific on-demand procedure as often as the practitioner desires" and create a shorter learning curve. Other VR use cases, such as pain management and pediatrics, are being explored. The author also states that VR can bolster specialized and complex training use cases, such as astronaut preparation, institutional knowledge transfer to record workers' knowledge before they retire, empathy lessons for customer service employees, and soft skills training.

1.4.2 Uses of virtual reality in metaverse

Travel—VR enables users to travel across the world virtually. Users can visit beautiful locations and tourist places, enjoy mountains and monuments, eat multi-cuisine delicacies, and more. Users can also create digital memories through their digital identities. This metaverse-enabled experience is so versatile and vivid that it is tough to differentiate between real and virtual.

Medicine—Medical students, doctors, and specialists can use VR to perform digital surgeries on avatars. This can be repeated any number of times. The VR-powered training helps them hone their skills and enhance their confidence. Such technology-inspired learning ultimately helps eliminate any irreparable mistakes during actual surgery. With immersive surgical training, there is a noteworthy improvement in the quality of training and patient outcomes. Studies have also confirmed that VR improves the effectiveness of medical education programs.

Further on, real haptics increase accuracy and deliver complete skills transfer. A virtual learning platform, "Fundamental Surgery" (https://fundamentalsurgery.com/), enables medical teams to perfect their precision skills. It instills confidence in surgeons to operate in real-life scenarios with the utmost clarity, alacrity, and competence.

Games and entertainment—This is a well-known and widely used domain artistically embracing the growing power of the metaverse. With VR headsets, players can get a mesmerizing gaming experience. Players can also play and practice. 3D cinemas are also gaining attention.

Education—Teachers can use VR-supported screens to create engrossing learning experiences for students. They can easily create a virtual display to illustrate any problematic concept. This facility sharply empowers students to unlearn and learn complex things quite quickly. Virtual tours to difficult places like the moon or planets keep students happy.

Virtual events—VR allows users to attend a music concert, sports extravaganza, technology conference, etc., right from the comfort of their homes. This saves a lot of time and money.

Military and athletics—VR facilitates training sessions for soldiers in a simulated combat environment. Military personnel get good exposure to real-world and real-time situations to prepare for any undesired eventuality.

VR is transforming the way athletes of all levels train. It allows them to analyze their movements and cognitive skills deeper, enhancing their confidence and competence.

In short, VR is the foundational and fundamental base on which the riveting concept of metaverse operates. The mind-boggling VR domain decides the pace and power of the metaverse technology. VR aids in creating a 3D virtual world wherein users can immerse and express themselves. People can get interactive experiences that are hard in the physical environment. The growing interest in the metaverse will push product engineers to stretch further and strive to bring scores of slim, sleek, trendy, handy, and multifaceted VR headsets.

Mixed Reality (MR) establishes natural and intuitive interactions between humans, computers, and the surrounding environments by blending physical and digital worlds. The radical and rapid technological innovations in artificial intelligence (AI) algorithms, AI-centric processors, and AI applications like computer vision and remote sensing enable MR, typically the hybrid version of virtual and augmented realities. In particular, holographic devices with see-through displays allow users to interact with physical objects, while immersive devices allow interaction with virtual objects in the virtual world. Headsets with visual displays are increasingly equipped with additional capabilities such as eye and hand-tracking, anchors, and spatial mapping to understand the environment neatly. By using advanced sensors such as gyroscopes, these devices can correctly track the locations and positions of objects in virtual spaces. These devices are increasingly used for several purposes, including educational training, three-dimensional animations, entertainment, games, sports, engineering, and construction. Hololems2 is an advanced headset that enables users to view holograms. Mixed reality has many versions and displays. Here are four types of MR displays to experience mixed reality (https://metaverseinsider.tech/2022/10/24/what-is-mixed-reality/)

MR uses various sensors, cameras, and complex image processing algorithms to superimpose 3D virtual elements onto the physical realm. This is similar to augmented reality (AR), but AR allows individuals to interact with 3D virtual objects. It is also possible to have haptic feedback through sensors, and such a facility makes the entire experience delightfully immersive.

When we use an MR headset, the cameras and sensors in the glasses will connect and collect all the information in our surroundings. It will then create a virtual physical world map to position 3D objects correctly. It has in-built hand and movement tracking that enables users to interact with the virtual elements. Through that map, MR creates holographic content and images in the digital world by using projections of 3D elements. MR can track the items, boundaries, and surfaces to work effectively.

MR combines the best properties of AR and VR to guarantee a delectable experience for users. Wearing a headset is essential. The headset scans and maps the surroundings and positions the virtual objects accordingly.

A 2D picture may not serve much but a 3D object allows interaction within a person's surroundings, and this capability can open up a myriad of fresh possibilities and opportunities. Talking with our friends using holograms from our homes is touted as a robust use case of MR. MR will promote business prospects. Rather than seeing small images on our laptops or mobile phones, potential customers can view 3D versions of products through holograms. Thus, stunning visuals can captivate clients and consumers. With MR infrastructure, newer use cases can be envisaged and delivered to explore fresh avenues towards increased revenues.

1.4.3 The applications of mixed reality

Many sectors are exploring, experimenting with, and expounding on the unique capabilities of MR.

Education—Through interactive environments, MR is being used to train students and promote their inborn abilities to learn and retain knowledge. This immersive technology is an excellent tool for teachers, learners, and practitioners in their pursuit.

Engineering—The engineering sector is benefiting immensely from the growing power of MR. MR is simplifying and speeding up real-time simulations of industrial processes, creating virtual models of architecture and product prototypes, training field workers, and more. Engineers get actionable and accurate insights in time to resolve current and future problems.

Healthcare—Performing surgeries need a lot of education, expertise, and experience. MR comes in handy here in empowering surgeons through practical training. Teachers teaching anatomy to their students can use MR. Students can see holograms of different layers of the human body and learn everything with all the clarity and convenience. Pre-operative and intra-operative planning get a boost with MR. Patient-specific holograms are more intuitive and informative than MRIs and CT scans. This can facilitate efficient operations by eliminating unnecessary complications. MR is effective in managing chronic pain. By putting patients in multiple realities through MR, sensor experiences can be studied to make medications right and relevant.

Equipment repair in unreachable situations—By using MR, NASA made one of their astronauts in outer space upgrade the Cold Atom Lab, their quantum lab abroad, present in the International Space Station. MR is used for water purification, wind farms, and desalination of plants.

The automotive and aerospace industries utilize MR technology. The primary difference between augmented reality and mixed reality is that while both technologies overlay 3D virtual images onto the physical realm, only mixed reality allows users to interact with these images.

Extended reality (XR)—AR, MR, and VR have been termed standalone technologies for immersive experiences in learning, shopping, etc., in the offline world. XR is an umbrella term encompassing VR, AR, MR, and everything in between.

As discussed above, the metaverse can bring unprecedented disruptions and innovations across industries ranging from tourism to fashion. Multiple noteworthy developments exist in the ICT landscape. Digitization and digitalization technologies are slated and stated to contribute immeasurably to the grandiose success of the metaverse conundrum. Many reality technologies like VR, AR, and MR are vital building blocks for metaverse system engineering.

However, experts point out that extended reality (XR) is indispensable for making the metaverse appealing to people at large. With pioneering use cases, the concept of the metaverse is bound to grow and glow. In time, the metaverse idea will touch all of our personal, social, and professional lives. XR will uplift the user experience in the metaverse through AR smart glasses and VR headsets, haptics, hologram displays, etc. Such devices are handy for enjoying and experiencing increasing physical services in the virtual world.

In the tourism industry, VR can help travelers gain a first-hand experience of their preferred tourist spots before physically visiting them. AR and VR technologies can combine to empower travelers to experience potential hotels beforehand and make hotel bookings with confidence and clarity. For farmers, the metaverse can help increase farm outputs. Warehouses, farms, weather conditions, and other relevant parameters can be closely monitored and managed remotely. Such a setup helps improve yields.

Brain—computer interfaces—Brain–computer interface (BCI) technology allows users to interact and control using brain signals. This is to enable direct communication between the brain and the external world. As inscribed in the beginning, blockchain guarantees transparency, data security, and integrity. Transactions cannot be tampered with. Therefore, all interactions and collaborations within the metaverse are tightly secured and shielded. The 5G communication network offers a high data transmission rate and low latency. Thus, communication becomes instantaneous. Also, 5G promises to connect many IoT edge devices compared to 4G communication. The metaverse idea will be severely adopted as the world works on 6G communication standard specifications. As detailed in this chapter, the 6G-enabled metaverse will be sagaciously mesmerizing. These technologies can ultimately result in multi-dimensional, multifaceted, highly interactive, and immersive digital space. Businesses will foresee a lot of path-breaking use cases and finalize a suite of premium services for their partners, employees, and end-users.

Metaverse systems will succulently empower people in their everyday deals, deeds, and decisions. Our imagination is the boundary for the metaverse paradigm.

Experts have pointed out that the metaverse concept is to see many improvisations with the faster maturity of metaverse technologies. The hardware and communication limitations can be overcome through various breakthrough technologies. Specific equipment simulates only a few visual or auditory sensations. The future belongs to the brain-integrated metaverse. This can help in experiencing the sensory details emitted from the external environment through electrical signals instead of VR and XR equipment. The conventional interaction happens through keyboards, mice, gaze-based interactions, gestures, and voice instructions. These are simple but need additional devices. Thus, interactions are not direct as intermediaries are involved.

Through brainwave signals, AR-BCI directly connects the user's brain and the virtual environment. This enables immersive and personalized interactions, and AR-BCI is the way forward for people with physical infirmities.

1.5 Web 3.0

The pandemic showed us how vital the internet infrastructure, platforms, software services, and content are for personal, social, and professional reasons. It all started with Web 1.0 (simple web) and then proceeded to Web 2.0 (social web). Now, Web 3.0 is fully decentralized, with the belief that no individual or institution can completely control it. Decentralization takes several forms: blockchain (decentralized digital ledger), cryptocurrency (decentralized finance, or DeFi), non-fungible tokens (NFTs), decentralized autonomous organizations (DAOs), decentralized wireless (DeWi), decentralized apps (DApps) and decentralized storage (filecoin.)

Web3 is open (public blockchains), permissionless (no need for centralized intermediaries to approve transactions), and trustless (no need for centralized third parties to provide authorization.). More can be found on this page (https://www.ciena.com/insights/articles/2023/what-is-web3-and-how-does-it-relate-to-the-metaverse).

Web 3.0, or Web3, aims to be fully decentralized, putting content creation in the hands of creators, not platform owners. According to an online blog (https://www.techtarget.com/whatis/feature/Web3-vs-metaverse-Whats-the-difference), Web3 consists of five components.

1. **Semantic web**—The web uses AI to understand what a user or customer may mean or intend. The idea is to understand user queries' meaning and context and provide contextually proper and relevant responses.
2. **AI.** The AI of Web3 helps better understand what a user is trying to search for.
3. **3D graphics and spatial web.** Virtual reality (VR) headsets and realistic graphics make websites more realistic.
4. **Blockchain and cryptocurrency** eliminate intermediaries and enable direct transactions between parties.
5. **Ubiquitous connectivity**—Web3 applications are always connected via 5G cellular communication and other connectivity methods such as Wi-Fi, NB-IoT, Bluetooth, ZigBee, etc.

As stated above, in the fully realized spatial web, every element of every building in the physical world will be entirely digitized. Every human being will have virtual avatars; one can roam around in any virtual workplace or meeting place. Thus, every piece of information around the world will become spatial. The spatial web consists of IoT sensors and wearables such as smart glasses.

The most significant difference between the two technologies is that people use Web3 to access the metaverse, much like an automobile uses a road. Web3 is about decentralized ownership and control and putting the web in the hands of its users and the community. On the other hand, the metaverse is a shared digital reality that enables users to connect, build economies, and interact in real time, and they do not care who owns it.

1.6 The metaverse implications

The gaming industry is to change drastically. In other words, with 6G communication networks in place, gaming experiences will be altogether different. Creating real-time games demands immediate decisions. Undoubtedly, 6G is the way forward. Setting up virtual meeting rooms with real-time collaboration is being streamlined through the power of metaverse technologies.

Similarly, other industry verticals explore, experiment, and expound the metaverse's radically and rapidly growing power. Such technology-inspired empowerment is perceived as a positive signal to visualize trendsetting metaverse applications. The metaverse is an appropriate answer for unexpected situations such as the unprecedented health impact of the coronavirus. Our way of living, working, and socializing has dramatically changed. With metaverse technologies, new interaction capabilities can be brought to educate and excite users.

The 6G-enabled metaverse can completely change how we design, build, and enhance many infrastructures (city, connectivity, social, cyber, industrial, entertainment, etc.). City architects and urban planning experts can use the growing power of the metaverse to create digital models of city buildings, hospitals, retail stores, warehouses, etc. The digital models come in handy for starting the physical construction with all the confidence and clarity. Similarly, the metaverse and 6G, in combination, can create sophisticated and sustainable transportation systems, power energy grids, etc.

Users in metaverse environments can readily interact with one another in real time. This requirement is met through next-generation network infrastructures, which can efficiently handle massive multi-structured data in real time. According to telecommunication experts, 6G technology is expected to achieve a theoretical speed of 1 Tbps.

Product engineers and suppliers can collaborate in the virtual world using the metaverse technology to simplify and speed up product design and develop processes. One of the most essential needs for this to happen is a reliable and high-speed network. The data transmission rate has to be on the higher side to enable real-time team interaction. Lightning-fast speed is crucial for the metaverse idea to flourish. Therefore, the world is keenly waiting to deploy 6G communication networks. The current networks need to be improved in several ways, such as limited coverage and reliability. 5G networks, which are becoming penetrative and pervasive across the globe, could fulfill the network requirements for making and running basic metaverse applications in autonomous driving, augmented reality (AR), etc. However, technology experts believe that 6G is the way forward to establish and deploy path-breaking metaverse systems. AI-centric, energy-efficient, and high-performance chips are also insisted as the primary ingredient to achieve the intended success in the metaverse era.

Another critical facet of the metaverse is its ability to cope with a large user base. With billions of people set to use the metaverse, the communication network infrastructure must be top-class. Today, we have a cloud-native digital infrastructure that has to be supplanted by a digital network infrastructure that guarantees 1 or 2 μs latency. Experts focusing on 6G specification development expect that 6G can support one million edge devices within a kilometer radius. Energy efficiency is another vital factor. With connected devices already billions at this point, all set to join mainstream computing, the amount of data getting generated, transmitted, stocked, and processed is humongous. Hence, energy consumption is bound to go up rapidly. As a result, much heat can get dissipated into our fragile environment. Thus, with advanced technologies, newer opportunities and possibilities are bound to emerge, evolve, and emancipate. Conversely, with extensive usage of technological components in our personal, social, and professional locations, a considerable amount of energy could be better spent, severely degrading our environment. Thus, energy evangelists and exponents insist on devising pioneering methods to reduce energy consumption sharply.

6G, coupled with the IoT and AI, is a unique combination in setting up and sustaining 3D environments, a prominent metaverse application. A magazine article says that auto manufacturers collaboratively develop new lightweight AR glasses, which must collect and aggregate data from multiple sources, including dashboards, IoT edge devices and sensors, and displays. By fusing different devices within a car, it is possible to give and guarantee an augmented reality (AR) experience to car drivers. However, producing AR glasses, a well-known new-generation wearable, has several challenges in fulfilling the above features and functionalities. There is a need for competent and cognitive products, solutions, and services to readily achieve next-generation requirements such as advanced radio interconnection and multi-sensor fusion capability. All these have to be performed with less power consumption.

1.7 The metaverse benefits

It provides a way for users to interact with each other through VR, AR, and related technologies. Extending this to the workspace, virtual offices can be set up in the metaverse, and employees can set up their cubicles. Each cubicle could be branded by the employer or set up as the employee chooses, should the employer allow it.

The metaverse is an extension of the corporate office to the virtual world, and we expect the environment and work culture to follow those of the actual brand and office.

As articulated above, with the availability of high-throughput computing and broadband connectivity capabilities, the intriguing concept of the metaverse is being explored, experimented with, and expounded upon. Many business domains are vigorously formulating their strategy to infuse the power of the metaverse to produce and deliver a suite of premium service offerings to their clients and consumers. This section will highlight the metaverse paradigm's key benefits across a few leading industry verticals.

Improving product design and development—This is one of the prominent advantages of the metaverse. Newer product design and development gets a fillip through the metaverse, which can effectively establish real-time interaction between product sponsors and end users. Such an interaction can finetune the product design to meet user requirements fully. Users can be situated across cities, counties, and countries. That is, user-centric product design gets a boost through the metaverse. Product development, user acceptance testing, deployment in production environments, and continuous improvement can be accelerated through the intelligent leverage of the metaverse. Thus, bringing quality and people-centric products to the knowledge-driven market is getting speeded up and shaped by the advancements in metaverse technologies. 6G communication will allow people to interact seamlessly and spontaneously with their surroundings and critical assets.

Increasing sustainability—Power conservation is critical as everyday devices join mainstream computing in large numbers. Industry 4.0 and advanced healthcare applications typically involve many automated tools, electronic devices, connected machinery, AI-enabled robots, drones, etc. The result is an increased wastage of power energy. It is indicated that with the metaverse, it is possible to monitor, measure, and manage the energy consumption of all kinds of energy-guzzling appliances, equipment, wares, utilities, and consumer electronics. The much-dreaded carbon dioxide (CO_2) emission can be substantially reduced using DTs for the physical assets mentioned above. DTs are being built for factories and warehouses and deployed in cloud environments to monitor every asset and aspect of industry activities in a minute. Metaverse applications in the form of well-designed DTs come in handy for exploring the ways and means of achieving less carbon emissions to sustain our environments.

The metaverse is expected to reduce travel across places by bringing together multiple team members dispersed across the world virtually. Online meetings and conferences can be quickly set up through the 6G-enabled metaverse. Therefore, travel needs can be considerably reduced. Such a travel reduction results in fewer greenhouse gas (GHG) emissions. As per an online report, the transportation sector generates the largest share of GHG emissions from burning fossil fuel for our buses, trucks, ships, trains, and airplanes.

Another exciting use case for sustainability is given below. We have fitting rooms in physical clothing stores to check whether the chosen dresses fit well. Online retailers are, therefore, adding virtual fitting rooms (alternatively termed the try-on facility) for shoppers to choose and get the correct apparel. Such an advanced feature significantly reduces product returns. The packaging, shipping, inventory, and replenishment costs come down remarkably with the addition of this feature.

Driving creativity—The metaverse will eloquently create and sustain virtual relationships between people at large. These relationships can eliminate barriers, such as physical distance, culture, language, etc. Such virtual relationships can facilitate knowledge-sharing and boundaryless information flow. The creativity level can be further expanded and enhanced through metaverse-inspired knowledge communities. Medical diagnosis and medication can be astutely advanced through virtual interactions. The education sector will undergo drastic transformation with the widespread adoption of the metaverse.

1.7.1 The metaverse challenges

Network latency is being told as a significant constraint for rolling out people-centric and technologically advanced metaverse solutions. Therefore, the world is keenly yearning to formalize and finalize 6G communication standards. Metaverse developers must focus on high performance to relay the data streams in real time. There should not be any interruption or disruption when data gets streamed, even if data streams originate from and travel for a more considerable distance. Experts believe 6G is the only option to achieve this hard requirement.

The upload and download throughput must be significantly higher to support the illusion of presence. That is, ensuring seamless and spontaneous connectivity is indispensable to providing immersive experiences, which the participants ambitiously expect. Real-time collaboration is required for mission-critical and high-risk fields such as aerospace, defense, automotive, and healthcare. The flourishing concepts such as edge computing, edge device cluster/cloud, and edge data analytics (through traditional analytical methods and powerful AI models) must be meticulously nourished through a host of cutting-edge technologies and tools to shape up the formative yet transformative paradigm of the metaverse. Another widely known challenge is integrating disparate technologies to build end-to-end communication systems. The system complexity gets amplified with the participation of the IoT devices and sensors. With the overwhelming incorporation of artificial intelligence (AI) capabilities across purpose-specific and agnostic systems, the complexity is bound to go more complicated. Thus, overcoming these challenges technologically is essential for enabling a wide range of next-generation metaverse applications.

Technology giants are keenly investing their talents, treasures, and time in 6G communication technology. Though the metaverse is slowly yet steadily beginning its long and arduous journey, 6G technology can play a vital role in shaping it.

Several technical challenges must be surmounted for the metaverse to grow and glow in the coming days. To reach its full potential, there are miles to traverse. We need state-of-the-art hardware, middleware, and software solutions to produce and release pioneering metaverse systems.

Data privacy and security are being accepted as top challenges of the metaverse. Users typically create and maintain the metaverse. This raises concerns about who owns the data created in the metaverse and how it will be used. Another challenge that needs to be addressed is none other than scalability. As known to everyone, the metaverse is a persistent and online environment. Therefore, the metaverse has to support a tremendous number of users concurrently. A 6G communication infrastructure can tackle many users without jitter.

One challenge that needs to be addressed before metaverse can be widely adopted is data privacy and security. Metaverse is a user-created online space, meaning users create and maintain the metaverse.

Metaverse is a virtual world wherein users can interact with one another and digital objects with all the elegance and exuberance. Metaverse is being seen as a transformative technology capable of revolutionizing how we live, socialize, relax, and work. However, for the ideals of the metaverse to be fulfilled, there is a need for a few breakthrough digital technologies. The most important are the IoT, 6G communication networks, and artificial intelligence (AI) technologies. The IoT is mainly used as a data generator, collector, and aggregator. 6G is the primary data transmitter. AI is an advanced data cruncher that emits actionable insights in time. These technologies should be primed with high-performing digital infrastructures and platforms to realize the metaverse's power. Cloud-native environments are highly optimized and organized digital IT infrastructure. 6G network infrastructure has to be widely deployed. Thus, with the continued innovations and disruptions in the digital technology ecosystem, the metaverse dream is all set to shine and be sustainable.

The world is slowly yet steadily moving from the digital to the metaverse era. In the digital era, every tangible/concrete thing gets digitized, connected, and enabled to purposefully interact with one another in the vicinity and with remotely held (cloud-hosted) software applications. The deep and extreme connectivity empowers digitized entities to discover, connect, and communicate to generate massive amounts of multi-structured digital data. Digital technologies collect, cleanse, and analyze digital data to produce actionable insights, which, in turn, enable business workloads, ICT services, digital devices, and software packages to operate intelligently in their processes, outputs, and offerings. Thus, timely knowledge discovery and dissemination of digital data go a long way in laying down a stimulating and sparkling foundation for digital living.

Now, there is a twist. There is a transition from the digital world to the metaverse, wherein a person will feel immersed in a virtual, three-dimensional (3D) world. This transformation is to increase data transmission and usage sharply. An online report says that data usage will go up by 20 times across the globe by 2032. Telecommunication companies are to benefit immensely from this heightened data usage. High-fidelity video transmission, which will become the new normal in the metaverse era, will lead to higher bandwidth consumption. Metaverse will power new use cases such as gaming and entertainment. People can engage in many ways and purposes that were not done before. Unforeseen use cases will emerge and thrive when the 6G-enabled metaverse flourishes. 3D virtual options open up for the entertainment industry for film, television, and music. In the metaverse era, a user can be viewed as a hologram in another place, teleported to any remote location, etc. Higher data transmission rates and lower latency are the prime needs for envisioning fresh metaverse systems.

6G, in conjunction with edge computing, is being pitched as the most crucial technological paradigm for setting up and sustaining people-centric and business-critical metaverse applications.

We have discussed how the metaverse idea will become a prime mover across multiple business domains. With the convergence of powerful technologies, building metaverse systems and environments become a simple and speedy affair. Experts envisage new possibilities and opportunities emerging and evolving with a deep and decisive understanding of the metaverse paradigm. Experts have pointed out that the intended success of the metaverse squarely depends on the roll-out of 6G communication infrastructure. That is, real-time sensing, communication, processing, decision-making, and actuation are becoming positive with the surging popularity of edge computing, which fully complies with the ideals of distributed and decentralized processing and storage precepts.

The possibilities of the metaverse seem endless, yet those tantalizing benefits can only be resiliently realized atop a dependable 6G infrastructure. The flexibility and capability of the network, the global coverage it provides, and the use of distributed computing and sensing systems will result in a more seamless interworking of various communications technologies.

1.7.2 The cloud-native infrastructures for the metaverse

We need cloud-native infrastructure to power the metaverse vision and mission. All kinds of IoT sensors and devices are being integrated with cloud-hosted applications. Enterprise-grade applications are becoming microservices-centric and containerized, deployed, and managed through container orchestration platforms like Kubernetes. DevOps practices and site reliability engineering (SRE) principles are gaining the attention of many for speedy software delivery and management. Metaverse applications, being complicated and composite, are being recommended to be built on the cloud-native architecture (CNA) precepts. With the CNA tool ecosystem growing consistently, building and releasing cloud-native applications attracts more significant attention.

AI has to become the core and central aspect of 6G to guarantee higher bandwidth and lower latency amid cognitive uncertainties. AI can dramatically improve bandwidth while reducing network latency. Further on, 6G network infrastructures will enable us to realize the grandiose vision of the metaverse where a person will feel immersed in a virtual and three-dimensional world. 6G technology will open up fresh possibilities and opportunities. Unknown things will be foreseen in the metaverse era to provide society with premium and path-breaking products, solutions, and services. 6G networks will have the capacity and capability to transmit, process, and analyze the massive amount of poly-structured data. 6G can accommodate a more significant number of users. Billions of connected devices are to participate and benefit immensely through the breakthrough 6G technologies. 6G will ensure 1 μs latency for latency-critical applications such as metaverse systems.

Thus, compute, network, storage, and security infrastructure resources must be resilient and versatile to support the enigmatic metaverse era.

1.8 6G for the metaverse

6G communication networks will guarantee high reliability. Discussions are happening around incorporating advanced features in 6G. AI will be the critical technology for the projected strength and success of 6G communication. The adaptability, resiliency, maneuverability, and reliability of 6G help visualize sophisticated metaverse systems. Metaverse in sync with 6G can lead to many ground-breaking and trendsetting systems, solutions, and services. Product engineers, owners, and end-users collaborate in the virtual world to accelerate product design and development.

One of the critical features of the metaverse is its fully immersive and interactive environment. Users will be able to interact with each other in real time, which means that the network infrastructure will need to handle a massive amount of data in real time. 6G technology is expected to achieve speeds of up to 1 Tbps.

Another critical aspect of the metaverse is that it has to support many users. 6G technology is expected to support up to 1 million devices per square kilometer. Metaverse has to guarantee a low-latency network infrastructure. 6G technology is expected to support 1-ms latency. The metaverse will consume a lot of computing power and a high amount of power energy. It is speculated that 6G technology is energy-efficient. That is, the 6G-enabled metaverse can handle a massive amount of data without the less wastage of energy.

Metaverse is a virtual world wherein users can interact with each other and digital objects. The metaverse has the innate strength to revolutionize how we live, learn, work, contribute, and socialize. With the introduction of 6G technology, the metaverse is poised to provide better and bigger things. Today, Zoom calls are prevalent and productive. Remote work, collaboration, and immersive gaming will become the new normal. With 6G communication networks, it is possible to create virtual meeting rooms, which guarantee real-time collaboration between people and digital objects across national boundaries.

The metaverse through 6G enablement can change how city designers and dwellers develop, run, and manage city infrastructures (healthcare, social, connectivity, and cyber). City architects and urban planners can confidently use the metaverse to create digital models of office buildings and infrastructures. Digital models can be subjected to various investigations to understand everything needed to build and improve mesmerizing buildings, manufacturing floors, nuclear installations, expressways, tunnels, stadiums, airports, etc. The metaverse with 6G can be a crucial driver in creating modern and sustainable transportation systems, energy grids, etc. In the healthcare industry, metaverse can be applicable across areas, including holographic medical imaging, or by enabling real-time interactions between patients, healthcare professionals, and caregivers, irrespective of geographical boundaries.

The metaverse can help significantly improve the manufacturing process, particularly in product design and development, by facilitating an improved relationship and interaction between the key stakeholders—business owners, suppliers, and end customers. Apart from this, customers in the metaverse could have much better and improved visibility into the supply chain process with 3D representations of how products are designed, built, distributed, and sold. Overall, the future of the metaverse holds immense potential to revolutionize a wide range of sectors, and 6G can enable us to realize the metaverse vision.

6G will be an exponentially powerful successor to 5G cellular technology within the next decade. 6G will use higher frequencies to provide significantly higher data transmission capacity at extremely low latency. The 6G Internet is to support 1-μs latency. This is 1,000 times faster, or 1/1000th the latency, than 1 ms throughput.

1.8.1 6G-enabled edge AI for the metaverse

Edge AI is the strategically sound combination of two powerful edge computing paradigms and artificial intelligence (AI). Increasingly, data processing and analytics are being performed on the edge. With the growing deployment of resource-intensive connected devices at ground level, edge data processing gains speed. By directly deploying highly optimized AI models (machine and deep learning models) in edge devices with some memory, storage, and processing power, edge devices are intelligent in their contributions. Precisely speaking, the paradigm of edge intelligence is emerging and evolving with the widespread adoption of edge AI technologies, frameworks, libraries, toolsets, AI accelerators, the heightened usage of resourceful edge devices across environments such as homes, hotels, hospitals, warehouses, manufacturing floors, stadiums, transport vehicles, etc. Edge AI and cloud AI are flourishing.

Edge AI enables edge devices to process diverse inputs (audio, images, videos, etc.) at the edge. 6G is projected to be the best-in-class communication technology for receiving such a massive volume of data. Edge intelligence is the need of the hour to make real-world interactions between physical and virtual worlds a new standard.

Performing data analytics at the edge brings in a suite of advantages. Real-time knowledge discovery and dissemination are vital for producing and improving real-time services and applications. Making sense of data heaps instantly is essential for envisaging next-generation metaverse applications. By processing data locally, there is less need to send edge data to faraway clouds. Further on, data security and privacy are fully ensured through such a setup. Acquiring the distinct capability of data interpretation in real time can lead to the realization of sophisticated software applications. 6G is the way forward to fulfill this fabulous and futuristic transition. 6G will gain the inherent strength and sagacity to adapt to varying connectivity situations. In short, knowing edge insights in real time goes a long way in ensuring every individual's safety, smartness, and privacy.

Data filtering at the source results in less data being transmitted to off-premise, online, and on-demand clouds. The bandwidth gets preserved, and local data processing can eliminate the dire implications of sending confidential, customer, and corporate data in open and public networks. 6G greatly supplements edge computing and vice versa. 6G propels the data transmission rate.

By using the improvisations being achieved in the blockchain technology space, it is possible to ensure the tightest security for private data. Data breaches can be stopped.

With the higher reliability being inherently guaranteed by 6G communication, edge processing becomes reliable. Machine-to-machine (M2M) interactions become speedier and more intelligent. Such 6G enablement will directly result in next-generation metaverse systems.

1.9 Conclusion

Metaverse refers to virtual worlds that are created and maintained by their users. It is an online space wherein people can interact with each other and with computer-generated virtual environments and characters. Virtual reality (VR) is a simulated environment accessed through a VR headset or other device. VR allows users to experience a different world or scenario, which can be realistic or fantastical. Augmented reality (AR) overlays digital information in the real world. This can be done using a head-mounted display, smartphone, or other personal digital assistant. Thus, the metaverse is a user-created online space, VR is a simulated environment, and AR overlays digital content in the real world.

Chapter 2

Metaverse enabling technologies and industry use cases

Pethuru Raj[1]

Abstract

The Internet paradigm is proliferating. The early version of the Internet (Web 1.0) supported only the read mode. Then came the second version (Web 2.0), which supports both read and write modes. The next evolution is Web 3.0, a decentralized and interoperable version of the Internet. The dreamt era of the metaverse is to be primarily realized through the power of Web 3.0 in association with extended reality, AI, 5G, edge computing, and IoT technologies. Metaverse is a 3D shared virtual space that is hyper-realistic, immersive, instinctive, and interactive. The metaverse is posed to reflect the real world digitally and diametrically.

The much-discussed metaverse represents the next-generation universe, and the prime implementation infrastructure for the metaverse is the future Internet (Web 3.0), which leads to a kind of 3D virtual world wherein users interact with various spaces and virtual reality components using digital avatars. In a nutshell, the metaverse is the grandiose intersection and seamless crossover between real and digital worlds. The potential and promising digital technologies are a huge enabler of the metaverse dream. A dazzling array of pulsating metaverse applications is being envisaged and realized through the intelligent leverage of pioneering digital technologies and tools. There are specific challenges and concerns widely associated with the metaverse era. This chapter delineates the various versatile metaverse applications, implementation technologies, and use cases (individual and industrial).

Keywords: Artificial Intelligence (AI); Edge Intelligence; Generative Intelligence; Adaptive Metaverse; Non-Fungible Token (NFT); Digital Payments

2.1 Introduction

The data communication happened in text, images, audio, and videos. Now, communication is evolving further to accommodate new and different dimensions. This

[1]Edge AI Division, Reliance Jio Platforms Ltd., Bangalore, India

has laid a stimulating and sparkling foundation for the ensuing era of the metaverse. The faster maturity and stability of digital platforms, processes, and products have decisively paved the way for envisioning and expressing the strategically sound advantages of the metaverse concept. The prominent metaverse technologies include artificial intelligence (AI) (machine and deep learning (ML/DL) algorithms), the Internet of things (IoT), 5G communication, digital twins, edge computing, blockchain, digital spaces, virtual, augmented and mixed realities (VR/AR/MR), etc. As is widely known, the metaverse is the next significant evolution of the current Internet. The metaverse guarantees an immersive and immaculate experience for users. Platform and tool vendors are coming out with integrated development and deployment platforms. Cloud service providers are jumping into the metaverse bandwagon. Gamers and other users are so excited about the vast prospects of the metaverse phenomenon. Several distinct possibilities are being propagated. Experts and exponents across the globe point out that newer and hitherto unheard opportunities are waiting for those who plunge into this futuristic field of study and research.

As an expert in this fast-growing field pointed out, the metaverse is not just a digital world. Metaverse is the seamless crossover between the real and digital worlds. It is all about leveraging extended (virtual, augmented, and mixed) reality technologies associated with multifaceted IoT sensors and devices to bring the real world into the digital world. Moreover, on the other side, it is about bringing the digital into the real world. This enigmatic and elegant fusion is to open a bevy of innovations and disruptions in the days to unfurl. The widely reported digital intelligence is bound to flourish with this combination. Real-time and real-world intelligent systems can be visualized and implemented through the spontaneous convergence of the digital and physical worlds. This strategically sound intersection has laid a stimulating foundation to build and release evolutionary and revolutionary metaverse applications for various industry verticals.

2.2 Describing the metaverse technologies and tools

Undoubtedly, the metaverse represents the next-generation universe, which will be mesmerizingly multi-dimensional, multi-purpose, and multifaceted. Users can enter a metaverse environment through a specialized VR headset (which is very expensive now). This costly and bulky gear can become a software library that can be pre-installed on our smartphones. A small additional hardware module can fully facilitate experimenting and experiencing the projected metaverse. The metaverse represents an extended virtual world. Here, in this shared virtual world, every participant can have his or her own augmented digital "body" (avatar) that he or she can easily customize. Also, the participant can have a home filled up with a growing collection of preferred artifacts, etc. He or she can visit hundreds of places and spaces virtually. He can interact with other users in the virtual world, accomplish complicated tasks collaboratively, play games intuitively and intensely, spend time usefully learning and sharing what is learned, etc. In short, whatever we do in our everyday environments (homes, hotels, hospitals, etc.) can be comfortably replicated in a virtual environment. The metaverse idea is blooming because it brings forth a dazzling array of individual and industrial use cases. For example, experts point out that the metaverse can reduce our travel needs across the globe. Instead, we can enjoy and experience different dream locations worldwide with all the comfort of our homes.

Conversely, augmented reality (AR) gears can substantially augment our physical places and products. In a 3D world, we can visualize and interact with any object easily. We can quickly switch between activities and locations by making a simple gesture. In the digital world, everything is connected, readily available, and accessible to understand its unique capabilities.

With more such pulsating and peculiar use cases emerging and evolving, building and releasing metaverse applications formally leveraging an end-to-end technology stack has gained momentum in the recent past. Fortunately, several development and deployment platforms and frameworks exist for producing and delivering new-generation metaverse offerings. However, building such applications is very tricky yet trendsetting. The mission of establishing and sustaining the metaverse is radically simplified through the power of a bevy of digital technologies. In this section, we will discuss the most indispensable technologies that can speed up the dawn of the metaverse era.

1. Artificial Intelligence (AI)
2. Integrated Analytics (Big and Streaming Data)
3. Blockchain Technology
4. The Internet of Things (IoT)—Digitized entities, connected devices, drones, robots, etc.
5. Data Fabric and Mesh
6. 5G and Wi-Fi 6 Communication
7. Digital Twins
8. Cloud-native Computing
9. Fog/Edge Computing
10. Serverless Computing
11. Microservices Architecture (MSA) and Service Mesh
12. Event-driven Architecture (EDA) and Event Mesh
13. Augmented and Virtual Reality (AR/VR) for Metaverse
14. Cybersecurity

2.3 The trends and transitions in the digital era

1. The Web is moving towards Web 3.0
2. The universe is heading toward the metaverse

2.3.1 About Web 3.0

With Web 3.0, applications and services use a decentralized blockchain instead of a centralized database. Communities will be developed as decentralized autonomous organizations (DAOs). Web 3.0 will also use AI to produce intelligent and adaptive applications. HTML will continue to be a foundational layer with Web 3.0, but how it connects to data sources and where those data sources reside are different.

1. **Decentralized**—Web applications and services will be architected and developed in a decentralized setup with no central authority.
2. **Blockchain-based**—Blockchain is an enabler for creating decentralized applications and services. It can also create a decentralized database, an immutable ledger of transactions and activities. Such an enablement helps provide verifiable authenticity in an increasingly decentralized world.
3. **Cryptocurrency-enabled**—Cryptocurrency usage will become a key feature of Web 3.0 services.
4. **Autonomous and AI-enabled**—Automation is a critical feature of Web 3.0, and it will essentially be powered by AI (machine and deep learning) algorithms and models.

As indicated above, Web 3.0 is the next evolution of the Internet paradigm. This represents the evolution of how users can create and control their identities, digital content, and services. Digital creators can make money by leveraging the popular blockchain technology in a highly secure manner. Non-fungible tokens (NFTs) are a famous use case for blockchain technology. NFTs are a shining example of owning, securing, and selling digital arts and assets with the aid of the powerful blockchain method. NFTs make it possible for items to exist uniquely in the increasingly digital and connected world. In the current web environment, anyone can cut, copy, and paste digital data and content. However, certain digital items are essential and memorable; hence, ensuring their ownership and manipulation is mandatory. Therefore, noteworthy digital arts are being formally tokenized and secured through the inherent strength of blockchain.

Web 3.0 is blossoming as an effective tool for decentralization and the future of governance, data management, and financial transactions. Web 3.0 is being built on the blockchain protocol, which is decentralized. This protocol does not mandate hosting and managing digital content and services in a centralized location. The point to be noted here is that the real power lies with the creator. In the current Web 2.0, everything is centralized and controlled. Digital creators have partial power. Instead, Web 2.0 service providers gain all the power of managing digital content and services. For example, Twitter can remove our account and content anytime without our approval because the operating control lies with Twitter.

Previously, the semantic Web was termed as Web 3.0. The Internet paradigm started with Web 1.0 (simple Web) and then moved to Web 2.0 (social Web). The world is moving towards Web 3.0 (semantic Web) with digital technologies' faster maturity and stability. However, the projected semantic Web is not the same as Web 3.0. The semantic Web is acquiring special significance because it has the potential to enable many web pages to be brought together and correlated using a semantic protocol. Such an arrangement helps users extract highly beneficial relationships between web pages. A comprehensive search is possible when the idea of a semantic web matures with the ready availability of enabling technologies and tools. Semantically correct content and services will be identified and supplied for any search query. All web pages can be indexed based on their relevance and affinity. Answering complex questions will be a correct and comprehensive affair.

The current web pages and portals provide two-dimensional experiences only. However, Web 3.0 may be three-dimensional, so users can get an immersive experience in the web world, as in the real world. Our everyday and industrial environments are increasingly stuffed and sandwiched with scores of multifaceted sensors, actuators, and other edge technologies. Therefore, people will get an interactive experience due to the environmental sensors' triggers. Gestures, voice commands, and other movements will guarantee a distinct experience. In simple terms, Web 3.0 is the decentralized Internet succulently built on blockchain technology. The economic value of Web 3.0 is bound to grow fast in the days to unfold. Web 3.0 can host NFTs, applications, and their data in a decentralized, publicly discoverable, network-accessible, highly usable, and secure manner. Web 3.0 applications, tokens, and data on the blockchain layer are being seen as a game-changer.

Blockchain and Web 3.0 data can be analyzed using AI algorithms and models to extract actionable insights. In the Web 3.0 world, making sense of data and making money is to thrive soon. Experts are pondering integrating Web 3.0 and blockchain to create a stimulating and sparkling foundation. With the deployment of 5G and 6G communication networks, the Web 3.0 paradigm will shine fully.

2.3.2 About the metaverse

Pundits and proponents proclaim that the metaverse is a convergence of physical, virtual, and augmented realities where people appear as digital avatars that can interact with one another in a shared 3D virtual space. The metaverse is an interoperable network consisting of real-time rendered 3D virtual spaces, which can be accessed with the help of special AR/VR devices. With the faster proliferation of social media, distributed gaming, NFTs, and cryptocurrencies, people started to experience the whole gamut of immersive and intuitive experiences in the increasingly virtual world.

As indicated above, once in the metaverse, people can create and customize their digital identities/representations (avatars) and choose their body parameters: hair style and color, clothes, accessories, and other related things. The metaverse reality brings many fresh possibilities and opportunities for individuals, innovators, and institutions. The projected metaverse has the innate potential to bring a paradigm shift in how people socialize, collaborate, innovate, work, play, shop, etc. Visitors can do immersive and intimate social chats with their friends. Gamers can explore a range of exuberant games. The metaverse can pave the way for the development of sophisticated virtual offices. Professionals can hold 3D meetings and bring new energy and enthusiasm to office life. The other possibilities include creating and making erudite presentations elegantly, working together on completing projects from geographically distributed locations, etc.

With continued support for the metaverse paradigm from different quarters, virtual clothing, accessories, and cosmetics will be available. As inscribed above, such virtual assets and spaces astutely coordinate to usher in a dazzling array of exciting and inspiring applications. Virtual living and collaboration will thrive ceaselessly. Brands and businesses will sustain their yearned edge through next-generation virtual products, solutions, and services.

2.3.3 Delineating metaverse

The metaverse is a three-dimensional immersive environment fully empowered by augmented, virtual, and mixed reality (AR/VR/MR) technologies. Such a setup allows users to interact calmly with different 3D objects in that environment.

The primary goal is to create a replica of the real world. Metaverse environments are entirely complete, with designated areas for work, play, and social activities. The beauty is that all of these virtual spaces are intrinsically interoperable. Multiple virtual environments can be seamlessly integrated, and they are, therefore, spontaneously and spatially interactive. Virtual objects and environments are hosted on the blockchain to achieve much-needed decentralization.

Cryptocurrencies are a foundational and fundamental mechanism for economically valuable assets and arts in the metaverse era. With the surging popularity of cryptocurrencies, all kinds of virtual shopping, gaming, financial transactions, work collaborations, knowledge sharing, etc., are getting simplified and speeded up in the metaverse as they are being done in the real world. Cryptocurrencies are popular as they eliminate intermediaries such as banks, clearinghouses, stock exchanges, and brokerages. The costs associated with intermediaries are enormous; hence, cryptocurrencies have acquired unprecedented attention and attraction these days from many quarters.

The Internet's future is bright and brilliant with the faster adoption and adaptation of Web 3.0 and blockchain technologies. Blockchain is famous for guaranteeing unbreakable and impenetrable data security. As described above, NFTs are immensely beneficial due to a string of advancements in the blockchain space. In the fast-evolving digital era, blockchain is expected to ensure exceptional security while providing the necessary, immutable financial infrastructure.

In conjunction with blockchain technology, the Internet of Things (IoT), and artificial intelligence (AI) concepts, the Web 3.0 phenomenon will grow dynamically and drastically in stature, fulfilling the much-anticipated decentralization and personalization requirements. For example, blockchain facilitates peer-to-peer (P2P) transactions without financial services providers such as banks in between users. Blockchain greatly simplifies storing and exchanging data within different metaverse platforms and ensures digital proof of ownership for assets within the metaverse.

2.4 3D modeling and recreation

3D modeling has set the idea of the metaverse to arrive and thrive. Inspired developers systematically build 3D models for various real-world products, which are being released for broader usage. To set up virtual environments, various physical objects must first be 3D-modeled. As we discuss below, there are multiple technologies to enable everyone to experience the power of 3D virtual spaces. Retail service providers have created competent virtual stores to improve the shoppers' experience and to drive away e-commerce. New avenues will emerge to explore fresh revenues. In the current and conventional e-commerce portals, high-resolution images and videos are being incorporated to excite and convince buyers. However, this works differently in the metaverse world. Still, dynamic images are sufficient in the physical world, but in the metaverse era, 3D digital avatars can imitate our real-world and real-time lives. That is, 3D goods are the way to march ahead. 3D recreations and representations are gaining immense attention and attraction to increase engagement and profit potential. That is, 3D representations give more details about an item than just an image of the item. The item can be viewed from different angles. When an item is virtually placed in a user's place using augmented reality, users can get a load of information, such as its exact size, fit, and look. Thus, the extended reality capability gives users much-needed confidence and clarity to decide quickly whether to buy the item. Market analysts and researchers say that retail giants can sell many items by embedding 3D content in their stuff. Thus, there is no doubt about the noteworthy contributions of 3D modeling. There are enabling platforms and toolsets for producing 3D models without much complications.

2.5 Virtual reality (VR)

Virtual reality (VR) is emerging as one of the most powerful technologies for the ensuing era of the metaverse. However, VR technology is at a very primitive stage as there are several challenges and concerns, as pointed out by experts. In order to experience the power of virtual reality fully and fabulously, the user needs to wear a special VR headset, which incidentally does not allow head or body movement to get the delightful experience. Many works remain to be accomplished so that the VR paradigm can prosper as a significant part of the metaverse. Thus, the field of VR has to go a long way to be pervasive and persuasive. 3D modeling will be mainly fused with VR technology to create an aura of the forthcoming metaverse.

2.6 Augmented reality (AR)

Augmented reality (AR) is seen as a solid enabler of the metaverse. AR fluently blends with VR to provide a seamless and spontaneous interaction between the real and the digital worlds. AR is about overlaying images and other relevant meta-information over real-world objects and environments. Any physical artifact can be empowered through AR technology. AR technology is being made available in most smartphones; hence, AR is a good substitute for experiencing the varying facets of the metaverse. Of course, AR does not guarantee a fully immersive experience. However, AR is an affordable and adaptive option for fulfilling the vision of the metaverse. Conceptually, VR facilitates participants to work in virtual worlds, whereas AR augments physical objects and environments with additional details in time. The physical world is augmented with much relevant knowledge to enable users.

For example, Meta Spark Studio (https://sparkar.facebook.com/ar-studio/) gives you all the right tools, from templates to asset libraries, to simplify and speed up customization needs. These noteworthy additions to its current Spark AR platform provide voice effects, improved depth mapping, and effects blending. Such features empower developers to bring forth breakthrough metaverse applications. Ultimately, this toolkit helps to build the most creative, complex, and immersive AR experiences.

Meta (https://about.fb.com/news/2021/10/facebook-company-is-now-meta/) is keenly strategizing to be a metaverse powerhouse. Meta is rolling out a powerful audio engine to achieve advanced audio integrations. This specialized engine will make clubbing together multiple audio sources easy and allow mesmerizing audio effects to be crafted. You can easily add voice, sound effects, and music tracks to engage and entertain dance. Such an enhancement will open up exciting possibilities, including building multisensory effects. This helps people use sight and sound artistically to get an immersive experience.

Machine vision and perception have become a common aspect of modern-day smartphones. These can accurately detect and interpret a simple scene to take better photos. With LiDAR sensors, smartphone cameras are also empowered to capture details of depth and distance. Several fresh features are consistently added to enhance the users' experience with VR and AR technology. An engaging and energizing environment is created and sustained through mixed reality (MR) software solutions.

With the faster maturity of the metaverse technologies, the era of traditional e-commerce is all set to an end. Today, buyers want a better and more profound experience while shopping online. They want to buy what they like by considering several features. Therefore, virtual fitting room solutions are readily and rewardingly attached to e-commerce sites. Such an addition can guarantee an immersive experience for shoppers. With a flurry of virtual and augmented reality technologies and tools, the shopping experience will reach a different level in the years ahead.

The much-celebrated AR technology is gradually being experimented with in retail stores to provide real-world immersive experiences to shoppers. This perfectly facilitates the "try before you buy" strategy. Through the capability of a virtual fitting room, shoppers can try on different clothes, dresses, and other items virtually with AR technology before making an informed decision on buying or rejecting them.

A virtual fitting room is the digital version of an in-store dressing room. Well-known e-commerce stores offer this innovative facility to their royal and loyal customers. Customers can try on a product virtually through this virtual room facility to visualize how it may look on their bodies. They can easily understand and evaluate features such as color, pattern, and style before purchasing. Virtual fitting rooms extensively utilize proven AR and AI technologies to digitally recreate the dressing room experience. These solutions can also help brands meet and even extend their business targets. YourFit (https://3dlook.me/yourfit/) turns shoppers into buyers by providing an ultimate virtual fitting experience.

Similarly, IKEA Place lets you virtually place true-to-scale 3D models in your space. This unique and technology-inspired functionality lets shoppers place virtual furniture in their house to see how it may look before buying it. Combining proven AR technology, IKEA's smart home solutions provide a new experience. This virtual fitting technology is profitably used for selling various accessories such as dresses, eyeglasses, watches, hats, furniture, etc.

Users increasingly view a virtual world using VR and AR-enabled gadgets such as headgear, smart glasses, and handles. There are plenty of easy-to-use wearables and handhelds to guarantee the metaverse experience. These unique hardware products help participants to view their stuff and surroundings in an extra dimension. This 3D visualization is accomplished by augmenting physical things. In the metaverse era, 3D images, sounds, texts, and videos are prevalent and paramount. Users can be immersed in doing multiple things in a digital environment with high-end security and transparency.

2.7 Artificial Intelligence (AI)

Artificial Intelligence is the most promising and potential technology for the forthcoming digital era. AI can comfortably use tremendous digital data to produce actionable insights in time. The most complicated task of accumulating and transitioning raw data to information and insights is being singlehandedly ensured through AI technologies and tools' intrinsic and envious power. That is, AI plays a pivotal role in shaping the knowledge era. The much-needed goals of automated knowledge discovery and dissemination towards bringing forth next-generation business workloads and IT services are being facilitated and fulfilled through the sagacious usage of the distinguished competencies of the AI paradigm. AI mission and vision are being enigmatically supplanted through AI technologies and tools. AI can work with different technologies to improve automation and optimization across industry verticals.

Experts have pointed out that extended reality technologies such as AR and VR have severe limitations. However, there is good news. Developers can overcome those identified lacunae and issues with the smart leverage of AI. AI can elegantly handle creating lifelike 3D spaces, delivering realistic and real-world experiences, running complex calculations necessary for AR face-tracking, and accomplishing other complicated tasks. As is widely known, AI can quickly complete such tasks more efficiently than humans.

2.8 Natural language processing (NLP)

Natural language processing is one of the prominent application domains of AI. Through the use of breakthrough AI algorithms (machine and deep learning

ML/DL algorithms), frameworks, platforms, accelerators, specialized engines, toolsets, libraries, etc., computer vision (CV) and NLP use cases can be ideally implemented and deployed as AI services in cloud environments to be publicly discoverable, network-accessible, horizontally scalable, composable, highly available and reliable, patchable, etc. Incidentally, the NLP capability being realized through the AI phenomenon is to contribute illustratively to the ensuing era of the metaverse. That is, numerous next-generation metaverse applications can be built and deployed through the bountiful contributions of the NLP ability. The NLP feature is embedded in today's computers, communicators, machines, gizmos, and gadgets.

The prime point of NLP is to understand human speech naturally and translate it into another communication language. Further on, speech can be converted into text. Similarly, text can be transitioned into human speech. Thus, speech recognition and translation, text summarization, text-to-speech conversion, etc., can all be meticulously done using AI-inspired NLP capability. We are increasingly comfortable with NLP-inspired chatbots. The new facet of conversational AI is emerging and capturing people's imagination through the ingenuity of the NLP concept. For example, Google Translate (https://translate.google.co.in/) is one of the most popular translation engines.

Today, man–machine interfacing is being extensively facilitated by AI. Humans can leisurely interact with machines on manufacturing floors, retail stores, warehouses, classic auditoriums, airports, etc. With digitization and edge technologies flourishing, all physical, mechanical, electrical, and electronic systems are digitized, connected, and embedded with edge AI capability. The pioneering edge AI paradigm enables edge devices (networked embedded systems) to gain a real-time understanding of their surroundings. By incorporating the much-celebrated edge AI property, device-to-device and human-to-device integration scenarios are gathering momentum. Precisely speaking, edge devices are interactive and augmented through AR technologies and tools to beneficially participate in constructing robust metaverse applications.

The NLP capability distinctively empowers all digital artifacts (computers and edge devices) to recognize and understand natural human languages. Written or spoken human speech is converted into a form that machinery, wearables, portables, and implantable, nomadic, and mobile devices can understand through NLP techniques. Several NLP-enabled use cases exist in our smartphones, such as spell-checkers, online search, translators, and voice assistants. Thus, NLP enables machine intelligence.

Several other tasks are being automated and accelerated through NLP power. Predicting the next word in a sentence is a crucial contribution of the NLP capability. Alibaba's DAMO Academy has developed the StructBERT NLP model (https://arxiv.org/pdf/1908.04577.pdf), which can analyze the text of medical records and epidemiological investigations. This NLP model comes in handy in treating COVID-19 patients effectively. NLP is constructive and cooperative in building and deploying impenetrable and unbreakable systems. NLP is powering up the realization of conversational AI. Slowly yet steadily, humans have been replaced by NLP-based chatbots. Essential questions are answered, and repetitive tasks are handled through NLP-based bots.

2.8.1 Computer vision (CV)

Computer vision (CV) is another prime use case of the AI paradigm. The widely reported CV capability empowers computers and embedded systems to see and understand their surroundings. The computer vision feature enables digital assets and machines to recognize any visual input, such as images, and to detect the specific objects in images. CV capability also helps machines uncover hidden patterns in images and videos. Context awareness and recognition of gestures and moods are facilitated through the mesmerizing CV functionality, accomplished through deep learning (DL) models.

As articulated above, one primary limitation of VR and AR experiences is the lack of control. Computer vision can overcome this problem through hand tracking. Users can naturally interact with their devices by aptly recognizing gestures and finger positions.

Here is an AR implementation. This includes working together with both the smartphone's video camera and LiDAR. Video camera captures the image or the video of the natural world and the user's hand. LiDAR then estimates the distance between the real-world objects and the user's hand. With those details, it is possible to place some virtual objects on the phone screen correctly. The virtual object looks like a part of the natural world for the user. Computer vision helps to recognize whether the user tries to interact with the virtual object with the hand. Through such interactions, it is possible to do many things. For example, a user can put a virtual object into a shopping cart in a virtual store.

The computer vision capability can do great things for the metaverse era. For example, ReadyPlayerMe (https://readyplayer.me/) uses face recognition to create a virtual avatar. To use a variety of video games and development platforms, users ought to create a brand-new avatar every time. However, when these avatars are created by computer vision, they can be used across different platforms. As indicated, users typically interact with the metaverse through digital avatars with bodies. Therefore, it is essential to have information on posture.

2.8.2 Human pose estimation (HPE)

Human pose estimation (HPE) is a prominent case of use in computer vision. HPE uses multiple motion-sensing devices like controllers, gloves, etc. HPE generally recognizes various body parts and their positions in an environment. The accuracy of pose estimation goes up through the accurate recognition of hand gestures, gait, eye tracking, and human expression. Users can choose an appropriate avatar through HPE and dive into the digital world. Simultaneously, the activity recognition capability can notice and understand interactive activities such as grabbing items or pushing buttons.

HPE typically predicts the poses of human body parts and joints in images or videos. Capturing a human's body pose is essential for recognizing specific human activities. 2D HPE estimates the location of human body key points from visuals (images and videos) in two-dimensional (2D) space. 3D HPE predicts the locations of body joints in 3D space.

While 2D human datasets can be easily obtained, collecting accurate 3D pose images is difficult. Going forward, making annotations on 3D pose images is time-consuming. In the recent past, 3D pose tracking has made considerable advancements. Still, many challenges remain. They are model generalization, robustness to occlusion, computation efficiency, etc. Fortunately, there is a growing array of state-of-the-art software solutions and libraries leveraging deep neural networks for real-time 3D HPE.

2.8.3 3D human body modeling

Through HPE, the location of various human body parts can be identified from visual data. This knowledge can be used to build a high-quality human body representation, a body skeleton pose. Therefore, human body modeling activity is vital in correctly estimating human poses. The body model generally illustrates the features and the key points squeezed out of visual input data. A human body model precisely describes and infers human body poses. This model can render 2D or 3D poses. Therefore, the skeleton pose estimation models capture the relations between different body parts.

Thus, HPE is a computer vision (CV) task that detects, associates, and tracks semantic key points. Examples of semantic vital points are "right shoulders," "left knees," etc. There are several multi-pose and single-pose methods emerging and evolving. The idea of single pose estimation is to correctly estimate the poses of a single object in a given scene. On the other hand, the multi-pose estimation is for rightly detecting poses for multiple objects. There are robust deep neural networks (DNNs), such as convolutional neural networks (CNNs), tailored for performing HPE.

Human post-estimation is to identify and classify specific parts of our bodies, such as limbs and joints. By leveraging this acquired knowledge, machines can finalize human poses. Empowering machines to do these can lead to envisaging and implementing a growing array of hitherto unheard applications such as fitness and rehabilitation. In a nutshell, the extracted knowledge helps to produce a concise and precise 2D or 3D representation of a human body. Performing the semantic key point tracking in live video footage demands a lot of computational resources. Researchers are unearthing several critical advancements and have several real-world and real-time applications. The prominent ones include self-driving vehicles and last-mile delivery robots.

Traditionally, object detection involves using a bounding box (a square) to perceive people or any object in an image or video. However, by performing pose detection and tracking, computers can capture and understand a lot about human body language. Tracking the human pose in real time helps understand human behavior clearly. This real-time capability solely drives the widely articulated use case of autonomous driving.

In summary, HPE can be used to track critical points on the human body and pass this data to the AR engine, which, in turn, will fit clothes on the user. This can be applied to clothes, face masks, etc. Pose estimation is popular in computer vision, which imitates human vision.

2.8.4 Human activity estimation

The previous sections discussed the significance of human body modeling and pose estimation. Pose estimation can track and measure human activity and movement. There are proven and potential architectures for activity, gesture, and gait recognition. Pose estimation neatly enables concrete examples of human activity tracking.

AR and VR applications empowered with pose estimation guarantee a better online experience. Users can virtually learn to play games like tennis via virtual tutors who are pose-represented. The United States Army experiments with augmented reality programs for combat use. These help soldiers distinguish between enemies and friendly troops and improve night vision. Other critical applications of pose estimation are in-game applications, where human subjects auto-generate and inject poses into the game environment for an intuitive and interactive gaming experience.

2.8.5 Providing surveillance services

Though online shopping is gathering momentum, retail sales still occur in brick-and-mortar stores. Shoppers in physical stores prefer checkout-free shopping. The facility of fully automated checkout is being provided in certain stores (Amazon Go, Tesco, Walmart, etc.) across the globe through the liberal usage of CCTV cameras. Computer vision's fast-maturing and stabilizing capability is the main driver for this sophisticated functionality. The above-discussed HPE comes in handy in understanding whether a person is taking some item from a retail store shelf. The HPE model analyzes the position of customers' hands and heads to understand if they took the product from the shelf or left it in its place. HPE is neither simple nor straightforward. HPE mandates a strong expertise across several technological domains.

2.9 The Internet of Things (IoT) for the metaverse era

We discussed the unique contributions of VR, AR, and AI technologies to streamlining the onset and sustenance of the metaverse era. This section will shed some light on how the IoT paradigm will be a game-changing phenomenon in this mesmerizing era.

We have a dazzling array of features-rich sensors and actuators being deployed in any mission-critical environment these days to capture and actuate many things in an automated manner. That is, digitized entities (all physical, mechanical, and electrical systems getting enabled to be digitized through a host of digitization and edge technologies) and the growing device ecosystem are decorating our everyday environments—homes, hotels, hospitals, etc. With the proliferation of IoT devices and sensors, there is a brighter and bigger scope for metaverse applications in the future. When interacting with themselves and their environments, the IoT artifacts generate massive multi-structured data. When applying AI-based processing to these data volumes, valuable insights are generated and used. Thus, for attaining the initially expressed benefits of the AI paradigm, the role and responsibility of the IoT phenomenon are becoming more significant.

IoT connectivity technologies—As indicated above, the IoT paradigm is to network many edge devices and connect edge devices with the cloud-hosted software platforms, services, and databases through the Internet, the most affordable, public, global-scale, and open communication infrastructure. There are short and long-range connectivity technologies. The world is looking forward to the 5G-advanced connectivity technology. Besides that, we have Wi-Fi 6, LPWAN, and satellite communications. Thus, all sorts of IoT devices connect locally and remotely to empower innovators to bring forth next-generation systems and services. Thus, the connectivity aspect is to produce mesmerizing use cases for institutions and individuals. Industry 4.0 and 5.0 applications can be developed through IoT devices (network embedded systems). Thus, connected entities are the most critical assets for implementing business and people empowerment solutions.

2.10 5G communication for the metaverse era

5G enables faster, more reliable, and secure connectivity for people to communicate and for all kinds of devices in our midst to interact and share their unique functionalities. Such a transition has resulted in a series of innovations and disruptions. Autonomous vehicles and cars are emerging; smart grids flourish globally; self-managing robots are found in manufacturing floors, warehouses, and other mission-critical environments. In short, all digitized artifacts across personal, social, and professional locations are connected to nearby and faraway cloud servers. Such seamless and spontaneous connectivity enables them to be empowered with extra capabilities. In short, a dazzling array of devices and sensors are getting digitized and networked by methodically applying proven and promising IoT technologies. Such transformation can usher in a series of game-changing use cases. The much-adored and adorned connectivity feature empowers our everyday devices to attain their individual and collective capacities and capabilities to accomplish more significant tasks.

There are anticipated to be billions of connected devices. However, the challenge is how to network them without compromising on requirements such as high speed, low latency, low cost, etc. The world has already started to experience 5G communication capability. 5G communication will become commonplace globally in the next couple of years. The specifications for the forthcoming 5G-advanced standard are under development. Around 2025 or after that, the 5G-advanced implementations will take shape.

To deliver ultra-high speeds with the lowest latencies, 5G networks leverage radio frequencies in two groups: FR1 is called the sub-6 GHz range, and FR2 stays between 24 and 52 GHz. FR2 is termed as the extremely high frequency (EHF) range. This is known as millimeter wave (mmWave) frequency, which lies between 30 GHz and 300 GHz. 5G supports massive Machine Type Communication (mMTC) or energy-efficient 5G by adopting the existing LTE LPWAN (Low Power Wide Area Network). This can efficiently transmit less data intermittently to and from devices that require comprehensive area coverage and long battery life. With more efficiency through 5G communication, handling tens of thousands of devices within a square kilometer is possible. This is ideal for smart meters. Narrowband IoT (NB-IoT) fits into the mMTC flavor of 5G technology, solidly addressing the LPWAN requirements of the IoT. LTE-M is another LPWAN technology fitting into the mMTC 5G category.

5G supports Ultra-Reliable Low Latency Communication (URLLC). This is termed mission-critical 5G, which guarantees high reliability while keeping the latency as low as 1 ms. This is ideal for highly reliable applications such as first responders, emergency services, and autonomous vehicles. Further, inspection drones, industrial IoT assets and robots, and AI-assisted smart medical devices need 5G communication to be correct and relevant in cases wherein milliseconds can eliminate disaster.

5G enables enhanced Mobile Broadband (eMBB). This is high-speed 5G, predominantly guaranteeing high data throughput by leveraging the greater bandwidth 5G spectrum. Besides the high bandwidth, data rate, and reliability, 5G communication networks achieve greater spectral efficiency. 5G delivers up to 10 Gbps. This is approximately ten times faster than 4G.

5G suits augmented and virtual reality (AR and VR). 5G is a game-changer for enterprises for smoothening industry automation. 5G provides lightning-fast speeds with imperceptible network latency. 5G eliminates energy leakage in order to strengthen sustainability. Thereby, innovative power-efficient design is incorporated for 5G networks. Along with new power management methods, higher throughput and reduced latency allow base stations and 5G networks to conserve energy. Data packets are being compressed to improve network traffic efficiency. Further on, the transmit and receive traffic is technologically controlled and optimized to increase rest time, and this mechanism can reduce energy consumption substantially.

There is a vast propagation loss of the millimeter wavelengths (mmWaves) employed in 5G new radio (NR) systems. Also, users demand high bandwidth. In order to meet these twin demands, beamforming techniques and massive multiple input and multiple output (MIMO) antennas are critical for increasing spectral efficiencies and providing reliable coverage. The other noteworthy improvisations include small cells, cloud-native network functions (CNFs), software-defined networks (SDNs), and network slicing. All these collaboratively reduce energy consumption.

Compartmentalizing (virtualization and containerization) networks help create multiple virtual networks over a shared network infrastructure to fulfill specific requirements. Such virtual networks are pronounced as the game-changer for the IoT world. The IoT idea can fulfill its initially expressed benefits only with higher data transfer throughput, expected to be delivered through 5G networks. Also, 5G ensures excellent coverage. That is, 5G networks can handle many IoT devices and sensors. Through slicing, 5G networks can quickly and elegantly meet the service level agreements (SLAs). A reliable and stable network condition is extremely important for any IoT system to benefit its users. With the faster maturity and stability of 5G communication, plenty of fresh opportunities and possibilities will exist. In summary, 5G is essential for the IoT era to shine.

As we know, various VR and AR tools are being rebranded as metaverse applications. High-speed connectivity is essential for these metaverse applications to succeed in their assignments. There is a greater emphasis on guaranteeing higher bandwidth and lower latency for the metaverse concept to provide its promises.

Currently, VR and AR applications need specialized equipment, which relies on users' data locally. To make these applications available to many, centralized data storage is needed. Cloud is the most appropriate platform for consolidated and centralized computing and storage. Fast streaming technologies are needed to experience genuinely immersive metaverse applications. There has to be a lower network latency between users' equipment and cloud-based data. As indicated above, 5G communication is the way forward. 5G gives lighting speed data transfer with single-digit milliseconds latency. The application scope for metaverse technologies is widening. In the subsequent sections, we will highlight the plausible use cases of the metaverse field.

Metaverse applications are succulently getting empowered through private 5G networks to bring forth a bevy of distinct innovations and disruptions. The advantages of embracing the metaverse domain are varied and vast: increasing business productivity, exploring new avenues for fresh revenues, creating optimized processes, achieving cost savings, generating premium and pulsating offerings to retain current customers and obtain new consumers, etc.

Multi-national companies offer products, solutions, and services across the world. Information and communication technologies (ICT) support businesses in their offerings. There are plenty of marketing and salespeople spread across the world. Further on, there are field workers providing product support and servicing. The field technicians offering repair and troubleshooting services can use the metaverse capability to complete their tasks neatly. During the pandemic period, personal and physical attention became risky and rare. Thereby, remote monitoring, diagnoses, and care flourished. Remote support and sustenance thrived with 5G communication. This works for companies of all sizes and sectors.

For the 5G and the forthcoming 6G communication networks, a metaverse is believed to add substantial economic value by surmounting some of the perpetual challenges. A 5G-connected metaverse can significantly help communication service providers get details about churn, making churn rate prediction easy. Besides benefiting consumers, the mesmerizing metaverse enables a range of business-to-business (B2B) and business-to-government (B2G) advantages. For example, a VR-powered metaverse can offer training to envisage and deliver premium offerings to users.

2.11 Non-fungible tokens (NFTs) and blockchain

Blockchain is the fountainhead for Web 3.0., which exhibits interoperability and automation by leveraging smart contracts and secure storage of data files. Blockchain plays a crucial role in changing conventional data storage and management approaches. Blockchain offers a unique collection of data (a universal state layer). This can be collectively managed. This unique state layer provides the opportunity to develop and use a value settlement layer on the Internet. That is why people call blockchain the fountainhead of the Internet of value. The state layer helps share files among peers in a highly secure manner. Blockchain eliminates intermediaries and still establishes much-needed trust when performing financial transactions.

The blockchain protocol ensures data security through a majority consensus from all network participants. Blockchain transforms data structures and supports the creation of a governance layer over the existing Internet. The governance layer fulfills the requirement of establishing trust between two unknown people. If there is any issue brewing, this governance layer can settle transactions over the Internet, which is the public, open, flexible, and affordable communication infrastructure across the globe.

Researchers are bringing forth several fresh use cases. Blockchain has become an essential protocol for data sharing and security. Blockchain presents an ideal foundation for Web 3.0 by natively supporting the elusive concept of decentralization. The current centralized control is beset with several challenges and concerns. Blockchain fully guarantees the security of data, whether transmitted or at rest. It also guarantees the accessibility, assessment, and availability of data.

Lately, we have extensively heard, read, and even experienced the noteworthy contributions of blockchain technology. Hundreds of books vividly illustrate the various features and functionalities of the futuristic blockchain, which intrinsically can enable users to interact with various online services (information, financial, commercial, etc.), which are powered and governed by a group of peers. This is a grandiose shift from the age-old practice of leveraging a centralized server cluster. On the other hand, a peer-to-peer (P2P) network of computers is essentially a decentralized network of computers. With such a transition, users can own their data and do permissionless and peer-to-peer transactions. There is no need for any intermediary, such as a bank, to establish and enforce the much-needed trust for trustworthy financial transactions. Users can save their intermediary costs. Anyone with Internet connectivity can use a cryptocurrency wallet to make direct payments.

2.11.1 NFTs

NFTs (https://readwrite.com/use-nfts-to-boost-brand-awareness/) represent physical and digital assets that can be uniquely tokenized, stocked, and traded through NFT marketplaces and platforms. NFTs are meticulously stored in blockchain systems and secured through crypto exchanges. Any digital items (memento, art, photo, image, audio, and video) can be turned into an NFT.

Many interesting characteristics are being supplied by NFTs. The token is unique and cannot be replaced. NFTs can be easily tracked and accounted for. All physical and digital assets can be methodically tokenized and secured through this brewing NFT concept. A token's unique ID and other metadata are used to track an NFT's ownership. The widely discussed concept of intelligent contracts comes in handy in assigning and managing tokens' ownership, and Smart contracts ensure the smooth transferability of NFTs. When an NFT owner sells his NFT, he can conveniently use a private key to initiate and authorize the transaction. The ownership of the NFT gets transferred and confirmed once the authenticity of the private key is verified.

The widely articulated blockchain phenomenon guarantees the tightest security for transaction data by enabling the creation and sustenance of a decentralized electronic ledger, which is famously tamper-proof. This establishes trust between the two parties involved, and there is no need for a central authority like a bank to verify the authenticity of each claim. In short, blockchain is the solid and sustainable foundation for the unprecedented success of the NFT paradigm.

NFTs have become mainstream in this blockchain era. Luxury fashion brands have launched NFT accessories to support their respective video games. NFT-based property registries have emerged as a secure and affordable alternative to traditional land registries. This is great for people who possess land but still need the title. Another use case is the establishment of virtual stock exchanges, which could empower companies from different regions to issue stock NFTs. All such enterprise-scale use cases are being made possible through the power of 5G networks. The emergence of cloud environments as highly optimized and organized IT centers is a real game-changer for the ensuing era of the metaverse.

NFTs are the tokens that are 100% unique. NFTs can be considered as certificates of ownership that exist on the blockchain. NFTs become vital because digital art and assets can be easily stolen and duplicated. NFTs guarantee a 100% confirmation of the designated owner of any digital art. Consumers are increasingly showing an interest in having ownership of digital goods. This is being simplified and streamlined by the stability of the paradigms such as non-fungible tokens (NFTs) and cryptocurrencies. The section below will discuss how NFTs contribute to producing metaverse applications.

2.11.2 Virtual marketplace

VRChat (https://hello.vrchat.com/) offers an endless collection of social VR experiences by giving its community the power of creation. These marketplaces serve as a fertile and famous ground for NFTs. Sellers can provide links and previews to assets on the web or mint assets directly in the VR landscape.

2.11.3 Art gallery

Virtual reality (VR) is emerging as a futuristic platform for viewing art. Through this platform, one can learn all the details of any art, which can be viewed from every angle. Many museums are placing NFT artwork in metaverses. For example, Voxels (https://www.voxels.com/) is a user-owned virtual world. Here, players can buy land, build on it, and customize their avatar with wearable NFTs.

Real estate can be a lucrative industry to work in not only in the physical world but also in the metaverse. When you buy a virtual property in the metaverse, you get an NFT of the virtual land. NFT eliminates real estate frauds such as forceful buying, cheating through fake documents, etc.

For example, take Decentraland (https://decentraland.org/), a virtual world owned by its users. Herein, one can create, explore, and trade. Plots of land can be sold as NFTs. This is to explore land parcels users own to experience incredible 3D scenes and structures. This has cryptocurrency, and VR gear users can access this metaverse.

2.12 Edge computing and analytics

As inscribed above, all tangible items are digitized and connected to the vicinity, along with the Web- and cloud-hosted applications at the ground level. These edge devices are increasingly stuffed with high memory capacity and processing capability. Thereby, edge devices are being prepared to join mainstream computing. That is, edge devices participate in processing edge data locally and logically. Therefore, edge computing makes the long-pending goal of real-time data capture and computing possible. Besides proximate processing, real-time data analytics, knowledge discovery, decision-making, and action also see reality.

Further, edge devices are hooked up to cloud platforms; thereby, the centralized monitoring of distributed and decentralized compute and storage resources is becoming the new normal. Edge devices gain additional capabilities as they are linked up with cloud-based software packages and platforms. Remote monitoring, measurement, and management of edge devices are being simplified through the direct and indirect connectivity between devices at the ground and cloud resources at the cyber level.

There are IoT middleware solutions in hubs, buses, gateways, brokers, queues, etc., to establish the linkage between edge devices (embedded systems) and cloud applications. A highly available, reliable, and secure cyberinfrastructure is very critical for attaining the propagated success of edge computing. With the grandiose success of containerization, a kind of compartmentalization, distributed and disparate edge devices are being clubbed together to form dynamic, transient, and purpose-specific device clusters and clouds to tackle process and data-intensive tasks. There are container orchestration and lifecycle management platform solutions such as Kubernetes that simplify and speed up the crafting and operation of containerized services and applications. Further, there are lightweight versions of the Kubernetes platform that establish and sustain edge device clouds to handle bigger and better tasks.

2.12.1 Edge AI

Lately, data analytics has happened through the intelligent leverage of AI algorithms and models. AI brings in several unique advantages. AI models continuously and automatically learn from fresh data to maximize prediction accuracy. AI algorithms untangle hidden patterns in data heaps to emit out actionable insights. Compared to traditional analytics methods, AI-enabled data analytics has several business, technical, and user advantages. The shrunken versions of AI models are being deployed in edge devices, which are continuously strengthened by embedding AI-centric processing units such as GPUs, TPUs, NPUs, etc. IoT devices with a reasonable amount of memory and processing power are being readied to be empowered through AI models. Such empowered edge devices can exhibit autonomy and adaptivity natively without human instruction, interpretation, and involvement. Thus, edge devices have on-device data processing to guarantee edge intelligence. In short, real-time edge-native applications and services are being envisaged and elegantly implemented through the growing and glowing power of the proven phenomenon of edge AI.

Real-time applications rely on edge computing and analytics rather than having a round-trip to centralized cloud platforms. Edge devices stay near the data sources and plunge into real-time data analytics to emit timely insights. Thus, real-time intelligent environments and enterprises can be visualized and realized to guarantee care, convenience, choice, and comfort for businesses and people. Edge data privacy and security are being fulfilled through edge computing. Factory automation is one of the prime use cases of edge computing. Autonomous vehicles are another futuristic use case of AI-based edge analytics.

2.12.2 Real-time pose estimation through edge AI

All kinds of audio, images, and videos are collected and transmitted to nearby or faraway cloud platforms and databases to extract actionable insights. The much-anticipated AI-enabled data processing gains momentum with the flourishing AI technologies and tools. AI-based data processing brings advanced capabilities in knowledge discovery and dissemination. Therefore, the aspects of cloud AI and edge AI started to flourish. Cloud AI is famous for comprehensive data analytics (through batch and stream processing), whereas edge AI is used for the real-time processing of drones and their environment data. For proximate data processing, edge devices must be stuffed with AI processing units such as GPUs, TPUs, VPUs, and NPUs. Pose estimation is computationally intensive and requires expensive AI hardware such as multiple NVIDIA GPUs.

With the blossoming of the edge AI paradigm, there is a glimmer of hope for envisaging real-time and real-world services and applications. Through AI model evaluation and optimization techniques, lean and lightweight AI models are being built and deployed in drones to automatically showcase adaptive behavior without any interpretation and involvement of human professionals. Post-estimation models are also refined, optimized, and run on devices with GPUs and other AI-centric processing units. Therefore, the pose estimation requirement is elegantly accomplished in edge devices. OpenPose is a real-time multi-person system to jointly detect human body, hand, facial, and foot key points (in total 135 key points) on single images, and the lightweight OpenPose is for real-time 2D multi-person pose

Estimation on CPU. The lightweight version is an AI model to empower edge devices to estimate poses.

2.13 Connected wearables for the metaverse

The device ecosystem has been growing dramatically. Medical instruments, humanoid robots, machinery on factory floors, kitchen utensils, toolsets for field workers, drones and satellites, defense equipment, personal gadgets, and gizmos are plentiful. In other words, we have a growing array of wearables, portables, implantables, wearables, mobiles, wireless, fixed and nomadic devices, etc., produced in large numbers. Hence, our everyday environments are stuffed and sandwiched with purpose-specific and agnostic devices.

Wearables like smartwatches, earbuds, and AR/VR headsets are flourishing. Their power goes up considerably with seamless integration with other devices nearby and with cloud-hosted software applications and data stores. All kinds of digitized artifacts collect and supply environmental, operational, and event data in time for wearables to accomplish bigger and better things for businesses and people.

As widely used, wearables help patients monitor their body parameters such as blood glucose level, blood pressure value, pulse rate, etc. Capturing the vitals and conveying them to caregivers in time through an IoT gateway (smartphone in his pocket) facilitates the caregivers to understand the problem and address it. Medication can be prescribed if there is any threshold break-in.

VR is paramount in providing expert training in the healthcare sector. Doctors, surgeons, and specialists can get virtual training to improve their education and expertise in performing surgeries astutely. In recent years, virtual reality (VR) has emerged as a potential method for treating a variety of phobias. Doctors can perform surgeries precisely with the perfect assistance of a head-mounted AR. Various wearables and sensors provide correct and relevant data to the surgeon through the head-mounted AR device, which then gives the information to surgeons to perfect the art of surgery. Head-mounted AR enables surgeons to use both hands to complete the surgery-related tasks with aplomb. Extended reality (XR) technologies can sharply surmount caregiving challenges and improve the healthcare industry by enabling remote surgeries. AR technology can also help nurses find veins to collect blood samples.

On the manufacturing side, a manufacturer can review a digital twin (simulation) of a factory layout in virtual reality. In the subsequent section, we have written about the immense contributions of the forthcoming metaverse era. A galaxy of multifaceted IoT sensors is deployed on a manufacturing floor to capture and share factory data. Such data can be shown alongside the digital twin for performance comparison. Thus, wearables are bound to play a vital role in shaping the metaverse era. Newer use cases in other industry verticals can be envisaged and implemented through the arrival of advanced AR and VR devices. Head-mounted display (HMD) devices can receive sensor data and real-time network information and empower field technicians, servicing professionals, etc., in their professions.

2.13.1 Empowering learners and workers

This is categorized as one of the prime application areas of the metaverse. There are a variety of process-intensive industries. For example, manufacturing and logistics rely upon numerous interconnected systems on multiple technology stacks. Therefore, new hires must be meticulously trained to operate and maintain connected and complicated machinery and equipment. However, training new employees to keep various systems running constantly is neither straightforward nor simple. Instead, it is tedious, risky, and time-consuming. This problem induces experts and technocrats to explore and expedite alternative approaches. Thus, learning and training methods are being completely overhauled with the emergence of new pioneering technologies. The teaching challenges get exacerbated in situations wherein the technology to be taught is not physically there. The faster proliferation and maturity of metaverse technologies and tools come in handy in helping industrial houses train their newly hired employees to get all that is required to operate and repair state-of-the-art industrial assets.

2.14 Digital twins for the metaverse

Digital twins are the virtual/cyber/logical/software versions of ground-level physical assets, equipment, robots, satellites, launchers, etc. Not only products but also processes are also codified as digital twins. With such virtual representations, several business and technical advantages are being derived. Having understood the growing significance of setting up and sustaining digital twins for connected physical systems at the ground, there is a heavy rush in producing corresponding digital twins for physical entities, and they are being deployed in cloud platforms along with other related entities such as data lakes, data analytics platforms, AI frameworks, knowledge visualization dashboards, etc. The idea of digital twins is being proclaimed as one of the enablers of the metaverse world. Training and empowering employees are being simplified and speeded up with digital twins for heavy industries and equipment. The training cost and time are bound to come down sharply.

For a suitable example, by leveraging the digital twins of an oil refinery and its various modules and processes, employees can better understand everything that is part and parcel of the oil and gas industry. Such technological empowerment makes enterprises proactive, prompt, and pre-emptive in their actions and articulations of changing business sentiments. The proven and potential AR and VR technologies can be used to create individual avatars for each employee under training so that every employee can consciously interact with the cloud-based digital twins and learn how to operate, manage, and maintain the machinery there. This interaction looks like they interact with and repair the physical systems. All these happen in an immersive and interactive manner in a virtual mode.

Employees are not trapped in risky conditions by interacting with virtual entities rather than physical ones. They can also learn everything comfortably. This empowers employees to explore the technology deeper and identify areas for potential improvements of the corresponding physical systems.

The brewing idea of metaverse relies heavily upon virtual worlds; 3D modeling is therefore seen as an essential skill to be gained and used as a part of the metaverse application development process. 3D modeling is needed for decorating homes, creating skins for avatars, etc. Thus, modeling is fundamental to shared virtual worlds. The prominent steps for setting up and sustaining virtual spaces are as follows. All tangible objects must be digitized and connected to create worthwhile virtual environments. With the ready availability and methodical application of multi-talented sensors, every common and concrete object in our everyday environments becomes a digitized artifact (IoT object). Physical things become digitized by tightly embedding different sensors and actuators. The implanted sensors can collect and send data points about the physical objects. Thus, there is a seamless and spontaneous connectivity between physical objects and sensors. Such integration helps in data capture and sharing by attaching purpose-specific sensors to objects in our everyday environments. Turning physical, mechanical, and electrical systems into digital entities is possible. That is, dumb objects become animated and dynamic elements.

Physical systems have their corresponding digital twins running on cloud platforms. Now, different sensors collect various information and send the captured data to digital twins for profit. Thus, digital twins are given a digital representation of physical objects. Such a representation brings several advantages, including a deeper understanding of systems' structural and behavioral characteristics. Making a digital twin is a kind of 3D modeling of an object. In other words, for the forthcoming era of the metaverse, forming digital twins acquires special significance.

2.15 The metaverse application domains

With metaverse-enablement platforms' faster maturity and stability, fresh use cases emerge and evolve fast. Pundits and proponents proclaim that the metaverse is a seamless and spontaneous convergence of physical, virtual, and augmented realities where people appear as avatars who can interact with one another in a shared 3D virtual space. The metaverse is an interoperable network consisting of real-time rendered 3D virtual worlds that can be accessed with the help of special AR/VR devices. With the faster proliferation of social media, distributed gaming, NFTs, and cryptocurrencies, people started to experience the whole gamut of immersive and intuitive experiences in the virtual world.

Once in the metaverse, people can create and customize their digital representations (avatars) and choose their body parameters: hair color, clothes, accessories, and other things according to their taste. The metaverse has the innate potential to bring a paradigm shift in how people socialize, collaborate, innovate, work, play, shop, etc.

Visitors can enjoy immersive and intimate social chats with their friends. Gamers can explore a range of exuberant games. The metaverse can pave the way for the development of sophisticated virtual offices. Professionals can hold 3D meetings and bring new energy and enthusiasm to office life. The other possibilities include creating and making erudite presentations, working together on completing projects from geographically distributed locations, etc.

With continued support for the metaverse paradigm from different quarters, virtual clothing, accessories, and cosmetics will be available. As inscribed above, such virtual assets and spaces coordinate to usher in a dazzling array of exciting and inspiring applications. Virtual living and collaboration will thrive ceaselessly. Brands and businesses will sustain their yearned edge through next-generation virtual products, solutions, and services. This potential and promising technology can introduce hitherto unknown capabilities for businesses and people.

2.15.1 Metaverse for the shopping

With a greater understanding of business leaders' and technocrats' strategic contributions of virtual, augmented, and mixed reality technologies, a renewed interest in fully embracing the metaverse paradigm exists. As indicated above, the metaverse idea is hugely beneficial for shoppers. Today, we have plenty of physical and online shops. B2C e-commerce applications are used by many businesses across the globe. However, modern and much-expected features like virtual fitting rooms are unavailable in online stores. Traditional online commerce will be remarkably empowered to give additional capabilities, such as virtual fitting rooms, as there is a realization that the metaverse domain has all that is needed to supply advanced features and functionalities across industry verticals. In short, with the power of the metaverse, it is possible to provide an extra experience for shoppers. For online shoppers, virtual reality (VR) and augmented reality (AR) technology rescue physical shoppers.

2.15.2 Metaverse for real estate

Web applications allow quick and easy registration of land parcels and properties. Sellers and buyers can visit those e-commerce portals to gain relevant details about the registered properties. Still, physically visiting and checking properties are mandatory for buyers to get more nuanced details before making any conclusive decision. The well-known and widely transacted properties include flats in apartments, houses in gated communities, independent villas, offices, shops, etc. Thus, the real estate business is booming these days. With the rapid proliferation of VR/AR gear, the phenomenon of the metaverse has brought in a slew of innovations to provide the ultimate virtual reality experience for any prospective buyer. With metaverse-empowered visualization of real estate properties, the buyer gets everything needed to make decisions remotely.

Prospective buyers can take a real-time and metaverse-enabled real estate tour, equal to the conventional physical property check. The extended reality (XR) feature lets buyers explore everything in greater detail. The beauty is that everything is finished very quickly. Further on, a virtual tour can be adapted to specific tastes, clients, and preferences. Augmented reality (AR) in the form of popups will make a metaverse virtual real estate site visit informative and intuitive. Thus, the metaverse's flourishing is seen as a silver bullet for the real-estate domain.

2.15.3 Metaverse for smart homes, hospitals, and hotels

The metaverse era is on the fast track with emerging path-breaking technologies and highly miniaturized AR/VR gadgets. Our homes, empowered through the metaverse phenomenon, can sharply enhance our interactive experience in our homes. Our everyday environments will become lively and lovely by incorporating extended reality methods. Head-mounted displays, simulators, and other VR/AR devices are emerging and evolving fast to bring in the dreamt metaverse era sooner rather than later. During the pandemic, the concept of work-from-home (WFH) became the new normal. Team members across multiple metaverse environments connect and collaborate calmly, consciously, and conveniently. With the surge of IoT devices and sensors in warehouses, airports, railway stations, restaurants, entertainment plazas, social environments, and factories; the steady maturity of AI algorithms and models; the development of metaverse technologies for creating well-defined simulated environments; the maturation of edge computing and analytics platforms; the emergence of Web 3.0 and digital twins; and the widespread deployment of 5G communication networks, the creation and maintenance of smarter environments that provide comfort, choice, convenience, and care for occupants and visitors are expected to become a reality soon. Technologically advanced environments will become the new ordinary, benefiting people and service providers alike.

2.15.4 Metaverse for tourism

The tourism sector has suffered dramatically recently due to the pandemic. The travel industry plummeted severely, and tourism revenue collection witnessed one of its biggest downfalls during the Covid era. The pandemic grossly restricted the people's movement. The growing concern for environmental sustainability also contributes to the slowdown of the tourism and travel industry. Metaverse came up strongly and sagaciously as a source of solace for the struggling industry. That is, the metaverse is being pronounced as the way forward to save the crippling tourism economy.

Tourism entrepreneurs and evangelists are passionately experimenting with metaverse and other virtual technologies to promote world exploration without physical traveling. There are gadgets to enjoy virtual tours and trips to places worldwide. The 360-degree videos converged with the 3D travel experience and laid a stimulating platform to change how we understand tourism. Travelers can quickly strike a balance between real and virtual travel. The highly proclaimed virtual tours bring forth new nuances and experiences.

The technology facilitates virtual tours of continents, countries, counties, and cities. Metaverse creates grandiose simulations of popular tourist locations and landmark areas. Thus, introducing the metaverse has created a workaround for the problems of the tourism industry. Further, the metaverse technology has created an interest in physically and personally exploring exotic places across the globe.

In summary, virtual tourism is gathering momentum with unprecedented developments in the metaverse domain. Technologies collectively let us travel in a virtual space. That means that we need to be there physically in some locations. Creating 3D digital environments by meticulously combining virtual and augmented reality methods will be a breakthrough for virtual tourism.

2.15.5 Metaverse for the entertainment industry

The entertainment domain has been hugely impacted by a series of noteworthy improvisations in the metaverse world. Digitization and digitalization technologies have brought unmatched user experiences. Within a metaverse entertainment cluster, it is possible to find digital concerts, technical symposiums, sports and games, etc. Participants can form knowledge-sharing groups. The intelligent usage of AI and AR/VR gadgets enriches users with personalized experiences. For instance, viewers can choose the angle at which they enjoy a digital event differently. Thus, possibilities and opportunities abound ceaselessly in simulated environments. The multi-view camera capability comes in handy in providing engrossing and enriching views.

The current social applications and entertainment platforms are predominantly two-dimensional systems. Shortly, they will evolve into full-fledged metaverses, wherein people interact with one another through their avatars or virtual representations. With the abundant and affordable production of VR and AR tools, there will be an interest in migrating from the traditional Web (web 1.0 and 2.0) to metaverses. The entertainment industry will significantly benefit from all the distinct accomplishments in the field of the metaverse. Multi-dimensional interactions will flourish to give a distinct feeling to the users.

2.15.6 Online gaming

Today, multiple gamers play exciting games online. People from geographically distributed places gather virtually to play games. Thus, the e-gaming sector has grown dramatically these days. This is a fertile ground for the faster adoption of the metaverse concept. A growing array of online gaming portals charge a small fee to sustain them. With metaverse, the gaming experience is to see tremendous improvement. Gamers can engross themselves in a more immersive and instinctive gaming environment. The entrance and endurance of blockchain technology ensures a provable gaming to eliminate any risk of misappropriation. Players can store their funds in a metaverse wallet to ensure their safety. With the steady growth of key technologies such as NFTs, cryptocurrencies, and blockchain, the game variety and experience will grow and glow in the days to unfold.

2.15.7 Metaverse in the education field

Education is a flourishing field across the globe. Knowledge sharing and enhancement are vital for any country to gain respect. For the education sector, the metaverse's faster maturity and stability are seen as a revolutionary step in the right direction. The metaverse's arrival is game-changing, especially for distance learning and online classes. The next-generation Internet (Web 3.0) is being empowered through various enabling technologies, and it can create a highly interactive and insightful learning environment. Virtual reality spaces and gadgets come in handy when explaining a complicated concept to learners. Thus, virtual classrooms can be easily, elegantly designed and developed in the metaverse era. Above all, the learning is all set to go through a paradigm shift. In short, education will be pragmatic, inspiring, and highly engrossing for students, scientists, and scholars.

For instance, a medical student can practice diagnoses and medications on patients in a virtual environment, which is being readily built using pioneering simulation technologies. Such a setup goes a long way in skilling and upskilling students to face the world with all the confidence and clarity. Another exciting feature is real-time feedback, which helps students to understand their competencies and to do course corrections on time. Thus, simulated environments prepare people to gain a prior and decisive understanding of real-world environments.

In summary, metaverse technology fundamentally and functionally changes the education sector. The realm of virtual reality can elevate the visual component of the educational process to a newer level. Learners will feel the excitement and elegance in the learning process. The knowledge discovery, dissemination, and assimilation will differ in the metaverse era. Traditional classroom training and teaching are bound to undergo a series of transformations by adopting and adapting the metaverse conundrum. The much-celebrated virtual learning environment might also eliminate the language barrier. Learners from different parts of the world can skilfully learn new things through a single virtual space. Multiple virtual environments can be dynamically integrated to tackle fast-changing requirements. Anyone from any corner of the world can easily and quickly benefit from virtual training, which is amply supported through VR toolkits. The education industry is poised to be quite different with the keen adoption of emerging technologies. Teaching will be spectacular and versatile with the power of metaverse technology. Many of the education industry challenges can be surmounted through the purposeful usage of advancements in the metaverse landscape.

2.15.8 Metaverse in the industry

Multiple industry verticals are keenly exploring and experimenting with metaverse technologies and tools to bring premium and patentable offerings to their clients and consumers. Manufacturing, warehousing, healthcare, logistics, supply chain, and education industries are interested in embracing the enigmatic and extempore metaverse paradigm to be correct and relevant to their customers. By unearthing and rolling out next-generation capabilities, the business world is bound to be on the right side. The virtual space facilitates immersive training for employees, educators, learners, surgeons, field workers, etc. They can try their hands on the work they will do in the future. The metaverse is expected to help expertly manage and maintain stocks and inventories for companies dealing with supply chain and transportation. The shift to digital spaces is to articulate inherent risks and rewards. Therefore, the capital and operational costs of setting up and sustaining physical spaces will decrease significantly.

With the steady growth of improvisations in the metaverse, newer use cases are bound to arise in the years to come.

2.16 Conclusion

Metaverse is a blockchain-enabled network comprising and coordinating multiple virtual spaces to unleash unheard digital experiences. Participants can mingle to finish assigned work, form a virtual team to play esoteric games, build virtual communities for knowledge sharing, and more. As illustrated in old films, the digital version of humans is an avatar that can connect, collaborate, and complete different things virtually.

The metaverse economy is to be driven by cryptocurrencies. Digital arts and assets are being tokenized and secured through NFTs. Blockchain is well-known for its power to enforce the tightest security for digital data. The metaverse IT infrastructure is none other than the cloud environments (public, private, and edge). Considering the value addition and productivity-enhancement capabilities of metaverse applications, several metaverse application development and deployment platforms are emerging and evolving fast to meet varying individual and industrial needs. These platforms are primarily run on cloud infrastructure modules. There are plenty of implementation technologies and tools. Virtual, augmented, and mixed reality (VR/AR/MR) technologies are paramount in realizing next-generation metaverse systems. As AI power is being understood across the board, AI is lustrously integrated with other digital technologies to showcase state-of-the-art metaverse systems. AI is to guarantee the mesmerizing experience of simulated virtual space. The virtual world strives to mirror the physical world with cutting-edge technologies and tools. Any activity or thing in a real-world physical environment can be realized and replicated in virtual spaces, too. Users can play games, shop, enjoy cinemas, and create digital spaces like offices.

With the delightful convergence of the digital and physical worlds, more personalized and reverberating experiences will await businesses and ordinary people. Many industry verticals have started to explore this futuristic and fabulous paradigm to retain their customers and obtain fresh consumers to enhance their brand value. In this chapter, we have concentrated on the growing array of renowned use cases. The key technologies are also discussed to invigorate our readers to visualize and realize advanced metaverse applications.

Chapter 3

Virtual, augmented, mixed, and extended reality for the metaverse

Prasanna Kumar[1]

Abstract

This chapter will concentrate on virtual, augmented, extended, and mixed reality (VR/AR/XR/MR) technologies and tools for the metaverse. In the previous chapters, we have discussed VR and AR products and how they empower people to experience the shared virtual world. The fusion of AR and VR can give highly beneficial results in achieving the needed levels of engagement while avoiding metaverse side effects. In this chapter, we will also cover MR and how it is going to be a game-changer in the forthcoming era of the metaverse.

Keywords: Reality–Virtuality Continuum; Augmented Realities; Mixed Realities; Extended Realities; XR Platform; Side Effects

3.1 The era of experience—VR, AR, MR, XR

In this era, all our activities of daily living are intertwined with devices and applications for experiences and productivity. Metaverse offers a range of technologies that deliver unified, immersive, shared, and persistent experiences. In particular, applications in education, entertainment, theme parks, virtual currencies, e-banking outlets, e-real estate, and e-party rooms are being set up on the metaverse platforms technologies. It is vital to first understand the metaverse terms and the RV (Reality–Virtuality) continuum (Figure 3.1) that clearly defines operating space for Physical Reality (PR), Augmented Reality (AR), Mixed Reality (MR), and Virtual Reality (VR).

XR stands for eXtended reality and is a catch-all term to refer to augmented reality, virtual reality, and mixed reality. The technology combines the physical world with a digital twin world. It is the composition of virtuality and reality that differentiates PR, AR, MR, and VR. However, one distinct technology stack difference is that AR and MR require visual processing of the physical environment. So it requires image processing of the camera feed to define the contour of the environment. However, in

[1]Business Optima, Fairfield, CA, USA

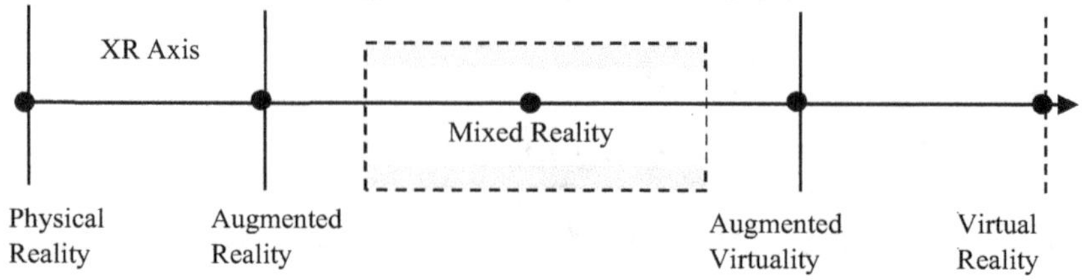

Figure 3.1 Reality–Virtuality continuum

VR it is optional and has a lesser dependency on the capture of visual aspects of the physical environment. Virtual Reality is only partially real and predominantly virtual, so the feed from the sensors is important to calibrate the user's action and relative position. VR stack is focused on rendering virtuality onto the head-mounted devices. That is one of the key differences at the stack level. On the contrary, Augmented Reality is predominantly real and partially virtual. AR brings in information overlay on top of the reliability. This could include text, images, audio into the mobile, handhelds, glasses, and wearables to augment the information dataset and overlay on top of users' existing reality. Finally, Mixed Reality is freely moving between Virtual Reality and Augmented Reality, essentially offering mobility of experiences.

3.2 Virtual reality world

VR technologies can deliver powerful sensations for all the senses in various combinations of visual, auditory, touch, thoughts, movements, and kinesthetics. Take for example the head mount display experiences in both VR and the AR experience through mobile and projection display. Beams emitted from ultralight laser modules onto the eye's retina. Compared to seeing real objects, images projected directly onto the retina will be sharper and clearer. Delivering greater experiences than the real world. The latest metaverse technologies powered by Virtual Reality, Augmented Reality, Mixed Reality, and Extended Reality are blurring the line between Physical Reality and Virtual Reality largely due to improvements in sensor integration technologies, streaming technologies, and high-definition rendering on head-mounted displays (HMD). Let us look at one of the latest HMD and its sensor ecosystem in the 2020s. Sensor Ecosystem includes Temperature Sensor, Pressure Monitoring, accelerometer, 3D position sensors, Head Movement, microphone for audio, speaker, compass, and motion detection. See Table 3.1 for more details.

The use of HMD started way back in 1968. Ivan Sutherland, a Harvard computer science professor, created this virtual reality HMD assisted by Bob Sproull (Student). Professor Ivan referred to this HMD as "The Sword of Damocles" since it required a large beam to support its weight. Since then HMDs have come a long way. They are available in tethered mode and untethered mode. Both are good entry point devices for Augmented Realities, Mixed realities, and Virtual Realities. Metaverse is the 4D version of the current internet, shared environment, and immersive experiences.

Table 3.1 Head mount and handheld sensor technologies

Sensor technologies	Description
MEMS IMU	Head movement, head tracking
E-Compass	Magnetometer Compass, head tracking
Temperature and Pressure Sensor	Body Temperature, Ambient Temperature, and Pressure Monitoring
MEMS Motion IMU	Controller Movement, Accelerometer
ToF Sensors	True 3D positioning, Motion detection, 3D position sensors
MEMS Microphone	Human Machine Interface, Microphone for audio, Speaker
Laser Module	Retina Projection
HaptX	Haptics Gloves provides a realistic touch
Connectivity and Framerate	Untethered (60FPS@16ms, 72 FPS@13ms) Tethered (90FPS@11ms, higher frame rates compared to untethered)

Facebook Horizon allows people to connect in virtual world rooms and helps create products for communities. On the rendering side, applications using Organic Light Emitting Diodes (referred to as OLED) with stereoscopic images plus a 90-degree field of vision with reprojection capabilities, augmented onto translucent surfaces have changed the way experiences are delivered. Oculus Rift OLED goggles are a case in point. Quest engine that brings out mixed reality has tremendous potential of merging and mixing environments that are physical reality into the virtual world.

3.3 Engineering the augmented realities

Engineering the Metaverse requires VR, AR, and MR toolkits and platforms such as Unity, Unreal Engine, VRTK, Nvidia Maxine, etc. The popular toolkits for augmented reality are ARToolKit, Google Arcore, Maxst AR. There is also a key requirement for platform-specific spatial computing since the coordinates between real-world rendering systems (e.g., Blender Engine) and metaverse world VR rendering are different (e.g., Unity Gaming Engine vs. Blender Engine). Each platform's Mesh, Skin, Renderer, Camera positions, LipSync, Avatars, Collider, Polygon count, VRChat Bot, Physical properties, and Scripting are platform specific and platform compatibility is essential for interoperability and streaming capabilities. Streaming applications are being rolled out with immersive rich content with 9dof/12dof (Degree of Freedom). The 4k–8k resolution images, video, and VR content delivered in life-scale 3D space is a much more enriching experience than what we see in normal non-augmented viewing. The non-VR reality looks foggy and less enriched as compared to the world viewed through VR goggles and augmented data. We use screen time to enrich our reality, whether it is a simple playout software that powers big news channels to smaller podcasts on YouTube. The overlays and augmentation have played a powerful role in disseminating content-rich experiences. These technologies are getting generational upgrades by several factors and further propelling the emergence of more metaverse applications for a range of domains. The following sections will cover broad applications, specific use cases, and a range of domains that can be leveraged for experiencing entertainment on game nights in the VR room or e-learning, eHealth, for every home. With gesture control and EKG headnet for clearly pinpointing thoughts, a new generation of VR devices is taking beyond the 27 degrees of freedom for the human hand (27 joints).

3.4 Mixed reality—the fusion of AR and VR

Metaverse applications are segmented based on their domains and within those domains more specifically based on the use cases, evolutions in technology, practical utility value, powerful user experience, affordability, scalability, and governance model. This requires a lot of experimental mix of Augmented Realities and Augmented Virtualities. The experiences and expectations from these Mixed Reality experiments are changing and keeping the metaverse in motion. Enriched by the confluence of different technologies on both sides of the V-R spectrum, hardened by data security and privacy, mixed reality offers a compelling value proposition for the future. MR is the perfect catalyst for adoption as it has the interplay between AR and VR, by offering the equilibrium spaces in the Reality–Virtuality spectrum continuum. Application and technology developers can experiment and find their sweet spot before going completely virtual. The key determinant is the experimental use of virtual reality, augmented reality, and mixed reality technologies combined in different permutations and combinations to build the metaverse applications for the present and future. Core features of the metaverse application domain are massive scalability, single sign-on identity, continuity of data, persistence, entitlements, objects and mutually transferability of data, configurations and relevant financial transactions across environments. Organizations position themselves in this Mixed Reality equilibrium space. In essence. Mixed Reality is a metaverse safe space that allows companies to take advantage of diverse technologies at the same time insulate their investments from down-cycles of the metaverse hype cycle. The leaders in the Mixed Reality space are Microsoft, with their HoloLens 2, Varjo, Magic Leap 2, and Meta with their Meta Quest Pro. A few of the other key challengers in the mixed reality space are DigiLens, Aptima, Mojo Vision, Thales, Healium, Resonai, and many more with the promised offering of a creative fusion of VR and AR.

The technology building blocks do require critical full-stack algorithms, components library, device drivers, connectors, and data integration. Common technology building blocks for metaverse include Spatial Computing using 3D engines, lifescale 3D Space, GeoSpatial Mapping, Games, Social Media Transformation with Metaverse AdNetwork, social Curation, 2nd life identities, Ratings, Agents, online Stores, Digital Dressing, and more. Metaverse Shopping, Immersive Movie Experience, Designing Experiences, Edge, AI, Blockchain, Microservices, and Gen 6.6G are all pervasive telecom connectivity and next-generation Mobile Phones with projectors. On the user interactivity front, we require Smartglasses, Mixed-Multi-Input Voice and Gesture Control systems, sub 1.4 nm silicon wafers, MEMs, and NVIDIA GPU (Table 3.2).

Metaverse Multi Creator to come up with unique and purpose-built infrastructure with differentiated QOS (quality of service). There will be commonly agreed engagement protocols and negotiated digital contracts. Buyers will own vast swaths of digital assets in this universe, allowing entry subscriptions, adoption habit formation access control, and billing in metaverse currency. Metaverse operators of these virtual worlds would indeed compete and collaborate at the same time for not just market share, mindshare, and wallet share, but also for the share of protestors. Metaverse is going to be bigger than countries and continents in delivering the highest realities for the maximum number of people. Its engagement using wearables delivers an immersive experience, easy-to-use gesture control, and secure identity (moving towards zero trust identities in the future). Metaverse building blocks include objects, scenes, subjects, images/panorama, 9dof, light fields voxel grids, layered representation, textual geometry, volumetric free viewpoint, video codec, depth, vector quantization of 2D and 4D tiles, compression, mesh tracking, Nvidia GPU compute chipsets. Structured classification of various Metaverse tools, technology stack, and trends are outlined in Table 3.3.

Table 3.2 XR platform and devices

XR platforms and plugins	Devices
Oculus XR Plugin	Meta Quest, Meta Quest 2
ARCore XR Plugin	Android devices (via AR Foundation)
ARKit XR Plugin	IOS devices (via AR Foundation)
OpenVR	Windows Mixed Reality headsets, HTC Vive, Oculus Rift
Ultraleap Hand Tracking	Ultraleap Leap Motion controller
Unreal Engine	HoloLens 2, Windows Mixed Reality, SteamVR
OpenXR	HoloLens 2, Windows MR headsets, Meta Quest, SteamVR devices
Windows XR Plugin	HoloLens, HoloLens 2, Windows Mixed Reality headsets

Table 3.3 Metaverse stack and toolset

Metaverse stacks and toolset	Description
Technology Platform	Meta Horizon World, Alphabet Google Starline, Microsoft Mesh, Apple VR, Autodesk, Unity
Chip Makers	NVIDIA, Qualcomm
Gaming Platforms	Activision Blizzard, Roblox, Tencent, Fortnite, Ready Player One, IMVU, Horizon Worlds, SecondLife, Decentraland, Roblox, Pokémon Go, Facebook
Spatial Computing Software Engine	Autodesk, Unity Software, NVIDIA Omniverse
Sensor Integration Company	Numerous SI and sensor integration technology providers exist in this Sensor Ecosystem for Temperature Sensing, Pressure Monitoring, accelerometer, 3D position sensors, Head Movement, microphone for

(Continues)

Table 3.3 (*Continued*)

Metaverse stacks and toolset	Description
	audio, speaker, compass, and motion detection. Notably, TDK Integrating a 3-axis magnetometer leads to the 9DoF sensing
Exchange Traded Funds	ProShares Metaverse ETF, Roundhill Ball Metaverse, Subversive Metaverse ETF
Immersive Gesture Control	Wearable, gesture control, secure zero trust identity, Apple's AR kit, MS PlayStation VR, Google Translate, 9DOF needed for rotation, AR rendering, and data fabric
Virtual world's scenery or content engine (Quixel Bridge)	Creating items that can be bought and sold, software solutions for content creation. Objects, Scenes, Panoramic image processing, 9dof, light fields 2D grid/3D grid, voxel grids, layered representation, textual geometry, volumetric free viewpoint, video codec, depth, vector quantization of 2D and 4D tiles, compression, mesh tracking, Nvidia GPU compute Photogrammetry, Light Fields, Voice Recognition
Next era of spatial computing	Acceleration, speed, gravity, deceleration
AT/MR/VR Toolkit	Apple's AR kit, reality composer, reality converter, MS PlayStation VR
Gaming Platforms and Applications	Valve Index, Oculus Rift, Meta Quest 2, HTC Vive, PS VR, PS VR2. Other popular VR games include Superhot VR, Beat Saber, Tetris Effect: Connected, Batman: Arkham VR, Elite: Dangerous VR, The Elder Scrolls V: Skyrim VR, No Man's Sky VR, Blade and Sorcery VR, Resident Evil 4 (+ Remake), Half-Life: Alyx, Demeo (dungeon crawler)
Data Mapping and Interplay of Real World, Virtual World and Roboworld Infrastructure	Streaming and Large Data Batch Processing, Data Mesh, Rendering, Enrichment, Data Transformation between Real world and Virtual worlds, and Roboworld
Personal Assistant Agents	Conversational AI, ChatBots, Self-Supervised Agents, Avatars, Human in the loop
Metadata	Jpeg Picture is now only worth a thousand JSON metadata information
Generative AI and Deep Fake	Text generation, summarization, sentiment and semantic analysis, Graph ML, music, content, video generation
Smart Tracking	Haptics data glove, exoskeleton, Eye tracking, head tracking, green screen, pointers, MEMS handhelds motion sensors (IMU)
Semantic Analysis	CoCoMetrics, Semantic Similarity, LFQA Evaluation
Vendor VR Gaming console and Wearable	Oculus Quest, Oculus Rift, Microsoft Hololens, Xbox, Apple ProVision, Amazon, Autodesk, Facebook, HTC, Sony PlayStation VR, Wii, Samsung, Intel, Lenovo Mirage, Nintendo Labo VR kit, Magic Leap, HoloLens and Samsung Gear VR

Table 3.4 Key XR metrics and trends

Key XR metrics	Current state	Future trends
XR Linked Experiences	Low on novelty, Low on utility	Trending toward high on utility
XR Linked Productivity Index	Low Productivity outcomes Lack of Productivity Index	Multiple Productivity Index, Outcome-based Indexes
XR Development Cost	High, Fewer Organizations	Low, Pervasive VR Dev Pods, and UX Pods
XR Devices Cost	\$300 (low-end) \$3,500–\$6,000 (high-end)	Cost Segmented per multi-class, Multiple midsegment options
XR Connectivity	Limited Spatial Data Fabric and Multiverse Connectivity	High Spatial Data Fabric and Multiverse Connectivity
Lifescale 3D Space	Low, ~3–6dof, 4k rendering	9DOF 16k and beyond rendering, light Projector, bendable displays,
XR Linked Commerce	Low	High, Digital Contracts
Data Privacy	Low	Zero Trust Data Privacy
Device and Network Latency	High, drives Impatiency	Low, increased engagement
High Availability	Low	Clustered and Containerized High Availability
Reliability and Resiliency	Low	Failover Capability, Experience Continuity, Data Recoverability
Observability and Recoverability	Low	Increased Instrumentation, Metrics, Measure Management
Ethics and Moral Dilemma	Limited	High Level of Complexity
Social Engagement	Low	High Social Engagement
Social Isolation	Low	Variable Social Isolation
Governance and Compliance	Low	Federated Distributed Governance, Digital Non-Repudiation led Compliance
XR Billing Models	Models not defined	Special Classes of Internets and Subscription Models
XR Data Consumption	Metered on GiB consumed	CSAT Experience Rating and Utility Driven Billing

Let us now look at some of the key XR metrics in the metaverse such as device cost, connectivity, data cost, development cost, experience, compliance, availability, latency, and several other key XR metrics for both the current state as well as some future trends (Table 3.4).

3.5 Metaverse benefits

In this section, XR (eXtended Realities) the catch-all terms for VR/MR/AR will be used to outline the common metaverse benefits. In the wellness space, Body Tracking sensors and Streaming technologies can be used for XR-based workouts. Metaverse-based buyers can perform product tryouts before making a high-value buy decision. Their preferences can be saved to metaverse personal data warehouses that can be further processed by analytical services. Recommendation systems can deliver personalized preferences by combining generalizing based on transfer requirements with specifics of graph-based relationships. XR Integration with Manufacturing units for fabrications with minimum order quantity can help in demand planning. In addition, companies can market the product on Metaverse and complete the purchase and deliver it via Amazon Prime or any shipping services to your doorstep or international addresses worldwide. You can sell the product to Metaverse warehouses and virtualize the order and keep the asset in Metaverse, blending the physical and digital realms. Projection technology can render images to windshield or HUD. Pilots can be better trained to hone flying skills with metaverse simulation and can be trained to handle even turbulent conditions in flight paths. HaptX Gloves provides a realistic touch for the enterprise metaverse. A multitude of microfluidic actuators distributed across your fingers and palms provide enhanced tactile feedback for immersive extended realities. Get ready for the plethora of benefits in an ocean of experiences.

3.6 Metaverse side effects

Metaverse experiences are principled around the concept that "virtual pleasure is greater than physical pleasure, minus physical pain." However, the excessive use of Metaverse is not devoid of side effects including proprioception, eye ailments, nausea, simulator sickness, and isolation effects. Table 3.5 provides a few of the key side effects.

Table 3.5 Metaverse side effects

Metaverse side effects	Symptoms and conditions
Eye Ailment	Dry eyes, Retinal detachment, Astigmatism
Bone and Joint pain	Carpal tunnel syndrome, repetitive use of devices
Sedentary ailment	Mental and Physical Fatigue
Isolation Problem and Pygmalion Spectacles	Escaping reality can lead to addiction to screen time and binge playing in the metaverse leads to isolation. Users decide to live in the digital world. Consequences of this brain in a vat, life-sustaining liquid
Distractions and Deaddiction	A continuous steady stream of distraction creates voidism and dyslexia. Metaverse can offer therapy for ADHD patients to focus, but it could also exacerbate the condition
Nausea	Users have reported the need for Dramamine and nausea medication

(Continues)

Table 3.5 (*Continued*)

Metaverse side effects	Symptoms and conditions
Proprioception (metaverse user's awareness contradiction)	Issues related to immersive elements that are different from the player's natural awareness of their body parts. Applications need to keep immersive experiences very realistic or keep them stylistic and abstract, not in the zone of contradiction leading to conditions of proprioception
Vection and Simulator Sickness	Visually induced motion sickness in Virtual Reality, illusion of moving in the opposite direction especially when a large part of the field of view move

Table 3.6 *Metaverse terms*

Metaverse terms	Description
VR—Virtual Reality	Computer-generated environment with realistic scenes, objects and surroundings to deliver immersive experiences
AR—Augmented Reality	View of the real world with an overlay of digital elements Information is rendered in real-time in the form of text, graphics, audio, virtual enhancements integrated with real-world objects e.g., Google Glass, Optinvent's ORA, Vuzix M100, monocular devices suited for augmented reality applications
MR—Mixed Reality	Fusion of AR and VR Describes assets interactions (physical assets and digital assets)
XR—Extended Reality	Broader term encapsulating Augmented Reality (AR), Virtual Reality (VR), Mixed Reality (MR), and everything in between
Ambient Computing	Connected technologies to collect and compute ambient inputs from wearables, monitoring devices, Voice assistants, and IoT-enabled sensors
Brain–Machine Interface	Neuralink, Facebook (Ctrl-Z Lab)
SLAM	SLAM stands for Simultaneous Localization and Mapping. It is the computational problem for constructing and updating a map of an environment while keeping track of an object or user's location within that environment

3.7 Metaverse glossary term

See Table 3.6 for Metaverse terms.

Further reading

[1] Matthew Ball (2022). *The Metaverse*. New York: Liveright.
[2] Neal Stephenson (1992). *Snow Crash*. New York: Bantam Books.
[3] Samuel Greengard (2019). *Virtual Reality*. Cambridge, MA: MIT Press.
[4] Cornel Hillmann (2021). *UX for XR: User Experience Design and Strategies for Immersive Technologies (Design Thinking)*. New York: Apress.
[5] M. Pell (2017). *Envisioning Holograms: Design Breakthrough Experiences for Mixed Reality*. New York: Apress.
[6] Erin Pangilinan, Steve Lukas, and Vasanth Mohan (2019). *Creating Augmented and Virtual Realities: Theory and Practice for Next-Generation Spatial Computing*. Sebastopol, CA: O'Reilly Media.
[7] Marcus Magnor and Alexander Sorkine-Hornung (Editors) (2020). *Real VR – Immersive Digital Reality: How to Import the Real World into Head-Mounted Immersive Displays (Lecture Notes in Computer Science Book 11900)*. 1st edn. Berlin: Springer.
[8] Amit Johri and Kalpesh Parikh (2023). *Revolutionizing Metaverse: Delve into the Building Blocks of Metaverse Commerce*. New Delhi: BPB Publications.
[9] Suchismit Mahapatra, Vladimir Blagojevic, Pablo Bertorello, Prasanna Kumar (2021). New methods and metrics. Suitable for evaluating LFQA tasks. *arXiv*: 13432. [Preprint]. doi: doi.org/10.48550/arXiv.2112.13432

Chapter 4

Immersive technologies for the metaverse

Harshavardhan Kosuri[1]

Abstract

Immersive technologies are a collection of sophisticated digital experiences that generate a sense of interaction and presence within a simulated environment. This category encompasses Virtual Reality (VR), which provides a fully immersive digital experience by obstructing the physical world with headsets; Augmented Reality (AR), which overlays digital content onto the real world using devices such as smartphones and AR glasses; and Mixed Reality (MR), which combines the physical and digital worlds to allow for real-time interaction. By enhancing engagement, training, visualization, and collaboration capabilities, these technologies are revolutionizing industries such as gaming, education, healthcare, and manufacturing.

Keywords: Immersive Technologies; Virtual Reality (VR); Augmented Reality (AR); Mixed Reality (MR); Extended Reality (XR); VR Headsets; Spatial Audio; Applications of VR

4.1 Three types of Virtual Reality

There are three types of Virtual Reality one (non-immersive) where you are not fully in it, another (semi-immersive) where you are halfway, and the coolest one (fully immersive) where you are totally inside a computer-made world. When people talk about all these VR types together, they call it extended reality (XR). Each type gives a different level of computer-made simulation.

1. **Non-immersive Virtual Reality:** Some VR is not super fancy; it is really common. In this type, you see a computer-made world, but you still know and control what is happening around you in the real world. Video games are a great example of this kind of VR.
2. **Semi-immersive Virtual Reality:** This VR is kind of in the middle. You get some of the experience in a computer-made world, but you are still connected to and aware of the real world around you. This VR is great for learning and practicing. It uses powerful computers and big projectors, like in-flight simulators for training pilots.

[1]PlanetMeta, Bengaluru, India

3. **Fully immersive Virtual Reality:** At the moment, there is no VR that completely takes you into another world, but things are changing really quickly. Soon, we might have super immersive VR! The best kind of VR makes everything feel super real—what you see, hear, and sometimes even smell! Games like car racing in VR make you feel like you are really driving fast. While it started with games, now we use this super immersive VR in lots of different areas too.

When we talk about virtual technology, it means it has a few important things. It is not just immersive (feels real), but it is also made by computers, feels like a real experience in many ways, and lets you interact with it.

4.1.1 Do you want to know how Virtual Reality works?

Making Virtual Reality (VR) involves both stuff you can touch (hardware) and computer programs (software). The hardware gives your senses things like sound, touch, smell, or heat, making it feel real. The software creates the made-up world you experience. Together, they trick your eyes and brain into feeling like you are really there.

4.2 Seeing and thinking

When we create a sense of reality, we mimic how our eyes and brains function. Our eyes are slightly different, so they perceive things differently. These tiny differences help our brains understand depth and make things 3D. Think of your eyes as two cameras, each taking two different pictures. Your brain takes these two views, combines them, and makes them look real. It is like magic, your brain creates depth or 3D, and it is all thanks to your eyes and brain working together like a team. That is why you can tell the difference between something close and far away.

When we create an immersive experience with technology, we use this trick. In Virtual Reality (VR), VR tries to mimic what happens naturally when we look around in the physical world. In VR, the hardware and software work together to play this eye-and-brain trick. Your eyes get slightly different images on a VR headset screen. The brain sees these images and makes you feel like you are really in that VR world. This is why VR can make you believe you are flying, underwater, or anywhere! It is all about making a cool and realistic experience. Imagine a robot with two eyes—that is how VR kind of works (Figure 4.1).

Figure 4.1 Metaverse web concept with people scenes set in flat style

4.3 Uses of immersive technologies

VR technology is like special gear, including things you wear on your head (Headsets) and tools you hold, like controllers. You use this gear (Motion trackers) to enter virtual worlds. These worlds are made either by downloading special apps or by going on the internet through a web browser. It is like putting on magic glasses to visit cool places!

4.4 Hardware used in immersive technologies

Virtual reality hardware includes sensory accessories such as controllers, as well as headsets, hand trackers, treadmills, and, for creators, 3D cameras.

1. **VR Headsets:**
   A VR headset is like special goggles you wear on your head. It is a screen that shows you things in a virtual world. These goggles can also have really good sound and sensors that track your eye and head movements, making it feel super real!
   There are three main types of VR Headsets:
   (a) **PC-based VR Headsets:** These VR headsets for computers cost more, but they give the best experiences. These headsets connect to the computer with a cable and need extra hardware to work. They have a special screen, sensors that track your head, and even an external camera to make everything look and sound amazing for a more real feeling.
   (b) **Standalone VR Headsets:** Some VR headsets are like all-in-one gadgets; they work on their own without wires. Think of them as special tablets or phones just for VR. But not all wireless VR headsets work alone. Some get information without wires from game consoles or computers nearby. Others might have a small wired pack you carry in a pocket or clip to your clothes.
   (c) **Mobile Headsets:** Some VR devices are like special shells that hold your smartphone. These shells have lenses that make the phone's screen show things in 3D. It is a cheap way to try VR, and you do not need wires because the phone does all the work. But phones are not as good as game consoles or computers for VR. They cannot show things as clearly, and you cannot move around to see things from different angles. It is like looking at a 3D picture that does not change when you move your head.

2. **VR Accessories:**
   VR accessories are extra gadgets that help make VR even better. People are always making new things to improve the experience. Some of these accessories include a special mouse for 3D, trackers that follow your movements, gloves with wires, controllers you move around, full-body suits, treadmills, and even devices that let you smell things in the virtual world!

Following are some of the accessories used today in VR

(a) **3D Mouse**: It is a special device made to help you move and point in 3D virtual spaces. This device uses different tricks like accelerometers, sensors, and lights to understand how you are moving in the virtual world. It is like a magic wand that helps you control things in your VR experience.

(b) **Optical Trackers**: Special cameras keep an eye on where the person or thing in VR is. They often use one or more cameras that stay in one place and watch what is happening in the virtual world. It is like having an invisible friend always watching and telling the VR system where you are.

(c) **Wired Gloves**: This device, often called cyber gloves or data gloves, is worn on the hands. It uses different sensors to track how your hands move. Like a tracking device, it captures rotation and position data. The software in the glove understands these movements. Some fancy gloves can even make you feel things, like a slight touch, making them not just for input but also for feeling things in the virtual world.

(d) **Motion Controllers**: These tools let people do things in a mix of the real and virtual worlds. Controllers are like magic wands that let you do very detailed things with digital objects because they know exactly where they are in space.

(e) **Omnidirectional Treadmills (ODTs)**: This cool machine lets you move around in any direction in the real world while you are in VR. It is like a special treadmill that helps you feel fully inside the virtual world by letting you move freely.

(f) **Smelling Devices**: There is a new accessory in VR—smell devices! A company in Tokyo, called Vaqso, made a special attachment for headsets that releases smells. It is like a fan with different scents, and the smells can get stronger or weaker based on what is happening on the screen. So, you can actually smell things in the virtual world!

4.5 Software used in immersive technology

People who implement Immersive Technologies use different computer programs. These include special kits for VR, programs to show things visually, tools to organize content, engines for making games, places to connect socially, and simulators for training.

1. **VR Content Management Systems Software:** Companies use this tool at work to gather, save, and study VR stuff all in one place.
2. **VR Game Engine Software:** People who make video games use these tools to create a VR experience.
3. **VR Software Development Kit (SDK):** SDKs provide a starting point to create, build, and try out VR experiences.
4. **VR Social Platforms Software:** Users collaborate from remote locations in VR with these tools.

5. **VR Training Simulator Software:** This software is good for many types of jobs to train employees in realistic, immersive situations.
6. **VR Visualization Software:** People see information combined in a pretend world. It helps them really get what the data is saying.

4.6 Role of audio in Virtual Reality

Virtual Reality design makes things feel real, therefore sound is super important in creating believable experiences. Both what you see and what you hear work together to make the virtual world feel more real and immersive. Sound helps to give a sense of presence and the feeling of being in a specific space. It is also important for giving clues or hints to users about what is happening in their virtual surroundings, guiding them through their digital adventure.

For VR to feel real, it is not just about good graphics. What you hear and see are key to how you sense space. Sound is even faster than what you see in making you react. To make VR truly immersive, you need realistic background noises and sounds that match the space you are in. It is like putting you in a virtual world where what you hear and see makes everything feel genuine and lifelike.

4.7 Spatial audio in Virtual Reality experience

When people hear, they can tell where a sound is coming from and roughly how far away it is. To make virtual sounds feel real, we use something called binaural or spatial audio. This makes the audio in a virtual experience mimic the way we hear in the real world, giving a more authentic and lifelike feel to the overall experience.

Binaural or spatial audio mimics how our ears and brain work together. Since we have ears on both sides of our head, sounds from one side take slightly longer to reach our ear on the opposite side. This time delay helps our brain figure out where the sound is coming from. So, with binaural or spatial audio in virtual experiences, we make it feel like the sound is coming from a specific spot in 3D space, just like it does in the real world.

Binaural and spatial audio make virtual worlds feel very real. To really feel the cool audio stuff in a VR experience, put on your best headphones and check out The Verge's audio infographic. It is like stepping into a world where the sounds make everything feel incredibly lifelike.

4.8 Applications of Virtual Reality in today's life

Virtual Reality technology is now not restricted to games but it is used in many ways like helping with sales, making education fun, simulating travel, and even for communication. After the COVID-19 pandemic, more people have started using VR for working from home, socializing online, and experiencing virtual travel. It has not just remained for gaming anymore; VR is helping us do lots of things in a whole new way.

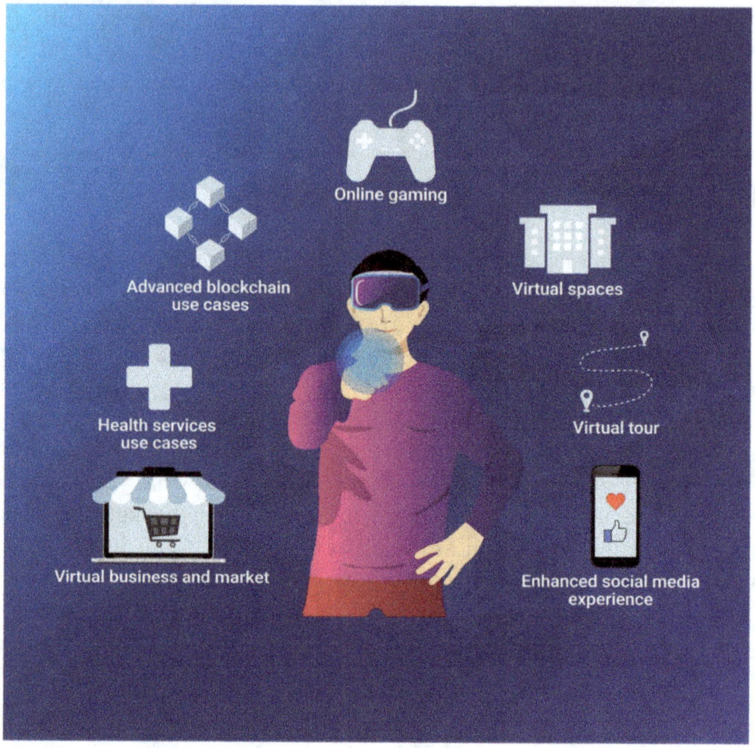

Figure 4.2 Use cases of metaverse vector illustration

VR has changed how businesses work, from medicine to tourism. It is a crucial part of many companies' plans to adapt and transform digitally. In simpler terms, VR is like a big building block in making businesses smarter and more modern (Figure 4.2).

4.9 Let us understand the difference between Virtual Reality and Augmented Reality

Virtual Reality is like stepping into a completely different, made-up world that covers everything around you. Augmented Reality, on the other hand, adds extra digital stuff to what you see in the real world.

VR makes fake worlds that you can feel and interact with. When you do things in these made-up places, it affects what happens there. These digital places look real but are separate from the real world you are in.

AR uses your actual surroundings that you see through a device, like a camera. Then, it adds extra computer-made things, like pictures, sound, or videos, to what

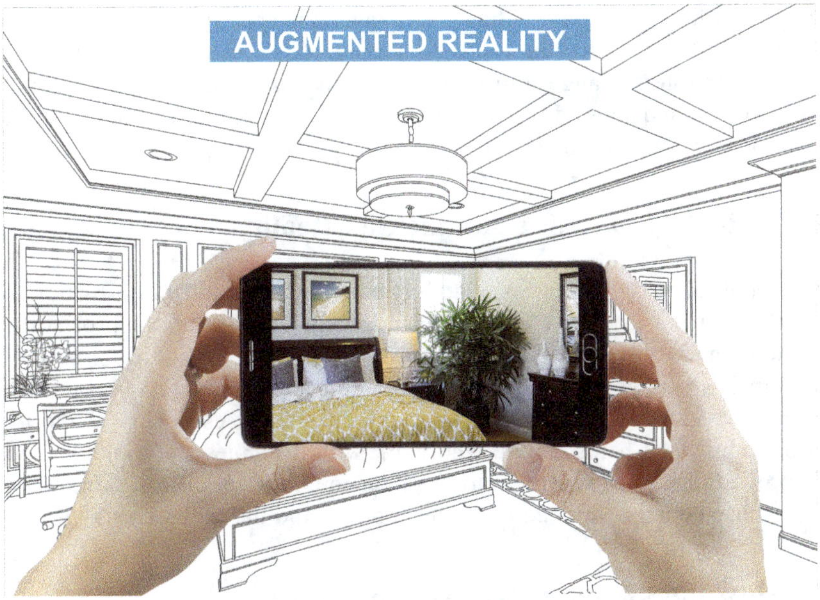

Figure 4.3 Hands-holding smartphone displaying a photo of a bedroom with Augmented Reality effect

you are already looking at. Unlike virtual reality, AR does not make a whole new world—it just adds cool stuff to what is already there.

4.9.1 What is Augmented Reality?

Augmented Reality is a blend of digital information and what you see in real life happening right now. Unlike Virtual Reality, AR does not create a completely false world. Instead, you are still seeing the real world but with additional computer-generated information added to it (Figure 4.3).

AR changes the way you see things or gives you more information about them. The interesting thing about AR is how it mixes computer-generated information with what is actually around you. AR is useful for decision-making as well as for entertainment.

AR shows you images, sound, and other information through a device such as a phone or a pair of glasses. It places this information on the device, blending it with what you actually see. This creates a blended experience, where digital things change how you perceive the real world. AR can add things to the real world or hide parts of it.

4.10 Augmented Reality overview

Augmented Reality is the addition of digital information to the real world. If you have ever browsed a neighborhood map before stepping foot in the door or tried out a piece of furniture in your sitting room with an app, then you have already experienced AR. In entertainment, there is a lot of AR in games and photos. For example, when filters change someone's appearance in an image, games blend real and fake worlds, and apps add virtual characters to your real environment. AR adds a digital element to your entertainment.

4.11 How do you define Augmented Reality

Augmented Reality is the process of adding computer-generated information to the real world to make it more interactive and engaging. With the help of software, applications, and tools such as AR glasses, AR puts digital content into the real world. It makes your environment more interesting and turns your environment into an interactive learning environment. This is very useful, especially in the manufacturing industry. It helps people who work with machines and systems blend in and improve them. It allows them to use their intelligence, observation, and creativity to enhance and add value to the technology and the IoT networks they use.

4.12 How does Augmented Reality work?

Augmented Reality comes in different forms like on smartphones, tablets, and glasses. They are even working on AR in contact lenses. To make it work, you need things like a brain (processor), sensors, a screen, and ways to give commands. Phones usually have the needed stuff for AR, like cameras, accelerometers, GPS, and compasses. These help make AR easy for regular people to use. GPS finds where you are, and the compass figures out which way your device is pointing (Figure 4.4).

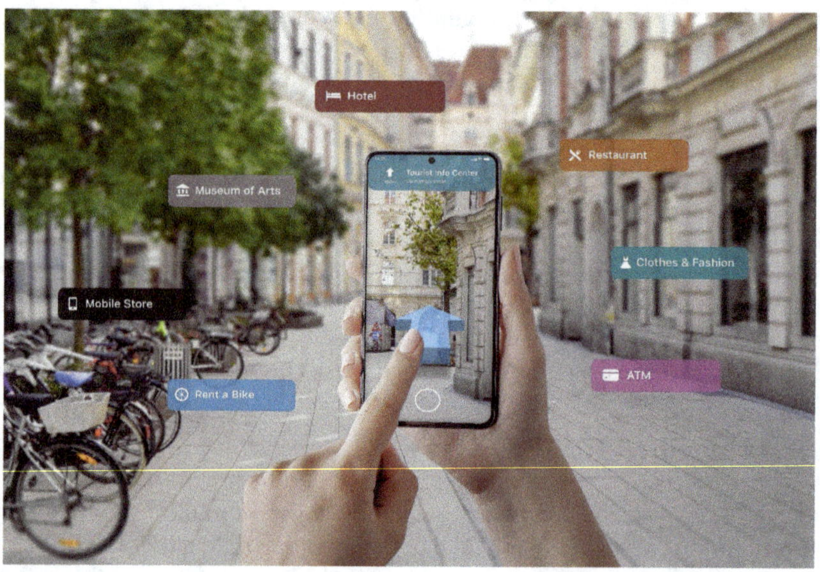

Figure 4.4 Tourist information and signposts on smartphones in tourist app

Military training uses advanced AR that can recognize objects and gestures. AR can be demanding on a device, so if it does not have enough power, some of the work can be done on another machine.

AR apps are made in special 3D programs that let developers connect animations or digital information in the computer to an AR marker in the real world. When the AR app gets digital information from a known marker, it follows the marker's instructions and adds the right images or animations on top of it.

4.13 Process of Augmented Reality

1. An AR device, like smart glasses, a tablet, or a smartphone with a camera, looks at a video to figure out what is around you. It can recognize things like machines or how a warehouse is set up.
2. A digital twin is like a digital copy of something in the cloud, a 3D version. It links the real world and the digital world together. It gathers information from both the actual thing and its digital version.
3. The AR device grabs information about an object from the cloud. It adds digital stuff to the object using markers or trackers, like GPS and sensors. This makes a mix of real and digital things in a 3D view.
4. Because live data is coming in from the things, you can play with the object or space by moving around and giving commands. You do this through a touchscreen, by speaking, or with hand movements.

4.14 Uses of Augmented Reality

- **Navigation:** AR can show you the way to where you are going by putting a route on top of what you see on the road. It can also tell you about nearby businesses as you walk or drive around.
- **Entertainment and gaming:** AR can be used to put a virtual game into the real world or let people do fun things with their faces on social media by adding creative animations.
- **Retail:** People can use a store's app online to check how things like furniture will appear in their own homes before they decide to buy.
- **Tools and measurements:** Phones and tablets can use AR to figure out the size and position of various points in the space around the user.
- **Architecture:** AR can help architects visualize a building project.
- **Military:** Information like directions, distances, weather, and road conditions can be shown on a car's windshield using augmented reality.
- **Archaeology:** AR has helped archaeologists by using 3D models to rebuild historical sites. This allows museum visitors and future archaeologists to feel like they are actually at the excavation site.

4.15 Examples of Augmented Reality

- **Target app:** The Target retail app has a feature called "See it in Your Space." With this, users can take a photo of a room in their home and use the app to see how a product, like a picture or a chair, will look in that space (Figure 4.5).
- **Apple Measure app:** The Measure app on Apple iOS is like a virtual tape measure. You can pick two points in the world around you, and the app will tell you how far apart they are.
- **Snapchat:** Snapchat filters use AR to add cool filters or masks over your pictures or snaps.
- **Pokémon Go:** Pokémon Go is a famous mobile game that uses AR. It figures out where you are using GPS and then makes Pokémon creatures show up in your real surroundings for you to catch.
- **Google Glass:** Google Glass is a kind of glass with a computer built in by Google. People can use it to work without using their hands. Companies like DHL and DB Schenker use Google Glass and special software to help workers be more efficient in tasks like managing global supply chains and personalized shipping.

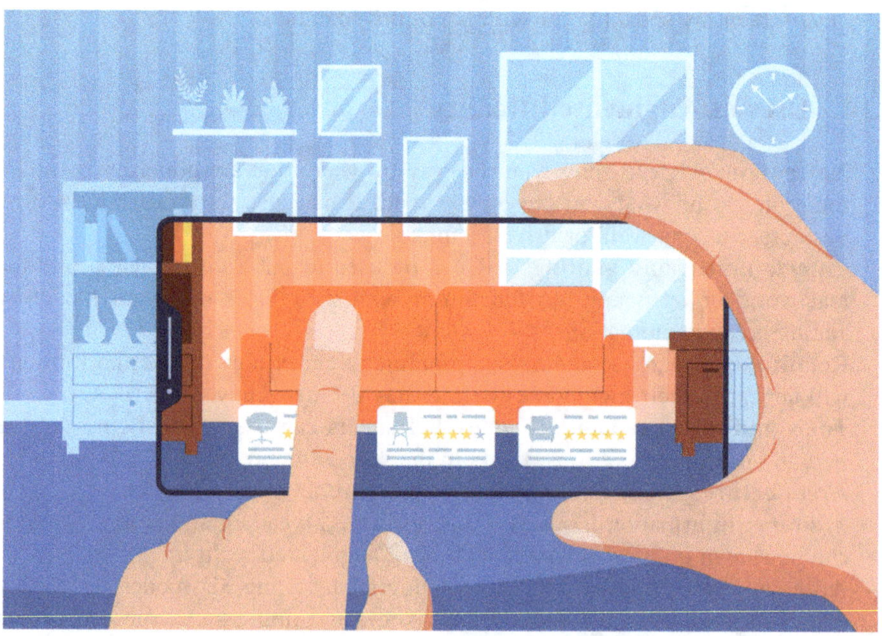

Figure 4.5 Augmented Reality concept with hand holding smartphone

4.15.1 *Future of Augmented Reality technology*

AR technology is getting bigger because more and more people are using apps and games like Pokémon Go or store AR apps. As 5G networks grow, it might become easier to have cool AR experiences online. This means AR apps could be faster and smoother with better internet connections.

Apple is making and improving a tool called ARKit for mobile augmented reality. Big companies like Target and Ikea use ARKit in their shopping apps for iPhones and iPads. The latest version, ARKit 6, makes AR look really sharp with high-quality images and videos. It also lets the camera understand the size and shape of things using depth information. Plus, it includes other upgrades to make AR even better.

The Android version of ARKit is called ARCore, and it keeps getting better. ARCore uses a geospatial API that gets information from 3D models on Google Earth and pictures from Street View on Google Maps. Just like ARKit, ARCore has made its Depth API better, especially for sensing depth over longer distances.

Exciting things are being made, like Google's smart glasses that turn spoken words into written text in real time. This could change how people who speak different languages talk to each other. Because AR is about immersive technology, we can expect more cool chances and experiences in various ways and places.

4.15.2 *Mixed Reality*

Mixed Reality (MR) is one of today's hippest technologies. It is a combination of Virtual Reality (VR) and Augmented Reality (AR). MR can create incredibly immersive experiences that make people feel they are in a virtual world, while also interacting with the real world. VR is like an entire digital universe compared to AR which overlays digital stuff on top of it. But in this context, what MR does is bring these digital things into your real world so you can hold and manipulate them as if they were really there (Figure 4.6).

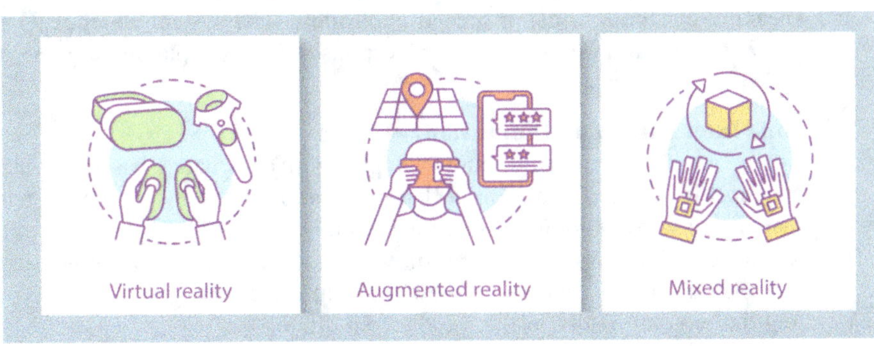

Figure 4.6 Immersive technologies

4.16 Let us see how Mixed Reality works

1. **Hardware:**
    - To enjoy mixed reality, you need special gear like MR headsets or glasses. These gadgets come with cameras, sensors, screens, and powerful chips to make the magic happen.
    - These devices watch how you move and use your hands, and they also keep an eye on the world around you. This helps them know exactly where you are and how you are moving, so you can play with digital stuff as if it is really there.
    - MR headsets usually have screens or cameras that let you see both the real world and virtual stuff at the same time. It is like having a mix of reality and virtual reality all in one view.
2. **Spatial Mapping and Tracking:**
    - Spatial mapping is like making a digital copy of the place where you are in real life. It helps mix virtual stuff into your surroundings accurately.
    - The sensors and cameras on MR devices take pictures and measurements of everything around you, like the floor, furniture, and walls. Then they use this information to create a 3D map, kind of like a digital blueprint, of your surroundings.
    - Once the MR device creates a map of your surroundings, it can put virtual stuff in the right places, like on a table or the floor. This makes it feel like the virtual stuff is really part of your world and can interact with things around you just like they would in real life.
3. **Integration of Virtual and Real Content:**
    - In mixed reality, cool digital things like 3D models, moving pictures, and holograms blend perfectly with the real world around you. It is like they are all together in one big playground.
    - In mixed reality, the digital stuff seems like it is right there with the real things, staying in the same spot no matter where you look from. It is like they are glued to the world around you from your point of view.
    - In mixed reality, you can play with digital things using hand movements, speaking out loud, or using special controllers. The system watches what you are doing and gives you instant responses, just like playing a game in real time.
4. **Dynamic Interaction and Immersion:**
    - In mixed reality, the digital things you play with can change based on what is happening around you right at that moment. It is like they are alive and reacting to what is going on in your world.
    - In mixed reality, you can touch, move, and play with digital things just like they are real. It feels like they are right there with you, making you feel like you are really in the middle of it all.
    - In mixed reality, fancy computer tricks like adjusting light and shadows make digital things look like they belong in the real world. It helps

everything blend together smoothly, making it seem even more realistic.

5. **Application Development:**
   - To develop mixed reality apps, you will have to make 3D artifacts, craft menus, and invent action mechanics for your MR experience.
   - These tools include development platforms like Unity or Unreal Engine that help build engaging MR solutions for different industries and application cases.
   - MR apps can range from amusements and games to learning, medicine, business, etc., making it a platform for endless innovation in this field.

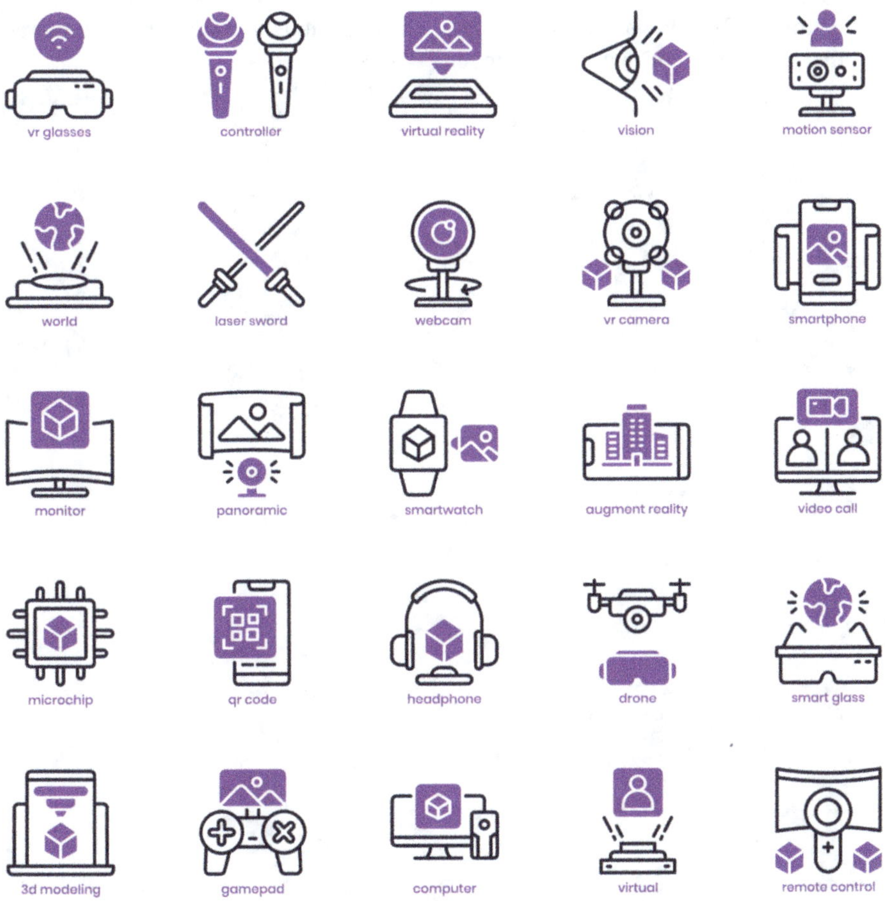

Figure 4.7 Virtual reality icons

Figure 4.8 Immersive technology use cases

It is an incredible combination of real-life surroundings and virtual world experiences whereby users can manipulate digital media using their hands as depicted in science fiction. As this technology progresses over time toward maturity, the implications of MR on various sectors could be enormous; the way humans interact with their environment may also change (Figures 4.7 and 4.8).

Chapter 5
3D modeling for the metaverse

Harshavardhan Kosuri[1]

Abstract

In the metaverse, 3D modeling is a critical technology that facilitates the development of interactive, immersive virtual environments. Users can engage with three-dimensional digital objects, avatars, and landscapes in real time through the design and visualization of these objects. The process involves the integration of a variety of components, such as geometry, texture mapping, lighting, and physics-based simulations, to generate lifelike or fantastical representations in virtual environments. These models are the foundation for a variety of metaverse applications, including education, social interactions, virtual commerce, and gaming. The development of virtual environments that are both more complex and accessible is being driven by advancements in 3D modeling technologies, such as AI-enhanced tools, real-time rendering, and hardware such as AR/VR devices. In the metaverse, 3D modeling not only facilitates aesthetic and functional aspects but also enables deep personalization, dynamic content generation, and cross-platform integration, thereby revolutionizing the way users interact with digital spaces. The metaverse ecosystem's development and sustainability are anticipated to be significantly influenced by the ongoing evolution of 3D modeling techniques.

Keywords: 3D Modeling; Metaverse; Virtual Environments; Avatars; Geometry and Texture Mapping; Optimization; Low Poly Models; VR/AR Platforms

5.1 3D modeling for the metaverse

3D modeling is the process of producing a digital model of a physical object using special software. Making a 3D model starts with basic shapes like cubes or spheres. The artist then tweaks and adds details to those shapes. They can change the colors and textures to make it look realistic. 3D artists work hard to get every little detail just right. Their work brings imaginary worlds to life on the big screen (Figure 5.1).

[1]PlanetMeta, Bengaluru, India

Figure 5.1 3D virtual office

5.2 Introduction to 3D modeling in the metaverse

The metaverse is an exciting new world. In this space, 3D modeling is very important. It helps create amazing digital experiences.

5.3 Building virtual worlds

With 3D modeling, you can make detailed virtual places. These could be busy cities or peaceful nature spots. Users get to explore interesting worlds.

5.3.1 Designing avatars

3D modeling also brings avatars and characters to life. Users can customize their virtual look. This helps them show their personality when interacting online.

5.3.2 Making virtual things and stuff easy

3D modeling lets you make all kinds of things like furniture, clothes, cars, and gadgets for the metaverse. These cool items make the metaverse fun. You can change your space and play games.

5.3.3 Feeling like you are there

Detailed 3D models make the metaverse seem real. You can go on adventures in fantasy worlds. You can learn, travel, and play games like you are really doing it (Figure 5.2).

Figure 5.2 Interior of modern office workplaces

5.3.4 Being creative and making new stuff

3D modeling tools let you make whatever you imagine for the metaverse. Creators can make their own content for virtual worlds. This brings new ideas and variety.

3D modeling makes the metaverse look real. With 3D models, people can see and do things in a digital world. It lets us explore new places that do not exist in the real world. 3D modeling builds the look of the metaverse. Without it, the metaverse would just be a blank space.

5.4 Process of making virtual items for 3D modeling

Making virtual items for 3D modeling in the metaverse is like making items for other virtual worlds, but you need to make sure they work with the specific platform you want to use. Here are the steps to get started:

- **Pick your metaverse platform:** There are many metaverse platforms coming up, and each one has its own rules and features. Some popular ones are Decentraland, Somnium Space, Cryptovoxels, and VRChat. Look into these platforms to see which one fits your project goals best.
- **Learn the platform's rules and tools:** Each metaverse platform usually gives guidelines and tools for making and importing 3D models. Learn these guidelines well, because they often have information on file formats, making assets work better, and other requirements.
- **Make your virtual stuff:** Use software like Blender, Maya, or 3ds Max to create the digital objects you want. Pay attention to size, detail amount, and polygon count, as these things can impact how well they work and fit in the metaverse space.
- **Improve your creations:** After making your models, optimize them for use in the metaverse. This might involve reducing the polygon count, improving textures, and simplifying complex shapes to boost performance and load times.

- **Convert files:** Export your 3D models in a file type the Metaverse platform accepts. Common ones include FBX, OBJ, and GLTF/GLB. Follow any special export settings suggested by the platform.
- **Put up stuff on the platform:** Use the tools that come with the platform to put your 3D things into the metaverse. Do the stuff the platform says to bring in things. Make sure your things are not too big or too little as the platform says.
- **See if it works right:** When your things are up, see if they look right and work right in the metaverse world. Make changes and fix things if the stuff is not working like it should.
- **Put things in your big project:** Put your virtual things in your big project in the metaverse. You can put them in places, have people play with them, or use them in games and worlds.

Creating cool virtual things for the metaverse is fun. By taking these steps and making them fit the metaverse platform you pick, you can make virtual objects that make the metaverse experience even better for users.

5.4.1 Fundamentals of 3D modeling

3D modeling is an essential factor in building immersive virtual environments, avatars, items, and experiences in the metaverse. The following are some basics of 3D modeling in the metaverse:

1. **Low Poly Modeling:** 3D models in the metaverse are often low poly due to performance reasons and the necessity of scalability wherein they contain relatively few polygons as compared to high-detail models used for offline rendering (Figure 5.3).

Figure 5.3 Low poly tropical island with the river

2. **Optimization:** To ensure smooth performance across various devices and platforms while in the metaverse, key consideration is given to efficiency. Among the methods used to optimize 3D models are: reducing polygon count, optimizing textures, and applying efficient rendering techniques.
3. **Modularity:** Reusability and flexibility are possible in the virtual environment development because of modular design. When the objects and structures are designed in modular pieces, it becomes easy to assemble and modify them. It also helps in scaling up very fast during content development; saving time for scaling up at a later stage.
4. **UV Mapping and Texture Atlases:** Memory usage reduction and rendering performance optimization are essential requirements for efficient UV mapping and texture atlases creation in the metaverse. Multiple textures are combined to form one image called a texture atlas which minimizes draw calls thereby improving rendering efficiency.
5. **Interactivity:** In the metaverse, 3D models often require interactivity like clickable objects, animated characters, and physics-based interactions. Implementing interactivity involves using scripting languages such as JavaScript or visual scripting tools provided by metaverse platforms.
6. **Avatar Creation:** Avatars, which are virtual representations of people in the metaverse, need to be created. For character creation, 3D modeling techniques will be employed in making customizable avatars. In animation, rigging must take place and for the purpose of deformation, skinning is necessary. There should be various customization options for avatars including changing clothes, accessories, and body parts (Figure 5.4).
7. **Standardized Formats:** Across various metaverse platforms, 3D models are often exported in standardized formats, such as GLTF (Graphics Library Transmission Format) and USDZ (Universal Scene Description), to ensure that they interoperate. These formats can handle animations, materials, metadata, and other features.
8. **Collaborative Design:** With real-time collaboration tools and workflows, multiple users can collaborate on 3D modeling projects concurrently, thus facilitating collaborative design and content creation towards the metaverse. They usually come with version control, commenting, and live editing functionalities.

By mastering these core skills, content creators will be able to produce captivating interactive 3D materials within the metaverse which will go a long way in

Figure 5.4 Boy cartoon avatars

creating diverse experiences and worlds virtually. They will be able to produce interactive 3D content to be used in the metaverse which will assist in creating different virtual worlds and experiences.

5.4.2 Different approaches to 3D modeling

5.4.2.1 Polygonal modeling

The creation of 3D models by geometric parameters like vertices, and edges among others as a way of creating complex shapes entails polygonal or mesh modeling. Users usually start with simple figures like: cubes, spheres, or even cylinders then use methods such as extruding, beveling, and subdivision to make them more detailed objects. The fact that this technique enables one to come up with accurate design models may account for its popularity within different sectors including but not limited to: gaming and animation industries, among others, character development plays a key role, as every character created should be unique in its own right, which highlights the need for customization capabilities possessed by polygonal modelers (Figure 5.5).

5.4.2.2 Sculpting

Modeling in 3D software packages usually involves "pushing around" vertices, edges, or faces individually. Using sculpting software, a designer can shape and mold the surface of a model as if it were real clay. Artists use the brushes to add or

Figure 5.5 Polygonal portrait of a wolf in low poly style

remove material, smooth, or carve away surfaces, and so on. This technique is particularly well-suited for creating complex organic forms such as creatures and characters which have an irregular layout. Blender's sculpt mode is popular among these programs.

5.4.2.3 Procedural modeling

Procedural modeling is the procedure of generating 3D models using predefined rules and parameters instead of manually sculpting or targeting geometry algorithmically. By defining rules and parameters that define the shape, structure, and appearance of an item, modelers can employ procedural modeling methods and tools to generate complex and very detailed objects. This technique is best suited for repetitive or pattern-based geometry such as plants, terrains, architectural elements, and procedural textures. Procedural modeling is ideal for creating large-scale procedural content efficiently with more flexibility making it suitable for assets with intricate geometries, environments, and landscapes.

5.4.2.4 Parametric modeling

Parametric modeling is a method that uses mathematical equations to define the shape of a 3D model. In parametric modeling software, designers create objects by specifying dimensions, constraints, and relationships between different features. These models can be easily modified or updated quickly through changes in their parameters which support fast iterations during design exploration processes. The technique is commonly applied in fields like engineering (e.g., automotive industry), product design/development as well architectural modeling where accurate measurements are combined with numerous iterations to realize an effective design solution. With parametric modeling tools such as Siemens NX or Solidworks, one can create accurate customizable designs easily adaptable according to specific needs (Figure 5.6).

5.4.2.5 Photogrammetry

Photogrammetry is a method of capturing real-world objects or environments using photographs and deriving 3D data from them. To create highly detailed and accurate 3D models, modelers analyze objects or scenes' geometry from multiple

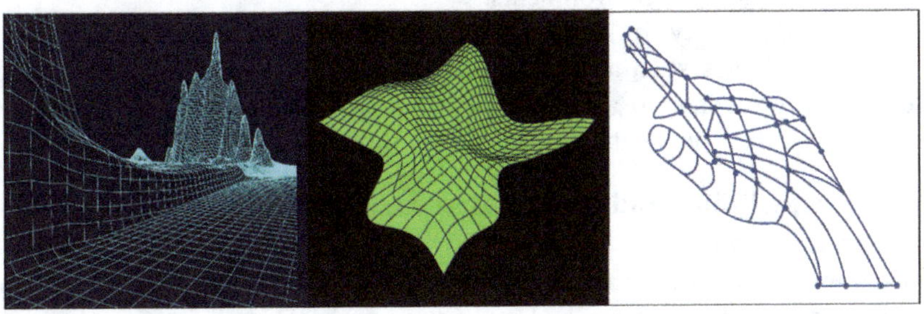

Figure 5.6 (a) 3d Terrain. (b) Cyberpunk-perspective-grid. (c) Hand of electric circuit.

Figure 5.7 (a) Stone pillar in the middle of a desert. (b) A stone pillar. (c) Stone column.

overlapping photos through photogrammetry software. In fields like archaeology, cultural heritage, and visual effects, photogrammetry finds common usage since it is necessary to capture real-world objects and environments with great fidelity. This method enables the generation of true-to-life 3D models with all the details present in the actual object or environment; therefore, it is suitable for building assets, scenes, and digital copies of tangible things from the data acquired through the same (Figure 5.7).

The reason why these different approaches to 3D modeling are valuable is that each technique offers essentially different tools and varies the way people create 3D content, modelers can make anything from very precise geometric models to organic-looking shapes or landscapes that have been procedurally generated as well depending upon what they need for their project and how much artistry they want involved with it. To produce not just any work but a specific kind of result, modelers may choose either one of the available methods or a combination, depending on what is needed most.

5.4.3 Challenges and opportunities in 3D modeling

5.4.3.1 Technical challenges in 3D modeling for the metaverse

Optimizing 3D models for real-time rendering in the metaverse is a major difficulty. To ensure that models perform smoothly on different platforms and devices, they must be constructed and textured efficiently.

Another technical challenge is metaverse cross-platform compatibility. Modeling for virtual reality (VR), augmented reality (AR), and traditional gaming environments may necessitate model adaptation or optimization to allow it to work concurrently across these environments.

Data interoperability for metaverse 3D models' integration needs to be solved with associated issues such as file format compatibility among others including data exchange protocols so as to allow for seamless communication and collaboration between various platforms as well as tools.

5.4.3.2 Accessibility and inclusivity considerations

User interface design

To make sure the metaverse is accessible and inclusive, user-friendly interfaces should be designed for creating and interacting with 3D models. To achieve this, intuitive controls, accessibility features, and assistive technology support must be at the forefront of tools and platforms to cater to people with different abilities.

Content diversity
In the metaverse, it is important that 3D models represent all walks of life because they help create an environment where everyone feels included. Therefore, those developing such content need to ensure variety when designing characters, avatars, or even whole virtual worlds which can be done by focusing on different cultures within our societies.

5.4.4 Intellectual property and copyright issues

5.4.4.1 Ownership and attribution

In the Metaverse, intellectual property rights are a big concern and so are copyright issues as that is where users come up with 3D content that they can share. You must set clear guidelines for owning these models and providing licenses for them as well as attributing any person who has worked on them which would ultimately safeguard the creator's rights against unauthorized exploitation or use of their work.

Content moderation
Copyright Act, 1998 restricts what you can do with someone else's work without permission. However, it is not always easy to tell if you have broken this law, as there are various types of infringement, including direct and indirect infringements. In addition to community guidelines, intellectual property laws must also be followed, and this necessitates the creation of robust screening systems to identify instances of plagiarism or unauthorized use of copyrighted materials in the Metaverse.

5.4.5 Emerging trends and future prospects

5.4.5.1 Generation of content by AI

The inclusion of AI measures in 3D modeling software is changing the creation of content in the metaverse. AI tools and algorithms can generate 3D models, procedural content and dynamic environments by themselves thus the process of creating them is simplified while the range of creative possibilities is broadened.

5.4.5.2 Blockchain and NFTs

The emergence of blockchain technology and NFTs brings fresh ways for developers to earn from their 3D models and digital art pieces in the metaverse. Blockchain-based systems provide peer-to-peer markets where people can buy or sell different items using cryptocurrencies like Bitcoin for example Ethereum Classic, etc. It also provides more control over wealth distribution due to its decentralized nature, where no central authority controls everything. This way, artists are paid what they deserve without being exploited, either internally or externally, as there are various revenue streams associated with their work, such as royalties from trading original pieces found online.

5.4.5.3 Spatial computing

VR, AR, and mixed reality (or MR) technology are coming together and driving spatial computing's rise in the metaverse. It is all about mixing digital content seamlessly into real-world spaces to a point where virtual boundaries no longer exist; instead, these kinds of interactions with traditional screens can become more immersive than ever before.

What is the future really holding for us when we talk about creating virtual worlds through 3D modeling while considering the social technicalities involved alongside legalities in place? Well, first off there are different kinds of things that need to be investigated but at the same time, this new world may offer opportunities for innovation which could in return result in collaborations of different people's creativity. All these aside, with every problem comes its own solution(s), and therefore by addressing each challenge accordingly while also embracing any new wave rippling through space, we get our own answer(s).

Overall, what might really change such a reality is how much fun it will be working there? That aside again.

5.5 Case studies

5.5.1 Decentraland

5.5.1.1 Platform overview

Decentraland is a virtual reality place based on the Ethereum blockchain where users can build, explore, and monetize applications and content.

5.5.1.2 3D modeling

Decentraland allows users to create and design their own virtual spaces using 3D modeling tools. The spaces could be anything from interactive games to virtual art galleries among others.

5.5.1.3 Impact

Virtual real estate, digital art, and social experiences have all been created within this new world fostered by Decentraland. Artwork, virtual land sales, or experiences can be monetized by artists who are now able to access previously unattainable markets through the metaverse thus creating economic value in it.

5.5.2 Roblox

5.5.2.1 Platform overview

Roblox stands as a platform that permits users to design, share and play games, as millions come together to participate in the creation process.

5.5.2.2 3D modeling

Roblox avails 3D modeling tools, allowing players to create their games and virtual worlds with ease; users may also design characters, along with the complex terrains and game mechanics they want in their environment.

5.5.2.3 Impact

Roblox lets people make a variety of games depending on their skills which is achieved by democratizing the process, this way, users at different levels can share

Figure 5.8 *(a) Roblox mobile game, (b) funny characters playing football, and (c) Lego warriors battling in a fierce epic*

what they develop, leading to the creation of everything from simple theme parks to more complex experiences like multiplayer environments. This, in turn, contributes to a growing number of features aimed at enhancing user engagement and retention within the system (Figure 5.8).

5.5.3 Spatial

5.5.3.1 Platform overview

Spatial is a collaborative virtual reality platform that allows users to manipulate digital content in the context of the physical world.

5.5.3.2 3D modeling

Spatial lets people bring in 3D models and assets to use within their VR environments. Teams can work together live, moving around and interacting with these virtual objects in real space.

5.5.3.3 Impact

By creating an immersive environment where meetings happen as though every one were really there, it has transformed remote team collaboration through communication. Spatial is not only for building models or designs—it is also ideal for virtual events like meetups when physical distance separates people, but sharing ideas is more vital than ever, as isolation can stifle innovation.

The diverse applications and the impact of 3D modeling in the metaverse are taught amply by these case studies, starting from virtual real estate and gaming to collaborative design and communication. 3D modeling will be playing an increasingly vital role in shaping immersive digital experiences and communities as the metaverse continues to grow and develop.

5.6 Tools and techniques

5.6.1 Tools for 3D modeling

5.6.1.1 Blender

It is an open-source software widely used in the metaverse for creating virtual environments, assets, and characters. This 3D modeling software offers tools such as sculpting, animation, texturing, or modeling among others that are comprehensive.

5.6.1.2 Maya

This industry's professionals often use other 3D modeling as well as animation software popularly known within gaming and entertainment sectors due to its robust features for rigging models then animating them too.

5.6.1.3 Unity and unreal engine

These two game engines primarily offer 3D modeling and asset creation modules, while also leveraging tools for performance optimization. Seamless integration is essential for virtual environment engagement, particularly through 3D object placement, which these engines handle effectively. The characterization of these engines has been thoroughly considered, ensuring they meet the needs of developers.

5.6.2 In-depth tutorials

For example, there are a lot of tutorials for 3D modeling techniques for Metaverse on websites like YouTube, Udemy, and Gumroad. The following are examples of such tutorials: character modeling, environment design with texture painting, and animation as well.

Many online communities and forums that focus solely on 3D modeling (e.g., Blender Artists or Polycount) often run regular activities including tutorials/workshops or even challenges that help people grow their skills while exchanging knowledge with each other.

5.6.3 Optimization techniques

5.6.3.1 Polygon reduction

If you optimize models for performance in virtual environments, you will often need to reduce polygon count without losing visual quality. Polygon reduction and LOD (Level of Detail) generation techniques as well as mesh simplification can be used to achieve this goal.

5.6.3.2 Texture atlasing

Having multiple textures could result in draw calls which are expensive operations and slow down rendering speed severely. Therefore, combining them into one texture atlas would be very beneficial for performance optimization.

5.6.3.3 Proper UV mapping

In order to make the models appropriate for performance, it is important to map UV efficiently and minimize their overlapping which would increase texture memory usage.

5.7 3D modeling tips and best practices

Design with modules: Convert complex environments and objects into modular parts that can be utilized again and copied. This method will help you manage assets well as you build them for an optimized-level design.

Focusing on platforms: As you optimize models, consider the performance needs and hardware constraints of your target devices such as: Virtual Reality goggles or handsets used for mobile devices. To be sure that they work best across different platforms, it is important to test these models on several gadgets.

Combine materials and shaders: You should decrease render overhead by reducing the number of materials and shaders in your model. This can be achieved without compromising performance through creating material instances or using shader variants.

By using these tools, tutorials, optimization techniques, and best practices, 3D artists can produce high-quality and visually impressive content for the metaverse. This will help in creating engaging experiences in various virtual environments and platforms.

5.7.1 Collaboration and community

In the world of 3D modeling for the metaverse, working together and building a community is very important. This collaboration helps to boost creativity, share knowledge, and promote innovation among 3D modelers. Below is a summary of online communities and tools designed to support collaboration among 3D modelers in the metaverse.

5.7.1.1 Online communities and forums

Polycount: Polycount is an online hub for 3D modelers, texture artists, and concept artists, where they share their work, receive feedback, and participate in discussions. The community also offers tutorials on 3D modeling software, techniques, and industry trends.

Blender artists: Blender artists is a community specifically for people who use the software, Blender. It provides forums, galleries, and tutorials for artists at any level of experience. Members can display their work, take part in challenges, and get guidance from more seasoned Blender users.

ArtStation: ArtStation is a popular website where digital artists can display their work, interact with other artists, and find job opportunities in industries like gaming, film, and entertainment. Although it is known for showcasing various types of artworks, it is particularly well-regarded for its support of 3D modeling.

5.7.1.2 Collaboration tools and platforms

GitHub: This platform has been widely used for years by software developers who need to work together on code, and maybe 3D modelers can benefit from it too if they are doing collaborative projects. When you are an artist collaborating with other people—especially if there is more than one of you contributing models or textures to a scene—using GitHub allows version control (keeping track of different drafts), as well as change tracking (seeing what has been altered from one version to another) and collaboration around 3D assets like models themselves but also their textures and scripts used within Unity3d or Unreal Engine 4 among other software applications. So basically, anything related to creating CG visualizations!

Google Drive and Dropbox: Google Drive as well as Dropbox which are examples of cloud storage platforms may come in handy while sharing huge data including 3D models, textures pictures (references) for team members during a project course. Furthermore, both offer tools such as real-time commenting or even editing documents and spreadsheets on the go thereby making it possible for people living miles away from each other to work jointly without necessarily being physically present in one place.

MURAL and Miro: When it comes to remote work, nothing beats MURAL not to forget Miro—they are platforms that enable brainstorming sessions among teams which are in different geographic areas besides organizing ideas visually as well as collaborating on them concurrently. In connection with this, we can say storyboards being created and used while making concept arts could also be reviewed through these two software thus eliminating any need for physical presence during such an activity but instead doing everything online.

Figma: Figma is a tool that allows multiple people to work together on designing things, such as the look and feel of websites and apps, as well as how users interact with them. It is mainly used for designing the visual and interactive parts of digital products, like buttons and menus. However, it can also be used for working together on creating 3D models. Teams can use Figma to make sketches, models, and example designs for 3D spaces and objects.

5.7.2 Virtual Reality (VR) collaboration platforms

Spatial: As specified before, is an AR medium that enables dispersed teams to collaborate in virtual environments, allowing them to bring in 3D models, label objects, and interact with digital data through VR headsets or mobile phones.

Mozilla Hubs: It is a web-based tool for generating and sharing virtual spaces where people are able to hang out, chat, and work together in real-time; it has support for 3D models, videos as well as web content and hence can be used in cooperative design sessions and virtual meetings.

In the digital realm, there are online communities, collaboration tools, and platforms that offer 3D modelers important resources and chances to come together, work together, and make things in the metaverse. This allows them to go beyond physical distance and build a feeling of belonging in the world of digital art.

5.7.2.1 Ethical considerations

Prioritizing inclusive design practices: In the metaverse, designers and creators of 3D models should focus more on inclusive designs that ensure a wide range of cultures, identities, and perspectives are represented in virtual worlds. This means having various characters, environments, and storylines among other aspects showing human diversity in depth.

Avoiding stereotypes: One needs to be careful not to sustain existing beliefs that are harmful through virtual reality characters but rather come up with authentic representations for different communities by challenging the usual norms held in the society as well as biases that might be present at any given time.

Accessibility: When creating 3D models, designers should also remember disability provisions so those people living with disabilities can have an easy time while interacting with these environments or objects virtually; for instance, there could be other sensory options apart from what has initially been provided plus designing interfaces which are user friendly with such considerations in mind diverse avatars, environments, and narratives that reflect the richness of human diversity.

5.7.3 Ethical implications of virtual experiences and interactions

Digital identity and privacy: The metaverse's virtual experiences bring up questions regarding digital identity and privacy. This can result in users providing their personal information or engaging in activities that will make it difficult to differentiate between what is real and what is not thus emphasizing the need for strong privacy protections as well as the ability to give informed consent (Figure 5.9).

Virtual harassment and abuse: Virtual environments are also susceptible to forms such as harassment and bullying among others. Therefore, 3D modelers and platform operators should take necessary measures to prevent harassment, while also implementing safe reporting systems that allow victims to report incidents easily. Additionally, it is important to foster a culture of responsibility and respect within the communities in these virtual worlds (Figure 5.10).

Impact on mental health: Prolonged immersion in virtual environments can affect mental health and general, characterized by loneliness, obsession as well as a shift from the real world. The moral issue is how to encourage the right habit of using them, offer assistance for mental problems that may arise, and come up with strategies to ensure the users are always alright (Figure 5.11).

Figure 5.9 Pensive crazy business worker

Figure 5.10 (a) Woman violence concept. (b) Business-woman portrait. (c) Recruitment employee.

Figure 5.11 (a) Businessman wearing virtual reality goggles. (b) Business-woman in bad mood. (c) Cheerful-couple having fun with VR.

5.7.4 Responsibility of creators and platform operators

Content moderation: Online content creators and platform operators have an obligation to regulate content and see that virtual environments abide by community standards and behavioral codes. This can mean setting up content filtering algorithms, human moderation teams, or systems driven by community reporting.

Transparency and accountability: Trust and responsibility within the virtual society can only be achieved by being honest about one's data practices as well as their rules for moderating information; transparency on how decisions are made via algorithms is also important. Creators alongside those who operate platforms must be open with users and request input so that they may address any worries that arise along the way while also creating accountability.

When creating 3D models for metaverse, inclusivity should come first above all things else followed by privacy, safety, and user well-being because without people feeling safe enough nothing can be achieved but this requires looking at everything 360 degrees thereby integrating principles into designs as well as governing bodies which run them, i.e., metaverse becomes more equitable space for everyone involved if ethical considerations are factored in during both planning stages and implementation process up to date.

5.7.5 Ethical considerations and regulation

Regulation and oversight: As the metaverse enlarges and becomes more enmeshed in everyday activities, the demand for ethical codes of conduct regulating the use of 3D modeling technology will shoot upwards. This might encompass laws determining how data should be kept private, monitoring what is shared online, and virtual land rights too.

Equity as well as variety: Increasing virtual environment access would require elevated attempts at fostering egalitarianism vis-a-vis differing human encounters and identity realization through 3D models.

Promising technological advancements are anticipated in the metaverse because of future 3D modeling. These advancements are expected to include realism improvements driven by artificial intelligence-generated content, mixed reality experiences, and enhanced social interaction, among other things. As technology advances, so will 3D modeling, which plays a key role in enriching the metaverse by redefining how we interact with digital information and with each other. Will technology continue to advance?

This is an insight into the influence of 3D modeling on the metaverse and its effects on different sectors and communities through this extensive exploration.

Chapter 6

Generative AI for the enterprise metaverse system engineering

Pethuru Raj[1]

Abstract

With digitization and digitalization technologies flourishing, the digital era is dawning upon us influentially. Every tangible entity becomes digitized to participate in mainstream computing fluidly. When digital entities interact with one another purposefully, a massive amount of multi-structured data gets produced, collected, cleansed, and stocked for posterior data analytics to extract hidden insights, patterns, and other knowledge bases. Artificial intelligence (AI), the most popular digital transformation technology on the planet Earth, is succulently capable of making sense out of accumulating digital datasets. Knowledge discovery is disseminated to the concerned systems to make them aware of the power of knowledge-enabled systems.

Notably, there are several illuminating and insightful improvisations (for example, multimodal generative AI) in the AI space. Blockchain, Web 3.0, the IoT, edge computing, cloud-native computing, immersive technologies such as virtual, augmented, mixed, and extended realities (VR, AR, MR and XR), multimodal LLMs for crafting 3D models for a variety of things including buildings, landscapes, etc., digital twins for complicated physical systems, processes and spaces, 5G communication, non-fungible tokens (NFTs), simulation tools, etc. are blending to establish 3D virtual environments to captivate users. Besides the consumer metaverse, enterprise metaverse systems emerge and evolve fast to bring delectable and decisive automation, acceleration, and augmentation to businesses. In this chapter, we have dug deep and dealt with the enterprise metaverse at length to educate and empower our esteemed readers.

Keywords: Cybersecurity; Digital Avatars; Internet of Things (IoT); Computer Vision; Immersive and Interactive Experience

6.1 Introduction

Over the past few years, the domain of natural language processing, understanding, and generation (NLP/U/G) has been gaining much attention with the bombardment

[1]Edge AI Division, Reliance Jio Platforms Ltd., Bengaluru, India

of several large language models (LLMs) from multiple organizations. With the flourishing of LLMs, devices, and machines around us, we have gained the capability of understanding conversations made using natural languages, and accurately responding has become the new standard these days. Therefore, machines and digital assistants are technologically empowered to gain the human capability of understanding and answering questions conversed in natural languages. Machine translation is becoming a reality with the realization of competent LLMs. Not only is understanding and processing prompts, instructions, queries, and other inputs accurate but language generation is also being realized. Slowly yet steadily, the distant goal of machine intelligence is being achieved. The arrival of LLMs has transformed the world of natural language processing (NLP).

The much-anticipated machine-to-machine, human-to-machine, and machine-to-cloud communications will thrive in the days to unfold. Such empowerment leads to the visualization and realization of scores of pioneering personal, social, and professional use cases. Several things can get automated, accelerated, and augmented through the intelligent leverage of the distinct advancements unveiled in NLP, one of the prominent applications of artificial intelligence (AI). The AI paradigm is becoming the talk of the town due to the consistent improvisations being accomplished in the NLP space. Suddenly, it looks like AI has attained a new life. Thus, a suite of technological innovations has resulted in business disruption and transformation.

6.2 About the Artificial Intelligence (AI) paradigm

AI is being brandished as the most popular and influential digital transformation technology. AI technology can streamline, simplify, and speed up data transitioning into information and knowledge. In a nutshell, AI leads in fulfilling the long-pending goal of knowledge discovery and dissemination, and thereby, AI facilitates the mantra of data-driven insights and insights-driven decisions and deeds. To begin with, every tangible artifact in our everyday environments (living, working, socializing, and relaxing) is methodically getting digitized and connected through the IoT, edge, and connectivity technologies. When interacting with one another purposefully, such empowered entities produce a massive quantity of poly-structured data, which becomes actionable insights when collected, cleansed, and crunched through AI algorithms and models. According to market watchers, analysts, and researchers, billions of IoT devices and trillions of IoT sensors will be across Earth by 2025. Such an enormous number of digital devices and objects create zettabytes of data daily.

The era of big data started here. This is the critical foundation for the concept of AI to commence its unique contributions. With the emergence of AI-centric processors, the computational requirements for AI-powered big data processing become simplified and swift. Data processing frameworks such as Apache Spark, Storm, Samza, etc., also enabled the need to pinpoint hidden patterns, beneficial associations, impending risks, and fresh possibilities and opportunities out of big data. The extensive data storage requirements are also met through advanced and adaptive storage appliances, parallel filesystems, database management systems, data storage types, etc. Thus, the concurrent arrival of big data processing, storage, and transmission technologies has set everything in motion toward the knowledge era.

The knowledge extracted through AI techniques and tools is fed into appropriate digital input/output (I/O) assistants, business workloads, information and communication technologies (ICT) services, and people in time to empower them to exhibit adaptive behavior in their assignments. The knowledge-filled devices make informed decisions and indulge in intelligent deeds with all the alacrity and clarity.

AI is moving from analytical to generative, opening fresh possibilities and opportunities. AI is captivating and propelling every industry vertical to greater heights. Besides fulfilling fundamental business transformation, AI is on the way to empowering people.

6.2.1 Generative AI

This is the latest buzzword in the AI landscape. Generative AI (GenAI) brings solid productivity improvements by automating and accelerating low-risk workflows and low-hanging fruits. GenAI has the unique capability of producing different kinds of data (text, music, image, video, and art). Generative technologies include generative adversarial networks (GANs), variational autoencoders (VAEs), diffusion models, etc. These turn out to be the foundational and fundamental technologies for guaranteeing the generative power of AI. For example, GenAI can quickly generate scanning electron microscope (SEM) images of rare defects. These generated images can then be used to train defect detection algorithms, and such an arrangement systematically increases the detection accuracy considerably. Numerous developments and disruptions are happening in the GenAI space, capturing and captivating business executives and technology professionals to jump onto the GenAI bandwagon to be in the limelight, yearn, and earn an unbeatable edge over their competitors. In the increasingly digitized world, the role and responsibility of GenAI frameworks, accelerators, platforms, toolsets, libraries, and knowledge guides have acquired special significance and delivered a suite of societal and industrial innovations.

Multiple industry verticals are also exploring, experimenting, and expounding GenAI's unique competencies to fulfill their functional and operational requirements delightfully. According to domain experts, GenAI is opening up a dazzling array of strategically sound opportunities for the semiconductor industry in advanced material design, circuit path-finding, fab simulation, and operation optimization.

6.3 Demystifying the flourishing idea of Large Language Models (LLMs)

LLMs represent the latest advancement in the thriving AI space. LLMs represent sophisticated deep learning (DL) algorithms trained on massive text data sourced primarily from the Web. LLMs are adept at understanding, interpreting, and generating human languages. DL is facilitated through deep neural networks (DNNs), which can process and learn from enormous amounts of text data. DNNs are the computational models inspired by the structure and functioning of the human brain. DNNs are composed of interconnected nodes (neurons) organized into layers. Each neuron receives input from other neurons, processes it, and passes the result to the neurons in the subsequent layer. Transmitting and processing information throughout a network allow the network to learn complex patterns. DNNs learn hierarchical representations of data and understand the relationships between words, phrases, and sentences.

LLMs are enormous as they are trained on tremendous amounts of text data (trillions of words). The resulting models possess billions of parameters and need ample server storage. The training time is in the range of days. The total amount of computational resources is simply enormous.

LLMs, the prominent DNNs, mimic the human brain and are pronounced as pattern recognition machines. LLMs develop the next word in an incomplete sentence as human brains visualize something. For example, consider the sentence "The apple falls from the ...." LLMs predict the missing word correctly based on training and learning.

The emergence and consolidation of the LLM concept have paved the way for a series of shifts in NLP—LLMs' grandiose ability to understand the context and generate coherent text. LLMs can help in text content generation, language translation (for example, English to French, etc.), sentiment analysis (for example, analyzing customers' review comments to design high-quality products or to enhance existing products, etc.), question-answering systems, intelligent chatbots, etc.

LLMs have taken shape with the introduction of the Transformer architecture in 2017. The idea of self-attention, a vital module of the Transformer architecture, has resulted in LLMs, which can understand and efficiently encode complex language patterns. In short, the maturity and stability of the Transformer architecture with a self-attention mechanism have led to the realization of ground-breaking LLMs. Here is a list of popular LLMs (https://www.peterindia.net/LLMs.html). With the abounding training data, high-performance processors, refined model architectures, fine-tuning, transfer learning techniques, etc., generic and specific language models are being produced and exposed through APIs.

6.3.1 Key concepts and components of LLMs

Besides computer vision (CV), NLP has been a critical use case of AI. Enabling computers and machines to understand human languages and to respond with clear-cut answers is the goal of the NLP domain. Text-to-speech, speech-to-text, and speech-to-speech translations remain the top goals of NLP. New world analytics, such as speech and text analytics, will get the required boost with noteworthy advancements in the NLP domain.

6.3.2 Transfer learning in LLMs

Transfer learning plays a vital role in the massive success of LLMs. LLMs are pre-trained, and foundation models are created through training on extensive text data.

Then, original LLMs are fine-tuned on a specific dataset to perform specific tasks efficiently. The fine-tuned model can leverage the knowledge it gained during the pre-training phase to deliver better services. This aspect is termed transfer learning. The pre-trained models can generalize well across NLP tasks and adapt elegantly to newer domains and tasks.

6.3.3 Transformer architecture

This architectural pattern is the game-changer for LLM development and adoption. Transformer architecture is advanced compared to the previous DNNs, such as convolutional and recurrent neural networks (CNNs and RNNs), and empowered with a self-attention mechanism that helps LLMs to weigh the significance of different words or tokens in any input sentence. This architecture helps in better understanding the relationships between words in a sentence. The self-attention method facilitates LLMs in processing input sequences in parallel, providing faster and more efficient training.

There are six essential components in transformer architecture.

1. **Inputs and input embeddings**—The tokens inputted by the user are considered inputs for the DL models, which understand numbers, not text. Therefore, any text input has to be translated into a numerical data format (widely referred to as input embeddings). That is, embeddings represent words as numbers that DL models can process. The embeddings help the model understand the meaning of words by placing similar words near each other. In short, during training, the model creates these embeddings so that similar vectors (a set of numbers) represent words with similar meanings.
2. **Positional encoding**—The order of words in a sentence helps determine the sentence's meaning. Positional encoding is the way forward to encode the position of each word in the input sequence as a set of numbers. These numbers can be fed into the Transformer model, along with the input embeddings. This ultimately contributes to generating syntactically and semantically correct output.
3. **Encoder**—The encoder module processes the input text and generates a series of hidden states that capture the meaning and context of the text. The encoder first tokenizes the input text into a sequence of tokens (such as individual words or sub-words). It then applies a series of self-attention layers to generate a series of hidden states that represent the input text at different levels of abstraction. Multiple layers of the encoder are used in the transformer.

> Imagine a sentence: "The cat sat on the mat." A transformer breaks down this sentence into smaller units called "tokens" (e.g., "The," "cat," "sat," "on," "the," "mat," and punctuation marks). Each token is represented as a vector, capturing its meaning and context. The transformer then learns to analyze the relationships between these tokens to understand the sentence's overall meaning (https://www.linkedin.com/pulse/transformers-llms-next-frontier-ai-vijay-chaudhary/).

4. **Output embeddings**—Output embeddings are similar to input embeddings and undergo positional encoding, which helps the model understand the order of words in a sentence. A loss function measures the difference between a model's predictions and target values.
5. **Decoder**—The positionally encoded input representation and the positionally encoded output embeddings go through the decoder. The decoder generates the output sequence based on the encoded input sequence. During training, the decoder learns how to guess the next word by looking at the words before it. Like an encoder, multiple layers of decoders are used in the transformer.
6. **Linear layer and softmax**—The decoder produces the output embeddings, and the linear layer maps them to a higher-dimensional space. T, transforming output embeddings into the original input space. Then, the softmax function generates probability distribution for each output token.

6.3.4 Training LLMs

Training involves many steps, as inscribed below.

6.3.4.1 Data collection and preparation

The success of any LLM lies in the quality and quantity of the text data on which it is trained. A diverse and extensive text dataset empowers the model to learn the nuances of language and generalize well across various tasks.

6.3.4.2 Tokenization and pre-processing

The text data must be pre-processed and tokenized before training to make it compatible with the LLM's input format. Tokenization involves breaking the text into smaller units, such as words or sub-words.

6.3.4.3 Model architecture and design

Transformer is the key and the latest architecture style for producing LLMs.

Configuring model parameters—Model parameters, such as the number of layers, hidden units, and attention heads, play a significant role in determining the model's capacity and performance. These hyperparameters should be configured accordingly to balance complexity and computational efficiency while avoiding overfitting.

Optimizing learning rates—The learning rate is a vital hyperparameter that can control the model's rate of adaptation during training. An appropriate learning rate can determine the model's performance and convergence speed.

Dealing with overfitting and regularization—Overfitting occurs when a model learns too much from the training data, and hence, the model may lose its ability to generalize to unseen data. Regularization techniques such as dropout, weight decay, and early stopping exist to surmount this limitation.

Metrics for assessing LLMs—There are metrics such as perplexity, BLEU score, ROUGE score, and F1 score for evaluating the performance of LLMs.

By collecting and curating data, choosing the best-in-class model architecture, and evaluating the model performance, LLMs are being built and released to be used through APIs. Purpose-specific LLMs are being developed through fine-tuning to target specific domains and tasks.

6.4 Applications of LLMs

LLMs have become penetrative, pervasive, and persuasive too. Several business domains leverage to bring forth sophisticated use cases. IT services are being strengthened through LLMs. Digital transformation initiatives and implementations are being facilitated through the power of LLMs. The forthcoming metaverse Internet will be succulently enabled through LLMs. LLMs will decisively and deeply impact all kinds of tasks associated with NLP. With the emergence of technologies and tools for enabling multimodal generative AI, there will be many new implications at the cusp of digital and real-world environments. Machines can fluently interact with machines in the vicinity and with remote machines without any hitch or hurdle. Further on, machines can unambiguously understand human languages and reciprocate accordingly. Therefore, human–machine interaction will go to the next level with such a series of notable advancements.

6.4.1 Machine translation

Text or speech translation from one language to another is automated through the unique contributions of LLMs.

6.4.2 Sentiment analysis (opinion mining)

People express their opinions, viewpoints, and emotions through text for various purposes. People write product reviews, contribute posts on social media platforms, and write news articles on online news platforms or print media. Sentiment analysis was performed through traditional data analytics platforms (big data, streaming, and real-time analytics). After that, with the solidity of AI platforms, sentiment analysis activity gets accomplished by AI models. With the popularity of LLMs, sentiment analysis is being comprehensively done by LLMs. LLMs can easily extract sentiment information from text data, enable businesses to gauge customer satisfaction, monitor brand reputation, and strategize new product design and development.

6.4.3 Intelligent chatbots and virtual assistants

LLMs enable language understanding and generation. This capability helps develop conversational agents to automate various activities, such as information retrieval, customer care, document processing, appointment scheduling, etc.

6.4.4 Text summarization

LLMs can generate concise and precise summaries of longer articles (white papers, research papers, e-books, case studies, etc.) without any quality degradation.

6.4.5 Natural language interface for databases

Today, technical experts are needed to write database queries using SQL. LLMs can convert natural language queries into structured database queries.

6.4.6 Content/Code generation and paraphrasing

LLMs are being fine-tuned to automatically generate text content and source code in any programming language. LLMs can help developers write code more efficiently, debug issues, and learn new programming languages by training on software source code snippets. Also, the requirement for paraphrasing is fulfilled through LLMs. Research papers, book chapters, legal documents, social media posts, magazine articles, etc., are being prepared to guarantee improved clarity and escape plagiarism.

LLMs will embark on an automation spree across industry verticals. With many improvisations to happen in the LLM space, the world can safely expect bigger and better things in the days ahead.

6.4.7 LLM challenges

LLMs are typically trained on vast text data, often stifled by biases and inaccuracies. Therefore, LLMs may inadvertently learn data-driven biases and throw discriminatory results at deliveries. That is, biases can quickly propagate into AI decisions. Researchers are working on bias mitigation techniques such as data balancing, detection, and model debiasing. The domains of ethical, responsible, and explainable/interpretable AI are capturing the attention of many to address AI systems' inherent fallacies. AI recommendations, predictions, and outcomes have to be unbiased and fair to all and all the time. The generative capacities of AI models are sometimes misused with malicious intent. Appropriate rules and regulations are being formulated and used to monitor the growing utility of AI capabilities closely.

LLMs emanate from a vast amount of data, which should contain some confidential customer and corporate information. Thus, data privacy and security remain a top research challenge in the LLM era. Experts say that data anonymization, privacy-preserving techniques, threat prediction AI models, and data security protocols are the steps to be initiated and implemented to ensure the tightest security for data security. With the broader adoption of LLMs, it is indispensable to ensure the much-needed accountability for the outcomes of these AI systems. Explainability and interpretability are essential to ensure trustworthy AI. That is, it is insisted to produce interpretable LLMs that can provide the correct explanations for their outputs. By incorporating an explainability layer, users can put more trust in LLM solutions.

As indicated in the beginning, training LLMs requires large-scale computational resources and power energy. With more power consumption, heat dissipation into our fragile environment increases, thereby increasing the carbon footprint in the LLM era. The environmental concerns expressed in different quarters have instigated AI experts and environmental scientists to work out workable schemes to build energy-efficient LLMs. AI model optimization and compression techniques, such as pruning, quantization, knowledge distillation, federated learning, etc., are being experimented with and expounded towards this cause.

6.4.8 The future of LLMs

The arrival of LLMs has remarkably boosted the adoption of the AI paradigm. The buzzing and blossoming concept of generative AI is progressing rapidly and drastically. The dormant domain of NLP has got a fresh life these days. Computers have been adept at processing formal languages (such as Python, Java, Scala, etc.) thus far. However, now computers and devices can understand and respond in informal languages (human communication languages such as English, French, Tamil, etc.). LLMs have laid an exciting foundation for envisaging bigger and better things in the future.

One immediate prospect is none other than multimodal LLMs. The current and classical LLMs are capable of text processing. With the emergence of new technologies and tools in the generative AI space, we can safely expect that the generative power of AI will go beyond what it is today. Text data, audio, art, videos, and images can be generated. With multimodal generative AI in place, individuals, innovators, and institutions can unearth next-generation business cases.

Today, LLM training, inferencing, and customization consume many computational and energy resources, profusely damaging our environment. We will discover new techniques to enhance training efficiency, reduce computational requirements, and minimize energy consumption. Knowledge distillation, mixed precision training, and asynchronous gradient updates are prescribed as the way forward.

More powerful LLMs are being created and deployed to provide advanced use cases with the ready availability of AI-specific processors in plenty. Cloud infrastructures (compute servers, storage appliances, networking, and security solutions) are being put up in multiple places worldwide. Further on, small language models (SLMs) are forthcoming to be deployed in IoT edge devices. Thus, language models are emerging as disruptive and transformative. LLMs can be cognitive, competitive, and constructive in delivering breakthrough AI systems. LLMs will be integrated with computer vision and deep reinforcement learning (DRL) systems to realize resilient and versatile AI systems. LLMs at edge devices such as robots, drones, etc., will become pervasive in unlocking trendy applications.

LLMs will be personalized to meet personal needs and preferences. People-centric AI systems will be ubiquitous, contributing to enhanced care and choice for people. AI systems will continuously learn to provide premium and personalized services to users. Context-aware capabilities will become the new normal. The adaptability of LLMs is seen as the biggest plus for LLMs in ever-changing and dynamic environments.

6.4.9 Overcoming the limitations of LLMs

LLMs are the latest buzzword in the GenAI space. They are the most potent AI models capable of processing, understanding, and generating text. LLMs' prominent contributions include intelligent chatbots, question-answering systems, and expert and decision-support systems.

In short, the arrival of LLMs has given AI a fresh lease of life. LLMs are being presented as the latest reverberating use case for AI. IT started its long innings as information processing technology. LLMs are being pronounced as language processing technology. Further on, the world is heading towards generating multimedia content (text, art, audio, image, and video), which is the cornerstone of multimodal generative AI. Visual LLMs are the latest sensation in the AI landscape. Sophisticated technologies are emerging and evolving fast; hence, it is safe to bet and bank on multimodal AI. However, LLMs have some severe limitations. Sometimes, LLMs hallucinate and even respond incorrectly to users' queries. For the increasingly dynamic world, retrieving correct and contextually relevant information is essential for LLMs to survive and thrive in the years to unfold. There are two competent approaches to overcome the limitations of LLMs.

- Retrieval Augmented Generation (RAG)
- Fine-Tuning

The RAG approach uses continuously updated external data stores such as vector databases and knowledge graphs (KGs) to get the latest and most accurate details. Externally provided and API-enabled document repositories are the way forward for surmounting the inherent limitations of LLMs. Well-written prompts are the other approach to getting relevant responses through LLMs. Using the RAG approach, the first step is to convert data documents and user queries into numerical representations using the embedding method. Embedding is the process by which text is given numerical representation (vectors). Thus, formed vectors are formally managed through a vector database management system. Vector databases acquire special significance as a viable and venerable tool for simplifying and speeding up information retrieval. As per the RAG model architecture, the embeddings of user queries are used to search the document embeddings stocked in the vector database. KGs are the other popular external data repositories gaining much attention these days. In some aspects, KGs are more tuned for information retrieval than vector databases. Data relationships can be profoundly and decisively represented in KGs. Contextually sensitive information can be acquired through KGs. More options exist to simplify knowledge discovery through the fast-evolving RAG concept.

Fine-tuning is another widely articulated approach for getting domain-specific responses. We have many foundational and pre-trained LLMs that fully comply with the Transformer architecture. Pre-trained models have broader and more generic capabilities. Fine-tuning is to train a pre-trained model on a domain-specific dataset. That is, fine-tuning is a customization method to train and tune the weights of the original model. This fine-tuning adapts the foundational model for particular tasks or domains. Fine-tuning empowers the model to be more adept in tasks like source code generation, question-answering, text summarization, expert and decision support systems, or sentiment analysis. Fine-tuning adapts the model to semiconductor, supply chain, or healthcare domains. Indeed, fine-tuned LLMs exhibit efficacy in specific scenarios. Specific domains do not need pre-trained LLMs as training, storing, and inferring through original LLMs is time-consuming, tedious, and expensive. Through fine-tuning, domain-specific answers will be more tuned, quick, and appropriate.

Fine-tuning takes much time and requires high-performance GPUs or TPUs. Therefore, researchers have prescribed some countermeasures to overcome the limitations of training and tuning. Parameter-efficient fine-tuning (PEFT) fine-tunes only a tiny subset of the model's parameters while freezing the weights of the original pretrained LLM. PEFT solves the problem of catastrophic forgetting. LoRA (Low-Rank Adaptation of Large Language Models) is a popular fine-tuning technique attracting the attention of both researchers and practitioners. LoRA introduces trainable rank decomposition matrices into each layer of transformer architecture and reduces trainable parameters for downstream tasks while keeping the pre-trained weights frozen.

Usually, the parameters of trained models are represented and stored in a 32-bit format. QLoRA is the quantized version of LoRA and is gaining popularity for producing highly optimized models. This optimization is achieved by allocating only 4 bits to represent and store each weight parameter in the pre-trained LLM. This reduces the memory footprint of the LLM. Such a transition leads to the deployment of LLMs on the Internet of Things (IoT) edge devices. Optimization and compression through pruning, quantization, knowledge distillation, etc., are some of the noteworthy advancements that are being accomplished in the GenAI space; hence, there is a glimpse and glimmer of hope for many industry verticals to benefit from GenAI immensely.

6.5 Tending towards multimodal generative AI

There is a conscious movement from single-modal AI towards multimodal generative AI. Multimodal generative systems can understand and generate many data types simultaneously. This shift is being seen as a significant milestone in the AI journey.

Multimodal AI is an emerging and evolving technology that cognitively perceives everything and responds accordingly, just as humans do in their everyday lives. That is, multimodal AI uses multiple sensory inputs, such as text, images, videos, and audio, to understand what is happening around it. This technology acquires special significance as it can generate images from text descriptions. This can summarize video content and help human-machine interactions through human languages. Multimodal AI does all of these through three core components.

1. The input module is a sophisticated neural network processing specific data types,
2. The middle module is to combine these data streams into a cohesive dataset to facilitate a comprehensive understanding without any ambiguity,
3. The output module is to generate multimodal responses.

The final step involves refining generated outputs to enhance the quality.

6.6 The advantages of multimodal generative AI

Several theses are being unearthed in this space. Fresh ideas are accruing, and several benefits and use cases are being worked out. Existing problems are being addressed. A concrete understanding of multimodal GenAI and how it transforms society is good.

6.6.1 Enhanced contextual comprehension

Context-aware systems are expected across industrial verticals. Unambiguously capturing context details is the first and foremost step in conceiving and concretizing people-centric and business transformation applications. Multimodal LLMs exhibit adeptness in accurately understanding sentences by thoroughly analyzing surrounding words and concepts. Heightened contextual understanding becomes a reality by seamlessly integrating linguistic and visual information. For example, image captioning models fuse visual data and linguistic cues to finalize a suitable image caption.

6.6.2 Increased precision

Multimodal AI systems can guarantee enhanced output accuracy by collecting and combining various modalities, such as images, videos, audio, and text. Image captions can be valid and vivid. Even in noisy environments, facial and speech recognition capabilities help pinpoint a speaker's emotions accurately.

6.6.3 Seamless natural interaction

Human–machine interaction will become advanced and accurate. By fusing multiple input modes, such as voice commands, visual cues, emotions, and gestures, machines can precisely understand users' needs and do what is necessary. Such a facility will sharply enhance user experiences and provide immersive interaction. Multimodal AI can provide nuanced recommendations for shopping, travel, entertainment, etc.

In short, besides guaranteeing contextually relevant actions, multimodal AI systems do their tasks in an effective and high-performant manner with accuracy.

Multimodal models significantly augment AI system capabilities by harnessing information from diverse modalities like image, text, and audio for contextual understanding. They execute diverse tasks with heightened effectiveness, accuracy, and performance.

On the other hand, multimodal GenAI faces a few critical challenges. Generative AI occasionally hallucinates. Safeguarding data privacy and security and ensuring data integrity are touted as essential challenges for the penetration and pervasiveness of GenAI systems across business domains. Therefore, AI's ethical, responsible, and explainable/interpretable aspects have generated much heat recently.

6.7 Multimodal generative AI use cases

LLMs are manifold these days and maturing and stabilizing fast. Several assistive and additional technologies, such as RAG, are supplanting the idea of LLMs.

However, multimodal LLMs need to catch up. Multimodal data is scarce compared to pure text data. Also, multimodal AI model training mandates a gargantuan amount of computational and storage resources compared with traditional LLMs. Image and speech recognition models are emerging and evolving. We can safely expect more robust and comprehensive multimodal AI systems to emerge and lay a stimulating and sparkling foundation for envisaging and implementing path-breaking and people-centric applications.

Some practical scenarios illustrate why multimodal AI is vital for insightful and immersive experiences.

6.7.1 Integrated and personalized content creation

Multimodal AI can help dynamically create multimedia content to enthrall users. Social media applications and personal blogs will become more encompassing and engaging.

6.7.1.1 Visual assistance

Smart glasses or augmented reality (AR) devices with multimodal AI capabilities can provide real-time information about surroundings. This helps individuals navigate unfamiliar places without any risks.

6.7.1.2 Health monitoring

Wearable and handheld devices empowered with multimodal AI capability can collect a variety of body condition details through a host of specialized body-attached sensors and provide specific details about fitness and health conditions in real time.

6.7.1.3 Smart homes

Increasingly, home networking and automation devices are equipped with multi-modal AI facilities. These can control home-bound sensors, actuators, instruments, equipment, appliances, kitchen utensils and wares, consumer electronics, humanoid robots, etc., and reversely collect much usable information. It is possible to activate home automation devices using voice commands and gestures. Thus, the energy management becomes efficient. The occupants and owners of smart homes can enjoy enhanced care, convenience, choice, and comfort.

6.7.1.4 Training and learning

Field workers and learners can significantly benefit from multimodal AI-powered tutoring platforms that offer personalized and interactive learning experiences.

6.7.1.5 Assistive technologies

Assistive technologies are critical for people with disabilities. Multimodal AI systems assist people by enabling hands-free communication, object recognition, and navigation support.

In a nutshell, multimodal generative AI has become an essential technological paradigm contributing to a high-quality life. Multimodal AI represents the next-generation AI. There is a movement from single-modal to multimodal AI. This transition is to open up a community of newer use cases. Hereafter, AI concurrently processes and makes sense out of multiple models, including text, images, videos, voice, and gestures. Machines will engage more intently. Humans and devices will interact more engagingly and elegantly.

6.8 A recap of metaverse paradigm

The domain of metaverse system engineering has gained much press these days. Metaverse is being projected as the next-generation Internet (Web 3.0). An expert says it will be at the intersection of the physical and digital worlds.

Building competent metaverse systems becomes simple and swift with metaverse technologies and fast maturing and stabilizing tools. Multiple industry domains keenly embrace the growing influence of the metaverse. The metaverse will undoubtedly be the center of attraction in the decades ahead, instigating creativity and curiosity across business verticals. Content creators can monetize their creations and contributions with non-fungible tokens (NFTs). Blockchain, Web 3.0, virtual, augmented, mixed, and extended realities (VR/AR/MR/XR), AI, the IoT/edge computing, cloud-native computing, 5G/6G, and cybersecurity in conjunction with a suite of metaverse platforms, frameworks, accelerators, and toolkits are being considered as the most critical technological paradigms for fulfilling the grandiose ideals of the metaverse era.

In the first Web era (simple Web), people would just read the content; in the second Web era (social Web), people could read and write. People will become creative in the third and next-generation Web (metaverse era). People ingeniously produce newer content, services, and applications to be deployed in a metaverse environment to be readily found and used by people worldwide. The metaverse Internet will guarantee immersive, interactive, insightful, and persistent online digital experiences. As there is only one Internet, there is only one metaverse. However, there can be multiple environments and experiences within the metaverse. People can learn, share, relax, interactively, and insightfully work in such spaces.

If built correctly, the metaverse can be open, decentralized, community-driven, and user-controlled on most occasions. Some metaverse environments can be private virtual spaces only accessible to people with authentication and authorization digital keys.

The metaverse is much more than virtual spaces. The fast-improving phenomenon of augmented reality (AR), which augments physical entities and environments, is closely integrated into the metaverse. The physical world will offer innumerable possibilities to be enriched through AR. AR will augment physical realities. Physical elements will be overlaid with the correct and relevant details, including entertainment, tourist and traffic information, and digital twin insights. This can be experienced with lightweight AR glasses or smart contact lenses. On the other side, typically, VR headsets are bulky and hence not conducive to being carried everywhere.

6.9 The emergence of immersive commerce

With the consistent contributions of product and platform vendors, solution and service providers, research labs, and ICT companies, the idea of the metaverse is continuously evolving and exciting. It has the innate strength to bring forth more significant opportunities for organizations, artists, and content creators to create value and make a living out of them. The mesmerizing metaverse Internet facilitates users with the integrated and immersive experience of blending the real and the digital worlds. Market watchers forecast that the metaverse can generate the value of trillions of dollars. The current Internet is the primary mechanism for the unprecedented success of e-commerce applications. The metaverse era will open a new channel for product owners and sellers to connect with consumers. Therefore, the metaverse world will enable immersive commerce. This new commerce is to create hitherto unforeseen interactive and insightful experiences for shoppers.

Immersive commerce will draw greater attention from buyers. The market value for such commercial activities will be more significant than the currently popular e-commerce. This next-generation commerce will revolutionize our way of shopping. There will be a distinct movement from "click and buy" to "experience and buy." This transition enables buyers to experience any product virtually before the physical version is delivered at the door.

IKEA's Place app uses this model to offer its customers a unique experience. In addition to the enhanced experience, sellers gain monetary benefits. Much user data is generated, which can be used to conduct deeper investigations to understand customer behavioral patterns and preferences.

This application lets users digitally try out furniture to see how it looks in their home environment beforehand. By meticulously gathering such digital customer interactions, sellers can capture the details of customers' leanings and interests. Such knowledge discovery goes a long way in designing new products that enthuse buyers.

The fashion industry is also using this new channel to find new avenues to improve the bottom-line revenues. The remarkable convergence of physical and digital shopping helps brands to sell the same product in the physical and virtual worlds. This is a new way of revenue generation for creative and curious minds. Experts point out that the metaverse is not an additional money-spinning opportunity but an entirely new distribution channel to enable creation and differentiation. Immersive commerce is a different ballgame and will provide infinite possibilities to attract consumers. As indicated above, immersive commerce provides virtual experiences and brings the digital into the physical world through magical mirrors. These intelligent dressing mirrors can show you wearing different outfits the mirror suggests. This hugely simplifies and speeds up the purchase decision. As fitting rooms are provided in physical stores to check how fit any chosen dress is, the virtual try-on feature is added to online stores to enable buyers to make quick decisions.

6.10 Demystifying the enterprise metaverse

When the Covid pandemic dawned, the world switched to remote work. The new concept of work-from-home (WfH) came up and flourished. People and knowledge workers started to interact and collaborate online. The Internet became the primary, open, flexible, and affordable communication infrastructure, enabling people to collaborate. The national governments-imposed lockdowns forced people to stay indoors. IT professionals could work from home comfortably to keep the economy of nations afloat. Several online conferencing, discussion, presentation platforms, and tools to facilitate remote meetings have come. All of a sudden, everything became digital.

While the pandemic brought fear, anger, despair, and grief to the world, it also drastically changed how we work. As soon as lockdowns happened worldwide, entire industries switched to remote collaboration without too much trouble, keeping the global economy afloat after the initial shock was over.

Remote working technologies will see several noteworthy advancements as the metaverse kicks in. These technologies will become more immersive and insightfully interactive. Communication and coordination will become cognitive, convenient, caring, and comforting. Sensing and actuation will become intuitive and informative. In conjunction with digital twins, the fast-maturing and stabilizing virtual and augmented reality tools help more nuanced collaboration accomplish more significant and better things. With all the pronounced advantages, enterprises must meticulously strategize, plan, and move over to embrace the growing idea of the enterprise metaverse.

Thus far, consumers are overwhelmingly using the metaverse capabilities for fun and frolic, shopping, education, entertainment, and gaming. With the steady growth of metaverse technologies and platforms, enterprises empower employees to work across time and space. It is insisted that the enterprise metaverse will be calmer, contaminative, and constructive. Platforms (Microsoft Teams, Zoom, etc.) enable remote work and represent the first version of the enterprise metaverse. Special tools (Slack, Miro, etc.) offer digital collaboration. With organizations embracing the metaverse, their employees are appropriately augmented to achieve more with less. By smartly leveraging proven and potential metaverse technologies (immersive technologies such as AR and VR, AI, blockchain, digital twins, edge computing, 5G/6G, etc.), the workforce and salesforce teams will be succulently strengthened to be innovative and transformative. Thus, with ubiquitous sensing, ambient communication, pervasive computing, and a plentiful of decentralized edge-native applications, the forthcoming enterprise metaverse will be more path-breaking, people-centric, service-oriented, event-driven, process-aware, context-sensitive, business-critical, and knowledge-filled.

The scope of the metaverse is fast expanding. It started with consumers, shoppers, gamers, knowledge workers, and business executives. The metaverse is journeying ceaselessly with adopting and adapting digital transformation, connectivity, and AI-driven data analytics technologies. Experts in this space write that the paradigm of digital twins contributes immeasurably to achieving the intended success of the metaverse. Digital twins represent the digital/software/logical/cyber version of any physical system on the ground. Digital twins run on cloud servers and continuously connect with their corresponding physical twins. The specific sensors attached to the physical twin collect many operational and behavioral data and transmit them to the digital twins. Real-time data collection, transmission, and processing help extract actionable insights in time. Such knowledge discovery data lakes and AI-powered data analytics platforms in the cloud assist digital twins in making informed decisions on time.

Digital twins, the replicas of physical twins, help to recreate and replicate the physical world in the digital environment. Digital twins are typically built and maintained for complex and mission-critical physical systems. Even cities are being logically represented through digital twins. Active and aware environments are being replicated through competent digital twins. Solution and service providers build and host digital twins for industry machinery, medical instruments, defense equipment, robots, drones, satellites, rocket launchers, etc. Digital twins, in sync with multifaceted sensors, AI, communication, etc., beneficially mimic physical systems and processes in microscopic detail. Digital twins are vital in setting up and sustaining exciting digital spaces.

The seamless and spontaneous integration of digital and physical worlds instigated by resilient digital twins has laid a stimulating and scintillating foundation for ingenuity. In a nutshell, the distinctions of digital twins are useful in envisaging robust metaverse systems. Digital twins represent the virtual model that accurately reflects real-world objects or systems. Any physical object or system change will lead to a straightforward change in digital representation and vice versa. In short, the concept of digital twins is the most essential ingredient for the enterprise metaverse.

The market and creativity values of the enterprise metaverse will easily surpass the consumer metaverse. Companies ought to collaborate and innovate to bring in newer competencies. As written above, digital twins will play a critical role in shaping and strengthening the enterprise metaverse. With digital twins, factories and their essential functions can be watched closely by executives sitting in a faraway place. As articulated widely, digital twins play a vital role in producing industry 4.0 and 5.0 applications. Factory automation equipment and machinery get digitized and linked up with the Web infrastructure through the power of the IoT and edge technologies. The connected devices plentifully deployed and leveraged in factory environments have become intelligent through the steadily growing power of AI. With sophisticated technologies, the system of records becomes the system of systems. By attaching VR and AR technologies, the interaction with the physical world is all set to be revolutionized entirely.

6.11 Metaverse opportunities for enterprises

Companies prefer immersive technologies to announce their financial health and product offerings publicly. Events such as conferences detailing new product releases, tie-ups, etc., will be held through immersive platforms that are incisive and decisive. The metaverse may be incredibly beneficial if enterprises focus on blockchain, e-learning, virtual marketplaces, NFTs, and gamification.

6.11.1 Improved sales

The primary purpose of any business establishment is to improve sales. A virtual environment is one in which every product offering looks like it is at hand. The product can be checked without much effort. Such a facility enabled and enhanced through the metaverse is to increase product sales prospects. The metaverse can arrange virtual meetings with potential purchasers, regardless of their physical presence. The geographical limitations get eliminated through the metaverse. This is to influence more people incisively.

6.11.2 Better networking and collaboration

Metaverse-inspired interaction is more effective than current communication methods such as emails, WhatsApp messages, etc. Both verbal and nonverbal communication is considered incredibly significant for networking. Therefore, establishing and sustaining client relationships inside a safe virtual environment may be more beneficial. Also, in the post-COVID era, metaverse telecommuting is preferred for strengthening the rapport between service providers and their consumers.

6.11.3 Marketing and advertising prospects

The Metaverse will technologically shift business communication and customer interaction. Avatars, the digital representations of humans participating in the metaverse, can understand human gestures, emotions, voice commands, visual cues, and tone. Avatars guarantee personalized communication. Next-generation customer service will use the metaverse as the core and central technology to offer intelligent communication. This empowers marketers and customers to envisage unheard innovations in making and selling products.

The 3D workspace facilitates more for providers and customers. Metaverse communication is more intimate, inspiring, informative, and intuitive. The metaverse-powered communication can be effective and impactful for sellers and buyers.

6.11.4 Remote work and control

With the flourishing of immersive technologies in the metaverse era, activity monitoring and remote management have become simple and sagacious affairs. Metaverse systems will make some serious improvements in ambient assisted living (AAL). Business executives can steer their businesses in the right direction sitting at their homes and offices, saving travel costs. Remote access to the metaverse system and complete control over everything in the virtual world make the idea of the Metaverse shine.

6.11.5 Cryptocurrencies and NFTs

Decentralization is seen as positively impacting the metaverse. Blockchain systems are inherently decentralized, and the much-insisted transparency is supported naturally in decentralized systems. Therefore, anything happening in the virtual world is innately secure. Any virtual world visitor can obtain and trade NFTs for creative products and services by involving and invoking cryptocurrencies.

6.11.6 Planning, architecting, and engineering

Digital twins are the virtual representations of physical products, infrastructures, and cities. Any physical entity, experience, and environment can be elegantly encoded as virtual things. Digital twins enable insightful product design, fabrication, and verification of complex systems. Product engineering is being substantially innovated through the intelligent leverage of digital twins. Any hidden risks in product engineering and management can be uncovered by digital twins. 3D visualization helps to conceive and concretize next-generation products. The carmaker (BMW) takes the unique advantage of Nvidia's Omniverse to design its cars more efficiently.

6.11.7 Employee training

Training field workers in a physical environment is beset with a few life-critical challenges. Therefore, the concept of metaverse training has propped up. Employees can acquire new skills through hands-on practice and education on operating procedures and emergency countermeasures in case of any unexpected incident inside virtual spaces comfortably without any life-threatening risks. The workforce productivity is bound to go up considerably through simulations. The employee onboarding time goes up remarkably.

6.11.8 Enhanced customer experience and support

We have plenty of high-quality chatbots to address customers' concerns and clarifications. With the integration of AI into classical chatbots, the customer experience becomes delightful. The recent buzzword of LLMs is another disruptor in the domain of customer care. Automated chats for customer service functions can use the metaverse capabilities to offer a new virtual-first model. Digital twins of customer service agents can do better in a shared and immersive space. Conversational AI agents will be supplemented with metaverse-backed additional capabilities to mesmerize customers in the years ahead. With the technology fusion, the customer support system is poised to reach greater heights soon.

6.11.9 Customer issue resolution

Technologies are extensively used to address a growing array of business problems comprehensively. Delighting customers is critical for business behemoths and start-ups to grow and glow ceaselessly.

Soon, businesses will exist in the same virtual space as customers. This transition will help businesses address their customers' issues and inquiries through AI-powered tools. The metaverse could provide seamless product demonstrations, feature and functionality explanations, and step-by-step instructions. For example, game developers can support their customers inside the metaverse in real time.

6.11.10 Omnichannel support

Omnichannel support means merging physical and digital shopping experiences. Businesses can fulfill customers' growing requirements through their preferred interaction channels. In the metaverse run on Web 3.0 infrastructure, users can interact, shop, and engage with businesses on multiple levels.

An enterprise metaverse creates fresh opportunities for an enterprise. The enterprise metaverse refers to immersive virtual environments through which businesses can create, offer, and promote breakthrough and premium services and solutions artistically and appealingly. The metaverse will drive intimate and intricate engagements, meaningful conversations, product demonstrations, and workers' training; with features-rich products, enterprises will quickly gain the much-needed global reach. Metaverse technologies and tools' distinct advantage is creating and delivering interactive and immersive 3D experiences at hyper-scale. The metaverse-activated business offerings will enthuse and entice millennials. The metaverse will provide customers with an enhanced physical world experience. In time, the metaverse will become the preferred digital space for consumers and businesses to engage beneficially. With the steady growth of the metaverse technology ecosystem, enterprises will steadily embrace and embark on the metaverse bandwagon to visualize and realize advanced services and applications.

The metaverse is a virtual immersive environment that mirrors our reality. As companies start to collaborate, innovate, and invent cogently, the actual value of the metaverse will be on the enterprise side. New capabilities will be acquired; current problems can be addressed; new use cases can be unveiled and proclaimed; business transformation can be sustained; unabating interest will be aroused and maintained using the metaverse, etc.

6.12 The convergence of Large Language Models (LLMs) with the metaverse

AI is journeying fast in understanding, and the latest trend in the AI space is none other than LLMs. We have discussed the unique properties of LLMs and how they are disrupting and transforming various industries. LLMs are being technologically empowered to create intricate 3D models. Thanks to the fusion of LLMs and 3D modeling capabilities, metaverse is becoming more advanced.

The thriving concept of LLMs is seen as a seismic shift in NLP. LLMs enhance natural language understanding and generation. Therefore, the long-pending goal of language translation from one language to another is being simplified and speeded up. Further on, text generation is being automated, so content and code generation activities have a fresh life. Researchers in the generative AI domain are stretching and strenuously working to advance the LLM idea. Besides text generation, empowering LLMs to generate all kinds of data (images, videos, art, music, etc.) is gaining importance nowadays.

Creating detailed 3D models in the past demanded extensive expertise in software toolkits and platforms. By providing textual descriptions or commands to LLMs, it is possible to generate intricate 3D models without getting drenched in complicated 3D modeling software. These 3D models can be anything ranging from everyday objects to fantastical creatures. LLMs are inherently capable of crafting these.

Architects can cogently describe their visions in natural language. LLMs take the descriptions as input instructions/prompts and then jump into action to generate 3D models of buildings, landscapes, etc. LLMs facilitate and proliferate creativity in the metaverse.

In the metaverse, avatars are undoubtedly our digital personas. LLMs can craft detailed descriptions of how users want their avatars to look. Further on, LLMs generate unique and personalized 3D representations. Such a customization capability offers an immersive experience in virtual spaces.

As discussed earlier, metaverse environments can be built and used to represent bustling cities and their happenings. LLMs can bring these cities to life by generating textual descriptions of landscapes, building structures, and tunnels, which can then be transformed into 3D models. This capability of generating 3D models by LLMs artistically accelerates the building of virtual cities, counties, countries, and continents. Building world-class cities physically then gets accelerated and accomplished in a risk-free manner.

LLMs are growing by leaps and bounds these days. Many educational institutions and IT organizations worldwide are competing with each other in producing and proclaiming powerful LLMs, which have surprisingly revolutionized 3D model generation in the recent past. However, ensuring generated models are visually coherent and accurate to textual descriptions is beset with technical challenges. Therefore, bridging the gap between textual descriptions and the corresponding 3D models generated presents a research problem for our research students, scholars, and scientists.

Going forward, leveraging highly efficient LLMs to produce realistic 3D models for empowering the metaverse idea will grow remarkably. With the multimodal generative AI technologies and tools maturing and stabilizing fast, the accuracy of 3D models becoming more sophisticated is guaranteed. Any gap between virtual and physical reality is sufficiently closed down. With all these LLM-induced 3D model generation capabilities gaining a wider adoption and adaptation, the metaverse conundrum is set to explode in the years to come. The power of language in producing appealing and artistic 3D models is to expand more to bring forth unprecedented virtual experiences for people. The affinity between LLMs and 3D modeling technologies has led to the visualization and realization of pioneering use cases. With a bevy of noteworthy improvisations in the LLM space, the metaverse will soon become a mesmerizing reality. The language and artistry combine to establish a reverberating and rewarding platform to exhibit human ingenuity.

AI is to breathe intelligence into the metaverse. AI empowers in setting up and sustaining self-managing, self-defending, self-healing, self-configuring, and self-organizing infrastructure, platforms, and services. Such AI-powered systems contribute profusely to achieving the intended success of the metaverse. AI specializes in creating intelligent chatbots, 3D models, avatars, virtual representations, etc.; hence, the user experience goes up elegantly. The latest sensations in the AI space, such as LLMs, visual language models (VLMs), multimodal LLMs, and SLMs, directly and drastically elevate and excite the metaverse era.

6.13 Conclusion

The bewildering idea of the metaverse is on the fast track. The metaverse concept fantastically captured the imagination of consumers. Gamers are influenced immensely by immersive technologies. With the metaverse technologies becoming proven and promising, enterprises started to explore how the metaverse can be influential and insightful for automating many enterprise-related activities. This chapter has articulated how the metaverse paradigm impacts worldwide enterprises. Also, we have talked about the captivating capabilities of artificial intelligence (AI) and its direct offshoots, such as generative AI and multimodal AI. Interestingly, we have written about how these innovations are empowering the metaverse to do more with less. That is, there is a perceptible transformation in the metaverse today. Enterprises are increasingly inclining and relying upon the metaverse to automate various everyday tasks. Business organizations are seriously searching for winning ways and means of improving revenue generation through the distinct power of the metaverse.

There are a series of fresh yet pulsating happenings in the form of shrunken VR headsets, smartphone applications, smart glasses, etc., to make the metaverse penetrative, pervasive, and persuasive. Many software and hardware solutions and innovations are needed to make this young concept flourish in the years to come. The metaverse represents the next-generation Internet, poised to guarantee users 3D immersive, intuitive, and informative experiences. The Web 2.0-powered e-commerce will zoom towards Web 3.0-backed immersive commerce. People-centric and business-critical use cases will be emerging and evolving to keep customers happy. In short, the metaverse is a futuristic and fabulous technology that offers spellbinding and sparkling experiences to people.

Chapter 7

Digital twin and metaverse

Kavita Saini[1] and Ritu Gupta[2]

Abstract

Digital twin technology has the potential to bridge the gap between physical and virtual systems. Virtual representation of any system or product can be created easily using the digital twin technology. The virtual products help to improve the productivity, efficiency, and accuracy of current and future systems and products.

Metaverse is an additive technology that will begin a new era of virtual reality. It introduces a new virtual world with more realistic experiences, where one can experience things and events in the same way as he/she can do being physically present there.

Nonetheless, there are inquiries that should be responded to prior to jumping into this future innovation. Questions about how to use the metaverse intuitively, for instance, still need to be figured out. Moreover, there are still a few unanswered inquiries concerning its drawn-out suitability. In any case, as the innovation keeps on creating, these difficulties will probably be settled.

Keywords: Digital Twin; Metaverse; Virtual Reality; Additive Technology; Artificial Intelligence; Blockchain; IoT

7.1 Introduction

In the year 2010, we took a step into the world of simulation, which bridges the gap between virtualization and the physical world. Digital twin technology made it possible for everyone to get the perfect prediction, visualization, and analysis of any product or service or system before its actual physical development. Digital twin technology proved itself as a real hero in the growing technical world. It gives the perfect visualization to the vision and assumption of any developer and creator. With digital twin technology, the world of imagination gets wings to fly in its journey to real-world implementation.

The digital twin has shown significant potential in various fields and has generated a lot of interest from both industry and academia. The degree to which a

[1]School of Computing Science and Engineering (SCSE), Galgotias University, India
[2]Penske Media Corporation, New York, NY, USA

digital twin resembles the real physical form depends on a variety of factors, including the amount of data used. A digital twin can be as complicated or as simple as needed. With the use of technology, users and stakeholders can gain a profound understanding of a system's internal workings, the interactions between its various components, and the behavior of its physical counterpart in the future. Users can explore opportunities to increase product development, extend a product's lifecycle, optimize production processes, and prototype utilizing a digital twin. In certain cases, a digital twin can graphically depict an issue, allowing for the formulation and testing of solutions inside of a computer program as opposed to in real life.

Digital twin technology mainly provides the 2D digital representation of any system and its operations. With digital twin technology, researchers and innovators can create a digital prototype of any system or product before its physical implementation. A digital prototype helps to predetermine and resolve the problems that may likely occur during the development cycle of that product. With the help of digital twin technology, the visualization, prediction, analysis, and maintainability of products or hardware are very easy, accessible, and reliable. Thus, it improves the performance and efficiency of the product gradually.

As the simulations developed using digital twin technology increase the efficacy and productivity of hardware-based products, in the same way, virtual reality technology has taken a boom in the past decade for the development of software-based products. VR technology is the one that can give us the experience of a new world that actually does not exist. With the help of VR, we can sense, feel, and experience the challenges of our imagination and thoughts. It is just like getting immersed in a new world. In the beginning, the VR technology was limited to the 2D simulations of the products and system, but with time we came across the 3D world of virtual reality. Which changed our experience and feel for the VR objects completely. With the 3D VR technique, the user gets more immersed into the virtual world and starts feeling more attached. Virtual Reality (VR) attempts to replicate what occurs naturally when we glance around the physical environment. In VR, the technology and software work together to perform this eye and brain trick. On a VR headset's screen, your eyes see slightly different visuals. The brain perceives these visuals and creates the illusion that you are actually in that virtual reality world. This is why virtual reality can make you believe you are flying, underwater, or in any place! It is all about providing a great and realistic experience. With VR technology, one can feel more connected with the virtual world and can make himself more related to it. For providing these experiences there are many VR accessories available with the VR software systems to provide a full realistic experience.

With the continuously growing technical world advancements, the era of virtual reality, augmented reality, and digital prototyping has begun. These technologies cover a broad range of application areas in almost every sector, whether it is healthcare, finance, IOT, business, banking, real estate, food industry, etc. Everywhere there is a tremendous change towards development growth and increasing customer demands. To meet the various criteria of this growing technical world, we are rapidly moving to the virtual world where one can give shape to his/her imagination or dreams.

The next evolution in this chain that provides us with a fully immersive experience of the virtual world is the metaverse. Metaverse is a technology of the coming future that will provide more realistic experiences, more connectivity, and the feeling of being together in the same place. This chapter focuses on metaverse technology, how it is connected to the digital twin technology, why the digital twin is considered the building block for metaverse technology, the need for metaverse technology, what are the key concepts, and applications followed by the conclusion.

7.2 Related work

The fourth wave of computer innovation is currently taking shape around immersive, spatial technologies like augmented reality (AR) and virtual reality (VR). This new era is predicted to create the next paradigm for ubiquitous computing, which might revolutionize distant work, business, education, and entertainment (especially for those who learn online). The Metaverse is this new paradigm [1]. The Metaverse, an emergent paradigm of the next-generation Internet, seeks to create a completely immersive, highly spatiotemporal, and self-sustaining virtual shared place for humans to play, work, and interact. Metaverse is transitioning from science fiction to reality, thanks to recent breakthroughs in new technologies such as extended reality, artificial intelligence, and blockchain [2].

The Metaverse differs from augmented and virtual reality in three ways. First, whereas VR-related research focuses on a physical approach and rendering, Metaverse stands out as a service with more long-term content and social meaning. Second, the Metaverse does not always incorporate AR and VR technology. Even if the platform does not support VR or AR, it is possible to create a Metaverse application. Finally, the Metaverse's scalable environment, which can handle a large number of users, is critical for reinforcing social meaning [3].

Metaverse development involves three stages: (I) digital twins, (II) digital natives, and (III) co-existence of physical and virtual reality, also known as surreality.

A digital twin is a virtual replica of an actual asset that allows for better real-time prediction, optimization, monitoring, and control capabilities. A digital twin is computer software that uses real-world data to simulate how a process or product may work. These systems can leverage artificial intelligence, software analytics, and the Internet of Things to improve their output [4].

Digital natives are today's youth who were born into the digital age and have grown up with the constant flow of digital information. Digital natives are a generation or group that has grown up in an environment dominated by digital technologies and considers computers and the Internet to be natural parts of their existence. They do not need to become acquainted with the technology by comparing it to something else. On the contrary, they suggest fresh ways to think about how technology may be used productively. Digital natives have a unique perspective on the world, seeing what is unfamiliar to digital immigrants as a normal part of their daily lives [5].

Surrealism is an artistic style that employs specialized strategies to elicit mental responses. These methods include frottage, grattage, and automatic drawing [6]. Surrealistic digital art is another genre that employs a computer as one of its distinguishing methods of creation. Surreal digital art's major genres include photo manipulation, digital collage, digital painting, CGI/3D rendering, algorithmic art, and digital animation [7].

Experts are optimistic about the metaverse's future capabilities and widespread adoption due to advancements in technologies such as high-speed (5G–6G) connectivity, digital twins, mirror worlds, avatars, virtual reality (VR), augmented reality (AR), and mixed reality (MR) [8]. Neal Stephenson's initial concept of the metaverse included technologies like VR, avatars, AI, high-speed connectivity, and fog computing, which have since become essential components [9].

Today, we characterize Metaverse as an immersive platform that we may access with augmented or virtual reality, and engage with any media using permanent avatars and sophisticated digital technology [10].

Metaverse is a promising development opportunity for the Internet. It requires industrial investment, legislation, industry integration, and technology advancements to thrive. The Metaverse is a virtual environment that combines many digital technologies, including video conferencing, games like Minecraft and Roblox, cryptocurrencies, email, virtual reality, social media, and live streaming. Previously, the Metaverse remained in the conceptual stage. The digital age and the rise of internet titans are blurring the line between virtual and real worlds [11].

According to [12,13] the future of virtual worlds may include a metaverse that combines immersive VR with physical actors, objects, interfaces, and networks, creating a social, virtual environment that can complement and even replace the real world. The gaming industry has pioneered Massively Multiplayer Online Gaming, featuring enormous, permanent environments with many human participants. A metaverse is defined by its immersive realism, ubiquity (universal, available, and interoperable), and scalability (number of users, scene complexity, and variety of interactions) [14].

The word Metaverse made its next big resurgence with the news that Meta (previously Facebook) would be developing its own Metaverse in 2021. A Metaverse could thus be utilized with standard 2D display devices, but one of the main notions driving the use of the Metaverse is frequently the concept of immersion, defined as the virtual diving into the Metaverse [15].

7.3 Digital twin: building block of metaverse

Digital twin technology provides the digital representation of any physical system or product. Using digital twin technology, we develop 2D or 3D simulators for the existing product or the future product for the purpose of visualization, analysis, performance, efficacy, accuracy, error finding, better prediction of the working module, time and cost-effectiveness, etc. There are various factors on which we can work together in order to generate a better physical device or product, before actually implementing it via digital twin technology. The key concepts of digital twin technology include prototype development, instance generation, aggregation, and digital twin environment. Digital twin technology is widely used and applicable in all sectors like power generation equipment, education, manufacturing, networking, healthcare, supply chain, automotive industry, smart cities, etc.

Metaverse can be defined as the generalization of the digital twin technology. Digital twin technology focuses on the simulation of the physical world products or devices. These simulators are developed so as to produce the same results virtually as a real-world product or equipment can provide. We can say that digital twin technology works as a bridge between the physical and virtual worlds. Metaverse, on the other hand, focuses on developing a fully immersive virtual world that behaves and acts exactly the same as the physical world does. Metaverse is not restricted to being a product-based device simulation, instead, it focuses on the environmental simulations which not only focus on the behavioral simulation but also provide the same realistic feel and experience to its user.

Digital twin is the building block of the metaverse as it adds realism to the virtual world. Businesses benefit greatly from this convergence of digital twins and the metaverse because it removes the risks and constraints associated with the real world and opens up new avenues for growth. Metaverse is considered a virtual world parallel to the real world with uncountable digital spaces where everything is completely digitized.

7.4 Key technologies: enabling metaverse

1. Artificial Intelligence: AI deals with a machine's ability to make decisions and constantly improve its performance intelligently without human intervention.
2. Internet of Things: The Internet of Things (IoT) depicts machines with sensors, the ability to handle, programming, and different advances that interface and trade information with different gadgets and frameworks over the Web or different correspondences organizations.
3. Blockchain: Blockchain is a record-keeping technology intended to make it difficult to hack the framework or produce the information put away on the blockchain, consequently making it secure and permanent. It is a sort of distributed ledger technology (DLT), a computerized record-saving framework for keeping exchanges and related information in different spots simultaneously.
4. Edge Computing: Edge computing is a dispersed registering system that carries venture applications nearer to information sources like IoT gadgets or nearby edge servers. This proximity to information at its source can provide significant benefits, including faster insights, improved response times, and better bandwidth availability.
5. 3D Modeling: 3D modeling is a method in PC illustrations for delivering a 3D computerized portrayal of any item or surface. A craftsman utilizes exceptional programming to control focuses in virtual space (called vertices) to shape a lattice: an assortment of vertices that structure an item.

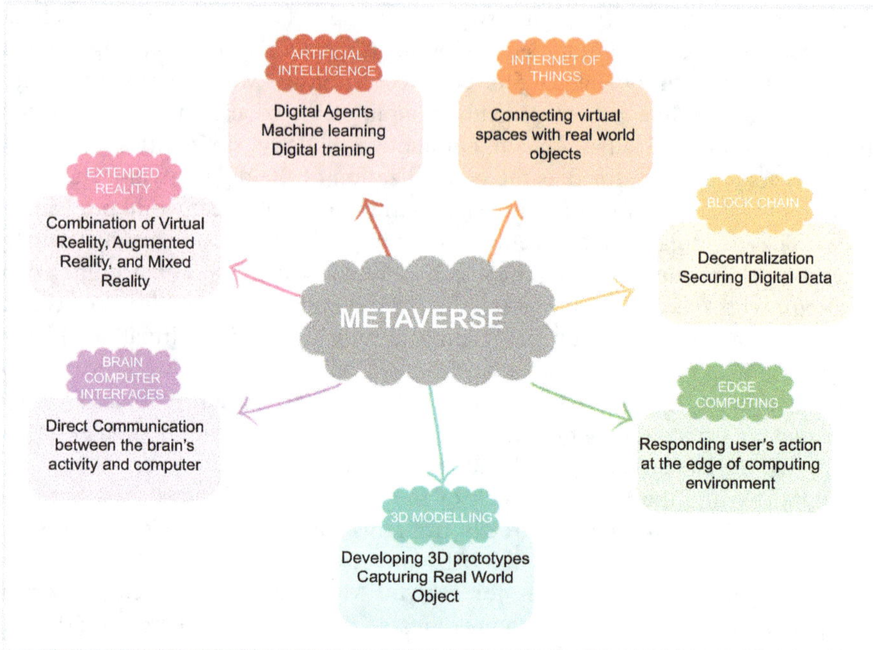

Figure 7.1 Key technologies for enabling metaverse

6. Brain–computer interface: Brain–computer interface (BCI) is a technology that enables direct communication between computing devices and human brain activity. This technology measures brain activity in the form of electrical signals and can control and command computing devices according to these signals.
7. Extended reality: Extended reality is a collective term for virtual reality, augmented reality, and mixed reality. Extended reality is intended to combine the physical world with the digital twin world to provide an immersive experience to the users (Figure 7.1).

7.5 Key features of the metaverse

1. Asset Digitization: Standardization, systems, tools, asset knowledge, and a workforce with the necessary skills are all part of the asset digitization strategy. It goes beyond an RFID label or bar code. It does more than just scan, store, and catalog data about assets. It consists of work procedures and analytics to measure and track data continually in real time.
2. Scenario-based Learning: One effective tactic to improve the learning process is scenario-based learning. Through the use of authentic and pertinent scenarios, this method allows students to apply their knowledge and abilities in a real-world setting.

3. Scope Economies: A reduction in the cost of manufacturing multiple different items is known as a scope economy. The strategy works on the factor, of reducing cost by increasing the variety of the product instead of increasing volume.
4. Industry Universality: Shared values, cross-sector cooperation, and the goal of sustainable development are what make the industry universal. Whether it is administration, education, or infrastructure, acknowledging these universal characteristics promotes advancement and creativity.
5. Integrated Innovation: Integrated Innovation is the term for the creation and execution of adaptable, advancement arrangements in areas of foundational breakdown, coming about in staggered, multi-useful enhancements across our interconnected financial, social, environmental, mechanical, and human frameworks. More basically, incorporated advancement implies finding market-based answers for the issues of manageable turn of events [16].
6. Platform Ecosystem: In the global economy, platform-based ecosystems are an essential source of innovation and dynamism for a wide range of technologies, goods, and services. Platforms have sparked innovation and improved efficiency by utilizing specialization and flexibility in a variety of industries, including computers, video games, mobile phones, cars, payment systems, e-commerce, government, and more [17] (Figure 7.2).

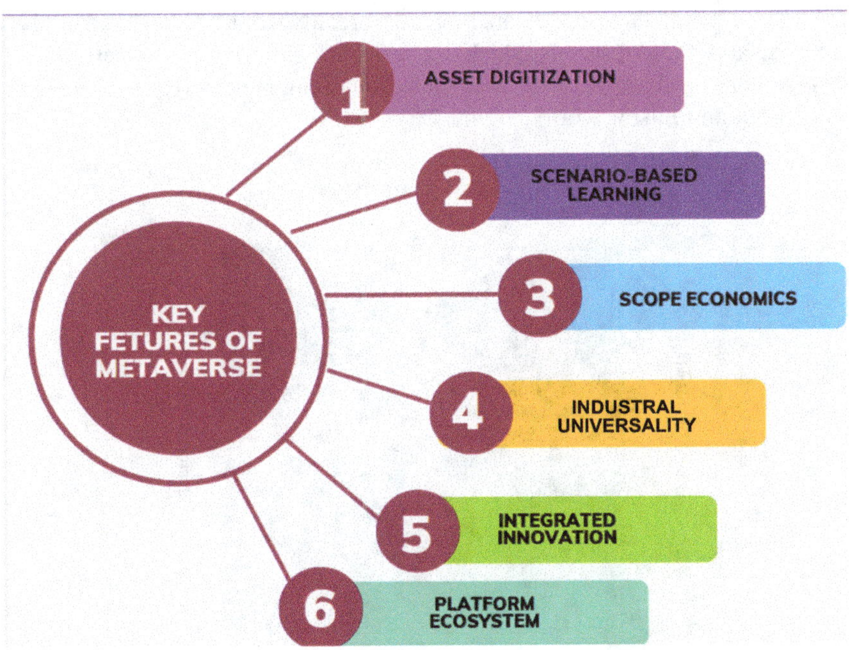

Figure 7.2 Key features of metaverse

7.6 Importance of metaverse

Metaverse technology is a yet growing technology that is developing and accelerating with a faster speed to cover almost every industrial, educational, and healthcare sector as well. The metaverse technology brings the 3D revolution of the internet. In today's online world, approximately 70% of the world's population uses the internet on a daily basis and is engaged in various social media platforms like Facebook, Instagram, and Twitter to stay connected with the rest of the world. Today's youth believe in staying connected online rather than in physical interactions or connectivity. Metaverse technology has been introduced in almost every social media sector and online gaming. With metaverse, people can interact through their social network with a completely immersive experience and feel rather than just chatting. In the online gaming sector too, we are moving at a very fast speed towards the fully immersive gaming experience. Till now there are many games that the semi-immersive gaming technology through avatars and other VR gadgets. The use of the metaverse is not restricted to online gaming and social media platforms rather it may prove very useful to other sectors also like education, healthcare, supply chain management, virtual businesses, digital currency monitoring, online banking, product management, digital marketing, etc.

7.7 Types of metaverse

Based on four prime factors, i.e., augmentation reality, user immersion, simulation techniques, and the degree to which the external environment is reflected, the metaverse can be classified into four categories: augmented reality, lifelogging, virtual world, and mirror world (Figure 7.3).

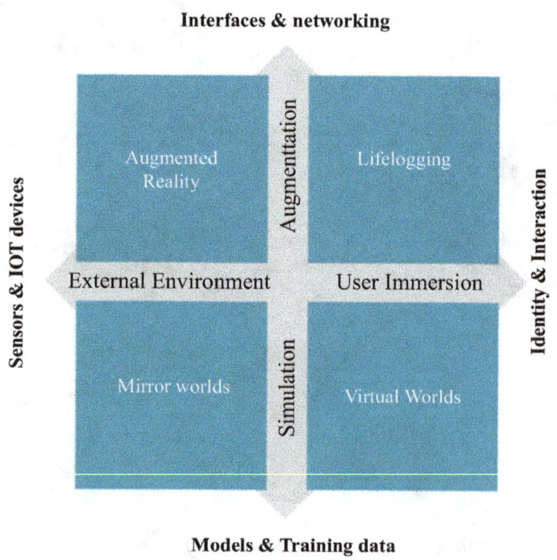

Figure 7.3 Different types of metaverse [23,31]

1. Augmented Reality: While virtual content is assumed to act as an intermediary between the viewer and the real world in augmented reality (AR), the degree of this intermediation and the ways in which it is meant to improve the real-world experience can differ depending on the tool and environment. There can be strong or weak connections between an overlay and the real world, and different AR experiences may place different emphasis on movement, location, and teamwork [18].
2. Lifelogging: Lifelogging, for the most part, is characterized as recording individual life including everyday encounters through wearable sensors like accelerometers, belts, FitBit, cameras, and others [19]. For instance, there is an expanded number of individuals who track their actual work involving wearable sensors to examine their presentation in an assortment of errands. Lifelogging turned into a fundamental help for our prosperity. This was a consequence of the intermingling of innovations to upgrade our way of life. For instance, individuals are accustomed to placing their wearable cameras in private spaces (like homes, vehicles, gardens, etc.) to record unforeseen occasions like mishaps or attacks, or to screen security basic circumstances for medical care help [20].
3. Virtual Worlds: Virtual worlds are everlasting online spaces where users can engage with others and feel as though they are there with them. Virtual worlds are persistent online social spaces that people perceive as ongoing throughout time, have vast populations, and are experienced as a world for social interaction with others. The phrase "virtual worlds" has been used to describe these environments. Because they are third spaces—online locations for socializing—virtual worlds can be distinguished from online gaming and massively multiplayer online roleplaying games (MMORPGs) [21].
4. Mirror Worlds: A mirror world is a digital duplicate of the physical environment that allows for real-time interaction. Mixed reality (MR) technology enables users to modify digital representations of real-world objects and environments. The mirror world concept allows users to engage with digital representations of real-world locales, buildings, and things. This technology can be accessible on smartphones, tablets, and VR/AR headsets. It could transform our interactions with the world and each other, enabling novel kinds of communication, entertainment, and education [22].

7.8 Applications on metaverse

1. Metaverse in education: Metaverse can add another dimension to the field of education technologies. Using metaverse technologies a fully immersive learning environment consists of 3D models, prototypes, training simulations, and digital labs. The educators, researchers, and learners can have their own digital space parallel to the physical world, where they can explore new terminologies, techniques, and ideas with a state of free mind to give shape to their innovative ideas. The two major things that bring a revolutionary change in the education system are digital labs and virtual educational spaces [23].

(a) Digital Labs: Virtual laboratories replace face-to-face lab activities by leveraging computerized models and simulations, as well as several other instructional tools. The most advanced virtual laboratories use interactive virtual reality simulations for lab exercises [24]. Using digital laboratories in lectures might enhance students' creativity and innovation by providing concrete experiences that transcend physical barriers. Digital labs enable the integration of Industry 4.0 features such as technical support, information transparency, networking, and decentralized decision-making into existing or new experiments [25].

(b) Virtual Educational Spaces: The virtual education area evolved from distributed e-learning, reflecting two key trends in the expansion of the Internet and Web. VES is an intelligent space capable of monitoring, communicating, making decisions, and acting on them. VES is context-aware, meaning it considers any information that can describe an identity's current state. The virtual education environment consists of e-learning services and educational situations accessible through an education portal [26].

2. Metaverse in marketing: Metaverse marketing enables firms to engage with customers in unique ways and differentiate themselves from the competition. Prioritizing interactive content helps engage the brand's target audience. Registering a brand's virtual presence boosts both its metadata exposure and real-world conversions. Metadata-based marketing enhances brand awareness and adapts to virtual contexts. Metaverse offers immersive storytelling experiences for brand marketing initiatives. Metaverse provides interactive branded installations and events, unlike traditional advertising [27].
3. Metaverse in healthcare: The Metaverse's healthcare system offers interactive, immersive, and entertaining healthcare experiences that are tailored to the needs of each individual patient. Metaverse technologies offer novel treatment options at cheaper costs, leading to better patient results. Metaverse technologies can help healthcare workers plan and diagnose diseases more effectively. The Metaverse environment improves surgical pre-operative planning by converting CT scans into 3D reconstructions via headsets. This enables surgeons to precisely inspect, isolate, and modify anatomical sections during essential surgeries [28].
4. Metaverse in business: Metaverse may work on the different key aspects of a business to benefit e-commerce business in various domains like enhancing customer service and experience, information gathering, promoting physical and digital goods and services, introducing the metaverse to benefit the customer, managing smooth payments, providing related hardware and software applications, etc. [29].

Key aspects of e-commerce business:

1. Hardware: various hardware devices like sensors, PCs, VR devices, VR headsets, mobile devices, microchips, and GPU devices support metaverse

technology and help to create and experience a fully immersive virtual environment.

2. Tools and Technologies: the tools and technologies that support the standardization and protocols of a business module like AI, blockchain digital twin, VR, AR, Avatar, etc.
3. Virtual platforms: virtual platforms support simulation, 3D modeling, and prototyping, which in turn smoothens and enhances the development, manufacturing procedure, training, and testing modules, visualization digital labs, and simulators.
4. Payment management: digital payment systems, managing digital currency exchange, operations and procedures via Blockchain technologies, and cryptocurrencies.
5. Content management: metaverse technology helps in designing content in the form of digital assets. For the purpose of sale, storage, management, security, and protection of digital assets are connected to user information.
6. User behaviors: focuses mainly on consumer and business behaviors for the purpose of investment, decision-making, profitability, management, etc.
7. Computations: computation power of a business can be improved via AI, machine learning, and other economical metaverse techniques.
8. Networking systems: enhance the existing networking capabilities via simulations, virtual reality, and augmented reality. These technologies provide a fully immersive user experience over 3D networking and make realistic interactions possible (Figure 7.4).
9. Metaverse in Supply Chain Management: the Metaverse will revolutionize client engagement, particularly in logistics. This technology will enhance process simulation and may lead to the creation of immersive virtual

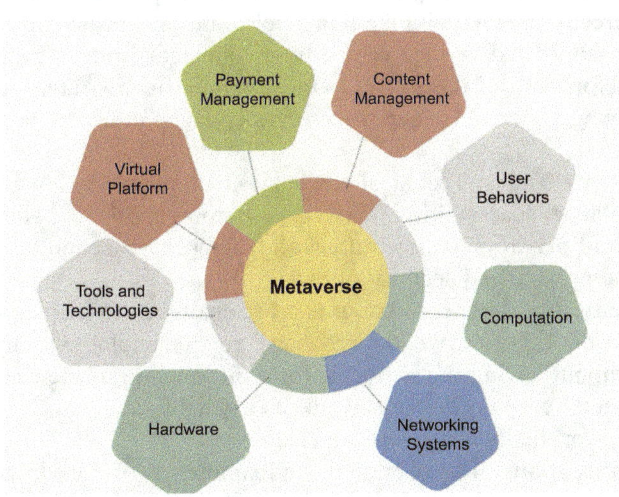

Figure 7.4 Metaverse—Key aspects of business

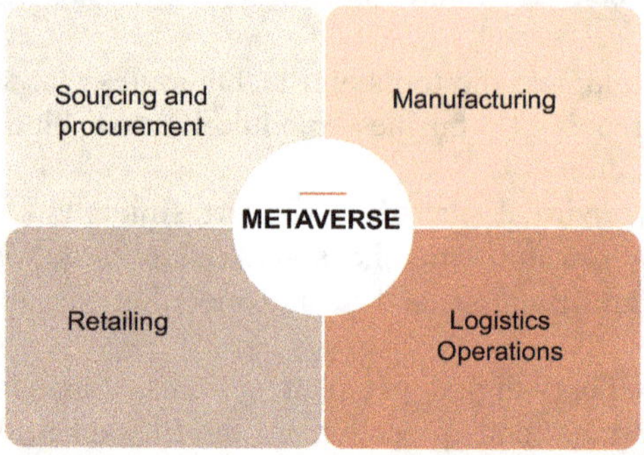

Figure 7.5 Metaverse—Functions of supply chain

environments for training in warehouses and industrial facilities. There are programs that create digital twins, improve work routines, identify inefficiencies, and boost productivity. A portion of the uses of metaverse across different elements of supply chains is sourcing and procurement, manufacturing, logistics operations, and retailing [30] (Figure 7.5).

7.9 Key challenges

Metaverse is an upcoming technology that might bring a great industrial and economic revolution in the near future. Being a multidisciplinary technology, metaverse can play a vital role in almost every public sector. It may generate a whole virtual world and is capable of providing a fully immersive user experience where the user can directly interact with the things related to the virtual world. The major application areas affected by metaverse till now are social media connectivity and the gaming sector, both of these are the most youth-affecting areas, as more than 80% of the young generation keep themselves engaged either on social media or online gaming.

Technical challenges: Technical challenges that metaverse have are related to security, acceptance, accessibility, maintenance, storage, privacy, etc.

Security and privacy: In the virtual world, blockchain technology is useful for maintaining the privacy and security of data.

Authenticity: For the metaverse, it is a big challenge to maintain the authenticity of the user, till now we do not have any technology to maintain user authenticity without having the physical world information of the user.

Acceptance: Acceptance of metaverse as a reliable and authentic technology throughout the world's industry is still a challenge.

Control operations: The operations and simulators of the virtual world will only be successful when we are able to control real-world objects and devices through it.

Storage: In the world of growing information, it is a big challenge for everyone to store a large amount of everyday increasing information and data using the metaverse's distributed environment.

Transformation: The applications and systems of the virtual world will only be successful when we are able to directly transfer them to the phenomenal systems of the real world.

7.10 Challenges for the human being

The above-mentioned are some of the challenges related to the technology and technical world. Now some other questions arise about the impact of metaverse on the human beings.

Socialism: No doubt, with metaverse social media connectivity and interaction of the people in their virtual space, will have a great experience and feel. But there are some questions that are still not in focus and may remain unanswered.

Q1. The young generation will get stuck completely into this virtual world?

Q2. The physical world connectivity of the youth may be finished completely.

Q3. The crimes and frauds that occur through social media platforms like deep fake will get a rapid increase.

Q4. Will it affect the mental health of the people and in what way? Either happiness will increase or it will have adverse effects like loneliness, depression, and hypertension.

Online gaming: With the help of 3D modeling and VR technologies we may have a fully immersive experience with the same realistic feeling like we can see our gaming characters simply walking on roads. One of the biggest unanswered questions is:

Q5. Till now only partially immersive gaming technology is available and we often come to know the crimes done by kids and youngsters are a result of some task allotted to them via the game they are playing. What are the control measures?

7.11 Conclusion

Metaverse is a multi-disciplinary technology that is able to create a parallel virtual world to the physical world. In the past decade, we have already gone through the technical advancements that occurred via digital twin technology. Metaverse is a generalization of the digital twin technology and is able to provide a complete virtual environment.

Every technology comes with its own pros and cons. Metaverse also has the same. The pros of the metaverse include enhanced connectivity, better social interactions, improved learning solutions, new business opportunities, advanced healthcare technologies, etc.

The cons of the metaverse include its adverse effects on human society, increased crime rate among youngsters, increased cybercrimes and online fraud, hacking, etc.

For this, there should be some defined protocols and standards that must be taken care of before moving ahead with this technology.

References

[1] Park, S. M., and Kim, Y. G. (2022). A metaverse: Taxonomy, components, applications, and open challenges. *IEEE Access*, *10*, 4209–4251.

[2] Dingli, A., and Seychell, D. (2015). Who are the digital natives? *In: The New Digital Natives.*, Berlin: Springer. https://doi.org/10.1007/978-3-662-46590-5_2

[3] Blumberg, N. (2024). *Claude Cahun*. Encyclopedia Britannica. https://www.britannica.com/biography/Claude-Cahun

[4] Mystakidis, S. (2022). Metaverse. *Encyclopedia*, *2*(1), 486–497.

[5] https://surrealismtoday.com/digital-art/

[6] Ioannidis, S. and Kontis, A.P. (2023). The emergence of metaverse in tourism literature: A mixed content analysis. *Proceedings MTCON2023*. 15–18 March, Istanbul (ahead-of-print).

[7] Ioannıdıs, S., and Kontıs, A. P. (2023). The 4 epochs of the metaverse. *Journal of Metaverse*, *3*(2), 152–165.

[8] Kayakoku, H. (2023). History and development of virtual worlds and metaverse. *In Metaverse: Technologies, Opportunities and Threats* (pp. 19–30). Singapore: Springer Nature.

[9] Huang, J., Sun, P., and Zhang, W. (2022). Analysis of the future prospects for the metaverse. *In 2022 7th International Conference on Financial Innovation and Economic Development* (ICFIED 2022) (pp. 1899–1904). Dordrecht: Atlantis Press.

[10] Smart, J., Cascio, J., and Paffendorf, J. 2007. *Metaverse Roadmap Overview: Pathways to the 3D Web*. Retrieved November 12, 2019 from http://www.metaverseroadmap.org/overview/

[11] Mason, W. 2015. *Why social VR is a huge priority for Oculus, but their metaverse is still far off. 015*. Retrieved November 12, 2019 from http://uploadvr.com/oculussocial-vr-metaverse-palmer-luckey/

[12] Huggett, J. (2020). Virtually real or really virtual: Towards a heritage metaverse. *Studies in Digital Heritage*, *4*(1), 1–15.

[13] Ritterbusch, G. D., and Teichmann, M. R. (2023). Defining the metaverse: A systematic literature review. *IEEE Access*, *11*, 12368–12377.

[14] Visser, W. Integrated innovation: Applying systems thinking to sustainable innovation and transformation. *Sustainability*. 2020; *12*(13):5247. https://doi.org/10.3390/su12135247

[15] https://onlinelibrary.wiley.com/doi/full/10.1002/smj.3250

[16] Yu, J-E. Exploration of educational possibilities by four metaverse types in physical education. *Technologies*. 2022; *10*(5):104. https://doi.org/10.3390/technologies10050104

[17] Kye, B., Han, N., Kim, E., Park, Y., and Jo, S. (2021). Educational applications of metaverse: possibilities and limitations. *Journal of Educational Evaluation for Health Professions*, *18*, 32. https://doi.org/10.3352/jeehp.2021.18.32

[18] Ksibi, A., Alluhaidan, A. S. D., Salhi, A., and El-Rahman, S. A. (2021). Overview of lifelogging: current challenges and advances. *IEEE Access*, *9*, 62630–62641.

[19] Schroeder, R. (2008). Defining virtual worlds and virtual environments. *Journal for Virtual Worlds Research*, *1*(1).

[20] Özkan, A., and Özkan, H. (2024). Meta: XR-AR-MR and Mirror World Technologies Business Impact of Metaverse. *Journal of Metaverse*, *4*(1), 21–32.

[21] Kammerlohr, V., Pfeiffer, A., and Uckelmann, D. (2021). Digital laboratories for educating the IoT-generation heatmap for digital lab competences. In *Cross Reality and Data Science in Engineering: Proceedings of the 17th International Conference on Remote Engineering and Virtual Instrumentation 17* (pp. 3–20). Cham: Springer International Publishing.

[22] Aubel, I., Zug, S., Dietrich, A., *et al.* (2022). Adaptable digital labs-motivation and vision of the crosslab project. In *2022 IEEE German Education Conference (GeCon)* (pp. 1–6). Piscataway, NJ: IEEE.

[23] MacCallum, K., and Parsons, D. (2019). Teacher perspectives on mobile augmented reality: The potential of metaverse for learning. *In World Conference on Mobile and Contextual Learning* (pp. 21–28).

[24] Valkanov, V., Stoyanov, S., and Valkanova, V. (2016). Virtual education space. *Journal of Communication and Computer*, *13*(2), 64–76.

[25] Efendioglu, I. H. (2023). Metaverse concepts and marketing. *Handbook of research on consumer behavioral analytics in metaverse and the adoption of a virtual World*, 224–252.

[26] Chengoden, R., Victor, N., Huynh-The, T., *et al.* (2023). Metaverse for healthcare: a survey on potential applications, challenges and future directions. *IEEE Access*, *11*, 12765–12795.

[27] Enache, M. C. (2022). Metaverse opportunities for businesses. *Annals of the University Dunarea de Jos of Galati: Fascicle: I, Economics & Applied Informatics*, *28*(1), 67–71.

[28] Trivedi, S., and Negi, S. (2023). The metaverse in supply chain management: application and benefits. *International Journal of Advanced Virtual Reality*, *1*(1), 36–43.

[29] Wang, Y., Su, Z., Zhang, N., *et al.* (2022). A survey on metaverse: Fundamentals, security, and privacy. *IEEE Communications Surveys & Tutorials*, *25*(1), 319–352.

[30] Yu, J-E. Exploration of educational possibilities by four metaverse types in physical education. *Technologies*. 2022; *10*(5):104. https://doi.org/10.3390/technologies10050104

[31] Lee, J. Y., Kim, J. Y., You, S. J., *et al.* (2019). Development and usability of a life-logging behavior monitoring application for obese patients. *Journal of Obesity & Metabolic Syndrome*, *28*(3), 194.

Chapter 8
Metaverse world and seven layers

Kavita Saini[1]

Abstract

Metaverse technology blends AI, IoT, augmented reality, and virtual reality into a hybrid of digital and physical experiences. It makes it possible for users to get engaged with digital content, obfuscating the distinction between virtual and actual encounters. Neil Stephenson first used the word "metaverse" in 1992. Roblox and other well-known games highlight how commonplace it is in the gaming industry, where real and virtual worlds interact.

The metaverse is a virtual environment with seven stages that are progressively turning into physical reality where users can engage, create, and explore immersive digital worlds.

These layers are experience, discovery, creator economy, spatial computing, decentralization, human interface, and infrastructure. Virtual reality, augmented reality, AI, and IoT devices are the main components of a metaverse environment, the chapter explains all these components in detail. Further, the chapter also covers a few more components including blockchain technology, 3D modeling and animation, and cloud computing. The chapter also talks about the digital twin, explainable AI, and similar other things.

Keywords: Virtual World; Metaverse; Virtual Reality; Artificial Intelligence; Blockchain Technology; Inbound; Outbound

8.1 Introduction

Metaverse technology represents the convergence of multiple advanced technologies to create a seamless blend of digital and physical experiences, offering new possibilities in how we interact with the world around us.

Metaverse technology refers to advanced, integrated systems designed to enhance and extend human capabilities by merging digital and physical realms. This technology encompasses several cutting-edge fields, including augmented reality (AR), virtual reality (VR), artificial intelligence (AI), and the Internet of Things (IoT). Through metaverse, users can interact with digital content in a more immersive and intuitive way, blurring the lines between virtual and real-world experiences.

[1]School of Computing Science and Engineering (SCSE), Galgotias University, India

Figure 8.1 Metaverse world

Neal Stephenson created the word "metaverse," which refers to a 3D virtual environment inhabited by avatars of actual people (1992). It refers to the digital technology that allows users to connect with other users via avatars. The term "metaverse" is an amalgamation of the terms "meta" and "verse" (universe). Roblox, one of the most popular games has shown the popularity of Metaverse technology in gaming. Metaverse where physical and virtual space coexist is a 3D web-enabled world built over AR and VR. The basic diagram of the metaverse is shown in Figure 8.1.

8.1.1 Interconnected virtual world

The metaverse, a fictional universe with virtual reality environments, is one of the rapidly growing technologies in research and academia. VR technology, particularly headsets, plays a crucial role in the emergence of the metaverse. VR headsets dominate the global market, while metaverse applications such as MeetinVR, Engage, Horizon Workrooms, and AltspaceVR are gaining significance in business and education. Future metaverse use and research topics are being actively discussed.

8.2 Seven layers of metaverse

Metaverse represents a collective virtual space where users can interact, create, and explore in immersive digital environments. The idea of the Metaverse is gradually becoming a tangible reality. Let us explore the seven levels that make up this intriguing virtual world (Figure 8.2).

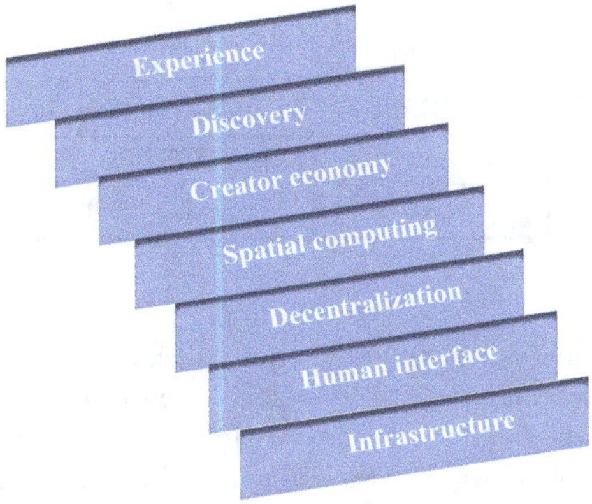

Figure 8.2 Seven layers of metaverse technology

8.2.1 Experience

Beyond the imagination, the metaverse is not just a 3D simulation or representation of the real world rather it is the exact depiction of spatial dimensions and distance of the real world.

It involves the dematerialization of real objects made possible by photorealistic visual elements, accurately representing physical dimensions and distances. With the help of metaverse dematerialization of the physical space, VR in the metaverse can provide experiences that are not possible in the real world.

Experiences are the central theme of the metaverse. The lifelike experiences it is prepared to offer are what have caused the excitement and money it has attracted. A true metaverse could revolutionize eSports, retail, theatre, gaming, and social interactions, among other human activities, because of its holistic and real-time nature.

8.2.2 Discovery

The actual discoveries that result from an ongoing "push and pull" of data are covered in this layer. "push and pull" introduces the real and new experience to the end users. Few examples of how inbound and outbound discoveries occur.

Inbound "pull" system, which involves users actively seeking out information and experiences.

Outbound "push" system informs users of the opportunities available in the Metaverse.

Inbound

COMMUNITY-DRIVEN CONTENT
REAL-TIME PRESENCE
SEARCH ENGINES

Outbound

DISPLAY ADVERTISING
NOTIFICATIONS
EMAILS AND SOCIAL MEDIA

Inbound: Community-generated material will be a significant inbound source for finding metaverse experiences. It is, in fact, one of the most affordable options for people eager to learn about the metaverse. Inbound Metaverse marketing covers search engines, app stores, user-driven content, and other related areas.

Outbound: With the help of metaverse technology, new experiences can be placed by using the relevant information in front of people through the outbound. The most efficient outbound is a discovery channel including display advertising, emails, social media, and alerts.

The metaverse has been a very important component of future industries and or personal use. Real-time engagement in the metaverse is essential to enhance the users' interaction in a virtual world and help in experience a better virtual world. This decentralization can help in exchanging ideas and experiences. It also helps in enhancing the users' interaction in the metaverse. The metaverse has the potential to disrupt the traditional digital landscapes with the help of a decentral identification framework. Among the most effective outbound routes for discovery is display advertising.

8.2.3 Creator economy

Metaverse creates a very realistic 3D virtual environment with the help of connected and realistic virtual areas. AR and VR are the one that helps in designing visitors who can do almost anything in the real world. The creation of content will be necessary to give impact to this new environment. One of the successful areas of the metaverse is the social media. The winners here are the creators, design tool platforms, e-commerce sites, and asset markets.

The metaverse involves the group of innovators of digital content like photos and videos, other artwork, webinars, and e-books. The metaverse helps raise the creative economy to a significant level. This technology is very helpful to gather fans of the same kind of liking.

8.2.4 Spatial computing

Spatial computing is being used everywhere including clothes in virtual changing rooms, education, driving, shopping, and other similar things. Spatial computing is a combination of Augmented reality, Virtual reality, and Mixed Reality. Where AR is a view of the real physical world with an overlay of digital elements. Virtual reality is a fully immersive digital environment. Mixed Reality (MR) is a view of the real world—the physical world—with an overlay of digital elements where physical and digital elements can interact. Virtual assistance is one of the major applications being used nowadays where it allows users to shop, socialize, and work as an avatar in a 3D world and enables the simulations. There is a need for specific hardware and software for its implementation. Many features of the software layer supporting the metaverse are given below:

Unity and unreal engine for displaying geometry and animation
Using object recognition and geographic mapping, one may map and analyze both the physical and digital worlds
Recognition of gestures and voices
Internet of Things to integrate device data
Biometrics of humans for identity reasons
UIs of the future generation built to handle simultaneous information streams and processing

8.2.5 Decentralization

The foundation of Web 3.0 and the Metaverse is decentralization. It lists a number of decentralized technologies—such as edge computing, DeFi, blockchain, and AI agents—that will rule the Metaverse. Here, is an example of a Facebook company that is running on a business model based on user data. This data is gathered and used to show the tailored advertising to the users.

A centralized metaverse could lead to security issues and privacy concerns. A solution is provided by blockchain technology, which makes decentralized finance, or DeFi, available to all parties without requiring brokerages or banks. By enabling users to access data without a social security number or proof of nationality, DeFi wallets like MetaMask and Trust Wallet guarantee anonymity and enhance privacy.

Various metaverse projects are utilizing the features of blockchain technology to make it decentralized and secure and hence provide user-owned experiences. The Ethereum blockchain is one which is being used to decentralize the virtual world and it runs on the DAO, i.e., a Decentralized Autonomous Organization whose rules are decided by public vote.

The main reason to use blockchain technology for the metaverse is, that blockchain makes the virtual environment transparent and traceable transactions and interactions. Within the virtual environment, NFT makes sure the property ownership is transparent and there is no dispute on the property. The metaverse is certainly an incredible technology in and of itself, but blockchain, cryptocurrency assets, and NFTs are going to be essential to this technology's ability to reach its full potential.

8.2.6 Human interface

This layer enables users to feel the actual enhancement of the metaverse technology. This layer incorporates various technologies including smart glasses and VR headsets, Smartwatches, eyewear, and smart rings. These devices help in human interaction within the virtual environment. Today's technology is very compact, smart, intelligent, and portable. However, an immersive metaverse experience depends on people and robots becoming closer, with advancements in spatial computing and interface design.

8.2.7 Infrastructure

The last layer of metaverse technology supports various platforms and devices. The most important technology here is telecommunications technology. With the innovation of 5G and 6G, a vast amount of data is being supported in the virtual environment. The reason to use 5G and 6G is, that users produce vast data in the metaverse. The cloud infrastructure and cloud services are also enhanced to support Metaverse.

The metaverse utilizes major five technologies:

- *The network and processing capacity: include GPU servers, real-time data transmission, edge computing, and spatial positioning algorithms*
- *Artificial Intelligence: includes AI and XAI*
- *Technologies used in video games: includes 3D game engines, animations, audio and video*
- *Display innovations like AR, VR, MR, ER, and XR*
- *Blockchain technology: includes smart contracts and decentralization.*

8.3 Components of metaverse technologies

See Figure 8.3 for metaverse components.

8.3.1 Application domains for the metaverse

The metaverse is transforming various industries, including education, entertainment, real estate, manufacturing, and healthcare, by empowering them with advanced applications and enhancing their understanding of the world.

With the help of motion capture technology, real-world movements are captured into digital form and create realistic objects and avatars.

Metaverse platforms can transform how companies interact with customers by providing immersive virtual experiences. Tour companies can offer personalized information in real time, while automakers can offer test drives in extended reality settings. This allows for a more immersive and personalized experience, enhancing customer experiences and allowing for more efficient marketing and outreach. The potential for metaverse applications is immense.

8.3.1.1 Gaming applications

The majority of people have been utilizing gaming applications for kids and teens in recent years, and a lot of businesses are now more concerned with producing experiences than with making games. Cities and rural areas can be created in virtual

Figure 8.3 Metaverse components

worlds using Roblox, Minecraft, Fortnite, and Farmville, among other platforms. Traditional fixed-location gaming has given way to augmented reality on tablets and smartphones, mixed reality, and fully virtualized reality with Oculus headsets. In the realm of gaming, smart wearables are likewise introducing 12 degrees of freedom. In the medieval fantasy game Dungeon & Dragons, players construct characters and listen to narrators. Superhot VR, Beat Sabre, Tetris Effect, Connected, Batman, Arkham VR, and Resident Evil 4 are a few more well-liked VR titles (Figure 8.4).

Gaming applications for children and young adults are playing games nowadays. With many companies now shifting their focus toward creating experiences rather than just being gaming companies. Virtual world platforms like Roblox, Minecraft, Fortnite, and Farmville offer world-building capabilities in urban and rural settings. People are not just playing games in a fixed physical world but rather

Figure 8.4 Gaming applications of metaverse

playing in a virtual environment. Smart wearables are also incorporating 12 degrees of freedom into the gaming domain. Dungeon & Dragons is a medieval fantasy game where players create characters and follow a storyteller.

8.3.1.2 Healthcare

Hospitals are utilizing VR technology for patient bedside assistance, particularly in postoperative care. Smart handheld devices and VR HMDs have been shown to increase patient engagement and endorphin-assisted recuperation. These metaverse experiences, combined with smart wearables, can provide therapeutic experiences for amputees. Robotic Assisted Surgeries, such as the DaVinci Surgery system, are also gaining popularity in large hospitals. Oculus and Hololens are used in medical technology applications, including surgical procedures. Augmented reality guides surgeons in surgical navigation for precision cuts and real-time inputs (Figure 8.5).

8.3.1.3 Finance and economics

The metaverse economy aims to balance demand for products and services with supply, requiring the minting of non-fungible tokens for metaverse transactions. Metaverse Exchanges control currency valuation, inflation, and deflation management. The net value of metaverse assets has grown due to privacy and secrecy. However, future cyber threats and cyber-attacks could cause difficulties in restoring order. Applications in the metaverse include capital market products, currency exchanges, position management, call-and-put options, forward contracts, and post-trade processing.

8.3.1.4 Metaverse real estate

Purchasing and selling virtual real estate within virtual worlds is known as metaverse real estate. Indians are spending more and more money in these online communities for socializing, business, and pleasure. Sites such as Decentraland and Sandbox provide chances for real estate development, opening up new channels for online communication and maybe generating income.

The turnaround time for villa sales is particularly high for homes that are priced higher.

Figure 8.5 Metaverse and healthcare

Real estate firms might use virtual tours and pictures of their projected villas to try to sell the property even before the building ever starts. However, the sales and marketing team for real estate is not giving the clients a clear enough picture of how the villa will appear and feel.

With Metaverse, the full residential township can be recreated, including the roads, clubhouse, and villas. The Residential township and the villas must be visible to you on your mobile device. You can build a digital doppelganger of your property in Metaverse, complete with interior and exterior elements. Using your avatar, you can access the real estate metaverse app and visually tour your home. You may view your property from the comfort of your home with Metaverse as well. You can explore your property virtually without leaving your house by using virtual tours and activities. This improves accessibility as well as broadens the audience for your real estate listings worldwide. The metaverse gives qualities of life (Figure 8.6).

8.3.1.5 Remote work and collaboration

Architects, designers, and developers of real estate are now able to work together in the metaverse. Teams can work together in real time regardless of their physical or geographic location by using virtual environments. Virtual collaboration facilitates more creative and participatory design exploration in addition to expediting decision-making. Traditional barriers are being broken down in the design and development stages of real estate developments by the use of metaverse virtual cooperation (Figure 8.7).

Figure 8.6 Metaverse and real estate

Figure 8.7 Metaverse and work collaboration

8.3.1.6 Metaverse in education and training

Virtual reality (VR) and augmented reality (AR) are used in metaverse education and training to create immersive, interactive learning environments. In virtual classrooms, trainees and students can work together, explore lifelike simulations, and access international resources. This technology makes learning settings more personalized to each student's needs, improves engagement, and offers practical experience.

The Metaverse is a novel idea that has gained popularity recently and has the power to completely transform a number of facets of our lives, including education. Teachers are investigating creative ways to use the metaverse to engage students, improve learning opportunities, and reimagine the traditional classroom setting as technology develops.

Virtual classrooms: Picture entering a classroom virtually, where distance is not a limitation. With the use of the metaverse, educators may design immersive virtual learning environments that go beyond traditional online learning to give students a sense of presence and interaction.

Further reading

[1] Dionisio, J. D. N., Burns III, W. G., and Gilbert, R. (2013). 3D virtual worlds and the metaverse: Current status and future possibilities. *ACM Computing Surveys (CSUR)*, 45(3), 1–38. https://doi.org/10.1145/2480741.2480751

[2] Saini, K. (2018). A future's dominant technology blockchain: Digital transformation. In *2018 International Conference on Computing, Power and Communication Technologies (GUCON)* (pp. 937–940). Piscataway, NJ: IEEE.

[3] Mystakidis, S. (2022). Metaverse. *Encyclopedia*, 2(1), 486–497. https://doi.org/10.3390/encyclopedia2010031

[4] Kye, B., Han, N., Kim, E., Park, Y., and Jo, S. (2021). Educational applications of metaverse: Possibilities and limitations. *Journal of Educational Evaluation for Health Professions*, 18, 32. https://doi.org/10.3352/jeehp.2021.18.32

[5] Lee, L. H., Braud, T., Zhou, P., *et al.* (2021). All one needs to know about metaverse: A complete survey on technological singularity, virtual ecosystem, and research agenda. *arXiv* preprint. https://arxiv.org/abs/2110.05352

[6] Raj, P., Saini, K., and Surianarayanan, C. (eds). (2020). *Blockchain Technology and Applications*. Boca Raton, FL: CRC Press.

[7] Kim, J. (2021). A study on the effect of metaverse platform characteristics on the satisfaction and continuous use intention of users: Focusing on the platform type. *Journal of Digital Convergence*, 19(10), 249–256. https://doi.org/10.14400/JDC.2021.19.10.249

[8] Park, S.-M., and Kim, Y.-G. (2022). A Metaverse: Taxonomy, components, applications, and open challenges. *IEEE Access*, 10, 4209–4251. https://doi.org/10.1109/ACCESS.2021.3140175

[9] Ning, H. S., Wang, H. T., Lin, Y., *et al.* (2021). A survey on metaverse: the state-of-the-art, technologies, applications, and challenges. *Journal of Internet Technology*, 22(7), 1469–1483. https://doi.org/10.3966/160792642021122207001

[10] Yan, J., and Li, H. (2022). Learning in the metaverse: Theoretical foundations and future research directions. *Educational Technology Research and Development*. https://doi.org/10.1007/s11423-022-10135-4

[11] Saini, K., Roy, A., Chelliah, P. R., and Patel, T. (2021). Blockchain 2.O: A smart contract. In *2021 International Conference on Computational Performance Evaluation (ComPE)* (pp. 524–528). Piscataway, NJ: IEEE.

[12] Han, S., Park, H., and Woo, J. (2021). Smart education and metaverse: Opportunities and challenges. *Journal of the Korea Convergence Society*, 12(10), 1–9. https://doi.org/10.15207/JKCS.2021.12.10.001

[13] Scholz, R. W., and Smahel, D. (2014). Digital technologies and the futures of education: Toward 'Non-Ideal' Metaverses? *International Journal of Digital Society (IJDS)*, 5(1), 1035–1043. https://doi.org/10.20533/ijds.2040.2570.2014.0128

[14] Dutta, A. (2021). Metaverse and marketing: Insights from a bibliometric analysis. *Journal of Internet Commerce*. https://doi.org/10.1080/15332861.2021.1995920

[15] Suh, W., and Ahn, S. (2021). Utilizing the metaverse for learner-centered constructivist education in the post-pandemic era: An analysis of elementary school students. *Journal of Educational Computing Research*. https://doi.org/10.1177/07356331211021777

[16] Jang, S. H., and Ryu, K. (2022). Development and application of a metaverse-based learning program for pre-service teachers. *Educational Technology & Society*, 25(1), 1–15. https://doi.org/10.30191/ETS.2022.25.1.1

[17] Kim, J., and Kim, H. (2022). The metaverse and digital twins for educators: A reflective analysis. *TechTrends*, 66, 410–421. https://doi.org/10.1007/s11528-021-00628-5

[18] Anshari, M., Almunawar, M. N., and Masri, M. (2021). Leveraging the metaverse in digital learning environments: A systematic review. *Journal of Information Technology Education: Research*, 20, 1–28. https://doi.org/10.28945/4826

Chapter 9

The convergence of spatial computing, edge computing, neuromorphic computing, HPC, quantum computing, and data analytics for the metaverse

D.P. Sharma[1]

Abstract

The convergence is a master enabler of new technological paradigms. The convergence of spatial computing, edge computing, neuromorphic computing, high-performance computing (HPC), quantum computing, and data analytics is composed to revolutionize the Metaverse, creating immersive, interactive, and intelligent virtual experiences. This chapter explores these technologies' synergistic potential, their unique contributions, and how they can be integrated to address the computational challenges inherent in building scalable, real-time, and personalized metaverse environments. We discuss the role of spatial computing in providing a sense of presence and interaction, edge computing for low-latency processing, neuromorphic computing for energy-efficient and biologically inspired computations, HPC for large-scale simulations and data processing, quantum computing for solving complex optimization problems, and data analytics for extracting valuable insights from vast amounts of metaverse data. By understanding the interaction between these technologies, we can visualize a future metaverse that like a dream blends the physical and digital worlds, offering extraordinary opportunities for collaboration, entertainment, education, and commerce.

Keywords: Convergence; Spatial Computing; Edge Computing; Neuromorphic Computing; HPC; Quantum Computing; Data Analytics; Metaverse

9.1 Introduction

In the era of digital transformation, the integration of immersive technologies has given rise to the Metaverse—a virtual realm where physical and digital realities unite. As the Metaverse evolves, the demand for real-time interactions, data

[1]Computer Scientist and Digital Diplomacy Expert, Jaipur, Rajasthan, India

processing, and seamless experiences becomes increasingly crucial. Traditional cloud-based architectures, while effective for many applications, face challenges in meeting the stringent requirements of the Metaverse.

This chapter explores the convergence of numerous computing in Metaverse for Reengineering the Virtualized and Augmented Operations and Data Analytics as a transformative solution to enhance the capabilities of the Metaverse. However, realizing the full potential of the metaverse requires addressing the challenges of real-time data processing, low latency, and security. Spatial computing, edge computing, and data analytics play crucial roles in overcoming these challenges and enabling a truly immersive and seamless metaverse experience [1].

Initially, as the Metaverse rises from digital dust, three technological pillars stand poised to shape its virtual landscape: Cloud computing is a model for delivering on-demand access to a shared pool of computing resources, including servers, storage, databases, networking, software, analytics, and intelligence, over the internet ("the cloud"); Edge Computing, an agile network performer reducing delay and latency; and Data Analytics, a wise vision whispering insights from user behavior. Together, they form a powerful trinity, ready to power the next frontier of human interaction. Prepare to step into a world where physics becomes pixels, responsiveness reigns supreme, and every choice echoes in the data verse. This is how these technologies cover the way for a Metaverse unlike any other [1–3].

Further, this immersive picture demands real-time data processing and analysis at the edge of the network, where edge computing steps onto the stage. By decentralizing processing power, edge computing empowers devices closer to users, ensuring responsive interactions and seamless experiences within the Metaverse [4].

However, the Metaverse's data deluge necessitates a shift beyond traditional computing architectures. Here, neuromorphic computing, inspired by the human brain's intricate structure emerges as a potential game-changer. By mimicking the neural networks that govern biological intelligence, neuromorphic chips offer low-power, high-throughput processing capabilities, ideal for handling the Metaverse's complex data streams in real-time [5].

But the true computational marvel of the Metaverse lies beyond the realm of classical physics. Quantum computing harnesses the strange properties of quantum mechanics to unlock unprecedented computational power. From tackling intractable optimization problems to simulating complex molecular interactions, quantum computing promises to revolutionize fields ranging from materials science and drug discovery to financial modeling and cryptography, all of which have profound implications for the Metaverse's development and evolution [6].

Finally, high-performance computing (HPC), the workhorse of scientific and engineering simulations provides the foundational muscle for this computational art. By harnessing the collective power of massive computing clusters, HPC underpins the development of complex Metaverse environments, from simulating physics and weather patterns to rendering realistic avatars and crafting intricate narratives [7].

This chapter embarks on a journey through this confluence of cutting-edge technologies, dividing their contributions and exploring their synergistic potential in shaping the Metaverse. The chapter investigates the data analytics pipelines that power these systems, highlighting the unique challenges and opportunities presented by this emerging virtual landscape. By explaining the intricate interplay of these technologies, we aim to equip readers with a roadmap to navigate the exciting frontiers of the Metaverse, where spatial interactions, real-time data analysis, and the power of quantum computation paint the picture for a revolutionary future of human experience.

9.2 Understanding the metaverse

The metaverse, a term coined by Neal Stephenson in his 1992 novel "Snow Crash," has gone from a science fiction concept to a buzzword. But what exactly is the metaverse? In essence, it is an emerging 3D virtual world or network of worlds accessible through various devices, including VR headsets, smartphones, and even smart glasses [8].

According to the modern definition, "The Metaverse is an open-source, decentralized virtual reality that facilitates interoperability between different providers." It is the next step in the virtual reality saga, whereby virtual reality aims to take over large aspects of physical life. Meta on the other hand is the parent company of Facebook and other companies and aims to become a large provider of virtual realities connected to the Metaverse [9].

9.3 Key characteristics of the metaverse and data-centric approach

- *Immersion*: The metaverse promises to be a revolutionary new space for human interaction and experience. It is a virtual world where people can connect, work, play, and learn in ways that are not possible in the physical world. To create a truly immersive and engaging metaverse, two key approaches are crucial: immersion and a data-centric approach. Immersion refers to the feeling of being completely present in the metaverse as if you are there. A data-centric approach is essential for making the metaverse truly interactive and personalized. This means using data to create personalized experiences, improve immersion, and drive decision-making. For example, it can be used to track traffic patterns in virtual worlds or identify areas where users are having trouble [10,11].
- *Interactivity*: The metaverse is not just a passive experience; it is a highly interactive space where users can connect with others, play games, work, shop, create, and participate in various activities. This interactivity is powered by social features and real-time communication tools [12].
- *Decentralization*: Unlike traditional online platforms controlled by a single entity, the metaverse is envisioned as a decentralized network. This means users will have more control over their data and experiences, fostering ownership and community building [12].
- *Openness*: The metaverse is designed to be an open platform, allowing for interoperability between different virtual worlds and services. This openness will encourage innovation and collaboration, leading to a diverse and ever-evolving virtual universe [12].

9.4 Data diversity in cross-disciplinary applications of the metaverse

The metaverse, a virtual world where digital and physical realities converge, holds immense potential across various fields. The extremely sophisticated and high-tech tools can only capture, organize, and analyze data in the virtual world of Metaverse. Here are some promising areas in which data analytics can play a critical role in consistently improving the Metaverse experiences in numerous applications [13,14]:

- *Entertainment*: The metaverse holds immense potential for entertainment, offering immersive gaming experiences, virtual concerts, and interactive storytelling [15]
- *Social Interaction:* The metaverse can facilitate meaningful social interactions and connections, regardless of physical location. Imagine attending virtual conferences, hanging out with friends in virtual spaces, or even exploring museums together remotely [16].
- *Work and Education:* The metaverse can revolutionize work and education by providing virtual workspaces, remote collaboration tools, and immersive learning experiences [17].
- *Commerce:* Businesses can leverage the metaverse to create virtual stores, offer personalized shopping experiences, and even host virtual events and conferences [18].
- *Healthcare:* The metaverse can be used for telehealth consultations, remote surgery simulations, and even virtual therapy sessions [18,19].

9.5 Data analytics for the metaverse

The Metaverse, a budding concept envisioning a persistent, immersive virtual world where humans interact through avatars, and incarnations stands poised to revolutionize social interaction, entertainment, and even work. However, this virtual realm will generate vast data over the edge, cloud, and pervasive devices, presenting both potential and challenges for the field of data analytics. This section investigates the details of data analytics in the Metaverse, exploring its unique opportunities and the specific analytical techniques required to navigate this complex digital landscape.

9.5.1 The data surge of the metaverse

The Metaverse promises an unprecedented level of digital immersion, generating data of diverse types and volumes. Avatars will leave complex trails of movement, interactions, and emotional states. Sensors within the virtual environment will capture biometric data, voice patterns, and real-time responses. Additionally, a vast treasure of data will stem from economic transactions, content creation, and user-generated content within the Metaverse. This data overflow necessitates the development of novel analytical approaches and infrastructures to process, analyze, and derive meaningful insights from the Metaverse's data streams [16,20].

9.5.2 The multidimensional treasure of data for the metaverse

Unlike the physical world, the metaverse offers a controlled environment where users' data of interactions, object movements, and environmental changes can be precisely captured and analyzed. This generates a rich treasure of multidimensional data for exploring opportunities to uncover hidden insights to improve the Metaverse experiences and alleviate future challenges, encompassing:

- *Spatial Data:* Location, movement patterns, and interactions within the virtual environment [8].
- *Behavioral Data:* User choices, actions, and responses to stimuli within the metaverse [21,22].
- *Physiological Data:* Biometric data (e.g., heart rate, eye tracking) captured through haptic interfaces and wearable devices [23].
- *Content Data:* Information generated from virtual objects, environments, and social interactions [24].

9.5.3 Hidden insights and opportunities for data-driven metaverse experiences

This data overflow presents both opportunities and challenges for analytics. Data analytics can unlock an ocean of possibilities in the metaverse:

- *Personalization and User Experience in Metaverse Environment:* Tailored experiences of Metaverse environment based on individual preferences, behaviors, and emotional responses can be analyzed to reveal hidden insights. Analyzing user behavior, preferences, and emotions can personalize the Metaverse experience, tailoring content, environments, and interactions to individual preferences. Machine learning models could anticipate user needs, recommend virtual experiences, and optimize avatar customization based on real-time data [25,26].

Enhanced Engagement in Metaverse: Dynamically adapt environments, challenges, and interactions to keep users engaged and immersed [27]

- *Economic Modeling and Virtual Market Optimization:* The growing virtual economy of the Metaverse will require sophisticated data analytics to track economic activity, model market trends, and optimize pricing strategies. Analyzing virtual transactions, resource consumption, and avatar behavior can inform the development of sustainable economic systems within the Metaverse. Analyzing market trends, user behavior, and resource utilization to optimize virtual economies and in-game monetization can help in predicting and controlling the market [28].
- *Immersive Storytelling, Content, and Social Interaction Analysis:* Understanding patterns of computing, communication, collaboration, and conflict within virtual communities of Metaverse to foster positive social interactions [29].

- Data-driven insights can inform the development of dynamic and emotionally engaging narratives within the Metaverse. By analyzing user engagement with virtual experiences, content creators can refine narratives, personalize story paths, and tailor content to maximize audience impact [30].
- *Safety and Security:* Monitoring user behavior, detecting anomalies, and predicting potential risks to ensure a safe and secure metaverse experience [31].
- *Virtual Society and Human-Avatar Interaction:* The Metaverse creates a unique opportunity to study human behavior and social dynamics in a controlled virtual environment. By analyzing avatar interactions, communication patterns, and emotional responses, researchers can gain valuable insights into human social behavior and develop models for fostering positive and productive interactions within the Metaverse [29]

9.5.4 Challenges and ethical considerations in data-driven analytics

While data analytics holds immense potential, it also presents challenges, and these challenges are required to be alleviated to enhance the potential applications and performance of the Metaverse environment:

- *Data Privacy and Security*: Data privacy and security are two important ethical concerns. The first concern is balancing the need for data-driven insights with user privacy and ethical data collection practices. The second concern is securing user data in the metaverse from cyberattacks and unauthorized access. The vast amount of personal data generated in the Metaverse raises these two concerns about privacy and security breaches. Robust data anonymization techniques and secure storage infrastructure are crucial to protect user privacy and prevent unauthorized access to sensitive data [31,32].
- *Algorithmic Bias and Fairness:* Data-driven algorithms used in the Metaverse must be closely scrutinized to avoid perpetuating existing societal biases and promoting fairness within the virtual environment. Bias detection and mitigation techniques are essential to ensure equitable access and opportunities for all users. So, the algorithms used for analysis are free from bias and discrimination, particularly in sensitive areas like virtual economies and social interactions [33].
- *Transparency and Explainability:* Ensuring transparency in how data is used and algorithms function to build user trust in the metaverse is essential. Addressing these challenges through responsible data governance and ethical AI development is crucial for building a booming and sustainable metaverse [33,34].
- *The Ethics of Avatars and Digital Identities:* The blurred lines between real and virtual in the Metaverse necessitate careful consideration of the ethical implications of avatar identities and interactions. Questions regarding user agency, accountability, and the potential for harm within the virtual realm require thoughtful discourse and ethical frameworks [35].

9.5.5 Navigating the data frontier of the metaverse and specialized computing

Data analytics stands poised to revolutionize the metaverse, shaping its experiences, economies, and social interactions. The emerging Metaverse presents a unique and challenging frontier for data analytics. By harnessing the power of data, we can unlock the potential of this virtual world for personalized experiences, engaging storytelling, and a thriving virtual economy. However, we must tread cautiously, mindful of the ethical considerations and potential pitfalls that accompany the Metaverse's data overflow. Only through responsible data practices and thoughtful consideration of ethical implications can we ensure that data analytics contributes to a positive and enriching future for humanity within the Metaverse. Numerous specialized computing used such as Neuromorphic Computing, Spatial Computing, Edge Computing, Quantum Computing, and High-Performance Computing to design the Metaverse environment [36].

9.6 Neuromorphic computing

Inspired by the human brain, neuromorphic computing utilizes artificial neural networks (ANNs) to process and analyze large volumes of data in real time, making it ideal for metaverse applications such as image recognition, natural language processing, and spatial awareness. Neuromorphic computing, a rapidly evolving field, aims to mimic the brain's structure and function to achieve efficient and powerful information processing. By drawing inspiration from biological neurons and networks, neuromorphic systems offer the potential to overcome the limitations of traditional computing architectures and unlock new possibilities in various domains [37].

9.6.1 Core principles of neuromorphic computing

- *Bio-inspired architecture:* Neuromorphic systems utilize neuromorphic hardware, consisting of artificial neurons and synapses, interconnected like the biological brain. This allows for parallel processing and distributed computation, offering significant advantages over von Neumann architectures [38].
- *Low power consumption:* Compared to traditional computers, neuromorphic systems can achieve significantly higher energy efficiency due to their inherent parallelism and analog nature. This makes them ideal for resource-constrained environments and mobile applications [39].
- *Adaptability and learning:* Neuromorphic systems are inherently adaptive and can learn from experience by modifying the strength of their connections. This enables them to perform tasks requiring real-time learning and adaptation, such as pattern recognition and signal processing [40].
- *Fault tolerance:* Inspired by the brain's resilience, neuromorphic systems can exhibit tolerance to hardware faults and noise. This makes them robust and reliable, even in harsh environments [41].

9.6.2 von Neumann vs. Neuromorphic architectures

von Neumann vs. Neuromorphic architecture: The two dominant paradigms in computing architecture, the von Neumann and Neuromorphic represent fundamentally different approaches to processing information. Understanding their strengths and weaknesses is crucial for navigating the future of computing, particularly in areas like artificial intelligence and machine learning.

The Legacy of the von Neumann: As depicted in Figure 9.1, the von Neumann architecture has the following specialties: (1) Structure: Based on a separate central processing unit (CPU) and memory unit, with data transferred between them through a communication bus. (2) Processing: Follows a sequential, linear instruction-based model, performing one operation at a time. (3) Strengths: Powerful for logic-intensive tasks, precise calculations, and well-defined algorithms. (4) Weaknesses: Limited parallelism, high energy consumption, and struggles with tasks mimicking natural intelligence [42].

The Growing Space for Neuromorphic Architecture: As depicted in Figure 9.2, neuromorphic architecture has the following specialties: (1) Structure: Inspired by the human brain, with interconnected artificial neurons and synapses performing computations and storing data simultaneously. (2) Processing: Utilizes massively parallel and distributed processing, mimicking the brain's ability to handle complex patterns and adapt to new information. (3) Strengths: Efficient for data-intensive tasks, pattern recognition, and tasks with inherent uncertainties. (4) Weaknesses: Still under development, less precise than von Neumann for specific calculations, and requires efficient algorithms for optimal performance [37,43].

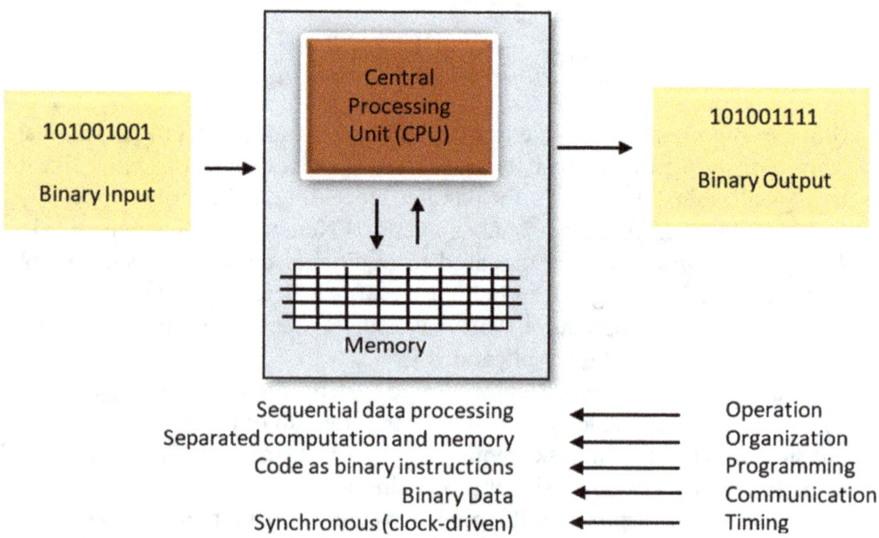

Figure 9.1 von Neumann architectural diagram

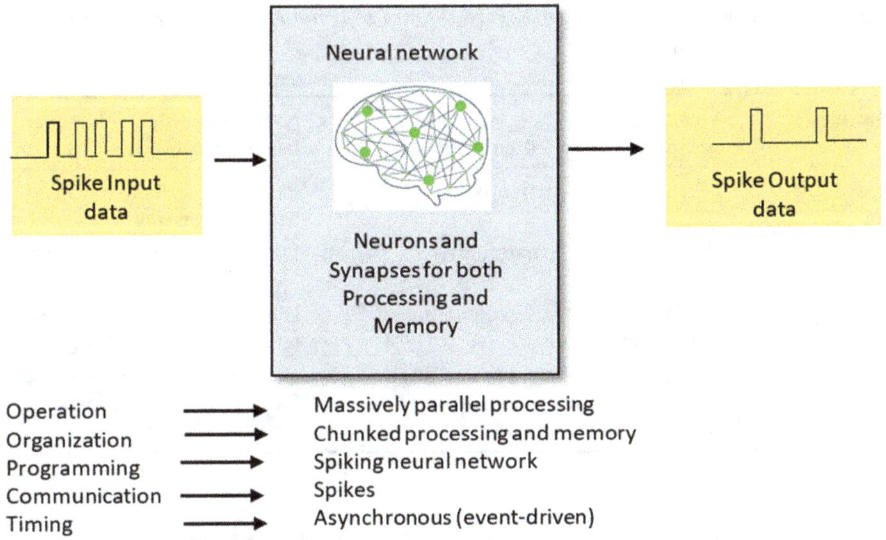

Figure 9.2 Neuromorphic architectural diagram

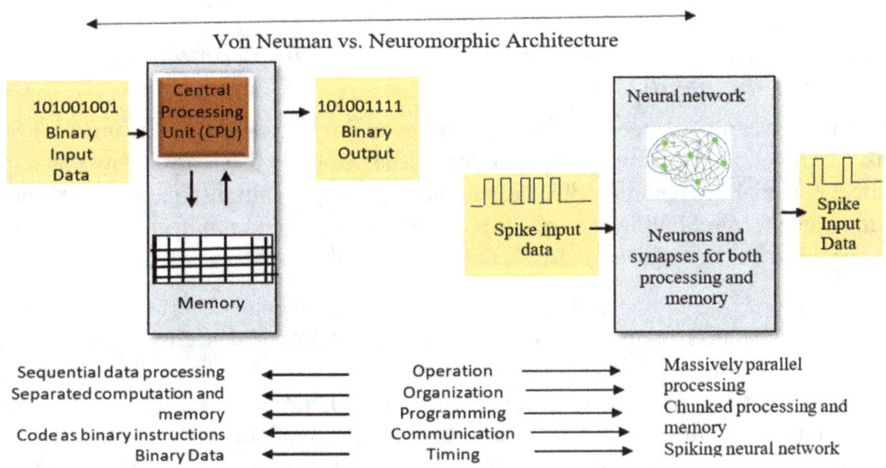

Figure 9.3 Comparison of neuromorphic architecture-based computing and von Neumann architecture-based computing

Key Differences in Design Artifacts of the von Neumann and Neuromorphic Computing Architectures: The feature-based key differences between von Neumann and neuromorphic architecture-based computing are depicted in Figure 9.3 and Table 9.1.

The Future of Computing: Both von Neumann and neuromorphic architectures have their place in the computational landscape. von Neumann remains dominant

Table 9.1 Comparison between von Neumann and neuromorphic computing architectures

Feature	von Neumann architecture-based computing	Neuromorphic architecture-based computing
Processing model	Sequential, instruction-based processing	Parallel, distributed system-based processing
Memory and processing	Provided in a separate unit	Provided in a unified manner
Advantages	Logic-based, precise calculation, defined algorithm	Data-intensive tasks, pattern recognition, adaptability
Disadvantages	Limited parallelism process, high energy consumption, struggle with neural intelligent tasks	Under development, less recise for specific calculations, algorithm dependence

for traditional tasks, while neuromorphic holds immense potential for AI, machine learning, and brain-inspired computing. The future likely lies in hybrid approaches that leverage the strengths of both architectures, combining von Neumann's precision with neuromorphic adaptability and efficiency.

9.6.3 Applications and impact of neuromorphic computing on the metaverse

The metaverse, a convergence of virtual worlds and interconnected experiences, promises to revolutionize how we interact, learn, and work. At the heart of this transformative potential lies neuromorphic computing, a paradigm shift inspired by the human brain's architecture. Following are some of the important and promising applications and potential impact of neuromorphic computing on the metaverse [37,44]:

- *Enhanced Interactivity:* By mimicking the brain's motor control mechanisms, neuromorphic systems can enable robots with improved dexterity, adaptability, and real-time decision-making capabilities. Unlike traditional computing, neuromorphic architectures excel at parallel processing and adaptation, enabling real-time responses to user actions and dynamic environments within the metaverse. This can empower intuitive interactions with virtual objects, immersive storytelling, and collaborative experiences that evolve based on user choices [45].
- *Hyper-Realistic Experiences:* Neuromorphic systems can process vast amounts of sensory data (visual, auditory, haptic) and simulate complex physical interactions, contributing to hyper-realistic experiences within the metaverse. This opens doors for virtual training simulations, remote physical therapy, and even realistic representations of historical events or distant locations [46].
- *AI-Powered Avatars and Companions:* Neuromorphic systems are well-suited for implementing ANNs and performing complex AI tasks such as image

recognition, natural language processing, and machine learning. Neuromorphic architectures can power sophisticated AI avatars and virtual companions that learn and adapt to user behavior, preferences, and emotions. This fosters deeper social engagement within the metaverse, personalized guidance and assistance, and potentially even therapeutic virtual companions [34,47].

- *Efficient Resource Utilization:* Neuromorphic computing can potentially reduce the energy consumption associated with complex metaverse simulations compared to traditional computing architectures. This aligns with the sustainability goals of many metaverse creators and contributes to a more environmentally friendly virtual world [45].
- *Healthcare Information Security and Privacy in Cyberspace:* Neuromorphic systems can be used for brain–computer interfaces, medical image analysis, and personalized medicine, leading to advancements in diagnostics, treatment, and rehabilitation. By analyzing large datasets and identifying complex patterns, neuromorphic systems can enhance cybersecurity systems and detect anomalies in real time [37].

9.6.4 Challenges and ethical considerations neuromorphic computing in metaverse

Micro-sized neurochips, often referred to as Brain–Computer Interfaces (BCIs), are miniature devices implanted in the human body to facilitate communication between the brain and computers. Inspired by the functioning of synapses, these neurochips emulate neuronal signals, enabling potential applications in neural rehabilitation, sensory restoration, and even communication and control of external devices.

While data processing speeds of current neurochips lag behind the human brain, advancements in this field are rapid. However, the ethical implications of BCIs extend beyond their medical potential. Applications such as cognitive enhancement, memory storage, or direct brain-to-brain communication raise complex questions about privacy, autonomy, and human enhancement [48].

Therefore, while the use of BCIs for therapeutic purposes, like restoring lost functions or facilitating communication, carries less ethical conflict, other applications warrant careful consideration and open dialogue. This includes establishing robust ethical frameworks to ensure informed consent, mitigate potential risks, and protect individual rights in the face of this powerful technology. While promising, neuromorphic computing for the metaverse faces challenges like algorithm development, energy efficiency optimization, and data privacy concerns. Additionally, ethical considerations regarding AI sentience, potential biases in learning algorithms, and responsible use of virtual avatars need careful examination and implementation of ethical frameworks [49].

9.7 Quantum computing

Quantum computing represents a groundbreaking leap in information processing, harnessing the principles of quantum mechanics to achieve remarkable computational power [50]. Unlike traditional computers that operate with bits (0s and 1s), quantum computers utilize qubits, capable of existing in a superposition of both states simultaneously [32,51]. This unlocks massive parallelism, enabling them to tackle problems intractable for even the most powerful classical computers [52]. These qubits, the fundamental building blocks of a quantum computer, can exist in a state of superposition, holding both 0 and 1 values at the same time. This allows for exponentially faster storage and processing of information compared to classical bits [37].

Furthermore, two or more qubits can become entangled, where their states are linked regardless of distance. This entanglement enables complex correlations and interactions, leading to enhanced computational capabilities. Specifically designed for quantum computers, quantum algorithms exploit the unique properties of qubits and entanglement to efficiently solve specific problems. Examples include Shor's algorithm for factoring large numbers and Grover's algorithm for searching unsorted databases [53].

Due to the delicate nature of qubits, quantum systems are susceptible to errors. Quantum error correction techniques are crucial for maintaining the integrity of quantum information and ensuring accurate computations [54]. This revolutionary technology holds immense potential across various domains, including Metaverse, Drug discovery, Cryptography, Finance, Machine learning, and Materials science. As the field continues to develop, we can expect quantum computing to revolutionize entire industries and solve problems currently deemed impossible [55].

9.7.1 Quantum computing convergence and application in metaverse engineering

The metaverse, a growing virtual reality space, promises to revolutionize human interaction and experience. Yet, its full potential cruxes on the ability to create complex, dynamic, and immersive worlds. The convergence of quantum computing (QC) and metaverse engineering, highlights how quantum technologies can boost the metaverse towards unprecedented levels of realism, interactivity, and computational power. As depicted in Figure 9.4, this integration helps in creating an amazing experience in the virtual environment of Metaverse.

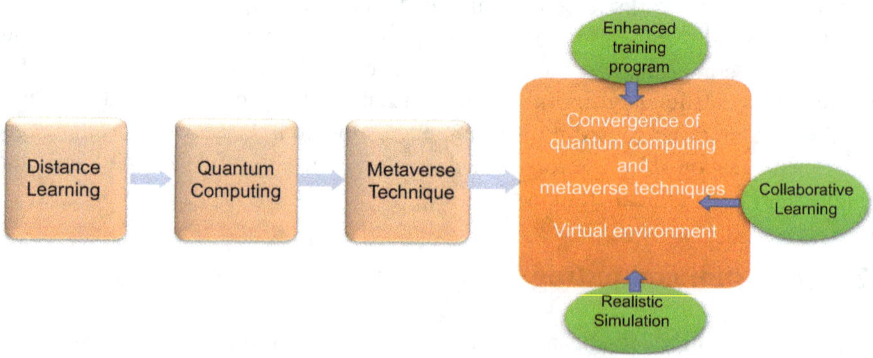

Figure 9.4 Convergence of quantum computing and metaverse techniques to create new frontiers virtual environments [56]

The Metaverse Landscape: A Challenge for Classical Computing: The metaverse envisions a persistent, interconnected network of virtual worlds where users can interact, collaborate, and even build their own realities. However, the computational demands of such a complex and dynamic environment are immense. Traditional computer architectures, based on the von Neumann model, struggle with tasks like real-time physics simulations, complex AI agents, and personalized content creation at the scale required for the metaverse.

The Unlocking New Possibilities through Quantum Computing: Quantum computers, harnessing the principles of superposition and entanglement, offer a paradigm shift in computational power. By manipulating qubits, the quantum equivalent of bits, they can perform certain calculations exponentially faster than classical computers. As depicted in Figure 9.5, Quantum computing along with other technologies such as Neuromorphic Computing, Cloud Computing, HPC, and Edge Computing creates opportunities and challenges in Metaverse engineering.

Quantum computing opens doors to new possibilities for metaverse engineering, including:

1. *Hyper-realistic environments:* Quantum algorithms can simulate complex physical phenomena with unprecedented accuracy, creating breathtakingly realistic virtual worlds for Metaverse with dynamic weather, fluid dynamics, and even quantum effects [56].
2. *Advanced AI and virtual agents:* Quantum machine learning algorithms can learn and adapt far faster than classical counterparts, enabling the creation of truly intelligent and interactive virtual agents that populate the metaverse [57,58].

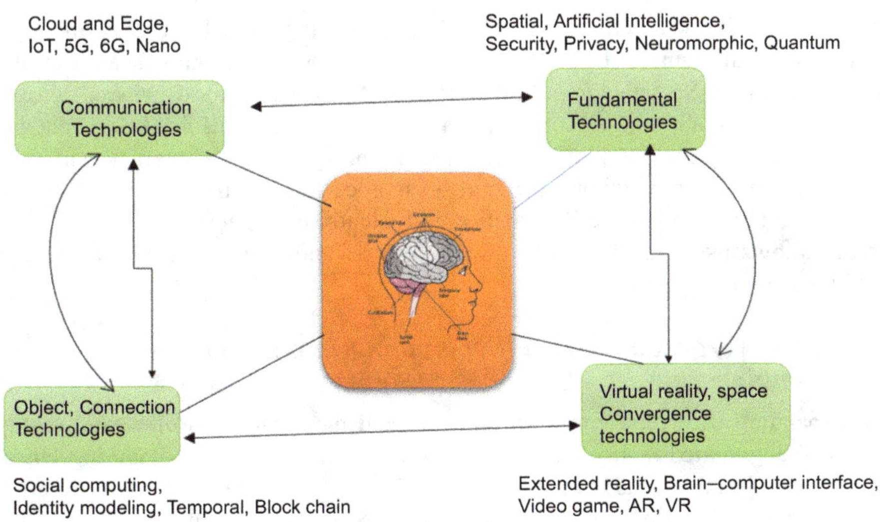

Figure 9.5 Opportunities and challenges of quantum computing, neuromorphic computing, cloud computing, HPC, and edge computing in metaverse [56]

3. *Personalized content and experiences:* Quantum algorithms can analyze vast amounts of user data and preferences to personalize every aspect of the metaverse experience, from the environment to the interactions with other users [59].
4. *Secure and efficient communication:* Quantum cryptography offers unbreakable encryption methods for secure communication within the metaverse, protecting user data and preventing cyberattacks [60].

9.7.2 Navigating the challenges and opportunities of quantum computing

While the potential of quantum computing for the metaverse is vast, several challenges remain. Quantum hardware is still in its early stages of development, and building large-scale, fault-tolerant quantum computers will require significant technological advancements. Additionally, developing efficient quantum algorithms for specific metaverse applications requires ongoing research and collaboration between computer scientists, metaverse engineers, and quantum physicists [78].

Despite these challenges, the convergence of quantum computing and metaverse engineering offers a transformative path toward a truly immersive and interactive virtual world. By addressing these challenges and fostering collaborative research, we can unlock the full potential of the metaverse and create a future where the boundaries between reality and virtual worlds become increasingly blurred.

9.8 Spatial computing

Spatial computing is an emerging technology that brings together digital and physical worlds, allowing users to interact with computers in more seamless and immersive ways. Spatial computing is truly a blending of the Real and Virtual Worlds. Spatial computing encompasses a range of technologies that bridge the gap between the physical and digital realms, enabling users to interact with and experience information within 3D spaces. It goes beyond traditional notions of computer interaction, where information is typically confined to flat screens, and instead allows users to physically move, gesture, and manipulate virtual objects within a spatial context [61].

9.8.1 Convergence of spatial computing in metaverse engineering

The expanding metaverse promises to transcend the limitations of virtual reality (VR) and augmented reality (AR), creating a new era of spatial computing where the real and virtual worlds seamlessly blend. The convergence of spatial computing technologies with metaverse engineering, and exploring how they will shape the next generation of immersive and interactive virtual worlds is paramount.

While redefining Human–Computer Interaction in the Metaverse, the Metaverse visualizes a persistent, interconnected network of virtual and augmented experiences where users engage in activities that exceed the boundaries of the physical world. This requires robust human–computer interaction (HCI) paradigms that bridge the gap between the digital and physical realms. Enter spatial computing—a constellation of technologies encompassing VR, AR, mixed reality (MR), and haptic interfaces, enabling intuitive interaction with 3D environments and digital objects in real time.

9.8.2 Spatial computing: The building blocks of immersive worlds

Spatial computing technologies like VR, AR, and MR break down the boundaries between the physical and digital realms. As depicted in Figure 9.6, using spatial computing technologies like VR, AR, and MR, users can physically move, interact with virtual objects, and experience information within 3D spaces, creating a sense of presence and immersion that traditional flat-screen interfaces lack. Imagine manipulating virtual objects on a table in your real-world living room with natural gestures, or attending a virtual meeting where anyone feels like he/she is actually in the same room as other participants.

9.8.3 Synergistic convergence: Unleashing the metaverse's potential

The convergence of these spatial computing technologies within metaverse engineering holds immense potential:

- *Enhanced spatial awareness:* Combining VR/AR with precise 3D mapping and localization technologies can enable users to navigate virtual environments with natural movements and gestures, mimicking real-world interactions [61].

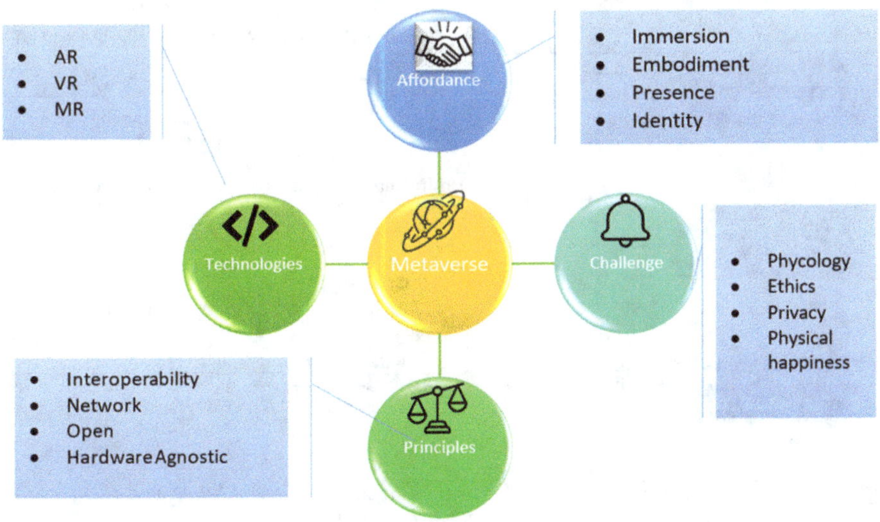

Figure 9.6 Spatial computing in Metaverse technologies, principles, affordances, and challenges [62]

- *Multimodal interaction*: Beyond traditional controllers, haptic interfaces and gesture recognition will allow users to manipulate virtual objects and interact with the metaverse intuitively, using touch, speech, and even eye tracking.
- *Real-world integration:* AR functionalities within the metaverse can bridge the gap between virtual and physical spaces, fostering collaboration and seamless transitions between the two worlds [61].
- *Hyper-realistic experiences:* Advanced rendering techniques, combined with spatial audio and haptic feedback, can create breathtakingly realistic virtual environments that blur the lines between real and digital [63].

9.8.4 The spatial revolution behind Web 3.0 and the metaverse

The internet is on the point of a transformative shift, poised to move beyond the boundaries of 2D screens and flat content towards a spatial revolution. This paradigm shift, intertwined with the emergence of Web 3.0 and the metaverse, is fueled by the power of spatial computing technologies like virtual reality (VR), augmented reality (AR), and mixed reality (MR). As depicted in Figure 9.7, let us explore this exciting intersection.

Web 3.0: Moving from centralized data ownership to a decentralized, user-centric web powered by blockchain technologies. This creates fertile ground for immersive and interactive experiences within the metaverse.

Metaverse: A persistent, interconnected network of virtual worlds where users can interact, collaborate, and socialize in 3D spaces. The metaverse booms on

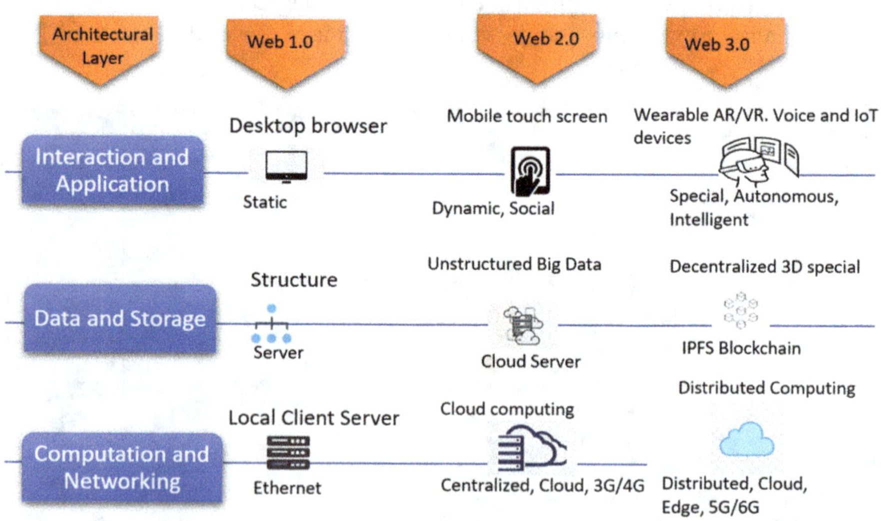

Figure 9.7 The spatial revolution behind Web 3.0 and the Metaverse (Source: Deloitte, "The Spatial Web and Web 3.0") [64]

spatial computing to create a sense of presence and embodiment within these virtual environments.

Spatial Computing: The foundation of this revolution, providing the tools to break free from flat screens and interact with the digital world in three dimensions. VR offers fully immersive virtual worlds, AR overlays digital information onto the real world, and MR seamlessly blends these two realities.

9.8.5 Challenges and opportunities: Navigating the spatial landscape

While the synergy between spatial computing and metaverse engineering promises an exciting future, challenges remain. Hardware limitations, battery life, and ensuring seamless transitions between different technologies require continuous research and development. Additionally, ethical considerations regarding privacy, user safety, and potential addiction to virtual experiences must be addressed carefully.

9.9 High-Performance Computing (HPC)

HPC systems provide the raw processing power needed to handle the massive computational demands of metaverse environments, including rendering complex virtual worlds, simulating real-time physics, and supporting a large number of concurrent users. HPC represents the cutting edge of information processing, harnessing immense computational power to tackle complex problems beyond the reach of traditional computers. By combining high-performance processors, specialized hardware, and sophisticated software, HPC facilitates breakthroughs in various scientific and technological fields. The key characteristics of HPC that explore its potential Metaverse engineering are as follows [7]:

- *Parallel processing:* HPC systems utilize multiple processors working simultaneously to achieve significantly faster computation speeds compared to single-processor systems.
- *High-speed data transfer:* Efficient communication channels allow data to flow rapidly between processors and other components within the HPC system, ensuring smooth program execution.
- Scalability: HPC systems can be scaled up by adding additional processors and memory, enabling them to handle progressively larger and more complex problems.
- *Specialized software:* HPC systems require specialized software tools and programming paradigms optimized for parallel processing and high-performance computing.

9.9.1 Convergence of HPC in metaverse engineering

The metaverse, a growing network of interconnected virtual worlds, promises a future where reality and virtuality seamlessly blend. To realize its full potential, however, the metaverse demands immense computational power to render complex environments, simulate physics, and power sophisticated AI agents. It is very essential to understand and explore the crucial role of one of the potential computing technologies, i.e., HPC in metaverse engineering. It is also important to highlight its convergence with other technologies for unlocking new possibilities for this emerging virtual world.

9.9.2 Challenges of traditional computing in metaverse

The metaverse visualizes a persistent and dynamic virtual space accessible to millions of users simultaneously. This requires real-time processing of vast amounts of data, including [52]:

- *Complex environment rendering:* Generating and maintaining intricate virtual worlds with dynamic weather, lighting, and realistic physical properties for Metaverse.
- *Sophisticated AI agents:* Powering intelligent virtual characters, non-player characters (NPCs), and advanced AI systems that adapt to user behavior and environment for Metaverse.
- *Massive user interaction:* Enabling unified and lag-free communication, collaboration, and interaction between millions of users within the metaverse.
- *Real-time simulations:* Simulating complex physical interactions, from fluid dynamics and particle systems to the movement of virtual objects and avatars in a Metaverse environment. Traditional computing architectures struggle with these demands due to their limitations in parallel processing, memory bandwidth, and data throughput. This is where HPC, with its vast computational power and specialized hardware, emerges as a critical enabler for metaverse engineering.

9.9.3 Challenges of High-Performance Computing in metaverse

Despite its impressive achievements, HPC faces significant hurdles in adapting to the metaverse's demanding needs. These challenges can be categorized into five main areas [47,65]:

- *Cost:* Running HPC infrastructure remains a substantial financial burden. With roughly half of current users citing high service and management costs as major barriers to adoption, the demand for resources often outpaces supply, leading to lost productivity.
- *Data Security and Privacy:* Concerns regarding data security and privacy loom large, particularly in cloud-based HPC environments where large-scale data transfers occur. Potential data breaches pose a serious threat to user trust and require robust security measures.
- *Performance Bottlenecks:* Current cloud-based HPC services often fall short of meeting users' performance requirements. Network latency and slow node speeds remain major pain points, hindering the smooth operation of demanding metaverse applications.

- *Energy Efficiency and Sustainability:* Training large AI models for the metaverse consumes vast amounts of energy. A single model can generate a staggering 284 metric tons of CO_2, with this figure only rising alongside demand. Striking a balance between performance and environmental impact is crucial.
- *Server Utilization:* Optimizing server utilization is a persistent challenge in the HPC industry. Studies indicate a worrying 30%–35% of servers remain idle, consuming unnecessary electricity and contributing to carbon emissions. Finding efficient resource allocation strategies is essential.

By addressing these challenges, HPC can unlock its full potential as a driving force behind the metaverse's development. Achieving cost-effectiveness, robust security, improved performance, sustainable practices, and efficient resource management is key to ensuring HPC plays a vital role in shaping this exciting virtual future.

9.9.4 HPC: The power for metaverse simulations

HPC systems, comprised of interconnected clusters of HPC, offer several advantages for the metaverse [66]:

- *Parallel processing:* HPC systems can distribute complex calculations across multiple processors simultaneously, significantly accelerating rendering, physics simulations, and AI algorithms.
- *High memory bandwidth*: These systems boast vast memory capacities and fast data transfer rates, crucial for handling the immense amount of data involved in rendering complex virtual environments and managing large numbers of users.
- *Scalability and flexibility*: HPC systems can be scaled to meet the ever-growing demands of the metaverse, adding more processing power and resources as needed.

9.9.5 Convergence and synergistic effects of HPC on metaverse

The convergence of HPC with other technologies further amplifies its impact in metaverse engineering:

- *Cloud Computing:* Cloud infrastructure can provide on-demand access to HPC resources, making HPC more accessible and affordable for metaverse development.
- *Artificial Intelligence*: HPC can power advanced AI algorithms for natural language processing, computer vision, and machine learning, enabling intelligent and adaptive virtual environments and AI-powered agents.
- *Edge Computing:* By placing processing power closer to users, edge computing can reduce latency and improve responsiveness within the metaverse, especially for geographically distributed users.

9.10 Edge computing

Edge computing, a paradigm shift in data processing, decentralizes computing power by moving it closer to data sources, often at the "edge" of the network. Edge computing moves data processing closer to data sources often directly to user devices or local gateways. This significantly reduces latency by minimizing the distance data needs to travel. The Metaverse architecture features the immersive and real-time physical-virtual world interaction presented in Figure 9.8. Think of it like having a mini-data center right on your doorstep, instead of relying on one across town. This approach offers significant advantages over traditional centralized computing, including [68,69]:

Reduced Latency: By processing data locally, edge computing eliminates the need for long-distance communication, minimizing delay and enabling real-time

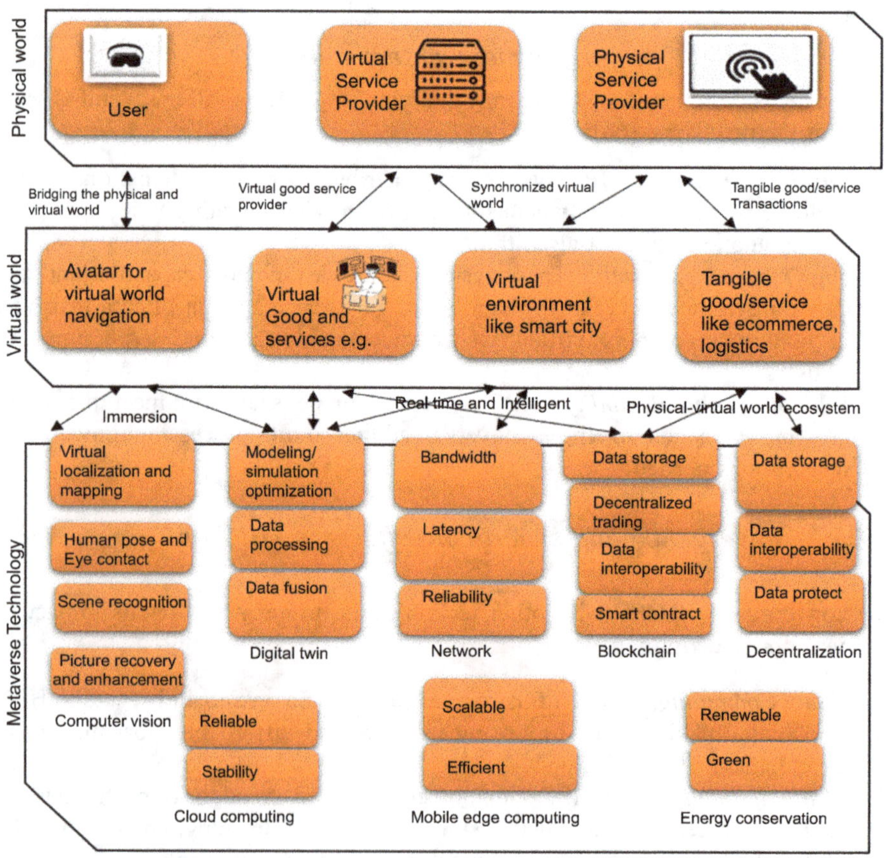

Figure 9.8 The Metaverse architecture features the immersive and real-time physical-virtual world interaction supported by the Metaverse technical layer [67]

responsiveness. This is critical for applications like the virtualized environment of Metaverse and autonomous vehicles, where latency can have serious consequences.

Improved Bandwidth Utilization: Offloading data processing from central servers frees up network bandwidth, leading to better performance and reduced congestion. This is especially beneficial for bandwidth-intensive applications like video streaming and IoT devices in the Metaverse environment.

Offline Functionality: Edge devices can continue to operate even when disconnected from the network, ensuring critical services remain available. This is crucial for Metaverse applications in remote locations or situations where network connectivity is unreliable.

Enhanced Security: Processing sensitive data locally reduces the risk of security breaches and data leaks. This is especially important for applications of Metaverse that handle confidential information [70].

Increased Scalability: The distributed nature of edge computing allows for easy scaling by adding more devices at the edge, and adapting to changing demands. This is crucial for Metaverse applications that require flexible and adaptable infrastructure.

9.10.1 Converging applications of cloud and edge computing in metaverse engineering

The metaverse, an increasing network of interconnected virtual worlds, promises to revolutionize how we interact, work, and play. However, its immersive, real-time experiences require a paradigm shift in computing infrastructure. The convergence of cloud and edge computing with metaverse engineering highlights its potential to overcome latency limitations and unlock new possibilities for this virtual frontier [67]. Cloud computing plays a crucial role in enabling this immersive and interactive experience by providing the necessary infrastructure and resources.

The metaverse demands a robust and scalable infrastructure to support the massive number of users and the demanding computational requirements of real-time simulations, graphics rendering, and data processing. Cloud computing provides the flexibility, scalability, and elasticity to address these challenges. Cloud-based services, such as HPC, artificial intelligence (AI), and machine learning (ML), can handle the immense computational demands of the metaverse [1–3].

Real-time simulations and graphics rendering are essential for creating immersive and realistic experiences in the metaverse. Cloud computing enables the processing of vast amounts of data to generate realistic graphics and simulate complex environments, allowing users to interact with objects and environments convincingly.

9.10.1.1 Computing, communication, and collaboration for cloud data in metaverse

The metaverse generates a vast amount of data, including user interactions, virtual world state, and digital assets. Cloud computing provides secure and scalable data storage solutions to manage this growing data volume and ensure data availability and accessibility. Cloud storage services offer the flexibility to store and retrieve data on demand, supporting the dynamic nature of the metaverse. The metaverse facilitates real-time collaboration and communication among users, enabling them to work together, socialize, and engage in shared experiences. Cloud-based collaboration tools, such as video conferencing and messaging platforms, enable seamless interaction and communication within the metaverse.

9.10.1.2 Converging extension of cloud towards edge computing for enhanced performance

To reduce latency and improve user experience, edge computing can be incorporated into the metaverse architecture. Edge computing brings computing resources closer to the users, reducing the need for data to travel long distances to and from the cloud. This can significantly improve the responsiveness and real-time performance of metaverse applications. The convergence of cloud computing and the metaverse is still in its early stages, but it holds immense potential to transform how we interact, work, and socialize. As the metaverse evolves, cloud computing will continue to play a critical role in providing the infrastructure, resources, and capabilities to support this immersive and interactive digital world.

9.10.1.3 Suitability of decentralized computing for metaverse

The metaverse envisions a persistent, dynamic, and highly interactive virtual space where users experience seamless interactions, real-time physics simulations, and intelligent AI agents. To achieve this, massive amounts of data need to be processed and analyzed in a real-time fashion. However, traditional centralized cloud computing architectures face latency challenges, hindering the responsiveness and immersion of the metaverse experience.

Imagine navigating a bustling virtual city where every movement, interaction, and environmental change needs to happen instantly. Lag or delay can break the illusion, creating a frustrating and disjointed experience. This is where edge computing comes in. Traditional cloud computing, where data is processed in centralized data centers far away from users, simply cannot keep up with the metaverse's demands. The physical distance between users and these centers introduces latency, the time it takes for data to travel back and forth, causing noticeable delays and hindering responsiveness.

9.10.2 Edge computing: Bridging the gap with decentralized processing

Edge computing offers a solution by placing processing power closer to the data source, at the network edge. As depicted in Figure 9.9, this decentralization provides several advantages for the metaverse applications such as:

- *Reduced Latency:* By processing data locally on edge devices, edge computing minimizes the time it takes for information to travel to and from central servers, resulting in significantly faster response times and smoother interactions.

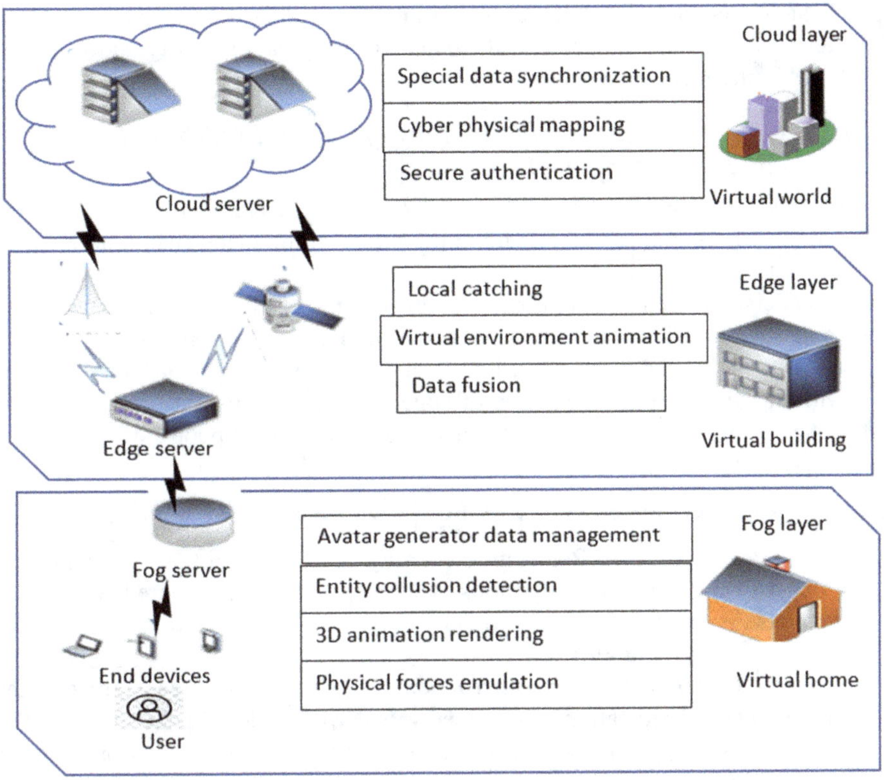

Figure 9.9 The proposed hybrid Fog-Edge architecture for metaverse applications [71]

- *Improved Scalability and Flexibility:* Edge computing allows for distributed processing across various devices, enabling the metaverse to scale efficiently and adapt to dynamic workloads.
- *Enhanced Security and Privacy:* Processing sensitive data locally on edge devices minimizes the risk of data breaches and improves user privacy.

9.10.3 Convergence and synergistic effects of the metaverse

The convergence of edge computing with other technologies further amplifies its impact in metaverse engineering:

Artificial Intelligence (AI): Edge computing can power AI-powered avatars, virtual assistants, and intelligent environments, enabling real-time decision-making and personalized experiences within the metaverse.

Internet of Things (IoT): Billions of connected devices at the edge can provide real-time data to the metaverse, enriching virtual worlds with environmental factors and facilitating seamless interactions between the physical and virtual realms.

Blockchain Technology: Secure and transparent data management through blockchain can be implemented at the edge, ensuring data integrity and fostering trust within the metaverse ecosystem.

9.10.4 Opportunities and challenges of 5G and 6G-based edge AI for metaverse

The advancements and convergence of 5G or 6G and edge artificial intelligence (AI) hold immense potential for shaping the future of the metaverse, a network of interconnected virtual worlds.

To understand the opportunities in advancements of ultra-modern networks in metaverse such as 5G or 6G, anyone needs to understand its functions. 5G or 6G with its ultra-high bandwidth, ultra-low latency, and pervasive connectivity, coupled with the distributed intelligence of edge AI, creates a potent cocktail for the metaverse. Let us try to redefine metaverse by exploring the opportunities of 5G or 6G-powered edge AI [67].

9.10.4.1 Opportunities of 5G or 6G-powered edge AI

- *Unbounded Immersion:* Real-time rendering of complex virtual environments, hyper-realistic physics simulations, and responsive AI-powered avatars of metaverse is achievable thanks to 5G or 6G's low latency and edge AI's real-time processing capabilities.
- *Seamless Collaboration and Interaction:* 5G or 6G's vast capacity enables massive user participation in the metaverse, while edge AI facilitates collaborative tasks, personalized experiences, and dynamic adaptation to user behavior in the metaverse.
- *Revolutionized Industries:* From healthcare and education to manufacturing and entertainment, various industries can leverage the combined power of 5G or 6G and edge AI to create transformative metaverse applications.

9.10.4.2 Bridging the gap and alleviating challenges of 5G- or 6G-powered edge AI

Despite the interesting opportunities, significant challenges need to be addressed in 5G- or 6G-powered edge AI [44,67]:

- *Infrastructure and Hardware:* Deploying a ubiquitous 5G or 6G network and developing energy-efficient edge AI hardware at scale for metaverse can pose significant infrastructure and technological challenges.
- *Security and Privacy:* Protecting user data, securing devices, and ensuring ethical AI practices within the metaverse require robust security protocols and transparent governance frameworks.
- *Resource Management and Optimization:* Efficiently allocating resources between distributed edge devices and optimizing computation for diverse metaverse applications remain essential areas of research.
- *Standardization and Interoperability:* Lack of standardized protocols for 5G or 6G and edge AI can hinder seamless data exchange and collaboration across platforms within the metaverse.

9.10.5 Futuristic research directions for 5G- or 6G-powered edge AI in the metaverse

Further research on the following dimensions is crucial to realize the full potential of this transformative technology [44,67]:

- *Heterogeneous Computing Architectures:* Developing efficient architectures that seamlessly integrate diverse computing resources at the edge and cloud will be critical for optimal performance.
- *Federated Computing and Collaborative AI*: Enabling secure and federated computing across edge devices without compromising user privacy will unlock data-driven intelligence within the metaverse.
- *Context-aware and Explainable AI:* Developing AI models that understand the contextual aspects of metaverse environments and provide transparent decision-making processes will be essential for user trust and ethical considerations.
- *Security and Privacy Enhancement Techniques:* Innovative cryptographic methods, secure multi-party computation, and secure enclave technologies will be required to build a secure and trusted metaverse infrastructure [72].

9.11 Data analytics fuels immersive experiences with fusion of computing

The metaverse, an expanding network of interconnected virtual worlds, is poised to revolutionize how we interact, work, and play. The crucial role of data analytics in shaping immersive experiences within the metaverse is an essential exercise in model data science. Exploring how it synergizes with spatial computing and edge computing to unlock its full potential in metaverse is an important aspect.

9.11.1 The data-driven meta: Beyond pixels and polygons

The metaverse excels in traditional graphical user interfaces and static content. It booms on real-time data streams, dynamic environments, and intelligent interactions, all powered by a robust data analytics infrastructure. This infrastructure goes beyond simply crunching numbers; it involves [73,74]:

Real-time Data Ingestion and Processing: Collecting and analyzing vast amounts of data generated by users, sensors, and virtual environments in real-time, requiring HPC capabilities. Thus, metaverse can use data capturing and analytical tools to uncover hidden insights through data analytics and knowing the behavior of the users and actors in the metaverse environment. Also, data analytics can help in improving the metaverse experiences.

Spatial Data Analysis: Understanding the spatial context of user interactions, object placements, and environmental changes within the metaverse, leveraging spatial computing technologies like virtual reality (VR) and augmented reality

(AR). This aspect can assist the metaverse system designers and engineers to improve the system progressively for the next generation of metaverse.

Predictive and Personalized Experiences: Leveraging data analytics can help to predict user behavior in advance, personalize experiences, and adapt virtual environments in real time, creating a dynamic and responsive metaverse.

9.11.2 The convergence data analytics of metaverse and mobile edge computing

A Fog-Edge hybrid computing architecture for metaverse applications leverages an edge-enabled distributed computing paradigm, utilizing edge devices' computing power to meet the required computational demands for heavy tasks, such as collision detection in a virtual universe and the computation of 3D physics in a virtual simulation. The latency count is the major issue to be handled carefully using real-time data analytics in "Transaction count" and "User count" for any computing, communication, or collaboration operation in the metaverse environment.

9.11.3 Data-driven immersion in spatial computing

Spatial computing technologies like VR and AR provide the sensory picture for data-driven experiences within the metaverse [75,76]:

VR Data Analysis and Visualization: VR environments can be designed based on user behavior and interaction data, creating visually compelling dashboards and immersive data visualizations.

AR-powered Contextual Insights: AR can overlay real-time data and analytics onto physical environments, enhancing user understanding and decision-making in the metaverse.

Spatial Data Structures and Algorithms: Developing efficient algorithms and data structures specifically for analyzing and utilizing spatial data within the metaverse is crucial for optimal performance.

9.11.4 Bringing intelligence to the virtual frontier using edge computing

Edge computing empowers real-time data processing and analysis closer to the source, playing a critical role in the metaverse [71,77]:

Low-Latency Analytics: By processing data at the edge, near users and virtual environments, edge computing minimizes latency, ensuring seamless and responsive interactions.

Decentralized Intelligence: Distributed edge computing platforms enable localized data analysis and decision-making within the metaverse, reducing reliance on centralized servers and improving scalability.

Privacy and Security Enhancements: Processing sensitive data at the edge minimizes the risk of data breaches and improves user privacy within the metaverse.

9.11.5 The data analytics in metaverse engineering

Data analytics plays a pivotal role in extracting meaningful insights from the vast datasets generated within the metaverse. By integrating analytics capabilities directly into edge devices, the metaverse gains the ability to derive actionable intelligence in real time.

Incorporating machine learning algorithms at the edge empowers the metaverse with on-the-fly data analysis. This enables adaptive and personalized experiences for users, as the system can dynamically respond to individual preferences and behaviors.

The metaverse generates vast amounts of data from user interactions, sensor readings, and environmental simulations. Data analytics plays a critical role in extracting insights from this data to improve the metaverse experience. Key applications of data analytics in the metaverse include:

- *User behavior analysis:* Understanding user behavior patterns helps personalize metaverse experiences, provide targeted recommendations, and identify potential issues.
- *Predictive analytics:* Predictive analytics can forecast trends, anticipate user needs, and optimize metaverse operations.
- *Anomaly detection:* Data analytics can detect anomalies and potential security threats in real time, ensuring the safety and integrity of the metaverse.

9.11.6 Navigating the data-driven metaverse

While the potential of data analytics in the metaverse is vast, challenges remain and hence these challenges are required to be alleviated:

Data Privacy and Security: Protecting user data within the metaverse and ensuring secure data collection and analysis processes require robust frameworks and ethical considerations.

Bias and Fairness in Algorithmic Decisions: Data-driven algorithms within the metaverse should be designed to be fair and unbiased, preventing discrimination and promoting inclusivity in virtual spaces.

9.11.7 Comparative analysis of computing paradigms in the metaverse engineering

The metaverse is a rapidly evolving concept that promises to revolutionize how we interact with the digital world. To support its complex demands, various computing paradigms are emerging, each with its own strengths and limitations. Here is a comparative table (Table 9.2) of Neuromorphic Computing, Spatial Computing, Quantum Computing, Edge Computing, and High-Performance Computing (HPC) in the context of the Metaverse.

Table 9.2 Feature-based comparative analysis of neuromorphic, spatial, edge, and HPC for the metaverse

Feature	Neuromorphic computing	Spatial computing	Quantum computing	Edge computing	High-Performance Computing (HPC)
Processing approach	Mimics the human brain's structure and function	Integrates physical space with digital information	Exploits the principles of quantum mechanics	Distributes processing power to the network edge	Employs powerful parallel processing architectures
Strengths	Efficient for real-time sensory processing and pattern recognition	Enables natural and intuitive interaction with virtual environments	Solves complex problems intractable for classical computers	Reduces latency and improves responsiveness for geographically distributed users	Delivers high computational power for demanding scientific and engineering simulations
Weaknesses	Still under development, limited programming tools	Requires specialized hardware and software, can be computationally expensive	Prone to errors, limited number of available qubits	Security and privacy concerns, limited network bandwidth at the edge	High energy consumption, complex infrastructure requirements
Data analytics for metaverse	Can handle unstructured, real-time sensory data from the physical world for avatar control, gesture recognition, and environment adaptation	Facilitates spatial data analysis and visualization for immersive experiences, navigation, and object manipulation	Can accelerate complex simulations and modeling for virtual world creation, physics simulation, and AI decision-making	Enables real-time data analysis at the edge for personalized experiences, anomaly detection, and edge-based AI	Provides powerful computational resources for large-scale data analysis, machine learning, and AI training for metaverse applications
Potential metaverse application	Autonomous avatars, haptic feedback, immersive virtual environments	Augmented reality experiences, spatial collaboration, 3D modeling and design	Drug discovery, materials science, financial modeling, AI for complex metaverse tasks	Real-time traffic management, smart cities, industrial automation, edge-based AI for metaverse interactions	Scientific research, climate modeling, engineering simulations, training large language models for metaverse AI

9.12 Metaverse technology disruptions: Reshaping realities, redefining interactions

The metaverse, an expanding network of interconnected virtual worlds, promises to blur the lines between the physical and digital, creating a wave of technological disruptions across various industries and paradigms.

New Frontiers of Human–Computer Interaction: The growing metaverse promises to upset our relationship with technology, splintering us beyond the boundaries of flat screens and into the heart of 3D virtual worlds. This disruptive force leverages a powerful store of technologies to blur the lines between real and virtual, fundamentally altering our perception of reality.

- *Virtual Reality (VR):* It leads this charge, crafting fully immersive digital realms experienced through headsets and controllers. These meticulously crafted landscapes indicate us, fostering a sense of embodiment and presence so profound that the physical world fades into the background. VR disrupts not just how we interact with technology, but how we experience the world itself.
- *Augmented Reality (AR*): On the other hand, AR does not eject the physical realm but rather augments it. Through smart glasses or mobile devices, AR seamlessly overlays digital information onto our surroundings, blurring the boundaries between real and virtual. Suddenly, our morning coffee table hosts a holographic chessboard, and city streets reveal hidden treasure hunts through our phone screens. AR disrupts not the existence of reality, but our perception of it.
- *Mixed Reality (MR):* Finally, MR emerges as the ultimate synthesis, seamlessly weaving VR and AR into a wall-hanging of interconnected realities. Digital objects seamlessly meld with physical spaces, enabling unparalleled collaboration and interaction between the two worlds. Imagine doctors performing surgery on holographic projections over a patient, or architects manipulating 3D models within the very room they are designing. MR disrupts not just the way we experience and interact with technology, but the very fabric of reality itself.

The metaverse, powered by these disruptive technologies, is not just another digital playground; it is a paradigm shift, poised to fundamentally reshape our relationship with technology and, perhaps, with reality itself. The question then becomes, are we ready to dive into this new reality, and what consequences, both positive and negative, await us on the other side?

Social Disruption: Redefining Communication and Collaboration: The metaverse fosters new forms of social interaction and collaboration:

- *Virtual Workspaces and Conferences:* Immersive meeting rooms and collaborative environments enable remote teams to work and interact side-by-side in virtual spaces, enhancing communication and engagement.
- *Social Events and Entertainment:* Virtual concerts, gatherings, and even shared gaming experiences bring people together across geographical boundaries, creating new avenues for community building and entertainment.

- *Digital Avatars and Identities:* Personalization takes center stage with customizable avatars that represent users within the metaverse, allowing for self-expression and exploration of new virtual identities.

Economic Disruption: New Markets and Opportunities: The metaverse opens doors to new economic models and revenue streams:

- *Virtual Economies and Decentralized Finance:* In-game currencies, digital assets, and blockchain-based transactions create thriving virtual economies within the metaverse, fostering new forms of ownership and financial interactions.
- *Virtual Real Estate and Marketplaces:* Digital land ownership and the development of virtual spaces within the metaverse can generate economic value, leading to the emergence of virtual real estate markets and related service industries.
- *Content Creation and Monetization:* Creators of virtual experiences, avatars, and digital assets can find new avenues for monetization within the metaverse, democratizing content creation and fostering a vibrant digital ecosystem.

Ethical and Psychological Disruptions: While the potential of metaverse technologies is vast, significant challenges remain:

- *Accessibility and Inclusivity:* Ensuring equitable access to the metaverse for users with disabilities and across different socioeconomic backgrounds requires careful consideration and development of inclusive technologies and experiences.
- *Privacy and Security:* Protecting user data and ensuring the security of virtual environments becomes paramount as more personal information and valuable assets exist within the metaverse.
- *Psychological and Social Impacts:* Potential issues like addiction to virtual experiences, social isolation, and the psychological effects of virtual interactions in the metaverse need careful study and ethical frameworks.

The metaverse represents a paradigm shift in human–computer interaction and offers transformative potential across various facets of society. By embracing the opportunities and addressing the challenges, we can navigate our future and lighten disruptions.

9.13 Conclusion

9.13.1 Building the metaverse—an art of computing and data analytics

As we stand at the precipice of the metaverse, an orchestra of diverse computing paradigms and data analytics takes center stage. Edge computing whispers near the nodes of reality, delivering lightning-fast responses and personalized experiences. Neuromorphic computing hums, mimicking the brain's dance to understand the ever-shifting virtual landscape. HPC orchestrates the grand simulations, crafting the intricate physics and vibrant worlds. Quantum computing, a wildcard maestro, promises solutions beyond classical limitations, while spatial computing seamlessly blends the digital and physical realms. Each paradigm plays its own vital role, but it is the data, the lifeblood of the metaverse, that binds them together. Data analytics, the gemstone of this digital world, translates every gesture, emotion, and interaction into actionable insights. By understanding the language of data, we refine avatars, personalize experiences, and build a metaverse that learns and adapts with each beat of its virtual heart.

However, amidst the art's climax, challenges remain. Security concerns need to be addressed, ethical considerations harmonized, and the digital divide bridged. Just as a conductor guides the orchestra, responsible development, and collaboration are crucial to prevent technological dissonance.

Ultimately, the success of the metaverse hinges on building bridges between these diverse paradigms, weaving them into an embroidery of computational power and data-driven intelligence. By fostering an environment of innovation and collaboration, we can ensure that the metaverse becomes not just a technological marvel, but a platform for human connection, creativity, and shared experiences beyond the limitations of our physical world. The final note of this chapter is not an ending, but a call to action: let us craft a metaverse that resonates with humanity, where computing and data analytics are not merely tools, but instruments in the art of a brighter future.

References

[1] R. Petersen, D. Santos, M. C. Smith, K. A. Wetzel, and G. Witte, "Workforce framework for cybersecurity (NICE Framework)," Gaithersburg, MD: National Institute of Standards and Technology, 2020. Available from: https://nvlpubs.nist.gov/nistpubs/SpecialPublications/NIST.SP.800-181r1.pdf.

[2] D. P. Sharma, A. J. Alade, and R. K. Sharma, "Convergence of intranetware in project management for effective enterprise management." *Journal of Global Information Technology (JGIT)-USA*, vol. 4, pp. 65–85, 2009.

[3] M. U. Bokhari, Q. Makki, and Y. K. Tamandani, "A survey on cloud computing," in *Advances in Intelligent Systems and Computing*, vol. 654, pp. 149–164, 2018. doi: 10.1007/978-981-10-6620-7_16.

[4] W. Shi, G. Pallis, and Z. Xu, "Edge computing [scanning the issue]," *Proc IEEE*, vol. 107, no. 8, pp. 1474–1481, 2019, doi: 10.1109/jproc.2019.2928287.

[5] E. O. Neftci, "Data and power efficient intelligence with neuromorphic learning machines," *iScience*, vol. 5, pp. 52–68, 2018, doi: 10.1016/J.ISCI.2018.06.010.

[6] B. Zygelman, "A quantum mechanic's toolbox," *A First Introduction to Quantum Computing and Information*. Cham: Springer; 2018, pp. 1–22, doi: 10.1007/978-3-319-91629-3_1.

[7] Y. Morikawa, M. Koh, H. Hashimoto, *et al.*, "A novel chiplet integration architecture employing pillar-suspended bridge with polymer fine-via

interconnect," in *Proceedings – Electronic Components and Technology Conference*, vol. 2023, pp. 34–39, 2023, doi: 10.1109/ECTC51909.2023.00014.

[8] Y. K. Dwivedi, L. Hughes, A. M. Baabdullah, *et al.*, "Metaverse beyond the hype: Multidisciplinary perspectives on emerging challenges, opportunities, and agenda for research, practice and policy," *Int J Inf Manage*, vol. 66, p. 102542, 2022, doi: 10.1016/J.IJINFOMGT.2022.102542.

[9] A. Mooij, "What is the metaverse?" *Regulating the Metaverse Economy*. Cham: Springer; 2024, pp. 5–10. doi: 10.1007/978-3-031-46417-1_2.

[10] R. T. Kreutzer and S. Klose, "What it is about," *Next Stop Metaverse. Business Guides on the Go*. Wiesbaden: Springer; 2023, pp. 1–20, doi: 10.1007/978-3-658-41180-0_1.

[11] "Metaverse market revenue worldwide from 2022 to 2032," Statista. Accessed: Jan. 10, 2024. [Online]. Available: https://www.statista.com/statistics/1295784/metaverse-market-size/

[12] "Global Future Council on the Future of Metaverse," World Economic Forum. Accessed: Jan. 10, 2024. [Online]. Available: https://www.weforum.org/communities/global-future-council-on-the-future-of-the-metaverse/

[13] The Institution of Engineering and Technology. *Safeguarding the Metaverse. IET*, 2022. Available: https://www.theiet.org/media/9836/safeguarding-the-metaverse.pdf.

[14] A. G. Atiyah, "Unveiling the quality perception of productivity from the senses of real-time multisensory social interactions strategies in metaverse," *Beyond Reality: Navigating the Power of Metaverse and Its Applications*. Cham: Springer; 2023, pp. 83–93, doi: 10.1007/978-3-031-51300-8_6.

[15] S. M. Park and Y. G. Kim, "A metaverse: Taxonomy, components, applications, and open challenges," *IEEE Access*, vol. 10, pp. 4209–4251, 2022, doi: 10.1109/ACCESS.2021.3140175.

[16] J. Simbaqueba-Uribe, A. Alvarez-Risco, S. Del-Aguila-Arcentales, M. Rojas-Osorio, C. R. Mejia, and J. A. Yañez, "Training courses by metaverse: intention of consumers in Colombia," *Dev Stud Res*, vol. 11, no. 1, 2024, doi: 10.1080/21665095.2023.2292474.

[17] S. H. Chang, C. W. Chang, H. H. Chen, and M. C. Wu, "Measuring the importance of smart E-learning education system," *ACM International Conference Proceeding Series*, pp. 421–428, 2022, doi: 10.1145/3568739.3568810.

[18] T. Hennig-Thurau, D. N. Aliman, A. M. Herting, G. P. Cziehso, M. Linder, and R. V. Kübler, "Social interactions in the metaverse: Framework, initial evidence, and research roadmap," *J Acad Mark Sci*, vol. 51, no. 4, pp. 889–913, 2023, doi: 10.1007/S11747-022-00908-0/TABLES/5.

[19] S. Gloeckler and N. Biller-Andorno, "Mental health services in the metaverse: potential and concerns," *Swiss Med Wkly*, vol. 153, no. 4, pp. 40089–40089, 2023, doi: 10.57187/SMW.2023.40089.

[20] O. S. Albahri and A. H. AlAmoodi, "Navigating the metaverse of big data: A bibliometric journey," *Mesopotamian J Big Data*, vol. 2023, pp. 92–106, 2023, doi: 10.58496/MJBD/2023/013.

[21] B. Chen, C. Song, B. Lin, *et al.*, "A cross-platform metaverse data management system," *2022 IEEE International Workshop on Metrology for Extended Reality, Artificial Intelligence and Neural Engineering, MetroXRAINE 2022 - Proceedings*, pp. 145–150, 2022, doi: 10.1109/METROXRAINE54828.2022.9967588.

[22] A. Kusiak, "Manufacturing metaverse," *J Intell Manuf*, vol. 34, no. 6, pp. 2511–2512, 2023, doi: 10.1007/S10845-023-02145-W/TABLES/1.

[23] M. Montola, "A ludological view on the pervasive mixed-reality game research paradigm," *Pers Ubiquitous Comput*, vol. 15, no. 1, pp. 3–12, 2011, doi: 10.1007/S00779-010-0307-7/METRICS.

[24] A. M. Al-Ansi, M. Jaboob, A. Garad, and A. Al-Ansi, "Analyzing augmented reality (AR) and virtual reality (VR) recent development in education," *Soc Sci Human Open*, vol. 8, no. 1, p. 100532, 2023, doi: 10.1016/J.SSAHO.2023.100532.

[25] M. Uddin, S. Manickam, H. Ullah, M. Obaidat, and A. Dandoush, "Unveiling the metaverse: Exploring emerging trends, multifaceted perspectives, and future challenges," *IEEE Access*, vol. 11. pp. 87087–87103, 2023. doi: 10.1109/ACCESS.2023.3281303.

[26] G. Moreno de Oliveira, A. Nascimento Carvalho, B. S. Lamego, I. T. Monteiro, E. J. T. Gonçalves, and A. F. Basilio, "Reporting the application of user experience tools and proxy users in an industrial process based on double diamond," *Lecture Notes in Computer Science (including subseries Lecture Notes in Artificial Intelligence and Lecture Notes in Bioinformatics)*, vol. 13321 LNCS, pp. 57–74, 2022, doi:10.1007/978-3-031-05897-4_5/COVER.

[27] M. Hendrix, T. Bellamy-Wood, S. McKay, V. Bloom, and I. Dunwell, "Implementing adaptive game difficulty balancing in serious games," *IEEE Trans Games*, vol. 11, no. 4, pp. 320–327, 2019, doi: 10.1109/TG.2018.2791019.

[28] A. Mooij, "Integration into the legal economy," *Regulating the Metaverse Economy*. Cham: Springer; 2024, pp. 87–99, doi: 10.1007/978-3-031-46417-1_7.

[29] N. de A. B. Navarro, C. A. da Costa, J. L. V. Barbosa, and R. da R. Righi, "Spontaneous social network: Toward dynamic virtual communities based on context-aware computing," *Expert Syst Appl*, vol. 95, pp. 72–87, 2018, doi: 10.1016/J.ESWA.2017.11.017.

[30] J. Hutson and P. Hutson, "Immersive technologies," *Inclusive Smart Mus*, pp. 153–228, 2024, doi: 10.1007/978-3-031-43615-4_5.

[31] A. Alismail, E. Altulaihan, M. M. H. Rahman, and A. Sufian, "A systematic literature review on cybersecurity threats of virtual reality (VR) and augmented reality (AR)," *Data Intelligence and Cognitive Informatics*. Singapore: Springer; 2023, pp. 761–774, doi: 10.1007/978-981-19-6004-8_57.

[32] Y. Wang, Z. Su, N. Zhang, *et al.*, "A survey on metaverse: Fundamentals, security, and privacy," *IEEE Commun Surv Tutor*, vol. 25, no. 1, pp. 319–352, 2023, doi: 10.1109/COMST.2022.3202047.

[33] J. R. Jim, M. T. Hosain, M. F. Mridha, M. M. Kabir, and J. Shin, "Toward trustworthy metaverse: Advancements and challenges," *IEEE Access*, vol. 11, pp. 118318–118347, 2023, doi: 10.1109/ACCESS.2023.3326258.

[34] G. Chemmalar Selvi, G. Yenduri, G. Srivastava, *et al.*, "Explainable AI for the metaverse: A short survey," *2023 International Conference on Intelligent Metaverse Technologies and Applications, iMETA 2023*, 2023, doi: 10.1109/IMETA59369.2023.10294907.

[35] J. N. Njoku, C. I. Nwakanma, G. C. Amaizu, and D. S. Kim, "Prospects and challenges of metaverse application in data-driven intelligent transportation systems," *IET Intell Transport Syst*, vol. 17, no. 1, pp. 1–21, 2023, doi: 10.1049/ITR2.12252.

[36] J. Knox, "The metaverse, or the serious business of tech frontiers," *Postdigital Sci Educ*, vol. 4, no. 2, pp. 207–215, 2022, doi: 10.1007/S42438-022-00300-9/METRICS.

[37] C. D. Schuman, S. R. Kulkarni, M. Parsa, J. P. Mitchell, P. Date, and B. Kay, "Opportunities for neuromorphic computing algorithms and applications," *Nat Comput Sci*, vol. 2, no. 1, pp. 10–19, 2022, doi: 10.1038/s43588-021-00184-y.

[38] H. Tang, T. Huang, J. L. Krichmar, G. Orchard, and A. Basu, "Guest editorial special issue on neuromorphic computing and cognitive systems," *IEEE Trans Cogn Dev Syst*, vol. 10, no. 2, pp. 122–124, 2018, doi: 10.1109/TCDS.2018.2835107.

[39] J. Kaiser, R. Stock, E. Müller, J. Schemmel, and S. Schmitt, "Simulation-based inference for model parameterization on analog neuromorphic hardware," *Neuromorphic Comput Eng*, vol. 3, no. 4, p. 044006, 2023, doi: 10.1088/2634-4386/AD046D.

[40] Z. Wang, X. Shi, X. Yao, Z. Wang, X. Shi, and X. Yao, "A brain-inspired hardware architecture for evolutionary algorithms based on memristive arrays," *ACM Transact Des Autom Electron Syst*, vol. 28, no. 5, 2023, doi: 10.1145/3598421.

[41] D. Ivanov, A. Chezhegov, M. Kiselev, A. Grunin, and D. Larionov, "Neuromorphic artificial intelligence systems," *Front Neurosci*, vol. 16, p. 959626, 2022, doi:10.3389/FNINS.2022.959626/BIBTEX.

[42] M. D. Godfrey and D. F. Hendry, "The Computer as von Neumann planned it," *IEEE Ann Hist Comput*, vol. 15, no. 1, pp. 11–21, 1993, doi: 10.1109/85.194088.

[43] R. V. Kutluyarov, A. G. Zakoyan, G. S. Voronkov, E. P. Grakhova, and M. A. Butt, "Neuromorphic photonics circuits: Contemporary review," *Nanomaterials*, vol. 13, no. 24, 2023, doi:10.3390/NANO13243139.

[44] T. Huynh-The, Q. V. Pham, X. Q. Pham, T. T. Nguyen, Z. Han, and D. S. Kim, "Artificial intelligence for the metaverse: A survey," *Eng Appl Artif Intell*, vol. 117, p. 105581, 2023, doi: 10.1016/J.ENGAPPAI.2022.105581.

[45] R. E. Pino, G. Genello, M. Bishop, M. J. Moore, and R. Linderman, "Emerging neuromorphic computing architectures & enabling hardware for cognitive information processing applications," *2010 2nd International*

Workshop on Cognitive Information Processing, CIP2010, pp. 35–39, 2010, doi: 10.1109/CIP.2010.5604236.

[46] D. V. Christensen, R. Dittmann, B. Linares-Barranco, *et al.*, "2022 roadmap on neuromorphic computing and engineering," *Neuromorphic Comput Eng*, vol. 2, no. 2, 2022, doi:10.1088/2634-4386/AC4A83.

[47] M. Getahun, M. Azath, D. P. Sharma, A. Tuni, and A. Adane, "Efficient energy utilization algorithm through energy harvesting for heterogeneous clustered wireless sensor network," *Wirel Commun Mob Comput*, vol. 2022, 2022, doi:10.1155/2022/4154742.

[48] A. T. Rabadán and A. Ammar, "Neurochips: An ethical consideration," *Learning and Career Development in Neurosurgery: Values-Based Medical Education*, pp. 101–109, 2022, doi: 10.1007/978-3-031-02078-0_11/COVER.

[49] V. R. Verma, D. P. Sharma, and C. S. Lamba, "QOS improvement in MANET routing by route optimization through convergence of mobile agent," *2018 5th IEEE Uttar Pradesh Section International Conference on Electrical, Electronics and Computer Engineering, UPCON 2018*, 2018, doi: 10.1109/UPCON.2018.8596852.

[50] M. Serda, G. Balint, B. Antala, *et al.*, "Synteza i aktywność biologiczna nowych analogów tiosemikarbazonowych chelatorów żelaza," *Uniwersytet śląski*, vol. 7, no. 1, pp. 343–354, 2013.

[51] U. Cali, M. Kuzlu, E. Karaarslan, and V. Jovanovic, "Opportunities and challenges in metaverse for Industry 4.0 and beyond applications," *2022 IEEE 1st Global Emerging Technology Blockchain Forum: Blockchain and Beyond, iGETblockchain 2022*, 2022, doi: 10.1109/IGETBLOCKCHAIN56591.2022.10087104.

[52] S. Banaeian Far, A. Imani Rad, S. M. Hosseini Bamakan, and M. Rajabzadeh Asaar, "Toward Metaverse of everything: Opportunities, challenges, and future directions of the next generation of visual/virtual communications," *J Netw Comput Appl*, vol. 217, p. 103675, 2023, doi: 10.1016/J.JNCA.2023.103675.

[53] G. Indiveri, "Introducing 'neuromorphic computing and engineering,'" *Neuromorphic Comput Eng,* vol. 1, no. 1, p. 010401, 2021, doi:10.1088/2634-4386/AC0A5B.

[54] E. Painkras, L. A. Plana, J. Garside, *et al.*, "SpiNNaker: A 1-W 18-core system-on-chip for massively-parallel neural network simulation," *IEEE J Solid-State Circuits*, vol. 48, no. 8, pp. 1943–1953, 2013, doi: 10.1109/JSSC.2013.2259038.

[55] M. Kjaergaard, M. E. Schwartz, J. Braumüller, *et al.*, "Superconducting qubits: current state of play," *Annual Review of Condensed Matter Physics*, vol. 11, pp. 369–395, 2020, doi: 10.1146/annurev-conmatphys-031119-050605.

[56] M. Chehimi and W. Saad, "Quantum technologies for the metaverse: Opportunities and challenges," *Metaverse Communication and Computing Networks: Applications, Technologies, and Approaches*, pp. 267–291, 2023, doi: 10.1002/9781394160013.CH11.

[57] Y. Liu and K. L. Siau, "Generative artificial intelligence and metaverse: Future of work, future of society, and future of humanity," *Commun Comput Inform Sci*, vol. 1946 CCIS, pp. 118–127, 2024, doi: 10.1007/978-981-99-7587-7_10.

[58] J. Zhao and W. Yu, "Quantum multi-agent reinforcement learning as an emerging AI technology: A survey and future directions," *Authorea Preprints*, 2023, doi: 10.36227/TECHRXIV.24563293.V1.

[59] S. Sihare and A. Khang, "Effects of quantum technology on the metaverse," *Handbook of Research on AI-Based Technologies and Applications in the Era of the Metaverse*. Hershey, PA: IGI Global, 2023, pp. 174–203, doi: 10.4018/978-1-6684-8851-5.CH009.

[60] Y. Meng, Z. Qu, G. Muhammad, and P. Tiwari, "Secure and efficient data transmission based on quantum dialogue with hyperentangled states in cloud office," *Internet of Things*, vol. 24, p. 100911, 2023, doi: 10.1016/J.IOT.2023.100911.

[61] K. S. Mohamed, "Deep learning for spatial computing: augmented reality and metaverse 'the digital universe,'" *Deep Learning-Powered Technologies*. Cham: Springer; 2023, pp. 131–150, doi: 10.1007/978-3-031-35737-4_4.

[62] M. Abrash, "Creating the future: Augmented reality, the next human-machine interface," *Technical Digest – International Electron Devices Meeting, IEDM*, vol. 2021, pp. 1.2.1–1.2.11, 2021, doi: 10.1109/IEDM19574.2021.9720526.

[63] L. Turchet, "Musical Metaverse: vision, opportunities, and challenges," *Pers Ubiquitous Comput*, vol. 27, no. 5, pp. 1811–1827, 2023, doi: 10.1007/S00779-023-01708-1/TABLES/1.

[64] "The Spatial Web and Web 3.0 A report from the Deloitte Center for Integrated Research." [Online]. Available: www.deloitte.com/us/cir.

[65] P. O. A. Navaux, A. F. Lorenzon, and M. da S. Serpa, "Challenges in high-performance computing," *J Braz Comput Soc*, vol. 29, no. 1, pp. 51–62, 2023, doi: 10.5753/JBCS.2023.2219.

[66] "A research framework for exascale simulations of distributed virtual world environments on high performance computing (HPC) clusters, *Proceedings of the Symposium on High Performance Computing*." Accessed: Jan. 10, 2024. [Online]. Available: https://dl.acm.org/doi/abs/10.5555/2872599.2872603

[67] L. Chang, Z. Zhang, P. Li, *et al.*, "6G-enabled edge AI for metaverse: Challenges, methods, and future research directions," *Journal of Communications and Information Networks*, vol. 7, no. 2, pp. 107–121, 2022.

[68] A. Mukherjee, D. De, S. K. Ghosh, and R. Buyya, "Introduction to mobile edge computing," *Mobile Edge Comput*, pp. 3–19, 2021, doi: 10.1007/978-3-030-69893-5_1/COVER.

[69] M. Alkhalaileh, R. N. Calheiros, Q. V. Nguyen, and B. Javadi, "Performance analysis of mobile, edge and cloud computing platforms for distributed applications," *Mobile Edge Comput*, pp. 21–45, 2021, doi: 10.1007/978-3-030-69893-5_2/COVER.

[70] N. Sharma, M. Sharma, and D. P. Sharma, "A trust-based scheme for spotting malicious node of wormhole in dynamic source routing protocol," *Proceedings of the 4th International Conference on IoT in Social, Mobile, Analytics and Cloud, ISMAC 2020*, pp. 1232–1237, 2020, doi: 10.1109/I-SMAC49090.2020.9243369.

[71] S. Karunarathna, S. Wijethilaka, P. Ranaweera, K. T. Hemachandra, T. Samarasinghe, and M. Liyanage, "The role of network slicing and edge computing in the metaverse realization," *IEEE Access*, vol. 11, pp. 25502–25530, 2023, doi: 10.1109/ACCESS.2023.3255510.

[72] T. Parlar, "Data privacy and security in the metaverse," *Stud Big Data*, vol. 133, pp. 123–133, 2023, doi: 10.1007/978-981-99-4641-9_8/COVER.

[73] M. Zhou, "Editorial: Evolution from AI, IoT and big data analytics to metaverse," *IEEE/CAA J Autom Sin*, vol. 9, no. 12. pp. 2041–2042, 2022. doi: 10.1109/JAS.2022.106100.

[74] D. Datta and M. Bhattacharya, "Development of cognitive intelligent mechanism for sustainability of bigdata: A future shape of metaverse," *Stud Big Data*, vol. 123, pp. 3–25, 2023, doi: 10.1007/978-3-031-29132-6_1/COVER.

[75] S. Banaeian Far, A. Imani Rad, and M. Rajabzadeh Asaar, "Blockchain and its derived technologies shape the future generation of digital businesses: A focus on decentralized finance and the metaverse," *Data Sci Manag*, vol. 6, no. 3, pp. 183–197, 2023, doi: 10.1016/J.DSM.2023.06.002.

[76] G. Gim, H. Bae, and S. Kang, "Metaverse learning: The relationship among quality of VR-based education, self-determination, and learner satisfaction," *Proceedings – 2022 IEEE/ACIS 7th International Conference on Big Data, Cloud Computing, and Data Science, BCD 2022*, pp. 279–284, 2022, doi: 10.1109/BCD54882.2022.9900629.

[77] Z. Yi, Y. Qian, M. Chen, S. A. Alqahtani, and M. S. Hossain, "Defending edge computing based metaverse AI against adversarial attacks," *Ad Hoc Netw*, vol. 150, p. 103263, 2023, doi: 10.1016/J.ADHOC.2023.103263.

[78] N. Aung, S. Dhelim, L. Chen, H. Ning, L. Atzori, and T. Kechadi, "Edge-enabled metaverse: The convergence of metaverse and mobile edge computing," *Tsinghua Sci Technol*, vol. 29, no. 3, pp. 795–805, 2022, doi: 10.26599/TST.2023.9010052.

Chapter 10

The convergence of Web 3.0 with AR, VR, IoT, and AI for shaping metaverse engineering

D.P. Sharma[1]

Abstract

The convergence of Web 3.0, Augmented Reality (AR), Virtual Reality (VR), Internet of Things (IoT), and Artificial Intelligence (AI) is composed to revolutionize metaverse engineering, creating immersive, interactive, and intelligent virtual environments. This chapter explores these technologies' collaborative potential, unique contributions, and how they can be integrated to address the computational challenges inherent in building scalable, real-time, and personalized metaverse environments. Web 3.0, with its decentralized and user-centric approach, offers a foundation for a more reasonable and transparent metaverse. AR and VR provide immersive experiences, blurring the lines between the physical and digital worlds. IoT enables the unified integration of physical objects into the metaverse, enhancing interactivity and realism. AI drives intelligent behavior within the metaverse, enabling personalized experiences, natural language interactions, and autonomous agents. The chapter discusses the key challenges and opportunities arising from the convergence of these technologies, including data privacy, scalability, interoperability, and ethical considerations. It explores potential use cases in various domains, such as gaming, education, healthcare, and social networking. By understanding the relationship between Web 3.0, AR, VR, IoT, and AI, we can visualize a future metaverse that is more decentralized, immersive, intelligent, and user-centric.

Keywords: Web 3.0; Augmented Reality; Virtual Reality; IoT; Artificial Intelligence; Metaverse; Convergence

10.1 Introduction

Change is the universal law of the universe. The concepts of science and technology are evolving quickly and transforming the world with mutual convergences. Amongst the numerous technologies, the metaverse is rapidly emerging and revolutionizing the world of computing, communication, and collaboration. The

[1]Computer Scientist, and Digital Diplomacy Expert, Jaipur, Rajasthan, India

metaverse is a shared virtual world that is envisioned to be the next generation of the internet and its allied networks. In the fast-changing technological world, the internet is undergoing a substantial transformation. These changes and transformations are driven by the advent of numerous technologies and Web 3.0 and its convergence with the metaverse is one of them.

The metaverse is a converged version of two distinct real and virtual worlds. The term 'Meta' refers to begin, vital, and consume. The convergence of Web 3.0 with the metaverse creates a new paradigm of the unimaginable and ubiquitously smarter and interactive world experience. In addition, the Web 3.0 building blocks offer lower-level support for designing and developing the metaverse featured applications. Numerous technologies such as augmented reality (AR), virtual reality (VR), and mixed reality (MR) have created a new world of amazing and incredible experiences of teaching, learning, entertaining, singing, dancing, etc. Also, in the connected world of people and systems, security and privacy of data are the two most important concerns today and almost certainly decentralized architecture of Web 3.0 plays a vital role in ensuring data protection and hence promotes metaverse security where anyone can enjoy control over their data usage privacy [1].

Starting from Web 1.0, the existing Web 2.0 was all about connecting people in which the social media platforms were invented, and the attention of extension was focused only on the application layer. Since Web 3.0 can be defined as an emerging technology and is still being developed, there is no universally accepted definition. Even the proper spelling and pronunciation are not still fixed and standardized. Organizations such as Forrester, Gartner, and IDC are switching between "Web3" and "Web 3.0." The new Web 3.0 or Web3 is referred to as distributed web technology primarily operated by decentralized blockchain and Artificial Intelligence. Today, Web 3.0 technologies have been revolutionizing and re-engineering industry 4.0, especially business, commerce, and digital currencies [2].

Today, Science and Technology are revolutionizing the way we work and think in the globalized world. The next generation's changes and transformations are inevitable and irreversible. Web 3.0 and the Metaverse are two distinct paradigms of the most exciting developments of the current era. The metaverse is a convergence or interconnection of the virtual and physical world, and it has the potential to revolutionize the way we interact with each other and with the world around us. The converging technologies of Web 3.0, such as artificial intelligence (AI), blockchain, machine learning (ML), or deep learning (DL) can play a critical role in the design, development, and adoption of the metaverse and its engineering and re-engineering aspects.

The metaverse, a budding yet exciting vision, promises to revolutionize how people interact, work, and play. To realize this ambitious dream, a potent convergence of cutting-edge technologies is taking center stage such as Web 3.0, TensorFlow, AWS SageMaker, and Blockchain. To embark on a tech journey through these key enablers, the key goal is to explore their transformative potential in shaping the metaverse landscape. Moving beyond the limitations of the centralized Web 1.0 and Web 2.0, Web 3.0 is in an era of distributed power and user-centricity. Imagine a metaverse built on open-source protocols, empowering users to own their data and participate actively in its governance [1]. Web 3.0 and its vision is to create a more open, secure, and democratic internet where users have full control over their data, information, and interactions. It is creating a new world where people can interact with each other, work, play virtual games, and devour content in more immersive ways. Web 3.0's prime goal is to develop a new internet infrastructure that is more secure, user-centric, and decentralized than the current web, facilitating individuals to own and control their data with greater ease [3].

Given cross-disciplinary convergence, Artificial Intelligence (AI) and Machine Learning (ML) or Deep Learning (DL) can be explored to create more immersive and realistic experiences in the metaverse domain. Towards building the master controller brains of the metaverse, Artificial Intelligence tools and Machine Learning (ML) techniques play a key role. Machine learning can be perceived as the lifeblood of the metaverse, and TensorFlow, a powerful open-source platform, fuels its intelligent core. From the inception of powering natural language processing for conversational AI avatars to driving content creation algorithms, TensorFlow plays a crucial role in shaping the dynamic and responsive virtual worlds of the metaverse [4].

AI needs huge computation power and easily upgradable and scalable high-performance machines with simplified AI development platforms. Developing and deploying the complex AI models needed for the metaverse can be discouraging if the computing, communication, and collaboration infrastructure is not on-demand scalable, with simple and desired performance. Amazon's AWS SageMaker, a comprehensive cloud platform that democratizes access to high-performance computing resources and simplifies the AI development lifecycle can be an alternative technology platform to make metaverse happen. Using SageMaker, even smaller teams can harness the full power of AI to build and scale their metaverse applications [5].

Trust and Security are the two major concerns in the metaverse world. Usually, a Blockchain offers a secure and transparent mechanism to manage and govern the digital assets and identities in the metaverse. The decentralized and secure nature of emerging blockchain technology provides a robust foundation for the metaverse environment. Starting from managing digital assets to ensuring secure peer-to-peer interactions, blockchain plays a critical role in promoting trust and security within the virtual world [6].

The emergence of these technologies is not mere bricks; they are the intertwined threads weaving the embroidery of the metaverse. Thus, weaving them together, Web 3.0 lays the decentralized basis, TensorFlow builds the intelligent models, AWS SageMaker empowers its creation, and Blockchain ensures its secure and trustworthy operations in the metaverse environment. This journey into the metaverse is just beginning, as these technologies evolve and converge, the possibilities for immersive experiences, meaningful connections, and even new forms of work and leisure become boundless. Therefore, try to brace yourselves, for the metaverse awaits, built on the converging foundation of Web 3.0, TensorFlow, AWS SageMaker, Blockchain, etc. in a new era of digital possibility.

The emerging business and technology complement each other in the connected world via the internet. Research of ReportLink indicates that the metaverse market could be worth 758.6 billion dollars by 2026. The future of metaverse engineering predicted by the research of Forbes, and GrayScale reaches up to a trillion dollars [7].

This chapter explores the synergy between the two distinct but interrelated concepts, i.e., Web 3.0 and Metaverse, and scrutinizes how they are trying to reshape the future of online systems and their augmented interactions. The key concepts, definitions, core and allied technologies along with the opportunities and challenges for Web 3.0 in the metaverse world are reviewed and described. Further, it discusses how numerous technologies such as Blockchain, Artificial intelligence, TensorFlow, AWS SageMaker, and Machine Learning can be explored to uncover the challenges and bridge them in constructing a user-friendly, secure, and promisingly scalable metaverse world [8].

10.2 Defining the metaverse

The metaverse is a hot topic of emerging technology, but pinning down a single, universally accepted definition can be difficult. The term "Metaverse" is still evolving, with various interpretations and perspectives. However, several standard publications define Metaverse by offering valuable insights from a technical perspective. However, here is a general and ideal definition: "At its core, the metaverse is envisioned as a network of interconnected, immersive virtual worlds where people can live, work, play, and socialize as avatars. Think of it as a 3D version of the internet, where physical and digital realities converge" [2,9].

10.3 Foundation of the metaverse

The foundation of the metaverse is a complex and multifaceted topic, with various layers contributing to its potential. Here are some key aspects to be considered for understanding the foundation design of the metaverse:

10.3.1 Technological foundations of metaverse

10.3.1.1 Connectivity

For the metaverse, a high-speed, low-latency internet infrastructure is crucial for seamless real-time interactions and immersive experiences. As depicted in Figure 10.1, advancements like 5G, 6G, and fiber optic networks are ways the way for the metaverse to evolve.

10.3.1.2 Computing power

The metaverse requires powerful, i.e., high-performance computing resources to extract complex virtual worlds, handle large datasets, and support huge AI capabilities. As depicted in Figure 10.2, cloud computing, distributed computing, and edge computing are the master enablers of on-demand high-performance computing.

Figure 10.1 High communication networks

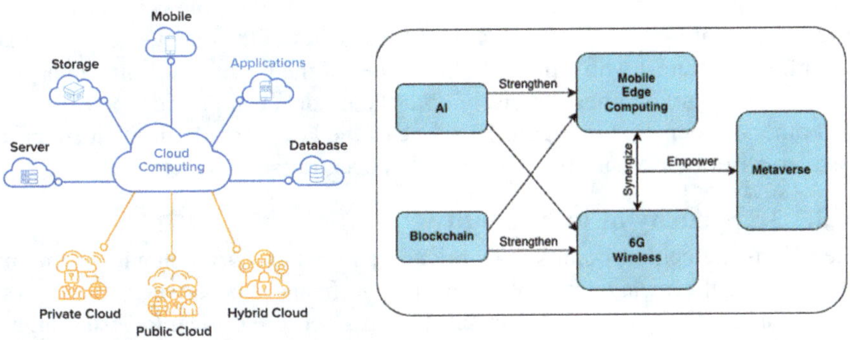

Figure 10.2 Cloud computing, distributed computing, and edge computing networks

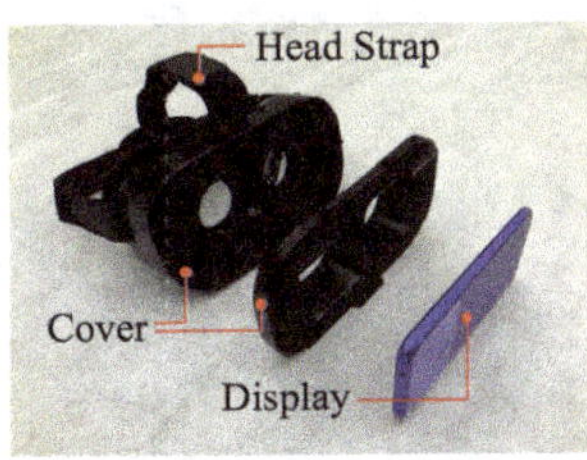

Figure 10.3 A virtual reality headset

10.3.1.3 Physical infrastructure resources

VR headsets, AR glasses, haptic suits, and other immersive technology are essential gateway instruments for the metaverse. A VR headset is depicted in Figure 10.3. Further advancements in these instruments will make the experience more natural and accessible.

10.3.1.4 Software platforms

Software entities are essential to run the metaverse instruments. Development platforms like Unity, Unreal Engine, and SpatialOS are laying the groundwork for building and interacting within the metaverse.

10.3.2 Conceptual foundations of metaverse [10]

10.3.2.1 Interoperability standards

Permitting users and content to move seamlessly between different metaverse platforms and experiences is vital for a unified, integrated, and thriving ecosystem. To make it happen, open standards and protocols are significant.

10.3.2.2 Centralization and decentralization

Both the Centralization and Decentralization models have their own merits and demerits while designing the metaverse environment. Still, the core tech designers have been debating on control and governance issues of the metaverse. It is a matter of conflict of interest who will be the controller of the metaverse, companies, or the decentralized communities. Precisely both the models can provide their benefits to each other. As depicted in Figure 10.4, one of the key technologies that support the metaverse is a blockchain that facilitates a decentralized architecture.

10.3.2.3 Security of user identity

The user is the central point whose privacy and data security should be the major concerns. In the metaverse environment, significant aspects such as ownership, privacy, and security of users' data and virtual assets are critical to ensure high-end trust and prevent undue exploitation.

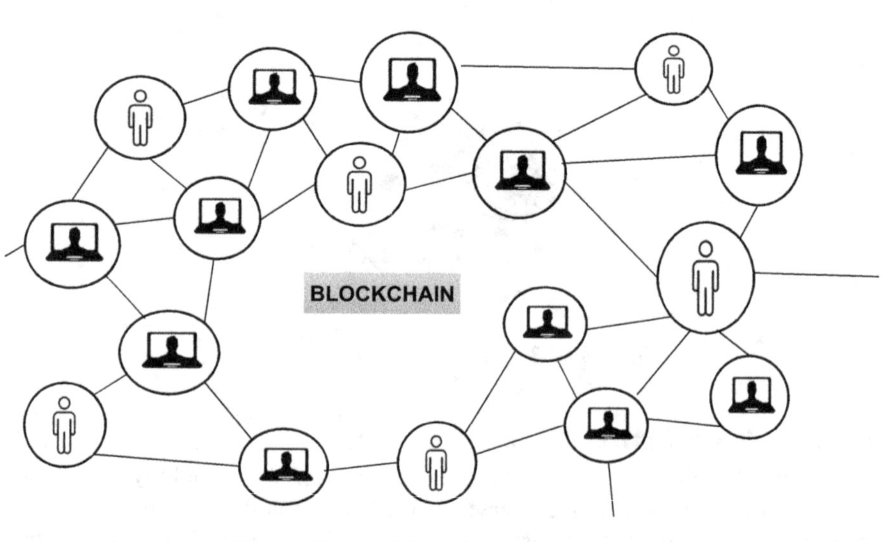

Figure 10.4 Blockchain in metaverse

10.3.2.4 Experience and design

In the Metaverse, creating intuitive, engaging, and diverse experiences that cater to different needs and preferences is essential for mass-level adoption in numerous areas.

10.3.3 Social and economic foundations of metaverse [9]

10.3.3.1 Community structure

Societal acceptance is one of the economic factors that need to be considered while designing or adopting the metaverse. Fostering a sense of community and belonging within the metaverse will be vital for its long-term and vibrant success. In the societal context, the key factors are social interactions, virtual economies, and shared experiences.

10.3.3.2 Digital economy

Every country is trying to introduce multidimensional digitalization. The exploration of metaverse for digital governance, administration, and economies has the potential to create new forms of commerce, employment, and creative appearance. In digital economies, the monetization models, virtual currencies, and NFTs are some of the key foundations for development.

10.3.3.3 Ethical governance

Equal opportunity, full participation, and protection of individual rights are key factors of any system, and the metaverse foundation and its design artifacts should be aligned accordingly. Issues like data privacy, discrimination, and potential harm within the metaverse require careful consideration of ethical standards and judicious governance frameworks. It is very crucial to understand that the metaverse is still in its early stages of development, and its foundations are constantly evolving. The continuing debate and collaboration between numerous stakeholders will help in shaping the future of the metaverse.

10.4 Converging technology attributes of the metaverse

The numerous converging technologies and their significant intersection points for the metaverse are depicted in Figure 10.5.

10.4.1 Virtual and real-world convergence

Technology convergence is a dynamic enabler. A technology platform where all roads of diverse technologies cross to create the emerging technology frontiers is popularly known as the convergence of technologies. Although there are numerous aspects of the metaverse's foundation, one of the most important aspects is the convergence of the technologies. The metaverse is often described as a convergence of virtual and real worlds, where users interact through avatars in immersive digital environments [2].

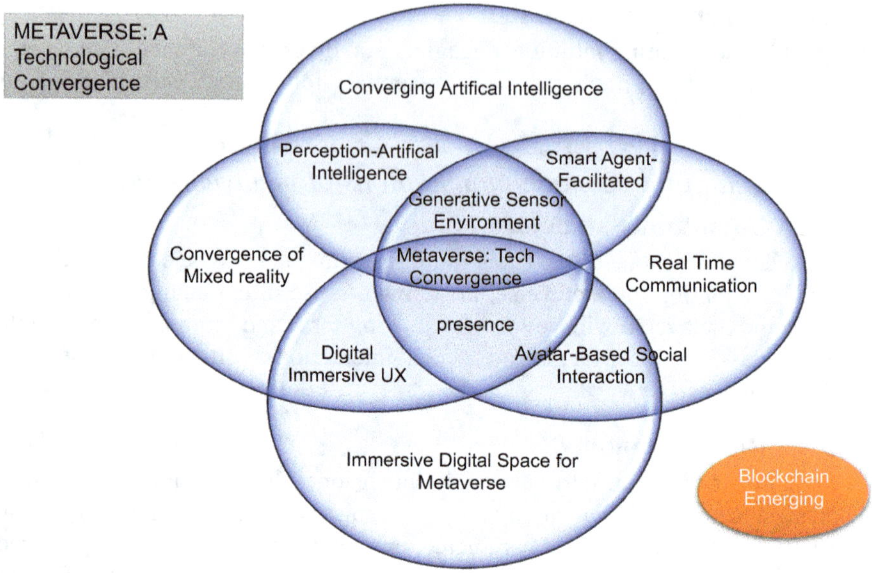

Figure 10.5 Technological convergences

10.4.2 Experiences of 3D world

The convergence of technologies such as AR and VR gives an immersive realization of the metaverse. A new world of metaverse experiences is the creation of 3D virtual spaces accessed through various technologies like VR, AR, and MR, providing a sense of presence and new incarnations.

10.4.3 Uncoupling from the physical world

The coupling of the numerous system components is redefined in the metaverse as a separate world of visual effects. While the metaverse may interact with the physical world through sensors and data, it exists as a separate digital space with its own rules and limitations [9].

10.4.4 Social communication and collaboration for interactivity

Incarnations or Avatars within the metaverse facilitate redesigning the social connection, interaction, collaboration, and even economic activity, creating a sense of community and shared experiences with multidimensional senses [9].

10.4.5 Technology-driven world

The metaverse relies heavily on various technologies like AR/VR hardware, TensorFlow, blockchain, and advanced networking for real-time data processing and user experience. As depicted in Figure 10.6, the metaverse will evolve through

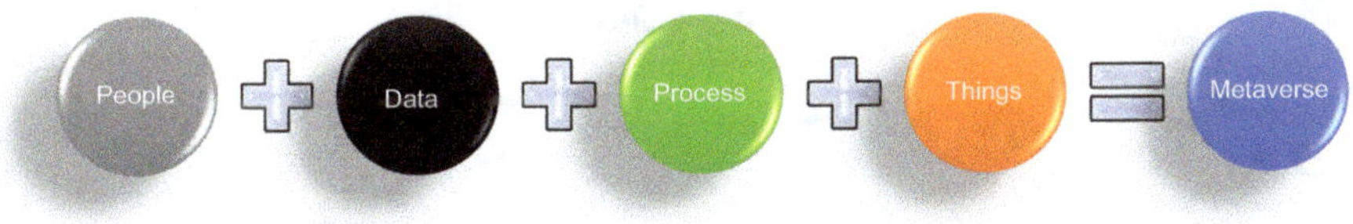

Figure 10.6 Converging components to form a metaverse environment

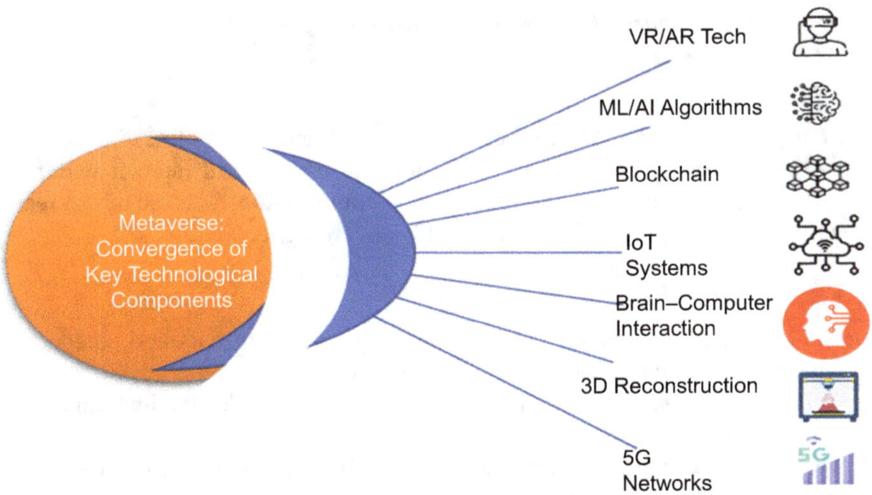

Figure 10.7 Converging technologies of metaverse

the convergence of People, Data, Processes, and Things. The upcoming era will provide a new experience of how people will be affected by the World-Driven Technology and the Technology-Driven World [2].

10.5 Key converging technologies of the metaverse

The metaverse, a vision of a future where virtual and physical worlds seamlessly blend, is fueled by the convergence of several key technologies. A breakdown of these technologies and their various roles and responsibilities is depicted in Figure 10.7.

10.5.1 Extended Reality (XR)

- *Virtual Reality (VR):* Virtual Reality creates immersive, 3D virtual environments for users to explore and interact with, often using headsets and controllers in the metaverse world.
- *Augmented Reality (AR):* Augmented Reality, overlays digital elements onto the real world through devices like smart glasses, enhancing perception and interaction with physical surroundings in the metaverse environment [11].

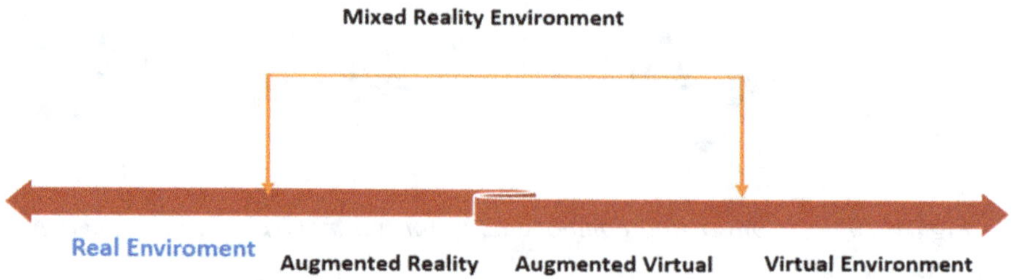

Figure 10.8 Mixed reality conceptualization

- *Mixed Reality (MR):* Mixed Reality blurs the demarcation lines between VR and AR, enabling real and virtual objects to coexist and interact within the same space of metaverse [12,13]. As depicted in Figure 10.8, the mixed reality has a typically blurred line between its converging technologies.

10.5.2 Artificial Intelligence (AI)

Natural Language Processing (NLP): Enables virtual assistants and chatbots for communication and interaction within the metaverse [14].

Computer Vision: Powers object recognition, scene understanding, and avatar creation for realistic experiences [15].

Machine Learning: Machine learning facilitates personalized experiences, content creation, and adaptation within the metaverse [16].

Multimodal AI: To create an artificial experience with human-like intelligence, AI plays a vital role. AI enables natural interactions within the metaverse by combining computer vision, natural language processing, and reinforcement learning.

Personalization and adaptation: Through a wide range of adaptations in numerous domains, AI can personalize metaverse experiences, tailor content, and naturally learn from user behavior [17].

Non-player characters (NPCs): AI-powered NPCs can populate the metaverse, offering companionship, assistance, and dynamic interactions in a metaverse environment [12].

10.5.3 Blockchain and Distributed Ledger Technology (DLT)

Decentralization and ownership: A decentralized blockchain technology can ensure the security of digital assets and enable ownership of virtual land, items, and experiences in the metaverse. Security of transactions and digital ownership enables secured asset management, identity verification, and data governance within the metaverse [18].

Blockchain facilitates decentralization and transparency to ensure a trust-less environment for interactions and transactions within the metaverse [19].

Secure and Smart Contracts: Provides a tamper-proof platform for digital ownership, identity, and transactions within the metaverse using automated agreements and transactions securely and transparently.

10.5.4 Web 3 for open and interoperable platforms

Web 3 principles can foster open and interoperable metaverse platforms, preventing siloed experiences [20].

Identity and reputation: Metaverse interoperability is the ability for different virtual worlds and platforms to interact with each other. This means that users on one platform can communicate and interact with users on another platform, as well as share data and content. Blockchain-based identity management can ensure secure and verifiable user profiles within the metaverse.

Non-Fungible Tokens (NFTs): Represent unique digital assets like avatars, virtual land, and in-game items, enabling ownership and trading within the metaverse.

10.5.5 High-speed networks and computing (5G/6G)

10.5.5.1 Real-time interaction with high-speed internet

Enables real-time data exchange, low latency, and seamless streaming for immersive experiences. Real-time interaction and low latency: Fast internet connections and powerful cloud computing are crucial for smooth and responsive experiences in the metaverse. Real-time interaction and low latency are cornerstones of immersive metaverse experiences. They enable seamless communication, collaboration, and natural interactions with virtual environments and other users. Realizing real-time interaction and low latency in the metaverse requires a multi-faceted approach that leverages edge computing, high-speed networks with advanced optimization techniques, predictive algorithms, optimized content delivery, and ongoing hardware and software advancements. Addressing these challenges will be crucial for creating truly immersive and interactive metaverse experiences [12,21].

10.5.5.2 5G and future networks

Provide the bandwidth and low latency necessary for real-time interaction and seamless data transfer within the metaverse. These technologies are not merely converging, they are actively influencing and shaping each other. For example, AI can personalize user interfaces within VR environments, while blockchain can secure the ownership of virtual assets created with AR tools, Cloud or Edge computing can offer the processing power and scalability necessary to support a vast number of users and complex metaverse environments.

10.5.5.3 The Internet of Things (IoT)

IoT is a network of physical devices embedded with sensors, software, and other technologies that allows them to connect and exchange data with each other, with the internet, and with external applications. These devices can range from simple everyday objects like thermostats and light bulbs to more complex industrial machines and medical devices [10].

10.5.5.4 Cloud computing and edge computing

The metaverse, as growing realm full of possibilities, demands robust computing power to—create and sustain its immersive digital landscapes. In this symphony of technology, two key players take center stage: cloud computing and edge computing. Each, like a talented magician, brings unique strengths and weaknesses, harmonizing to weave the intricate tapestry of metaverse experiences. The computing paradigms bring processing closer to users, reducing latency and improving performance in real-time metaverse applications. Cloud computing and edge computing offer the processing power and scalability necessary to support a vast number of users and complex metaverse environments—process data closer to users for faster response times and improved performance [12,22].

10.5.6 Human–computer interaction (HCI)

Intuitive and natural interfaces: Develop ways for users to interact with the metaverse using gestures, voice commands, and other natural methods [23].

Human–Computer Interaction (HCI): HCI is a vast and fascinating field that explores how people interact with and make sense of computer technology. Its goal is to design computer systems and technologies that are not only usable and efficient but also enjoyable and enriching to use. HCI draws upon a wide range of disciplines, including computer science, psychology, design, sociology, and anthropology [24].

Multimodal interaction: This enables users to interact with the metaverse through various modalities like touch, sight, sound, and smell [25].

10.5.7 Brain–computer interaction (BCI)

This is a fascinating technology that allows communication between the human brain and external devices without traditional physical input. It is revolutionizing fields like medicine, gaming, and prosthetics, opening doors to incredible possibilities. BCI works on three principles, i.e., (1) Brain Signal Acquisition: Sensors (EEG, MEG, etc.) capture brain activity like electrical signals or changes in magnetic fields, (2) Signal Processing: These signals are analyzed and translated into commands or instructions using algorithms and machine learning, and (3) Output Control: The decoded commands are then used to control various devices, such as cursors, robotic limbs [26].

10.5.8 3D reconstruction: building blocks of the immersive metaverse

3D reconstruction, the process of transforming real-world data into accurate 3D models, plays a crucial role in constructing the immersive landscapes and engaging experiences of the metaverse. Imagine stepping into a virtual replica of your favorite city, exploring a historical landmark brought to life in stunning detail, or interacting with a digital replica of yourself, all thanks to the magic of 3D reconstruction. The technology that contributes to shaping the metaverse are Multiple Data Sources, Photogrammetry, and Multi-sensor Fusion [27–29].

These are just some of the key catalytic technologies driving metaverse development. Each area faces its own set of challenges and research opportunities. The convergence of these technologies is still in its early stages, but it holds immense potential for revolutionizing various aspects of our lives, from work and education to entertainment and social interaction. As research and development progress, we can expect the metaverse to become increasingly immersive, interactive, and accessible.

10.6 The emergence of Web 3.0 for metaverse

The World Wide Web, a technology woven from information and interaction, has undergone a remarkable transformation since its inception. The web has transitioned through distinct phases, shedding its limitations and revealing new capabilities with each iteration. We call these phases "Web generations," each characterized by its defining technologies, user roles, and societal impacts. This section of the chapter embarks on a journey through these generations, analyzing their roles in the metaverse and tracing their lasting legacies.

10.6.1 Web 1.0 (Read-Only Web)

The budding web introduced in the 1990s, called "Web 1.0," resembled a vast library of static pages, meticulously crafted by experts and accessed primarily by passive readers. Pages were linked but not interactive, resembling brochures more than dynamic platforms. Information dissemination, not user engagement, was the primary goal. Websites hosted HTML documents, static images, and basic text formatting, relying on hyperlinks for navigation. In this generation, the dominant players were universities, research institutions, and government agencies, creating the web's foundational infrastructure. This generation was confined to HTML, hyperlinks, static websites, etc. [30,31].

10.6.2 Web 2.0 (Read-Write Web)

The beginning of the 21st century witnessed the explosive emergence of Web 2.0 in the 2000s, pertinently termed the "Read-Write Web." User participation exploded, transforming the web from a passive medium into a vibrant arena for collaboration and sharing. This shift was fueled by technologies like user-generated content platforms, blogs, social networks, and Wikis. Users became producers, not just consumers, of information, fostering online communities and generating dynamic, interactive experiences. Web 2.0 explored the era of social media, online collaboration, and personalized content [32,33].

10.6.3 Web 3.0 (Semantic Web)

The web continues to evolve, and from 2010 onwards Web 3.0, also known as the "Semantic Web," emerged as the master enabler of the intelligent and conversational content for the new world of metaverse. This generation emphasizes interconnectedness, machine-readable data, and artificial intelligence (AI) to personalize and automate user experiences in a converging world of technologies such as the metaverse. The semantic web aims to enrich web content with semantic annotations, enabling machines to understand its meaning and context, not just parse its syntax. This paves the way for semantic search, intelligent agents, and personalized recommendations, enhancing the web's utility and efficiency in various interactive technologies such as conversational AI and metaverse.

Web 3.0 is an emerging paradigm with the prime aim of creating a more intelligent, intuitive, and spontaneous experience for the World Wide Web users. It is envisioned as a web that is more interconnected, decentralized, and intelligent, where autonomic devices can understand and interpret data in numerous meaningful ways with multiple options and opinions [34–36].

In futuristic banking, current banking practices will be irrelevant as people exchange digital currencies and records without intermediaries. What is vibrant is that Web 3.0 has the capability of reengineering the concept of digital currency and its usage and banking [36,37].

As depicted in Figure 10.9, Web 3.0 is the futuristic technology of the internet. Web 3.0 is expected to re-engineer areas such as digital currency, e-commerce, e-business, social media, and real-time identity management uniquely with high security and privacy enforcement. The different versions of the Web are depicted in Table 10.1.

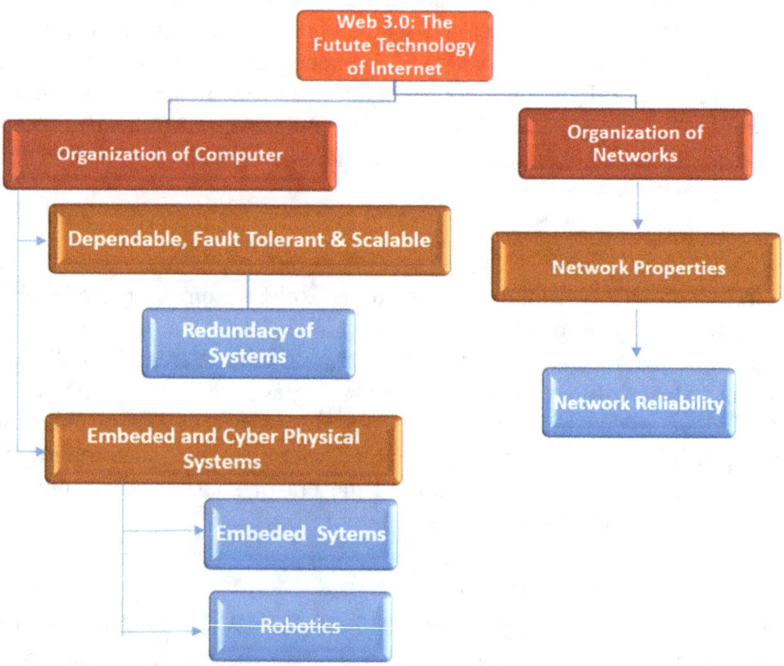

Figure 10.9 The Web 3.0: a future technology of the internet

Table 10.1 Differences among different versions of Webs

Web versions	Architectural designs	Representative products	Characteristics	Benefit distribution
Web 1.0	Centralized	Yahoo, Sina, Netscape	Host-generated content, Host-generated authority	Platform monopoly
Web 2.0	Centralized	Baidu, Google, Facebook	User-generated content, Host-generated authority	Profit-sharing (platforms and netizens)
Web 3.0	Distributed, and decentralized	Tor, Twin	User-generated content, User-generated authority	Peer to peer
Web3	Distributed, and decentralized	Ethereum, Binance	User-generated content, User-generated authority	Smart contract

10.6.4 Outside Web 3.0: (What is Next)?

As the web continues its mutation, future generations are emerging on the horizon. Web 4.0, dubbed the "Ubiquitous Web," envisions a seamless integration of the physical and virtual worlds, with pervasive computing and ambient intelligence becoming commonplace. Beyond Web 4.0, speculations about Web 5.0 and the "Sentient Web" explore possibilities of even more profound integration, with AI playing a central role in understanding and responding to human emotions and intentions. This is the junction point of technology convergence to shape up a new world of metaverse [38]. The emergence of Web generations is a testament to the web's dynamism and its continued adaptation to changing technologies and user needs. Studying these generations provides valuable insights into the ongoing evolution of the internet, helping us prepare for and shape its future trajectory. While challenges remain, like data privacy and ethical considerations surrounding AI, the Web's future.

Web 3.0 is not a completely new technology with a unique paradigm shift rather builds on the existing web technologies and standards, such as HTML, and JavaScript, but it converges with Blockchain, Internet of Things (IoTs), Artificial Intelligence, Machine Learning, etc. for further exploration of intelligent interventions. These technologies enable the web to become more decentralized, by transferring the power to individual users and minimizing the control of centralized authorities. Thus, Web 3.0 also ensures the empowerment of the users with more liberties than developers. The following Table 10.2 depicts the various generations of the Web. Web 3.0 protagonists advocate for numerous revolutionary changes to the internet, aiming for smarter, ubiquitous, and more intelligent usage of data and information. In the futuristic world, data will be unionized and unified with better human-like understanding capabilities, and these capabilities are usually referred to as the Semantic Web [38].

The Semantic Web is an idea for an extension of the current World Wide Web that provides software applications with machine-interpretable metadata of information or data that has been published. Thus, we can augment content and

Table 10.2 Various generations of the Web [38]

Parameters	Web 1.0	Web 2.0	Web 3.0	Web 4.0	Web 5.0
Nomenclature term	The web	The social web	The semantic web	The symbiotic web	The symbiont web
Year of establishment	1996	2006	2016	Near Future	Future
Inventor	Tim Berners Lee	Tim O' Reilly	Tim Berners Lee	–	–
Operational focus	Read	Read, and write	Read, write, and personalized	Read, write, and execute	Read, write, and emote
Orientations	Business	Society	Individual	Personal	Private
model	Client pulls	Two-way	Semantic	Ubiquitous	Decentralized
Technologies used	HTML	XML	RDF	WebOS	EEGs
Applications	CNN	Wikipedia	Facebook	Home Search	Emotion detector
Communications	Lectures	Conversations	Semantic	Interface	Emotional
Objective	Information sharing	Interaction	Immersion	Symbiosis	Smart communication

data that already exists on the Web with additional data descriptors. Using this, computers can be empowered to make meaningful interpretations like humans, i.e., comparable to how people use information to accomplish tasks. In other words, a characteristic of Web 3.0 is how to use semantic web technologies for machines or devices capable of understanding and interpreting the essence of data. These new capabilities of machines and devices can help users make better decisions using intelligent and contextually relevant searches and recommendations.

10.7 Converging features and playbacks of Web 3.0 in the metaverse

Engineering and re-engineering the next generation of the internet and making it suitable for metaverse, Web 3.0 can play a catalytic role in making the user's experience more intelligent, efficient, resourceful, and decentralized than the previous versions of Web 2.0 and Web 1.0. The metaverse, a concept of an immersive, interconnected virtual world, has captivated imaginations and spurred technological advancements.

Web 3.0's key features, including decentralization, interoperability, semantic web capabilities, immersive technologies, and economic empowerment, collectively lay a robust foundation for the development of the metaverse. As these technologies continue to mature and converge, they will play an increasingly crucial role in shaping the future of the metaverse, enabling a more decentralized, interconnected, and immersive virtual world where users can create, own, and experience value in unprecedented ways [39].

Some of the key features of Web 3.0 that are integral to the engineering and reengineering of the metaverse and potentially examine its future are presented in the below subsections.

10.7.1 Decentralization: a foundation for user ownership [40,41]

- *Decentralized architecture:* Web 3.0 applications are built on decentralized networks, like blockchains, where data and applications are distributed across multiple nodes, eliminating reliance on centralized servers or intermediaries. This ensures greater user control over their data, assets, and experiences within the metaverse.
- *Personal data ownership:* Users retain ownership of their data, choosing how it is shared and used within the metaverse. This contrasts with Web 2.0 models where platforms often control user data.
- *User-governed ecosystems:* Decentralized platforms empower users to participate in governance decisions, shaping the metaverse's evolution through voting mechanisms and community participation.

10.7.2 Interoperability: bridging virtual worlds [17,42]

- *Open standards and protocols:* Web 3.0 promotes the use of open standards and protocols, enabling seamless interoperability between different metaverse platforms and applications. Users can create avatars, transfer assets, and participate in experiences across diverse virtual environments.
- *Cross-platform compatibility*: This interoperability fosters a more expansive, interconnected metaverse, unbound by platform restrictions, fostering a richer and more diverse ecosystem.

10.7.3 Semantic Web: understanding meaning and context [40]

- *Machine-readable data:* Web 3.0 emphasizes semantic technologies that enable machines to understand the meaning and context of data within the metaverse. This facilitates intelligent search, content discovery, and personalized recommendations, enhancing user experiences.
- *Contextual awareness:* AI agents and virtual assistants can leverage semantic data to provide more relevant and contextually aware assistance to users within the metaverse, fostering a more intuitive and responsive virtual environment.

10.7.4 Immersive experiences: beyond the screen [42,43]

- *Virtual and Augmented Reality:* Web 3.0 technologies integrate seamlessly with virtual and augmented reality (VR/AR) platforms, enabling immersive metaverse experiences that transcend traditional screen-based interactions.

- *Spatial computing:* This integration creates a sense of presence and embodiment within the virtual world, allowing users to interact with virtual objects and environments naturally and intuitively.

10.7.5 Economic empowerment: digital ownership and value exchange [40]

- *Non-Fungible Tokens (NFTs):* Web 3.0 facilitates the creation and ownership of digital assets, including NFTs, which represent unique items within the metaverse, such as avatars, virtual land, or collectibles. This enables users to own, trade, and monetize their digital assets, fostering a creator economy within the metaverse.
- *Decentralized Finance (DeFi):* DeFi protocols enable secure and transparent financial transactions within the metaverse, supporting virtual economies and enabling users to engage in financial activities without relying on traditional intermediaries.

10.7.6 Inclusion of artificial intelligence and interoperability [44,45]

- *AI intervention:* Today systems are being made with precisely more and more intelligent features. To make the web more intelligent, intuitive, pervasive, and spontaneous, with personalized and context-aware experiences for the metaverse, Web 3.0 includes advanced features of artificial intelligence (AI), such as machine learning (ML), deep learning (DL), Few-Shot learning (FL), and natural language processing (NLP).
- *Rehabilitation for old age and disabled people*: The report of the United Nations 2020 reveals that most of the world's countries are experiencing growth in the old age (over 65) population, and the population is expected to double in the next 30 years. Developing a solid and judicious healthcare infrastructure that can deliver continuous care and support for older adults is a substantial necessity in terms of the social and economic welfare of these people. In this regard, many rehabilitation specialists say that Assistive Technologies that can be assistive, adaptive, and rehabilitative in the metaverse world can provide an alternative solution for these old-age needy people in day-to-day comforts [46].

  Assistive Intelligence and Ambient Intelligence are emerging areas of scientific convergence that bring intelligence to the smart environment and make it more sensitive, adaptive, and responsive to people who need special support preferences. It has been observed that ambient intelligence or context-aware systems have been gaining popularity and strengthened immensely as a result of tremendous technological advances in pervasive or ubiquitous computing, smart, and IoT environments [47].
- *Featuring interoperability:* For the metaverse, technology and their convergences have a mix of homogeneous and heterogeneous systems. Web 3.0 was developed to create a unified, interoperable web where diverse systems

and applications can easily converge, communicate, and share their data and information. Interoperability helps in eliminating data silos and creating a more unified web experience for the users.

10.7.7 Trust and security [40,48]

- *Trust interaction:* To create an interactive intelligent environment, a highly secured and trustworthy web experience is essential in the metaverse. Hence, Web 3.0 ensures prioritized trust and security along with decentralization of identity, secured channels of messaging, and tamper-free data repositories.
- *Enhanced security:* By architectural design, blockchain technology is decentralized itself. Since Web 3.0 is built on blockchain technology, and therefore it is very secure for open-world users in the emerging field such as metaverse. This provides enhanced security and hence it is very difficult to hack or tamper with data in the metaverse.
- *Empowerment of user:* Starting from Web 1.0 up to Web 3.0, the control over the data and information gradually shifted from the developer to the users. Web 3.0 provides users with more control over their data and information with better privacy. User empowerment is very important in the metaverse, where users may be sharing sensitive information about themselves.

10.8 Applications of Web 3.0 in the metaverse: use cases

Web 3.0, with its decentralized, user-centric, and semantically rich features, emerges as a crucial enabler for this emerging realm. The diverse applications of Web 3.0 within the metaverse, explore how its unique features unlock transformative use cases across various domains. Applications of Web 3.0 in the metaverse can be in a variety of ways, including:

4.7.0 Immersive Entertainment and Social Experiences [42,49].

- *Virtual worlds with user-generated content and governance:* Decentralized platforms built on Web 3.0 enable users to collaboratively create and govern virtual worlds within the metaverse. Imagine crafting stories, building landscapes, and shaping experiences together, fostering a sense of shared ownership and continuous evolution.
- *Identity management:* Citizen identity is a big concern for the smart city, campus, and office environments. In the metaverse, Web 3.0 can be used as a revolutionary tool to create and manage the digital identities of citizens or individuals with promised accuracy. This can be done using decentralized identity (DID) solutions and hence decentralized ID management can be a better security-promising platform than centralized or distributed.
- *Interactive and personalized entertainment:* Utilizing semantic technologies, AI agents within the metaverse can personalize entertainment experiences based on user preferences and contextual data. Think of dynamic musical performances that adapt to your mood, or interactive narratives that tailor themselves to your choices.

- *Decentralized social interactions:* Web 3.0 paves the way for secure and privacy-preserving social interactions within the metaverse. Users can own and control their avatars and data, engaging in genuine connections without fear of corporate surveillance or centralized control.

10.8.1 Professional training and education [50,51]

- *Interactive and immersive learning environments:* Web 3.0 enables the creation of virtual classrooms and laboratories within the metaverse, where students can experience complex concepts and scenarios firsthand. Imagine dissecting a virtual frog in biology class or exploring simulated historical events in a VR museum.
- *Skills development and collaborative training:* Virtual training simulations powered by Web 3.0 can provide immersive and personalized training experiences for professionals in various fields. Medical students can practice surgery in realistic virtual environments, or engineers can collaborate on designing complex structures within the metaverse.
- *Decentralized educational platforms:* Web 3.0 promotes open-source educational resources and collaborative knowledge sharing within the metaverse. Learners can contribute to knowledge repositories, earn rewards for their contributions, and democratize access to education.

10.8.2 Economic activities and digital ownership [52,53]

- *Virtual economies, Virtual Payments and decentralized marketplaces*: Web 3.0 facilitates the creation of self-sustaining virtual economies within the metaverse, where users can trade virtual goods and services using cryptocurrencies and NFTs. Imagine owning virtual land parcels, building businesses, and participating in a thriving decentralized marketplace. Another revolutionary application of Web 3.0 in the metaverse is to make digital payments. These emerging payment systems can be cryptocurrencies or stablecoins which are waiting for regulations in many countries.
- *Creative economy and monetization of digital assets*: Creators in the metaverse can leverage Web 3.0 technologies to own and monetize their digital creations, such as art, music, or virtual experiences. NFTs allow for transparent ownership and royalty distribution, empowering creators and fostering a flourishing virtual creative economy.
- *Decentralized finance and financial services*: DeFi protocols operating within the metaverse can offer secure and transparent financial services, such as loans, micropayments, and asset management. Imagine borrowing funds to purchase virtual land or receiving instant micropayments for your contributions to a collaborative virtual creation.
- *Data ownership and governance:* Web 3.0 can be used to give users ownership of their data in the metaverse. For the better governance of the metaverse, non-fungible tokens (NFTs) can be used as a better option. Thus, Web 3.0 can be used to govern the metaverse. This can be done using decentralized autonomous organizations (DAOs).

10.8.3 Sustainability and environmental initiatives [54–56]

- *Virtual simulations for environmental impact assessment:* Web 3.0-powered virtual simulations can be used to model the environmental impact of real-world projects, allowing for informed decision-making and promoting sustainable practices. Imagine testing the effects of a new dam construction on surrounding ecosystems within a virtual environment.
- *Decentralized carbon markets and conservation initiatives:* The metaverse can host transparent and efficient carbon markets powered by Web 3.0, enabling individuals and organizations to offset their carbon footprints and support conservation efforts.
- *Community-driven sustainability projects:* Web 3.0 communities within the metaverse can collaborate on environmental projects, such as virtual tree planting initiatives or educational campaigns to raise awareness about climate change.

10.8.4 Green Web 3.0 for metaverse: envisioning a sustainable virtual future [54,56,57]

At the intersection of virtual worlds and sustainability lies a vision for a greener metaverse, powered by the principles of Web 3.0. Key characteristics and potential impact of Green Web 3.0:

- *Decentralized infrastructure*: Distributing computing power across multiple nodes, reducing reliance on energy-intensive data centers.
- *Renewable energy sources*: Prioritizing solar, wind, and geothermal energy to power metaverse infrastructure.
- *Energy-efficient protocols*: Developing and adopting blockchain consensus mechanisms and data storage solutions that minimize energy consumption.
- *Circular economy models*: Reusing and recycling digital assets within the metaverse to reduce waste.
- *User empowerment*: Enabling individuals to choose renewable energy providers and track their carbon footprint in the metaverse.
- *Environmentally conscious design*: Prioritizing sustainable practices in virtual world development, such as using low-poly models and reducing unnecessary rendering.
- *Reduced carbon emissions*: Mitigating the environmental impact of the metaverse's energy consumption.
- *Promoting sustainable practices*: Fostering a culture of sustainability within virtual worlds and beyond.
- *Accelerating innovation*: Driving the development of cleaner technologies for Web 3.0 and the metaverse.

Green Web 3.0 offers a path towards a more sustainable and responsible metaverse. By embracing these principles, we can create virtual worlds that not only inspire and entertain but also contribute to a healthier planet.

10.9 Challenges in weaving Web 3.0 into the metaverse

While Web 3.0's features hold immense promise for the metaverse, harnessing its potential comes with a list of challenges. These intricate threads, explore technical, social, ethical, and legal hurdles that need to be overcome for a seamless and transformative integration.

10.9.1 Technological issues [53,58,59]

- *Scalability and interoperability:* Building decentralized platforms at the scale needed for massive metaverse experiences remains a technical challenge. Interoperability between diverse virtual environments, powered by different Web 3.0 technologies, requires the development and adoption of universal standards and protocols.
- *Latency and security*: Maintaining low latency and robust security in a decentralized metaverse is crucial for a smooth user experience. Ensuring secure transactions, protecting user data, and preventing cyberattacks necessitates innovative solutions on top of existing blockchain and cryptographic technologies.
- *Accessibility and user experience:* Making the metaverse accessible to users with varying technical skills and levels of comfort with virtual reality is crucial. User interfaces need to be intuitive and user-friendly while ensuring accessibility for people with disabilities.

10.9.2 Social and ethical concerns [53,58,59]

- *Digital divide and inequality:* Web 3.0's reliance on access to technology and cryptocurrency ownership could exacerbate existing inequalities if not addressed. Bridging the digital divide and ensuring equitable access to the Metaverse is crucial for inclusive participation and preventing further marginalization.
- *User safety and mental health:* Immersive virtual experiences can raise concerns about user safety, cyberbullying, and addiction. Ethical guidelines and regulations are needed to ensure the metaverse fosters positive social interactions and protects user well-being.
- *Digital data privacy and ownership:* Navigating digital data ownership and privacy within the metaverse requires careful consideration. Users need clear control over their data while ensuring transparency and preventing misuse of personal information.

10.9.3 Legal and regulatory frameworks

Every technology emerges with certain challenges and the following are some of the challenges being faced while applying Web 3.0 in the metaverse [60–62]:

- *Decentralized governance and regulatory uncertainty*: The decentralized nature of Web 3.0 raises questions about governance and legal frameworks within the metaverse. Establishing clear rules and regulations regarding intellectual property, financial transactions, and dispute resolution is vital for a well-functioning virtual world.

- *Emerging crime and law enforcement:* New forms of crime, such as virtual asset theft and harassment within the metaverse, pose challenges for traditional law enforcement agencies. Adapting legal frameworks and developing appropriate enforcement mechanisms are crucial for ensuring a safe and secure virtual environment.
- *Jurisdictional issues and international collaboration:* The global nature of the metaverse complicates issues of jurisdiction and enforcement. International collaboration and harmonization of laws are necessary to effectively address legal challenges arising in this borderless virtual space.
- *Usability and perception:* The metaverse, while promising immense potential, presents a unique set of usability challenges that designers need to address to ensure engaging and accessible experiences. Some of the key usability challenges in the metaverse to create a 3D environment are (1) *Navigation and spatial awareness*: Users need intuitive ways to navigate 3D spaces and understand their surroundings. Traditional 2D navigation methods may not translate well to a 3D environment, (2) *Object manipulation and interaction*: Users need natural and intuitive ways to interact with objects and environments in the metaverse. This requires new interaction models beyond traditional keyboard and mouse input, (3) *Perception and embodiment:* Users need to feel present and embodied in the metaverse. This requires careful design of avatars, physics, and sensory experiences.

The multifaceted challenges in weaving Web 3.0 into the metaverse are complex and intricate. Overcoming these hurdles requires a concerted effort from technology developers, policymakers, researchers, and users alike. By addressing these challenges with a balanced and inclusive approach, we can pave the way for a metaverse that is not only technologically dazzling but also socially responsible, ethically sound, and legally navigable. This will ensure that the integration of Web 3.0 empowers, rather than hinders, the transformative potential of the metaverse, shaping a future where virtual and physical worlds converge to create a more equitable and enriching experience for all.

10.10 Blockchain for metaverse

Blockchain, a distributed ledger technology, is a foundational fabric of the metaverse which plays a pivotal role in this convergence by addressing critical challenges within the metaverse. Some of the important roles are as follows [63,64]:

Decentralization: Blockchain eliminates the need for central authorities, enabling trustless and secure interactions between users and entities within the metaverse.

Ownership and scarcity: NFTs (non-fungible tokens) built on blockchain securely represent ownership of virtual assets, like land, avatars, and digital goods, creating a robust economy within the metaverse.

Immutability and transparency: Blockchain transactions are tamper-proof and publicly verifiable, ensuring trust and transparency in financial dealings and governance within the metaverse.

Smart Contracts: Self-executing contracts automate agreements and transactions in the metaverse, reducing friction and promoting trust-less interactions.

10.10.1 Blockchain: the base of the metaverse

The concept and the working principle of the metaverse as depicted in Figure 10.10, is a sprawling, interconnected virtual world that hinges on a foundational technology known as Blockchain. Here, blockchain's multifaceted role in building, powering, and enhancing the metaverse and exploring its applications in areas like decentralization, security, interoperability, and asset ownership are covered [65].

10.10.2 Decentralization (the cornerstone of a user-empowered metaverse)

Blockchains, inherently decentralized, distribute data and control across a network of nodes, eliminating the need for central authorities. This translates to several key benefits for the metaverse [53]:

User-owned data and assets: Users retain ownership and control over their digital assets and data within the metaverse, preventing corporate data-grabbing and empowering individuals to monetize their creations.

- *Democratized governance:* Decentralized platforms enable users to actively participate in shaping the metaverse, voting on governance decisions, and contributing to its evolution.

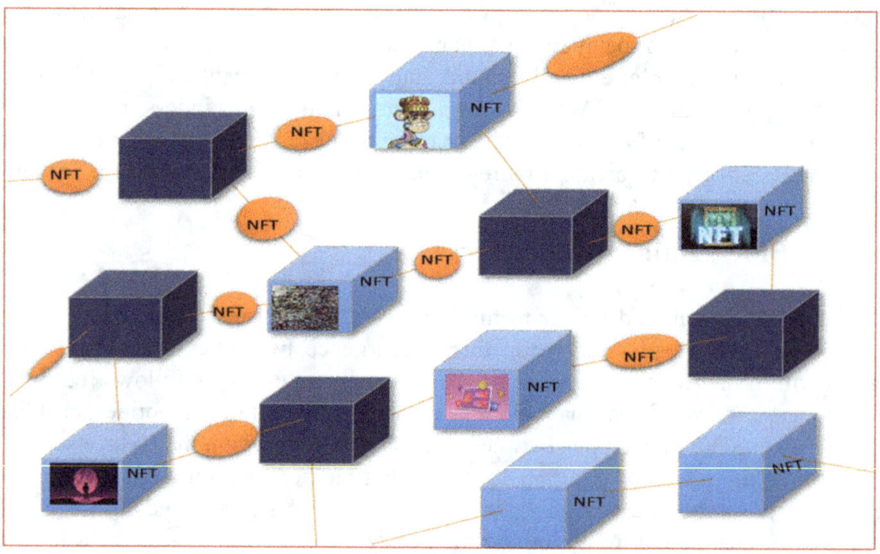

Figure 10.10 Working principle of blockchain

- *Resilient infrastructure with anticensorship:* Blockchain-based platforms are resistant to censorship and manipulation, fostering a free and open metaverse where diverse voices can be heard.

10.11 Harnessing the power of AWS SageMaker in building metaverse

Amazon Web Services (AWS) is an on-demand cloud platform offered by Amazon, that provides service over the internet. AWS services can be used to build, monitor, and deploy any application type in the cloud. Here's where the AWS SageMaker comes into play. Amazon SageMaker is a cloud-based machine-learning platform that helps users create, design, train, tune, and deploy machine-learning models in a production-ready hosted environment. The AWS SageMaker comes with a pool of advantages which are as follows.

The metaverse, a growing virtual world overflowing with potential, demands tools that can handle its intricate complexities. Amazon Web Services (AWS) SageMaker emerges as a powerful contender, offering a comprehensive suite of capabilities to architect, manage, and optimize machine learning (ML) solutions tailored to the metaverse's unique needs. Here, the key benefits AWS SageMaker provides for developers and creators seeking to navigate the metaverse frontier are covered.

10.11.1 Building immersive and dynamic experiences [51,66]

- *AI-powered content creation:* SageMaker empowers the creation of dynamic and personalized metaverse experiences. Generate realistic 3D assets, create immersive soundscapes, and craft adaptive narratives all powered by the magic of ML. Imagine AI-driven landscapes that morph based on user preferences or virtual characters that react and converse in real time.
- *Enhanced user engagement and interaction:* Utilize SageMaker for sentiment analysis, natural language processing, and computer vision to personalize user experiences within the metaverse. Imagine dynamic interactions with virtual beings, adaptive difficulty levels in virtual games, and tailored recommendations for virtual activities.

10.11.2 Optimizing performance and scalability [61,67–69]

- *Efficient resource management:* SageMaker's built-in tools and managed infrastructure streamline model training and deployment, optimizing resource utilization and reducing operational costs. This allows developers to focus on building groundbreaking metaverse experiences without getting bogged down in infrastructure complexities.
- *Seamless scaling and elasticity:* The metaverse demands solutions that can handle fluctuating user activity. SageMaker's auto-scaling capabilities ensure effortless adaptation to varying workloads, guaranteeing smooth experiences for users without compromising performance.

10.11.3 Streamlining ML workflows and collaboration [42]

- *Pre-built and customizable ML tools:* SageMaker offers a rich library of pre-built algorithms and templates, catering to diverse metaverse needs. From anomaly detection and image classification to recommendation systems and forecasting, developers can readily leverage these tools to accelerate their development cycles.
- *Collaborative and open environment:* SageMaker fosters collaboration within the metaverse development community. Share and adapt models, utilize open-source tools, leverage community-driven solutions to accelerate innovation, and push the boundaries of the metaverse.

10.11.4 Security and reliability

- *Secure and compliant platform:* AWS SageMaker operates within a robust security framework, ensuring data privacy and regulatory compliance for critical metaverse applications. Build trusted virtual environments where users can interact and create with confidence.
- *Reliable and fault-tolerant infrastructure:* Leverage the proven reliability and redundancy of AWS infrastructure to power your metaverse solutions. Deliver resilient experiences that are resistant to disruptions and maintain uptime even in high-demand scenarios.

10.11.5 Challenges and considerations

- *ML expertise required:* While SageMaker simplifies ML development, understanding core ML concepts remains crucial for effective utilization. Consider investing in team training or collaboration with experienced ML professionals.
- *Data acquisition and quality:* Building robust ML models for the metaverse requires high-quality and relevant data. Strategize effective data acquisition methods and ensure data quality to unlock the full potential of SageMaker.
- *Ethical considerations:* Responsible AI development is paramount within the metaverse. Address potential biases, transparency issues, and user privacy concerns when implementing ML solutions.

AWS SageMaker presents a compelling proposition for developers and creators exploring the metaverse. Its ability to empower immersive content creation, optimize performance, streamline workflows, and ensure security offers a significant advantage in this burgeoning landscape. By harnessing the power of SageMaker responsibly and creatively, developers can unlock the vast potential of the metaverse, shaping a future where virtual worlds push the boundaries of imagination and empower limitless possibilities.

10.11.6 Benefits of AWS SageMaker

Some of the advantages of SageMaker are below [55]:

- It enhances the productivity of learning and helps in creating and managing compute instances with the least amount of time

- It inspects raw data and automatically creates, deploys, and trains models with complete visibility to reduce the cost of building machine-learning models
- It reduces the time required for data labeling tasks and helps in storing all ML components in one place
- It is highly scalable and trains models faster.

10.11.7 Machine learning with AWS SageMaker

Machine Learning with AWS SageMaker helps in building, testing, tuning, and deploying machine learning models. Figure 10.11 shows how machine learning works with AWS SageMaker to support the operational intelligence in numerous systems.

10.11.8 Building ML models for various applications

AWS SageMaker provides numerous widely used ML algorithms for training purposes and facilitates the capability to select the required server size for a notebook instance where the user can write code (for creating model training jobs) using a notebook instance, select and optimize the necessary algorithm, such as K-means, linear regression, and logistic regression. AWS SageMaker also helps developers in customizing Machine Learning instances with the Jupyter Notebook interface as well.

10.11.9 Testing and tuning ML models

Initially, AWS Sage Maker helps set up and import required libraries then define environment variables and manage them for training the model. For training and tuning the model with SageMaker, it implements hyperparameter tuning by adding a suitable combination of algorithm parameters.

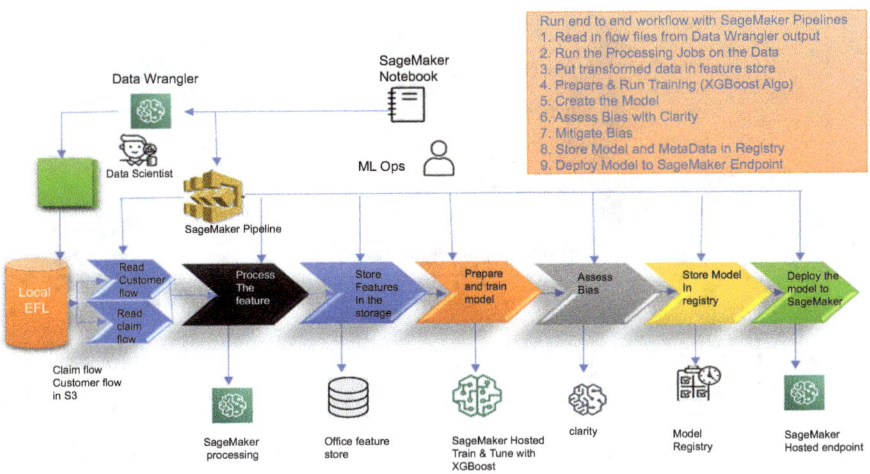

Figure 10.11 Machine learning with AWS SageMaker

In a homogenous computing environment, SageMaker uses Amazon S3 to store data as it is safe and secure. SageMaker uses ECR for managing Docker containers as it is highly scalable and ECR helps a user to save, monitor, and deploy Docker containers if containerization is preferred over virtualization. AWS SageMaker also divides the training data and stores it in Amazon S3, whereas the training algorithm code is stored in ECR and later, SageMaker sets up a cluster for the input data, trains, and stores it in Amazon S3 itself.

10.11.10 Deploying the ML model

Once tuning is done, models can be deployed to SageMaker endpoints where a real-time prediction is performed. Now, anyone can evaluate the model and determine whether the business goals are achieved or not.

10.11.11 Model training with AWS SageMaker

In SageMaker model training, as depicted in Figure 10.12, is done on machine learning compute instances. When a user wants to train a model in SageMaker a training job is required to be created. A training job includes:

- S3 bucket (within the compute instance): The URL of the Amazon S3 bucket where the training data is stored

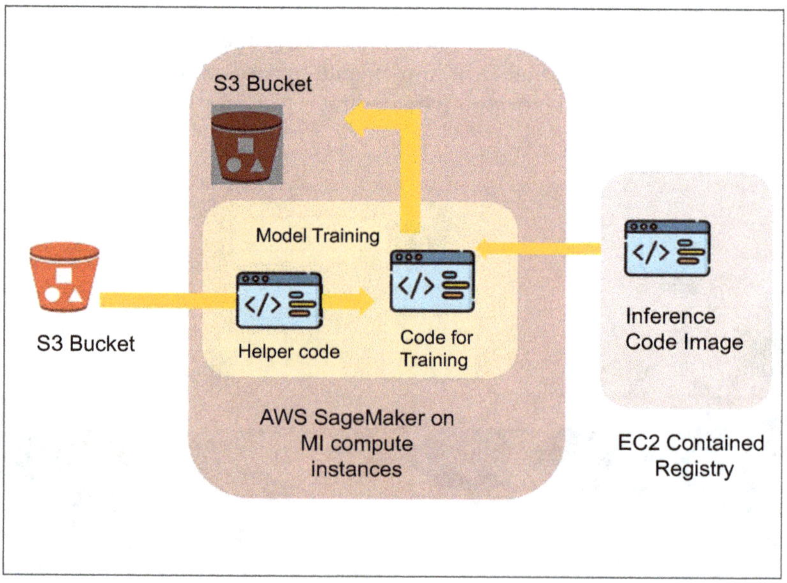

Figure 10.12 Steps to build and train a machine learning model using AWS SageMaker

- AWS SageMaker on ML instance: Compute resources or Machine Learning compute instances
- S3 bucket (outside the compute instance): The URL of the Amazon S3 bucket where the output will be stored
- Inference code image: The path of AWS elastic container registry path where the code data is saved.

In this manner, the input data is fetched from the specified Amazon S3 bucket and once the training job is done, Amazon SageMaker launches the ML compute instances and then it trains the model with the training code and dataset. Generally, SageMaker stores the output and model artifacts in the AWS S3 bucket but in case the training code fails, the helper code performs the remaining task. The interference code consists of multiple linear sequence containers that process the request for inferences on data.

In SageMaker EC2 container registry is a storage registry that helps users save, monitor, and deploy container images and note that container images are the ready applications to Run. Once the data is trained, the output is stored in the specified Amazon S3 bucket to prevent the algorithm from being deleted, save the data in Amazon SageMaker critical system processes on your ML compute instances.

10.11.12 Validating a model with SageMaker

Validation is essential for the evaluation of the developed models. Anyone can evaluate their model using offline or historical data over SageMaker. The steps to be followed for validation are as follows:

- *Offline testing:* This testing uses historical data to send requests to the model through Jupyter Notebook in Amazon SageMaker for evaluation.
- *Online testing with live data:* This testing deploys multiple models into the endpoint of Amazon SageMaker and directs live traffic to the model for validation.
- *Validating using a "Holdout Set":* In this, a part of the data is set aside, which is called a "holdout set ". Later, the model is trained with the remaining input data and generalizes the data based on what it learned initially.
- *K-fold validation:* In this, the input data is split into two parts. One part is called k, which is the validation data for testing the model, and the other part is k−1 which is used as training data. Now, based on the input data, the machine learning models can evaluate the final output.

10.11.13 Applications of AWS SageMaker for Web 3.0 in the metaverse

The convergence of Web 3.0 and the metaverse presents exciting opportunities for building decentralized, immersive, and user-controlled virtual worlds. There are examples, and the potential applications of AWS SageMaker for Web 3.0 in the metaverse are vast and continuously evolving. As the metaverse and Web 3.0 technologies mature, we can expect to see even more innovative and transformative applications of machine learning in this exciting space.

Building secure machine learning environments with Amazon SageMaker is an essential aspect of the metaverse environment. As businesses and metaverse experts look to accelerate the adoption of machine learning (ML) and artificial intelligence (AI), there is a growing need to understand how to build secure and compliant ML environments that meet enterprise requirements.

One major and ***first*** challenge faced is integrating ML workflows into existing metaverse and business work streams. A ***second*** challenge is convergence, i.e., bringing together stakeholders from business leadership, data science, engineering, risk and compliance, and cybersecurity to define the requirements and guardrails for the organization. ***Third***, because building secure ML environments in the cloud or edge is a relatively new topic, understanding recommended practices is also helpful.

Thus, AWS SageMaker, a machine learning platform, can play a crucial role in this process by enabling various applications, including:

Personalized metaverse experiences: (1) Recommendation Systems: SageMaker can be used to train recommendation models on user data (e.g., preferences, interactions) to recommend personalized avatars, virtual spaces, and experiences within the metaverse [70,71]. (2) Adaptive Content Generation: Based on user behavior and preferences, SageMaker can generate dynamic content and adjust the metaverse environment in real time, creating a more engaging and personalized experience [72,73].

Decentralized AI for the metaverse: (1) Federated Learning: Train AI models collaboratively across different metaverse nodes without compromising user data privacy. SageMaker supports federated learning, enabling secure and distributed model training [74]. (2) Predictions through Machine Learning: Deploy AI models directly on blockchain platforms using SageMaker Neo, enabling transparent and verifiable predictions within the metaverse [75–77].

Secure and efficient metaverse infrastructure: (1) Fraud Detection and Anomaly Recognition: Train anomaly detection models on blockchain transaction data to identify fraudulent activities and ensure the security of the metaverse economy [78]. (2) Resource Optimization: Use SageMaker to optimize resource allocation for metaverse infrastructure, ensuring efficient and cost-effective operation of virtual worlds [6].

Building intelligent metaverse avatars: (1) Natural Language Processing (NLP): Train NLP models with SageMaker to enable avatars to understand and respond to natural language, facilitating more realistic and interactive communication within the metaverse [79]. (2) Computer Vision (CV): Develop CV models using SageMaker to allow avatars to recognize objects, gestures, and emotions, enhancing the realism and interactivity of metaverse interactions [80].

10.12 TensorFlow: building the brains of Web 3.0 in the metaverse

The convergence of Web 3.0 and the metaverse presents exciting opportunities for building decentralized, immersive, and interactive experiences. TensorFlow, a powerful open-source library for machine learning, plays a crucial role in enabling various applications within this evolving landscape. In TensorFlow, we explore some potential applications of TensorFlow for Web 3.0 in the metaverse.

The metaverse is an emerging digital realm with enormous possibilities and demands a robust technological foundation. Web 3.0, with its emphasis on decentralization, user ownership, and semantic richness, emerges as a key building block. However, bridging the gap between theoretical concepts and immersive experiences requires powerful tools. Here, TensorFlow, a leading open-source machine learning (ML) framework and its potential as the driving force behind Web 3.0 applications within the Metaverse are described [65].

10.12.1 TensorFlow's strengths (building blocks for a decentralized metaverse) [42]

- *Open-source and community-driven:* TensorFlow's open-source nature fosters collaboration and innovation. Developers worldwide can contribute to the framework, ensuring its continuous evolution and adaptation to the ever-changing metaverse landscape.
- *Versatility and scalability:* TensorFlow's flexible architecture and powerful computational libraries cater to diverse Web 3.0 applications within the metaverse. From natural language processing for decentralized social interactions to computer vision for immersive virtual experiences, TensorFlow offers a comprehensive toolbox.
- *Federated learning:* This unique capability allows for distributed ML training across decentralized networks, protecting user data privacy while enabling collaborative model development for the metaverse. Imagine training AI agents for virtual assistants across individual users' devices, ensuring personalized experiences without compromising data security.

10.12.2 Web 3.0 applications powered by TensorFlow [65]

- *Decentralized AI platforms:* TensorFlow facilitates the creation of open and transparent AI platforms within the metaverse. Users can contribute their data and computing resources to train and utilize ML models, fostering a collaborative and community-driven approach to AI development.
- *Personalized and interactive experiences:* Web 3.0's semantic web capabilities enable the creation of context-aware AI agents within the metaverse. TensorFlow can power these agents to understand user preferences, recommend relevant virtual experiences, and personalize interactions in real time.

- *Self-governing virtual communities*: Decentralized communities within the metaverse can leverage TensorFlow to develop AI-powered governance systems. Imagine using sentiment analysis to gauge community opinion on virtual world rules or utilizing predictive models to optimize resource allocation within self-governing virtual environments.

10.12.3 Challenges and considerations [81]

- *Resource requirements:* Training complex ML models for the metaverse can be computationally intensive. Addressing resource constraints and ensuring efficient model deployment on decentralized networks remains a challenge.
- *Data security and privacy:* Balancing the benefits of decentralized AI with user data privacy is crucial. Secure enclaves and federated learning techniques must be employed to ensure user data remains under their control.
- *Explainability and transparency:* As AI plays an increasingly prominent role in the metaverse, understanding how models make decisions and ensuring their transparency is paramount. Develop and implement explainable AI techniques to build trust and empower users within this decentralized virtual landscape.

TensorFlow, with its open-source nature, versatility, and federated learning capabilities, holds immense potential for powering Web 3.0 applications within the metaverse. By harnessing its power, we can build a decentralized, user-centric, and intelligent virtual world where AI serves as a tool for empowerment, personalization, and collaboration. Addressing resource limitations, prioritizing data privacy, and ensuring transparency in AI decision-making are crucial challenges to overcome. By navigating these challenges with thoughtful design and ethical considerations, TensorFlow can become the brainpower behind a thriving Web 3.0 metaverse, shaping a future where virtual and physical worlds converge in a seamless and empowering experience for all.

Web 3.0 has the potential to revolutionize the metaverse. It can make the metaverse more decentralized, secure, and user-controlled. However, there are still some challenges to using Web 3.0 in the metaverse, such as scalability, usability, and interoperability.

10.13 Feature-based comparison of Web 3.0, Blockchain, IoT, AR/VR, AI/ML, and 5G

Table 10.3 highlights the key strengths and limitations of each technology in the metaverse. Web 3.0 and Blockchain provide the foundational infrastructure for a decentralized and secure virtual world, while IoT and AR/VR offer real-time interaction and immersive experiences. AI/ML personalizes the user experience and powers intelligent agents within the metaverse. 5G ensures fast and reliable connectivity. The success of the metaverse will depend on the seamless integration and collaboration between these diverse technologies.

Table 10.3 Comparison of Web 3.0 for metaverse and its converging technologies—Blockchain, IoT, AR/VR, AI/ML, and 5G

Core features	Web 3.0	Blockchain	IoT	AR/VR	AI/ML	5G
Core focus	Decentralized web, user ownership, semantic web	Distributed ledger technology, secure data storage, and transactions	Connecting devices and collecting data	Enhancing physical world perception with virtual elements	Leveraging data to learn and automate tasks	High-speed, low-latency wireless communication
Decentralization	Highly decentralized, user-controlled data and assets	Core principle, eliminates reliance on central servers	Varied, depends on network design	Not inherent, but can be combined with blockchain for decentralized experiences	Not directly, but can be used to create decentralized AI models	Not inherently decentralized, but can be used to connect decentralized devices
Security and privacy	Emphasis on user-controlled data and encryption, the potential for improved privacy	Strong cryptography ensures data security and immutability	Security varies depending on device and network protocols	This can raise privacy concerns due to access to real-world data	Requires careful data governance and ethical considerations	Enhanced security through encryption and authentication protocols
Interoperability and openness	Open standards and protocols promote interoperability across platforms	Varies depending on blockchain implementation	Emphasis on standardization for device communication	Requires common standards for content and hardware	Open-source tools and frameworks encourage collaboration	Standardized protocols facilitate global connectivity
User experience	Focus on user empowerment and customization	Varies depending on the application	Enhances physical world experiences with digital overlays	Can be immersive and interactive, but hardware limitations exist	Personalized and adaptive experiences based on user data	Increased responsiveness and real-time capabilities
Potential applications	Decentralized marketplaces, social media, personalized learning, virtual economies	Supply chain management, digital identity, secure transactions, voting systems	Smart homes, connected cities, industrial automation, wearables	Gaming, entertainment, education, healthcare, tourism	Facial recognition, predictive maintenance, fraud detection, content creation	Autonomous vehicles, remote surgery, immersive entertainment, real-time communication

Note: Table 10.3 provides a general overview and specific features and applications may vary within each technology. References are provided for further exploration.

10.14 Conclusion

The metaverse foundation rests on the convergence of cutting-edge technologies, each playing a critical role in intertwining the threads of this immersive virtual world. Among these, Web 3.0 emerges as the connective component, the force that binds these diverse elements into an embroidery of interoperable, user-centric, and empowering experiences.

Blockchain, the bedrock of decentralization, lays the groundwork for a metaverse free from centralized control. Users own their data and assets, shaping the virtual landscape through governance mechanisms empowered by distributed networks.

The Internet of Things (IoT) weaves the physical world into the fabric of the metaverse. Sensor-laden objects bridge the digital and physical realms, allowing real-time data to inform and enrich virtual experiences. Imagine cities adjusting virtual traffic flows based on real-time sensor data or virtual avatars mirroring the emotions of their human counterparts thanks to physiological sensors.

Augmented Reality (AR) and Virtual Reality (VR) are the brushes that paint the metaverse on our canvas of perception. These immersive technologies blur the lines between real and virtual, transporting us into dynamic worlds limited only by our imaginations.

Artificial Intelligence (AI) and Machine Learning (ML) are the engines that breathe life into the metaverse. These powerful tools process data, learn from user interactions, and drive dynamic content generation, making virtual experiences ever more responsive and personalized. AI agents can guide us through virtual worlds, tailor educational experiences to individual needs, and even create art and music on the fly, pushing the boundaries of what is possible.

5G, the next generation of cellular network technology, forms the invisible nervous system of the metaverse. Its blazing speed and ultra-low latency ensure seamless data transmission, supporting the demands of VR/AR experiences, real-time interactions, and high-fidelity content streaming. As 5G networks permeate the physical world, they become invisible gateways to the metaverse, allowing us to seamlessly teleport between digital and physical realities.

However, this convergence is not without its challenges. Issues of data privacy, ethical considerations surrounding AI, and the need for interoperability across diverse technologies must be addressed with foresight and responsible implementation. We must ensure that the metaverse is an inclusive, sustainable, and secure space for all, harnessing the power of these technologies for good.

In conclusion, Web 3.0 stands as the bridge between these converging technologies, weaving them into a cohesive fabric that forms the very essence of the metaverse. By embracing decentralization, fostering user empowerment, and ensuring responsible development, we can unlock the vast potential of this digital realm, shaping a future where the metaverse is not just a virtual playground, but a transformative force for human interaction, creativity, and societal progress. The metaverse awaits, and Web 3.0 holds the key to unlocking its boundless possibilities.

References

[1] W. Gan, Z. Ye, S. Wan, *et al.*, "Web 3.0: The future of Internet," presented at the *Companion Proceedings of the ACM Web Conference 2023*, Austin, TX, USA, 2023. https://doi.org/10.1145/3543873.3587583.

[2] G. D. Ritterbusch and A. Teichmann, "Defining the metaverse: A systematic literature review," *IEEE Access*, pp. 12368–12377, 2023. https://doi.org/10.1145/3543873.3587583.

[3] L. Gasser, "WEB3," *Trends in Data Protection and Encryption Technologies*. Cham: Springer, pp. 209–213, 2023. doi:10.1007/978-3-031-33386-6.

[4] M. Abadi, A. Agarwal, P. Barham, *et al.*, "Tensorflow: Large-scale machine learning on heterogeneous distributed systems," *arXiv preprint arXiv*, 2016. https://doi.org/10.48550arXiv:1603.04467.

[5] D. Nigenda, Z. Karnin, M. B. Zafar, *et al.*, "Amazon Sagemaker model monitor: A system for real-time insights into deployed machine learning models," in *Proceedings of the 28th ACM SIGKDD Conference on Knowledge Discovery and Data Mining*, 2022, pp. 3671–3681. https://doi.org/10.1145/3534678.3539145.

[6] L. Turchet, "Musical metaverse: Vision, opportunities, and challenges," pp. 1–17, 2023. https://doi.org/10.1007/s00779-023-01708-1.

[7] L. Floridi, "Metaverse: a matter of experience," vol. 35, no. 3, p. 73, 2022. doi: https://doi.org/10.1007/s13347-022-00568-6.

[8] A. M. Al-Ghaili, H. Kasim, N. M. Al-Hada, *et al.*, "A review of metaverse's definitions, architecture, applications, challenges, issues, solutions, and future trends," 2022. doi: 10.1109/ACCESS.2022.3225638.

[9] T. Chen, H. Zhou, H. Yang, *et al.*, "A review of research on metaverse defining taxonomy and adaptive architecture," in *2022 5th International Conference on Pattern Recognition and Artificial Intelligence (PRAI)*, 2022, pp. 960–965. Piscataway, NJ: IEEE. doi:10.1109/PRAI55851.2022.9904076.

[10] V. R. Verma, D. P. Sharma, and C. Lamba, "QoS improvement in MANET routing by route optimization through convergence of mobile agent," in *2018 5th IEEE Uttar Pradesh Section International Conference on Electrical, Electronics and Computer Engineering (UPCON)*, 2018, pp. 1–6. Piscataway, NJ: IEEE. doi:10.1109/UPCON.2018.8596852.

[11] G. Tang, Chau, A. Kwok, *et al.*, "A systematic review of immersive technology applications for medical practice and education-trends, application areas, recipients, teaching contents, evaluation methods, and performance," vol. 35, p. 100429, 2022. https://doi.org/10.1016/j.edurev.2021.100429.

[12] F. Shi, H. Ning, X. Zhang, *et al.*, "A new technology perspective of the Metaverse: Its essence, framework and challenges," 2023. https://doi.org/10.1016/j.dcan.2023.02.017.

[13] N.-N. Zhou and Y. L. Deng, "Virtual reality: A state-of-the-art survey," vol. 6, no. 4, pp. 319–325, 2009. https://doi.org/10.1007/s11633-009-0319-9.

[14] B. Min, H. Ross, E. Sulem, *et al.*, "Recent advances in natural language processing via large pre-trained language models: A survey," vol. 56, no. 2, pp. 1–40, 2023. https://doi.org/10.1145/3605943.

[15] Z. Zou, K. Chen, Z. Shi, *et al.*, "Object detection in 20 years: A survey," 2023. doi: 10.1109/JPROC.2023.3238524.

[16] H.-n. Wang, N. Liu, Y.-y. Zhang, *et al.*, "Deep reinforcement learning: a survey," vol. 21, no. 12, pp. 1726–1744, 2020. https://doi.org/10.1631/FITEE.1900533.

[17] H. Ning, H. Wang, Y. Lin, *et al.*, "A survey on the metaverse: The state-of-the-art, technologies, applications, and challenges," 2023. doi: 10.1109/JIOT.2023.3278329.

[18] T. R. Gadekallu, T. Huynh-The, W. Wang, *et al.*, "Blockchain for the metaverse: A review," *arXiv preprint arXiv*, 2022. https://doi.org/10.48550/arXiv.2203.09738.

[19] T. Paul, A. Famulari, and T. J. C. N. Strufe, "A survey on decentralized online social networks," vol. 75, pp. 437–452, 2014. https://doi.org/10.1016/j.comnet.2014.10.005.

[20] A. Dwinggo Samala, T. A. Usmeldi, L. Bojić, *et al.*, "Metaverse technologies in education: A systematic literature review using PRISMA," vol. 18, no. 5, 2023. https://doi.org/10.3991/ijet.v18i05.35501.

[21] L. U. Khan, I. Yaqoob, M. Imran, *et al.*, "6G wireless systems: A vision, architectural elements, and future directions," vol. 8, pp. 147029–147044, 2020. doi: 10.1109/ACCESS.2020.3015289.

[22] F. Liu, G. Tang, Y. Li, *et al.*, "A survey on edge computing systems and tools," vol. 107, no. 8, pp. 1537–1562, 2019. doi: 10.1109/JPROC.2019.2920341.

[23] Z. Lyu, "State-of-the-art human–computer-interaction in metaverse," pp. 1–19, 2023. https://doi.org/10.1080/10447318.2023.2248833.

[24] G. Sinha, R. Shahi, and M. Shankar, "Human computer interaction," in *2010 3rd International Conference on Emerging Trends in Engineering and Technology*, 2010, pp. 1–4. Piscataway, NJ: IEEE.

[25] D. Martin, S. Malpica, D. Gutierrez, *et al.*, "Multimodality in VR: A survey," vol. 54, no. 10, pp. 1–36, 2022. https://doi.org/10.1145/3508361.

[26] A. Vallabhaneni, T. Wang, and B. He, "Brain–computer interface," in *Neural Engineering*. Berlin: Springer, 2005, pp. 85–121. https://doi.org/10.1007/0-306-48610-5-3.

[27] Z. Huang, Y. Wen, Z. Wang, *et al.*, "Surface reconstruction from point clouds: A survey and a benchmark," *arXiv preprint arXiv*, 2022. https://doi.org/10.48550/arXiv.2205.02413.

[28] L. Zhao, H. Zhang, and M. Jasper, "Multi-sensor data fusion for 3D reconstruction of complex structures: A case study on a real high formwork project," vol. 15, no. 5, p. 1264, 2023. https://doi.org/10.3390/rs15051264.

[29] A. Bandyopadhyay, A. Sarkar, S. Swain, *et al.*, "A game-theoretic approach for rendering immersive experiences in the metaverse," vol. 11, no. 6, p. 1286, 2023. https://doi.org/10.3390/math11061286.

[30] T. Berners-Lee, R. T. Fielding, and H. F. J. R. Nielsen, "Hypertext transfer protocol – HTTP/1.0," vol. 1945, pp. 1–60, 1996.

[31] J. December and N. Randall, *World Wide Web Unleashed*. Sams, 1995.

[32] T. O'reilly, "What is Web 2.0: Design patterns and business models for the next generation of software," no. 1, p. 17, 2007. https://ssrn.com/abstract=1008839.

[33] J. Zhao, T. Guo, S. Shang, *et al.*, "Work along both lines: The positive impact of work-based social media use on job performance," vol. 18, no. 21, p. 11578, 2021. https://doi.org/10.3390/ijerph182111578.

[34] S. Staab and R. Studer, *Handbook on Ontologies*. Berlin: Springer Science & Business Media, 2010.

[35] V. K. Venkatesan, M. T. Ramakrishna, A. Batyuk, *et al.*, "High-performance artificial intelligence recommendation of quality research papers using effective collaborative approach," vol. 11, no. 2, p. 81, 2023. https://doi.org/10.3390/systems11020081.

[36] B. K. Singh, D. P. Sharma, T. Choudhury, *et al.*, "Autonomic resource management in a cloud-based infrastructure environment," in *Autonomic Computing in Cloud Resource Management in Industry 4.0*. Cham: Springer, pp. 325–345, 2021. https://doi.org/10.1007/978-3-030-71756-8_18.

[37] T. Choudhury, B. K. Dewangan, R. Tomar, *et al.*, *Autonomic Computing in Cloud Resource Management in Industry 4.0*. Cham: Springer, 2021. https://doi.org/10.1007/978-3-030-71756-8.

[38] P. Tambe and D. Vora, "Evolution of the web and E-learning application," in *2016 3rd International Conference on Computing for Sustainable Global Development (INDIACom)*, 2016, pp. 1110–1113. Piscataway, NJ: IEEE.

[39] T. Berners, J. Hendler, and O. Lassila, "The semantic web," vol. 284, no. 5, pp. 34–43, 2001.

[40] N. Shadbolt, T. Berners-Lee, and *et al.* "The semantic web revisited," vol. 21, no. 3, pp. 96–101, 2006. doi: 10.1109/MIS.2006.62.

[41] M. Atzori, "Blockchain technology and decentralized governance: Is the state still necessary?" 2015. https://ssrn.com/abstract=2709713.

[42] A. B. Mahmoud, "The metaverse and Web 3.0: Revolutionising consumption and communication for the future," in *Handbook of Research on Consumer Behavioral Analytics in Metaverse and the Adoption of a Virtual World*. Hershey, PA: IGI Global, 2023, pp. 322–345. doi:10.4018/978-1-6684-7029-9.ch015.

[43] G. Bansal, K. Rajgopal, V. Chamola, *et al.*, "Healthcare in metaverse: A survey on current metaverse applications in healthcare," vol. 10, pp. 119914–119946, 2022. doi: 10.1109/ACCESS.2022.3219845.

[44] F. Ricci, L. Rokach, and B. Shapira, "Introduction to recommender systems handbook," in *Recommender Systems Handbook*. Berlin: Springer, 2010, pp. 1–35. https://doi.org/10.1007/978-0-387-85820-3_1.

[45] R. Burke, "Hybrid recommender systems: Survey and experiments," vol. 12, pp. 331–370, 2002. https://doi.org/10.1023/A:1021240730564.

[46] M. Leo, G. Medioni, M. Trivedi, *et al.*, "Computer vision for assistive technologies," vol. 154, pp. 1–15, 2017. https://doi.org/10.1016/j.cviu.2016.09.001.

[47] N. Gershenfeld, R. Krikorian, and D. J. S. A. Cohen, "The Internet of Things," vol. 291, no. 4, pp. 76–81, 2004. https://doi.org/10.1038/scientificamerican1004-76.

[48] C. Bizer, T. Heath, and T. Berners-Lee, "Linked data: The story so far," *Semantic Services, Interoperability and Web Applications: Emerging Concepts*. Hershey, PA: IGI Global, 2011, pp. 205–227, doi: 10.4018/978-1-60960-593-3.ch008.

[49] S. Yang, "Storytelling and user experience in the cultural metaverse," vol. 9, no. 4, p. e14759, 2023. https://doi.org/10.1016/j.heliyon.2023.e14759.

[50] K. Kim, H. Yang, J. Lee, *et al.*, "Metaverse wearables for immersive digital healthcare: a review," vol. 10, no. 31, p. 2303234, 2023. https://doi.org/10.1002/advs.202303234.

[51] P. Onu, A. Pradhan, and C. Mbohwa, "Potential to use metaverse for future teaching and learning," vol. 29, pp. 8893–8924, 2024. https://doi.org/10.1007/s10639-023-12167-9.

[52] D. Vidal, "The illusion of the metaverse and meta-economy," vol. 86, p. 102560, 2023. https://doi.org/10.1016/j.irfa.2023.102560.

[53] H. Chen, H. Duan, M. Abdallah, *et al.*, "Web3 metaverse: State-of-the-art and vision," vol. 20, no. 4, pp. 1–42, 2023. https://doi.org/10.1145/3630258.

[54] Ş. Vlăduţescu and S. Stănescu, "Environmental sustainability of metaverse: Perspectives from Romanian developers," vol. 15, no. 15, p. 11704, 2023. https://doi.org/10.3390/su151511704.

[55] S. Rathor, M. Zhang, and T. Im, "Web 3.0 and sustainability: Challenges and research opportunities," vol. 15, no. 20, p. 15126, 2023. https://doi.org/10.3390/su152015126.

[56] Z. Ma, "Energy metaverse: A virtual living lab of the energy ecosystem," vol. 6, no. 1, p. 3, 2023.

[57] M. Getahun, M. Azath, D.P. Sharma, *et al.*, "Efficient energy utilization algorithm through energy harvesting for heterogeneous clustered wireless sensor network," vol. 2022, 2022. https://doi.org/10.1155/2022/4154742.

[58] F. Boccia and D. Covino, "Knowledge and food sustainability: The metaverse as a new economic-environmental paradigm," pp. 1–14, 2023. https://doi.org/10.1007/s13132-023-01626-w.

[59] A. Pellegrino, R. Wang, and A. Stasi, "Exploring the intersection of sustainable consumption and the Metaverse: A review of current literature and future research directions," vol. 9, no. 9, p. e19190, 2023. https://doi.org/10.1016/j.heliyon.2023.e19190.

[60] B. Cheong, "Avatars in the metaverse: potential legal issues and remedies," vol. 3, no. 2, pp. 467–494, 2022. https://doi.org/10.1365/s43439-022-00056-9.

[61] B. Yu, Y. Liu, S. Ren, *et al.*, "METAseen: Analyzing network traffic and privacy policies in Web 3.0 based Metaverse," 2023. https://doi.org/10.1016/j.dcan.2023.11.006.

[62] A. Gupta, H. U. Khan, S. Nazir, M. Shafiq, and M. Shabaz, "Metaverse security: Issues, challenges and a viable ZTA model," vol. 12, no. 2, p. 391, 2023. https://doi.org/10.3390/electronics12020391.

[63] Y. Fu, C. Li, F. R. Yu, T. H. Luan, P. Zhao, and S. Liu, "A survey of blockchain and intelligent networking for the metaverse," vol. 10, no. 4, pp. 3587–3610, 2023. doi: 10.1109/JIOT.2022.3222521.

[64] A. Gupta, H. U. Khan, S. Nazir, *et al.*, "Metaverse security: Issues, challenges and a viable ZTA model," vol. 12, no. 2, p. 391, 2023. https://doi.org/10.3390/electronics12020391.

[65] D. M. Doe, J. Li, N. Dusit, *et al.*, "Promoting the sustainability of blockchain in Web 3.0 and the metaverse through diversified incentive mechanism design," 2023. vol. 4, pp. 171–184, doi: 10.1109/OJCS.2023.3260829.

[66] Y. K. Dwivedi, L. Hughes, A. M. Baabdullah, *et al.*, "Metaverse beyond the hype: Multidisciplinary perspectives on emerging challenges, opportunities, and agenda for research, practice and policy," vol. 66, p. 102542, 2022. https://doi.org/10.1016/j.ijinfomgt.2022.102542.

[67] K. A. Awan, I. Ud Din, A. Almogren, *et al.*, "Enhancing performance and security in the metaverse: Latency reduction using trust and reputation management," vol. 12, no. 15, p. 3362, 2023. https://doi.org/10.3390/electronics12153362.

[68] B. Liu, *Artificial Intelligence and Machine Learning Capabilities and Application Programming Interfaces at Amazon, Google, and Microsoft*, Massachusetts Institute of Technology, 2022. Available from: https://dspace.mit.edu/handle/1721.1/146689.

[69] Y. Huang, Y. J. Li, and Z. Cai, "Security and privacy in metaverse: A comprehensive survey," vol. 6, no. 2, pp. 234–247, 2023. doi: 10.26599/BDMA.2022.9020047.

[70] Z. Chen, W. Gan, J. Wu, *et al.*, "Data scarcity in recommendation systems: A survey," *arXiv preprint arXiv*, 2023. https://doi.org/10.48550/arXiv.2312.10073.

[71] L. Wei, X. Wang, T. Wang, *et al.*, "Recommendation systems for the metaverse," vol. 1, no. 1, pp. 19–33, 2023. https://doi.org/10.3390/blockchains1010003.

[72] K. Jiang, J. Hu, C. Fang, *et al.*, "Adaptive anti-jitter optimization for immersive streaming in metaverse scenarios," in *Proceedings of the 2023 7th International Conference on High Performance Compilation, Computing and Communications*, 2023, pp. 310–319. https://doi.org/10.1145/3606043.3606087.

[73] J. Wang, S. Chen, Y. Liu, *et al.*, "Intelligent metaverse scene content construction," vol. 11, pp. 76222–76241, 2023. doi: 10.1109/ACCESS.2023.3297873.

[74] P. Mammen, "Federated learning: Opportunities and challenges," *arXiv preprint arXiv*, 2021. https://doi.org/10.48550/arXiv.2101.05428.

[75] T. Huynh-The, Q.-V. Pham, X.-Q. Pham, *et al.*, "Artificial intelligence for the metaverse: A survey," vol. 117, p. 105581, 2023. https://doi.org/10.1016/j.engappai.2022.105581.

[76] L. Cao, "Decentralized AI: Edge intelligence and smart blockchain, metaverse, Web3, and DeSci," vol. 37, no. 3, pp. 6–19, 2022. doi: 10.1109/MIS.2022.3181504.

[77] L. A. Ajao and S. T. Apeh, "Blockchain integration with machine learning for securing fog computing vulnerability in smart city sustainability," in *2023 1st International Conference on Advanced Innovations in Smart Cities (ICAISC)*, 2023, pp. 1–6. Piscataway, NJ: IEEE. doi:10.1109/ICAISC56366.2023.10085192.

[78] N. C. Tran, J. H. Wang, T. H. Vu, *et al.*, "Anti-aliasing convolution neural network of finger vein recognition for virtual reality (VR) human–robot equipment of metaverse," vol. 79, no. 3, pp. 2767–2782, 2023. https://doi.org/10.1007/s11227-022-04680-4.

[79] T. Huynh-The, Q.-V. Pham, X.-Q. Pham, *et al.*, "Artificial intelligence for the metaverse: A survey," *arXiv preprint arXiv*, 2022. https://doi.org/10.48550/arXiv.2202.10336.

[80] K. Nalbant and Ş. Uyanik, "Computer vision in the metaverse," vol. 1, no. 1, pp. 9–12, 2021. https://dergipark.org.tr/en/download/article-file/2167684.

[81] S. Banaeian Far and S. Hosseini "NFT-based identity management in metaverses: challenges and opportunities," vol. 5, no. 10, p. 260, 2023. https://doi.org/10.1007/s42452-023-05487-5.

Chapter 11

Detailing the unique power of the blockchain technology for the metaverse world

Kavita Saini[1], K. Sivakumar[2], B.S. Vidhyasagar[3] and H. Anwar Basha[4]

Abstract

Leveraging the use of VR, AI, and blockchain technology, the metaverse platform provides users with 3D complete immersion. The process of decentralized concealment and various other security aspects of a blockchain-based metaverse have recently attracted interest. By incorporating blockchain technology into the metaverse, we can foster the growth of a shared ecosystem, safeguard personal information, and ensure the safety of digital assets in both the physical and digital realms. The use of blockchain technology in developing and administering the metaverse platform is investigated in this article. Researchers and practitioners in the discipline of the blockchain-based metaverse will find it a useful resource. Digital currency, like bitcoin, has effectively implemented blockchain technology a potential method for decentralized consensus—to function as a public record of transactions. Many people throughout the globe are interested in it because of its safe architecture, which may support a fault-tolerant distributed computing system. If blockchain technology can successfully reduce costs, increase resource utilization, and establish trust between humans and machines, it could lay the groundwork for new socioeconomic systems. First, blockchain technology is going to be crucial for the safe decentralization of many new areas, including the following: the Internet of Things (IoT), cyber-physical systems, edge computing, social media, crowdfunding, and next-gen mobile communication. Scalability, privacy, efficiency, availability, security, privacy, flexibility, true decentralization, and high reliability are some areas where its development might use improvement.

Keywords: Blockchain; Metaverse; Privacy; Vertical Applications; Digital Transformation; DeFi; NFTs; BaaS

[1]School of Computing Science and Engineering (SCSE), Galgotias University, India
[2]Department of Computer Science and Engineering, SEGi University, Malaysia
[3]Amrita School of Computing, Amrita Vishwa Vidyapeetham, India
[4]Department of Computer Science and Engineering, Rajalakshmi Institute of Technology, India

11.1 Introduction

The concept of a "metaverse" was first introduced in Neal Stephenson's 1992 science fiction novel "Snow Crash," in which it is described as a virtual reality shared by millions of users (Stephenson, 2003). The metaverse is a collective virtual shared space, created by the convergence of the internet and virtual reality (VR), where users can interact and engage with each other, as well as virtual objects and environments [1] (Figure 11.1). It is a virtual world that allows users to create and explore their own digital identities and experiences, and connect with others in real time. The metaverse is often seen as a potential future evolution of the internet and has been discussed [2].

11.2 Prospects and challenges of blockchain technology in digital transformation

Digital transformation is the process by which companies and industries leverage technology to transform their internal and external operations. This includes data management, customer experience optimization, and digitalization of products and services. In other words, digital transformations such as receipts and tax invoices on your mobile phone, personal product recommendations, and real-time delivery tracking are all experiences we encounter in everyday life. Blockchain technology plays a key role in this digital transformation, proving its value in various industries by strengthening the security and transparency of data and improving the efficiency of asset transactions [3].

The concept of asset tokenization refers to the creation of digital tokens on the blockchain that represent digital or physical assets. These tokens represent ownership, and the blockchain ensures that no single authority can revoke or change ownership. Moreover, these tokenized digital assets play a crucial role in bridging the gap between the real and digital realms, thereby accelerating digital transformation. For instance, in blockchain usage, assets can be tokenized to ensure proof

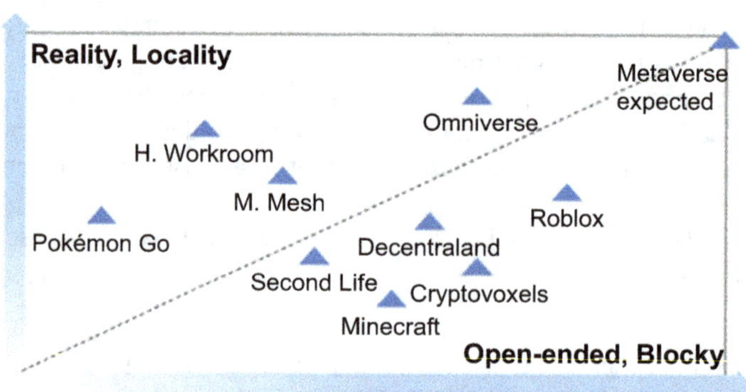

Figure 11.1 Roadmap of metaverse

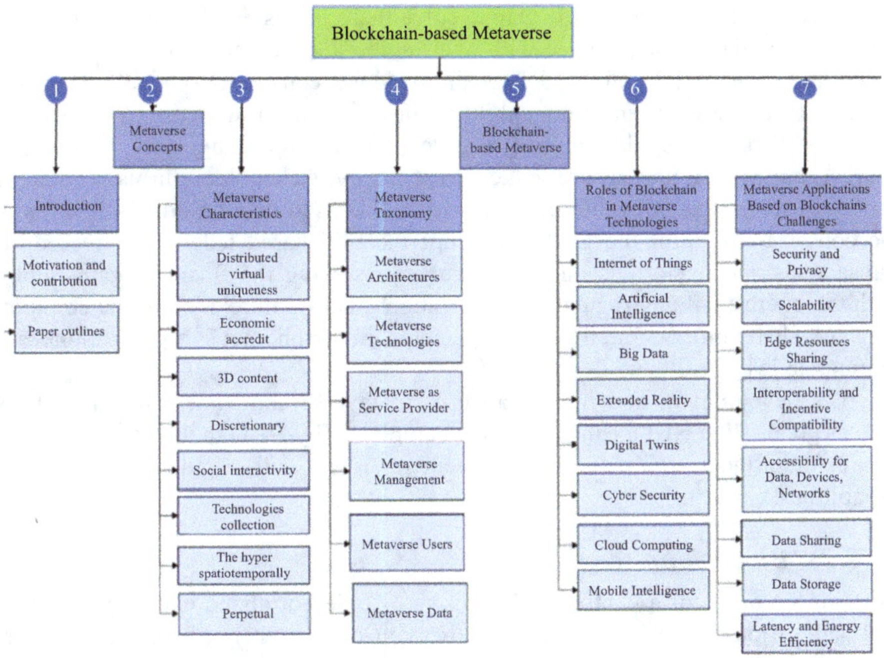

Figure 11.2 Flow chart of blockchain-based metaverse

of ownership and transparency (Figure 11.2). This increases the mobility of assets. Therefore, it is applied to various areas such as premium memberships, art, intellectual property, and real estate, bringing more participants and liquidity to the market and providing more investment opportunities to market players. These examples demonstrate not only how blockchain contributes to creating new business models and increasing efficiency in various fields, but also how they have the potential to bring revolutionary changes to the financial landscape [4].

11.2.1 Protecting user material

In its pursuit of providing the best possible experiences for its users, the metaverse gathers massive amounts of personally identifiable information. In order to build efficient targeting infrastructure, the companies or applications require this data. The wrong people might use the information to attack users in the real world if it spilled. Users are given full control over their data by blockchain, which secures their data privacy through authentication, access control, and consensus processes. Information in the metaverse is protected via the Bitcoin blockchain's usage of algorithmic hashing and asymmetrical key protection.

Most significant selections in classically organizational structures have historically rested with directors and area supervisors; these choices are prone to error and risk since they are based on human judgment. Distributed autonomous organizations (DAOs) are a new way to solve these issues by allowing anonymous users to share data in accordance with a self-enforcing protocol. The smart contract algorithms that reside on a blockchain network control DAOs, allowing for increased transparency and immutability while reducing transaction management expenses. A DAO regulations are recorded on the blockchain network's open-source, transparent, and secure ledger. Importantly, stakeholders in native tokens cannot bypass restrictions, but they can utilize tokens to vote on proposals through the consensus rules of the DAO. An impermeable shared ledger will record all transactions and operations on the network, preserving the financial gains along with the interests of any regulated organizations. This is in relation to the common aims of shareholders. Intelligent agreements in autonomous organizations are immutable [5].

The development and maintenance of metaverse companies (like DeFi), as well as goods (like NFT), can be handled completely by DAO in the not-too-distant future. Intelligent contracts and agreement rules will regulate all primary capabilities.

11.2.2 Blockchain technology

Without the need for a central broker, users of a decentralized exchange can buy and sell various cryptocurrencies directly with one another. There are no intermediaries in decentralized exchanges because they are both issued and operated on blockchain technology. Different kinds of decentralized exchanges exist. One of the most typical forms is a p2p exchange. Buyers and sellers engage in this form of transaction face-to-face. When trading digital assets, this sort of decentralized market is ideal. There are two types of order books: centralized and decentralized. Customers can purchase and sell coins directly with the exchange operator in a central book by depositing monies. With the help of smart contracts, a decentralized book may function without an intermediary [6].

11.2.3 Non-fungible tokens (NFTs)

Non-fungible tokens, or NFTs, are digital representations of non-fungible assets, such as real estate. They help bring underutilized assets into the mainstream and open up new markets. Among the many possible uses for NFTs are in-game purchases, in-game awards for content creators and viewers, and in-game suggestions for content reviewers. Due to their permanent storage on the blockchain, NFTs can never be replaced. So, they are just like any other marketable asset: you can buy, sell, and trade them. A single token cannot be exchanged for more than one NFT, in contrast to tradable assets like stocks or commodities, which are divisible and marketable in limitless amounts. To summarize, NFTs are digital tokens that are authenticated by the blockchain. They enable digital goods, such as artwork or photos, to possess a distinct value that is determined by their scarcity, provenance, and authenticity, which is confirmed through on-chain transactions [7].

The concept of smart contracts and business as a service: Solidity is a widely used language for building smart contracts. One of the most widely used blockchain

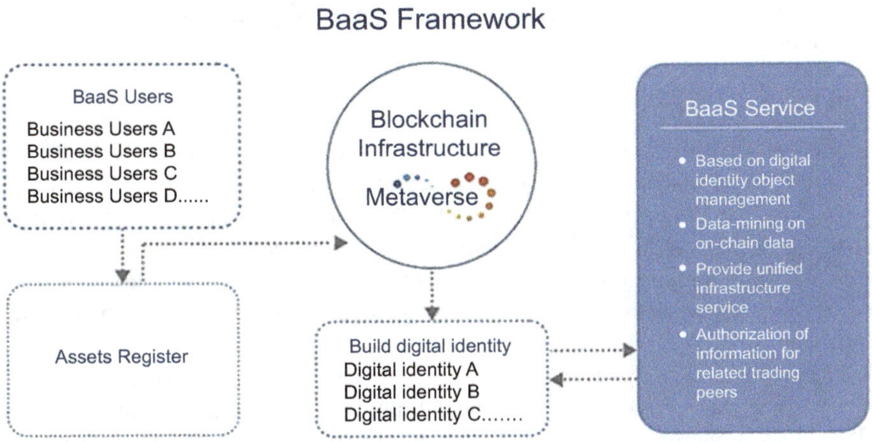

Figure 11.3 BaaS framework

platforms, Ethereum is the network that enables smart contracts. One of the most prevalent applications of blockchain technology is BaaS, or blockchain-based application service. Decentralized apps (dApps) on blockchain networks can be easily created and launched with the help of BaaS, a software service (Figure 11.3). There are few more important applications of blockchain technology than this. With BaaS, you can create blockchain-based apps and grant users access to them.

Innovation abounds in the digital realm. However, the development and use of blockchain technology are swiftly altering the digital asset landscape and the very nature of banking. As digitization progresses, we may expect to witness an ever-increasing number of changes. There will be no letup in the profound and pervasive ways in which the ever-expanding digital world impacts our day-to-day lives [8].

The rate of digitalization's impact on society, banks, industries, and enterprises will grow exponentially. We are more ready than ever before to deal with the additional changes that are on the horizon. Our perception of reality is undergoing a metamorphosis right now. The rapid pace of technological advancement is reshaping and carving out our future in ways we could never have imagined. Digital is where the world is headed, and the world will end when digital is no longer relevant. Now that we are living in the digital age, new kinds of records are needed, such as digital identities, electronic signatures, and blockchain transactions. Although some may find these innovations difficult to grasp and implement, you and/or your company must change to fit in with the exciting new world that blockchain technology is creating. To name just a few ways in which the internet has altered our daily routines, consider the following. The development of blockchain technology has undoubtedly accelerated the mysterious and paradoxical trend that could lead to the complete fusion of humans and machines. This trend is making the digital world feel more "real" while the natural world becomes increasingly uninhabitable without the help of these astounding technological advancements [8–12].

11.2.4 Data quality

The metaverse collects information from many sources, including the healthcare and entertainment industries. Metaverse artificial intelligence algorithms use this information to make important decisions for those involved. The accuracy of users' real-world data is crucial to the metaverse item generation process. Anyone or any entity may validate any transaction using blockchain since it gives full audit trails on every single transaction. As a result, the metaverse's quality of information will improve.

Passwords and usernames have mostly replaced other forms of digital identification since the advent of the Internet. A number of non-governmental organizations and government agencies use inefficient identification systems and laborious verification procedures. Also, by making users register many times, these systems may be wasting time and resources and cannot ensure the safety of users' personal information. In order to find appropriate answers, this scenario prompted a substantial study on digital identities based on the blockchain. Digital assets and digital identities are all part of the metaverse, an autonomous open system built on public blockchain technologies. Metaverse maximizes market effectiveness by creating a 2B2C broad technology platform that digitally stores assets including intellectual property, rare objects (paintings and collectibles), and entitlements to income from instruments of finance. To create a network of value, metaverse uses online identities to link disparate value stores (Figure 11.4). In the future, digital identities will revolve around the metaverse and all the things it can do. Use cases will revolve around Blockchain as a Service (BaaS) and the Metaverse Wallet, with the overarching goal of providing authentic and reliable infrastructure services to everyone. The term "digital identity" is used to describe the overall label provided

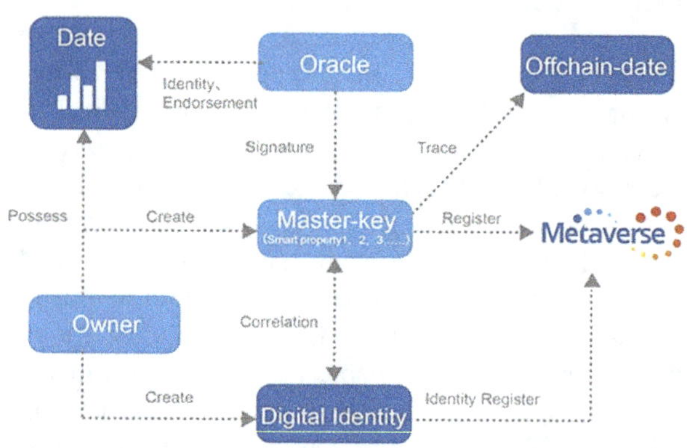

Figure 11.4 Data processing in metaverse

to a user's profile data that corresponds to their personal private key. Metaverse assigns a distinct identity for every profile, which is termed DID (Digital Identity). Everyone with an online identity can apply to be an Oracle or an ordinary user, and anyone can use their online persona to engage in projects. Digital identities and master private keys are related in a one-to-many fashion; anybody or any organization can generate a digital identity and associate it with their private key. In addition to facilitating the issuance of assets on the blockchain and the utilization of permission and inquiry functionalities, identities can also serve as successful networks of evidence [13–15].

11.2.5 Qualifying unified and secured data allocation

A more interconnected and immersive environment is the outcome of the metaverse's reliance on augmented and virtual reality gadgets, which enable seamless and safe sharing of information. When used in conjunction with augmented reality (AR) on both digital and physical items, the metaverse truly shines. The development of the metaverse hinges on the smooth exchange of data between AR and VR and opens the door to the creation of cutting-edge apps that help address real-life issues. The powerful encoding technology of the blockchain allows for the safe and efficient interchange of data in the metaverse.

11.2.6 Assisting data interoperability

Stakeholders in the metaverse must acquire and manage assets in several virtual worlds using a wide range of apps. Due to the diverse contexts in which these computer simulations are constructed, data interchange is severely hampered. A cross-chain communication mechanism allows for the transfer of data between blockchains that are situated in different virtual environments. The interactivity of the blockchain makes it easier for users to move between different simulated worlds [16].

Starting from the first version of Bitcoin's peer-to-peer system, the blockchain concept continued to grow and evolve as a multi-purpose technology, enabling use cases that went far beyond the functionalities of cryptocurrencies (Table 11.1). DLT and blockchain technologies enable transactions ensuring complete transparency since they are available to everyone. They also ensure complete security, as these blocks cannot be altered and this, of course, guarantees data integrity over time. In the long run, this concept could revolutionize the way we interact and do business across new digital platform ecosystems, because it can guarantee complete, transparent, and safe information exchange [17–19].

Key advantages: Blockchain is robust enough to be built upon. It can serve as an important first layer that enables non-discriminatory and uncensored access. The industry of blockchain-powered apps is thriving, and the different approaches to blockchain technology are developing. Most use an in-browser, or in-device (VR sets, phones) approach to connect individual users to a decentralized network (Table 11.2).

Table 11.1 Blockchain Distributed Ledger Technologies (DLT)

	Blockchain	DLT
Definition	Belongs to the category of DLT in which every single node holds a copy of the ledger. Every time someone adds a new transaction, a new copy of the ledger is created.	DLT is a database decentralized across several computers or nodes. Every node maintains the ledger, and each node is authorized to update the distributed ledgers independently from the others but under the consensual control of the other nodes.
Structure	Data and information represent a chain of blocks. This structure is not the real structure of distributed ledgers.	It is a database distributed across several nodes. Data is represented differently for different ledgers.
Sequence of block	You can find all the blocks in a particular sequence.	You do not need to follow the blockchain sequence of data.
Consensus	Wide usage of proof-of-work mechanisms in blockchain.	No particular kind of consensus is needed, thus more scalable than blockchain.
Implementation in real case	Many enterprises and startups are already using blockchain.	DLT projects and usage are still under development. Few real-world implementations exist.
Tokens	Many blockchain platforms involve some sort of token economy.	No tokens or any other kind of currency are needed on the network.

Table 11.2 Architecture DLT

Property	Public	Private	Consortium
Consensus	All the miners	Centralized organization	A set of nodes
Permission	Public	Public or restricted	Public or restricted
Immutability	Nearly impossible	Could be tampered with	Could be tempered with
Efficiency	Low	High	High
Consensus process	Permission-less	Permissioned	Permissioned

There are three key advantages of the use of blockchain in the metaverse:

1. Cryptographic protection of personal data and the network increases the possible solutions for personal data privacy.
2. There is potential for fast and direct transactions between users without the third party or validator.
3. Digital assets are publicly authenticated.

One of the key challenges facing blockchain technology is the speed and cost of processing transactions, as each transaction is required to be validated across a large number of nodes in order to be secure. Greater adoption and complex processes, which are likely to become commonplace in a thriving metaverse ecosystem, will create a heavy load jamming up the traffic. The weakest point of blockchain technology is scaling. This type of authenticated information system is slow and resource-demanding. Decentralization affects the overall capacity, as propagation and synchronization between nodes in the network require time and careful handling of cryptography.

As we mentioned, blockchain can be used as a layer one solution to be built upon. Along with this comes new solutions for bringing the best from both worlds—authentication and immutability of blockchain, and the speed of centralized solutions—all as one [20].

11.3 A thrustless architecture of blockchain-enabled metaverse

Undoubtedly, a metaverse is a system that relies heavily on vast amounts of data. Unfortunately, developers have to choose between realism and openness because present computing capabilities have not evolved enough to meet the massive processing power required of metaverses. A modest virtual situation can become a reality with the help of high-performance gadgets, particularly Graphics Processing Units (GPUs), which can handle complicated rendering demands. Unfortunately, because of a lack of resources, rendering an entire metaverse is practically unfeasible. As a result, if we want the metaverse to be open-ended, we have to give up some of reality. As a whole, the limitations of today's processing and networking capabilities prevent us from having the metaverse we envision.

As a result, we suggest a new design that combines blockchain with edge computing to unite the cloud, edge, and device computing resources. A blockchain links all the resources in a big network by acting as an underlying trustworthy middleman. Our blockchain, inspired by Sky computing, aims to connect all the separate services offered by big and small businesses in order to pool the resources we have for creating a metaverse. On top of that, the network is transformed into a resource pool through virtualization, where computing activities are distributed among computing units according to consumption situations. By combining blockchain technology with other processing resources, a kind of supercomputer may be created, and all the necessary gear can be used to its full potential.

Following this, we will go over a few scenarios where blockchain technology could be useful in the metaverse.

- A method for handling money that is secure, accessible, and transparent among blockchain's four notable features is decentralization. There needs to be a way to ensure the safety and efficiency of the millions of transactions that take place in the metaverse every second for the exchange of goods.

These characteristics make blockchain-based cryptocurrency an attractive option for building scalable and large-scale economic systems in the virtual world.

Digital currencies that are built on the blockchain enable transactions to take place between users in the metaverse. Virtual currencies allow for cheap, easy, and instantaneous online purchases in the metaverse. Coinbase and Finance and similar crypto exchanges are vital since not every metaverse uses the same coin.

- Deploying smart contracts: There is no need for a third-party verification platform when using smart contracts because of the blockchain's built-in capabilities, which include smart contracts being automated, programmable, open, transparent, and verifiable. Metaverse financial systems that are built on blockchain technology have the potential to decentralize contract operations in a trustworthy, verifiable, and non-custodial way. This could greatly reduce instances of rent-seeking, corruption, and underhanded operations in the system. Smart contracts have many applications in the financial, social, and gaming industries.
- Non-fungible tokens (NFTs): NFTs' primary characteristics—indivision and uniqueness—make them well-suited to identity representation. NFTs can be freely exchanged and transferred assets that are exclusive and indivisible. These digital possessions are accompanied by ownership certificates known as NFTs in the metaverse.

In the healthcare industry, blockchain technology has the potential to enhance the safety and efficacy of metaverse healthcare services.

Data such as patient records can be safely stored on a distributed ledger using this technology. Smart contracts built on the blockchain might also eliminate the need for human intervention or middlemen in the payment process by automating transactions between healthcare providers and insurance companies. Patients could have more say over their personal health data and only authorized professionals could access it using decentralized identification methods on blockchains like Ethereum [21,22].

The metaverse ecology relies on data collection. When customers pay, we get some of their sensitive information, such as their bank or credit card numbers. Furthermore, in order to develop digital avatars, it is necessary to gather sensitive data in the metaverse, including biometric information, user poses, and gestures. Decision support, digital product creation, suggestion system design, and metaverse marketing can all benefit from data collection, which in turn trains algorithms for artificial intelligence and machine learning. Systems will benefit from metaverse data capture in the form of improved insights that can evolve and adapt to new circumstances (Figure 11.5). The metaverse will function as an online market where users can transact, play, communicate, and work through the use of a variety of gadgets. This will lead to the creation of vast quantities of diverse data. Listed below are a few examples of data acquisition methods that can be employed in the metaverse. One way that users' information can be gathered in the metaverse is through the use of web forms. Before being allowed access to the metaverse capabilities, clients can easily and rapidly fill out information utilizing web forms. Users' social security numbers and other sensitive information can be collected by bots. In the metaverse, a high-definition camera records the user's bodily

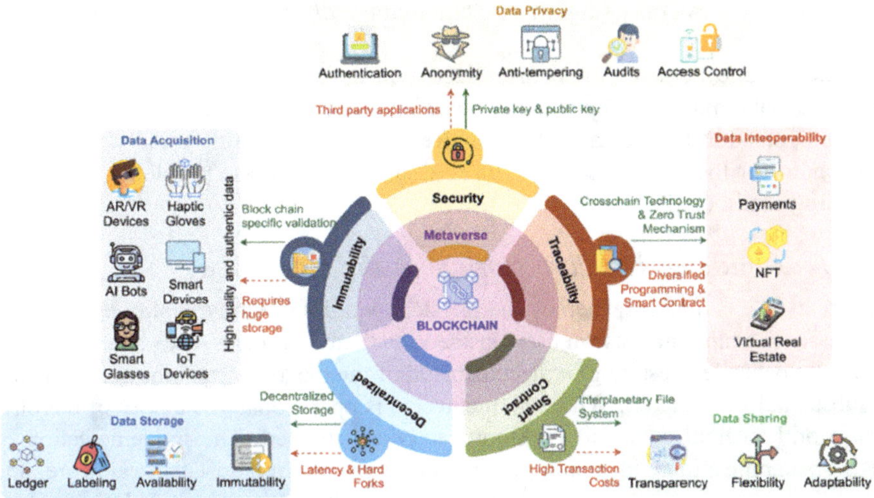

Figure 11.5 Blockchain for technical aspects in the metaverse

characteristics. A user's physical characteristics are utilized to construct a digital likeness of the user within the virtual environment. Using augmented and virtual reality devices to investigate the metaverse will be useful for the customer. The purpose of these devices is to record the user's actions.

11.4 Maintaining confidentiality difficulties throughout the metaverse

Digital applications operating in the metaverse, such as Wi_Fund, Etheria, 4G Capital, and Amplifying Art, will produce massive amounts of data that are both real time and unstructured. Acquiring the massive amounts of data being produced is a major obstacle. Applications like recommendation engines in the metaverse are going to depend more on data assurance or integrity. The dependability of such systems may become compromised if data is collected from unreliable sources. The provision of excellent digital offerings in the metaverse, such as the Horizon Worlds and Horizon Venues apps for virtual reality headsets, will cause the volume of data to explode. The proliferation of streaming media for various purposes will put a strain on data-collecting infrastructure. The data quality could be compromised if erroneous or duplicate information is also obtained. Gathering data in the metaverse while guaranteeing outstanding and precise information is challenging. In spite of its potential speed advantages, the complexity and decentralization of blockchain technology mean that it may be cumbersome to implement in data collection systems. The time it takes to complete a transaction using blockchain technology can be quite lengthy. The entire process can take many days. Because of this, the network can only support a certain number of users and transaction charges are increased.

The storage demand for data collected in a blockchain system is increased since the data must be duplicated down the chain. Additional storage space is required for additional data collection. Research into creating a fully developed blockchain for the metaverse can still be done to solve these problems with data-collecting methods [23].

11.4.1 Challenges of data storage in the metaverse

The metaverse is a realm whereby the physical world and virtual reality exist simultaneously. The rapid increase in users inside virtual environments leads to a significant growth of data files, resulting in the expansion of the metaverse and the accumulation of substantial information. When the metaverse is operational, the ability of the physical world to hold data will be significantly constrained. The implementation of metaverse applications, including gaming, entertainment, real estate, healthcare, and others, will encounter a significant challenge in terms of data storage. Relying on a centralized storage system in the metaverse heightens the risk of data leakage, alteration, or destruction. The metaverse's personal details, speech pronunciations, and vital signs are in jeopardy because of the significant probability of data loss and corruption in centrally located apps. Due to the vast quantities of data produced by metaverse systems, the task of data labeling and categorization will provide a significant challenge. The distributed architecture of the digital currency blockchain will allow data scientists to collaborate more effectively and reduce the time needed for data categorization and identification. The blockchain guarantees the accessibility, clarity, and reliability of data in the metaverse. Each block in the blockchain will function as a redundant copy of the data. In order to enhance security and reduce the vulnerability of metaverse data to replication and unauthorized alterations, a distributed ledger system that relies on consensus can be employed. Given that every new piece of data needs to be duplicated along the entire chain, further examination of delay is required. Considering the impossibility of data manipulation in cryptocurrencies, it is worth considering the implementation of a hard fork [24,25].

11.4.2 Obstacles associated with sharing knowledge across the metaverse

Various stakeholders in the metaverse can benefit from data sharing. As applications and users transition to a common platform, their collaboration and productivity can be significantly enhanced. Sharing knowledge from the metaverse will benefit a wide range of individuals, including researchers and ordinary individuals. The metaverse will utilize augmented reality.

Augmented reality (AR), virtual reality (VR), and Internet of Things, or IoT-based gadgets gather data with the purpose of creating personalized solutions for users. Consequently, a multitude of diverse applications will be capable of delivering an enhanced user experience. Through the act of exchanging data across different platforms, firms will get the capability to do data analytics within the metaverse. Shared data enables a deeper understanding of customers, a more accurate evaluation of adverts, customized material, the establishment of communication strategies, and the development of metaverse businesses.

11.4.2.1 Data sharing in central platforms for exchanging information might open

Data owners' personal and sensitive information is highly vulnerable in the metaverse. There is a lot of latency and not enough data available because data in the conventional sharing environment is very changeable. In contrast to unchangeable data, scaling changeable data is difficult. There will be a plethora of real-time applications in the metaverse that produce massive amounts of data, including medical treatment, news, entertainment, and congestion efficiency.

When the need for real-time data grows in a conventional data-sharing setting, data flexibility becomes a problem [26].

11.4.3 Challenges related to privacy preservation in the metaverse

In the metaverse, privacy preservation faces significant challenges due to the massive amount of personal data being collected, including our actions, preferences, and interactions. This raises the possibility of illegal tracking and spying, which may result in the unintentional disclosure of private data. Concerns about identity theft and the abuse of digital avatars are also growing since bad actors can easily exploit them. Additionally, attempts to maintain privacy are made more difficult by third parties' access to personal data, often without explicit consent. Finally, efforts to safeguard users' privacy rights are hindered by inadequate legislation in the metaverse [27].

11.4.4 Challenges related to digital twins in the metaverse

The merging of multiple virtual worlds will give rise to the metaverse. There is a lack of cohesion and organization in the existing conventional centralized digital platforms. To take part in various worlds, users need to configure their accounts, avatars, equipment, and payment methods (Figure 11.6). There are restricted ways for users to transfer their digital goods, such as NFT and avatar, to another virtual environment. Because of the lack of transparency, moving about in simulated environments is not easy. For instance, you cannot use the same Roblox account as you do in Decentraland. The interoperability of the virtual worlds determines the possibilities for using applications within them. There should be no barriers to data exchange between apps in the digital world, regardless of physical location or the technology in use. One major drawback of the conventional method is that it does not account for the need to properly manage interactions among virtual worlds in order to ensure metaverse compatibility [28].

11.4.5 Challenges related to AI in the metaverse

When used to metaverse data, blockchain technology will increase its adaptability and versatility. There is more latency in data transfers on a blockchain because

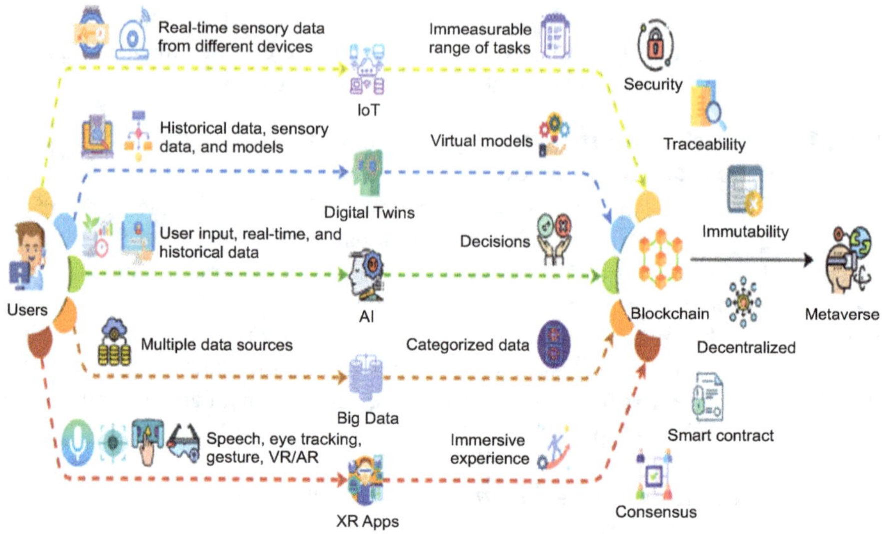

Figure 11.6 Blockchain is utilized as a fundamental technology for the primary supporting aspects of the virtual world

copies of data must be replicated down the chain. Extensive computing resources will be required to accommodate the inevitable growth in the number of users in the metaverse, which will lead to an increase in the number of blocks. Due to this, users should expect to pay more when their pooled transactions are validated. Addressing this issue is crucial for future-generation blockchains to ensure effective data exchange in the metaverse. It is going to be challenging to build AI in the metaverse, which is the latest frontier in science and technology. The ownership of content driven by artificial intelligence is hard to trace. In the virtual world, users are unable to tell if the person they are chatting with is an actual person or an avatar created by a computer. Users can take advantage of AI programming to dominate games and steal materials from other players, among other ways they can illicitly access assets within the metaverse. Consumers may lose trust in the metaverse if AI makes mistakes, another possibility. It also makes it harder to use the same blockchain for different metaverse applications involving artificial intelligence [29].

11.5 Blockchain's effects on metaverse-enabling systems

Bitcoin exemplifies first-generation citizens' blockchain technology, essentially merely fostering decentralized documentation of transactions. Blockchain was once thought to be only a ledger, but later it was discovered that it can handle a lot more, including managing wealth and family trust (Figure 11.7). So, Ethereum, the second generation of blockchain, entered the scene. The advent of intelligent

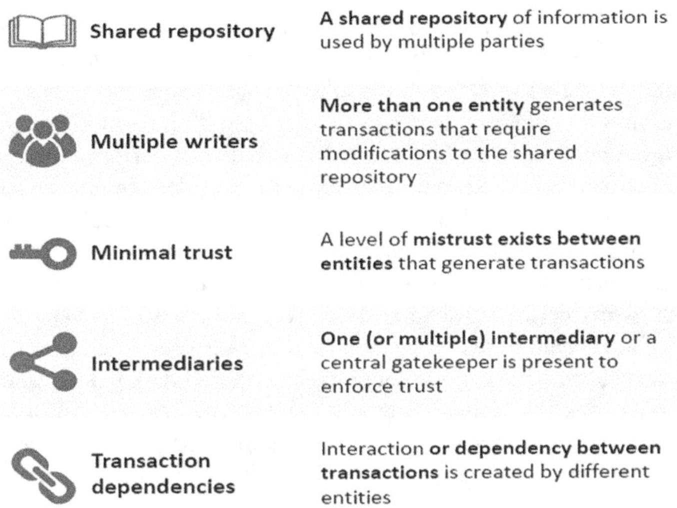

Figure 11.7 High-potential application traits

agreements is the most significant innovation that Ethereum introduced. A guide to an intelligent blockchain is where all legally binding contracts are recorded. Smart contractual arrangements provide functionalities that can be triggered by transactions, allowing for the automatic transfer of funds. Alternatively, notify the specified accounts. Smart contracts enable users to establish a chain in a short amount of time. Blockchain-based programs can autonomously verify and certify the reliability of payments, ensuring trust and transparency [30].

11.6 Conclusion and additional research

Research on blockchain's technological and business case application within the metaverse suggests it may change the immersive sector. Consensus mechanisms and network management, like interoperability, are being studied further in all blockchain versions. There are several consensus approaches that produce low latency and great throughput, but security, scalability, and decentralization cannot all be maintained simultaneously. Negotiation techniques ensure that all designated nodes in a distributed system agree on data states. To solve these issues, new and enhanced hybrid consensus techniques like Proof-of-Capability, Proof-of-Burn, and Leased Proof-of-Stake are needed. Governments and blockchain communities worldwide acknowledge the detrimental climate-related and ecological consequences of running a large number of nodes in a network, which includes high usage of energy and emission of greenhouse gases. The interstellar consensus mechanism authenticates transactions using a set of reliable nodes, this speeds along the entire procedure and saves energy usage, resulting in an environmentally conscious choice.

As a result of the proliferation of blockchains and networks tailored to particular uses by various nonprofits and public agencies, it is imperative that new and existing chains be interconnected in order to expedite the advancement of metaverse technology. The introduction of cross-chain technology represents the pinnacle of blockchain interoperability, enabling users to effectively perform value and information transactions across several blockchain networks simultaneously. As an example, users might transfer data between other blockchains, such as Ethereum and Polygon. The growing number of completely decentralized systems that use cross-chain bridges is also driven by this interoperability mechanism. With omni-chain, a blockchain-as-a-service infrastructure service that can connect to various enterprise networks, the blockchain relies on applications and services (such as asset management, smart contracts, handling transactions, and shared data ledger) and can offer numerous advantages, including faster processing times, more security, increased openness, and increased traceability. These features are crucial for the future of blockchain technology, which aims to achieve multi-chain interoperability.

11.7 Future approach

Today, more and more people are drawn to the idea of digital transactions being more trustworthy and transparent. Blockchain technology has many potential applications because of its essential properties. One possible use case for blockchain technology is the creation of a distributed ledger system that would make it impossible for any one entity to alter or fabricate data, regardless of how powerful they are. This idea has a lot of potential.

References

[1] M.A.I. Mozumder, M.M. Sheeraz, A. Athar, S. Aich, H.-C. Kim, Overview: Technology roadmap of the future trend of metaverse based on IoT, blockchain, AI technique, and medical domain metaverse activity. In: *2022 24th International Conference on Advanced Communication Technology (ICACT)*. 2022, pp. 256–261. https://dx.doi.org/10.23919/ICACT53585.2022.9728808.

[2] M. Abraham, P. Saeghe, M. Mcgill, M. Khamis, Implications of XR on privacy, security and behaviour: Insights from experts. In: *Nordic Human-Computer Interaction Conference*. 2022, pp. 1–12. http://dx.doi.org/10.1145/3546155.3546691.

[3] A. Ahmed, M. Agus, M. Alzubaidi, *et al.*, Overview of the role of big data in mental health: A scoping review. *Comput. Methods Programs Biomed.* 2 (2022) 100076.

[4] R.A. Ainsworth, D.J. Sandin, J.P. Schulze, A. Prudhomme, T.A. DeFanti, M. Srinivasan, Acquisition of stereo panoramas for display in VR environments. In: *IS&T/SPIE Three-Dimensional Imaging, Interaction, and Measurement*. 2011, p. 786416. http://dx.doi.org/10.1117/12.872521.

[5] M.F. Alam, S. Katsikas, O. Beltramello, S. Hadjiefthymiades, Augmented and virtual reality based monitoring and safety system: A prototype IoT platform. *J. Netw. Comput. Appl.* 89, (2017) 109–119.

[6] M. Ali, F. Naeem, G. Kaddoum, E. Hossain, Metaverse communications, networking, security, and applications: Research issues, state-of-the-art, and future directions. 2022, arXiv preprint arXiv:2212.13993.

[7] I. Goodfellow, J. Pouget-Abadie, M. Mirza, *et al.*, Generative adversarial nets. In: Ghahramani, Z., Welling, M., Cortes, C., Lawrence, N., Weinberger, K. (eds.), In: *Advances in Neural Information Processing Systems (NeurIPS)*, vol. 27, Curran Associates, Inc., 2014, pp. 1–9, https://proceedings.neurips.cc/paper/2014/file/5ca3e9b122f61f8f06494c97b1afccf3-Paper.pdf.

[8] A.K. Graham, R.S. Weissman, D.C. Mohr, Resolving key barriers to advancing mental health equity in rural communities using digital mental health interventions. *JAMA Health Forum*, 2(6) (2021), e211149. http://dx.doi.org/10.1001/jamahealthforum.2021.1149.

[9] N.H. Nam, Impact of cryptocurrencies on financial markets. *VMOST J. Soc. Sci. Humanit.* 65(2) (2023), 3–15.

[10] R. Napolitano, I. Douglas, M. Garlock, B. Glisic, Virtual tour environment of Cuba's national school of art. *Int. Arch. Photogramm., Remote Sens. Spat. Inf. Sci.* 42 (2017), 547–551.

[11] Y. Hajjaji, W. Boulila, I.R. Farah, I. Romdhani, A. Hussain, Big data and IoT-based applications in smart environments: A systematic review, *Comp. Sci. Rev.*, 39 (2021) 100318.

[12] U. Majeed, L.U. Khan, I. Yaqoob, S.A. Kazmi, K. Salah, C.S. Hong, Blockchain for IoT-based smart cities: Recent advances, requirements, and future challenges, *J. Netw. Comput. Appl.* 181 (2021) 103007.

[13] A. Dorri, F. Luo, S. Karumba, S. Kanhere, R. Jurdak, Z.Y. Dong, Temporary immutability: A removable blockchain solution for prosumer-side energy trading, *J. Netw. Comput. Appl.* 180 (2021) 103018.

[14] M.A. Uddin, A. Stranieri, I. Gondal, V. Balasubramanian, A survey on the adoption of blockchain in IoT: Challenges and solutions, *Blockchain: Res. Appl.* 2(2) (2021) 100006.

[15] Q. Chen, S.-J. Lee, Research status and trend of digital twin: Visual knowledge mapping analysis, *Int. J. Adv. Smart Convergence* 10 (4) (2021) 84–97.

[16] K. Yoon, S.-K. Kim, S.P. Jeong, J.-H. Choi, Interfacing cyber and physical worlds: Introduction to IEEE 2888 standards, in: *IEEE International Conference on Intelligent Reality*, ICIR, 2021, pp. 49–50.

[17] C. Zhuang, J. Gong, J. Liu, Digital twin-based assembly data management and process traceability for complex products, *J. Manuf. Syst.* 58 (2021) 118–131.

[18] L.U. Khan, W. Saad, D. Niyato, Z. Han, C.S. Hong, Digital-twin-enabled 6G: Vision, architectural trends, and future directions, *IEEE Commun. Mag.* 60(1) (2022) 74–80.

[19] D. Lee, S.H. Lee, N. Masoud, M. Krishnan, V.C. Li, Integrated digital twin and blockchain framework to support accountable information sharing in construction projects, *Autom. Constr.* 127 (2021) 103688.

[20] W. Shen, T. Hu, C. Zhang, S. Ma, Secure sharing of big digital twin data for smart manufacturing based on blockchain, *J. Manuf. Syst.* 61 (2021) 338–350.

[21] T. Huynh-The, Q.-V. Pham, X.-Q. Pham, T.T. Nguyen, Z. Han, D.-S. Kim, Artificial intelligence for the metaverse: A survey, *Eng. Appl. Artif. Intell.* 117 (2023) 105581.

[22] B.K. Wiederhold, Ready (or not) player one: Initial musings on the metaverse, 2022.

[23] A.A. Hussain, F. Al-Turjman, Artificial intelligence and blockchain: A review, *Trans. Emerg. Telecommun. Technol.* 32(9) (2021) e4268.

[24] S. Han, T. Kim, News big data analysis of 'metaverse' using topic modeling analysis, *J. Digit. Contents Soc.* 22(7) (2021) 1091–1099.

[25] N. Deepa, Q.-V. Pham, D.C. Nguyen, *et al.*, A survey on blockchain for big data: approaches, opportunities, and future directions, *Future Gener. Comput. Syst.* 131 (2022) 209–226.

[26] D.M. Gligor, K.G. Pillai, I. Golgeci, Theorizing the dark side of business-to-business relationships in the era of AI, big data, and blockchain, *J. Bus. Res.* 133 (2021) 79–88.

[27] J.O. Yang, J.S. Lee, Utilization exercise rehabilitation using metaverse (VR·AR· MR·XR), *Korean J. Sport Biomech.* 31(4) (2021) 249–258.

[28] P. Bhattacharya, D. Saraswat, A. Dave, *et al.*, Coalition of 6G and blockchain in AR/VR space: Challenges and future directions, *IEEE Access* 9 (2021) 168455–168484.

[29] S. Kumar, A.K. Bharti, R. Amin, Decentralized secure storage of medical records using blockchain and IPFS: A comparative analysis with future directions, *Secur. Privacy* 4(5) (2021) e162.

[30] D.G. Johnson, N. Diakopoulos, What to do about deepfakes, *Commun. ACM* 64(3) (2021) 33–35.

Chapter 12

Metaverse use cases (individual and industrial) and application domains

Harshavardhan Kosuri[1]

Abstract

The metaverse is revolutionizing industries and redefining the way people interact, work, and play in digital spaces by presenting a diverse array of use cases. Virtual social interactions are among the most significant applications, as they enable users to establish connections in immersive 3D environments through avatars, thereby establishing novel forms of communication and collaboration. The metaverse enables the creation of expansive, persistent virtual worlds in the gaming industry, enabling users to participate in interactive, shared experiences. The metaverse is also revolutionizing commerce by providing virtual marketplaces for digital goods, NFTs, and services, which allows businesses to engage with global audiences in inventive ways.

The metaverse offers immersive learning environments in the fields of education and training, which simulate real-world scenarios to provide hands-on learning experiences. These environments range from virtual classrooms to professional training simulations. Furthermore, the metaverse is being utilized by the healthcare, entertainment, and real estate sectors to facilitate virtual property visits, telemedicine consultations, and live performances, respectively. The metaverse is poised to unleash new opportunities across a variety of sectors, thereby establishing a more interconnected and experiential digital economy, as technological advancements, such as AR/VR, blockchain, and AI, continue.

Keywords: Metaverse; Virtual Reality (VR); Augmented Reality (AR); Immersive Experiences; Virtual Collaboration; Education in Metaverse; Metaverse Real Estate; Metaverse Gaming

12.1 Metaverse real estate

For high-priced properties, the turnaround time for villa sales is very high.

Real estate companies may attempt to sell the property long before the construction begins by showing photos and virtual videos of their proposed villas.

[1]PlanetMeta, Bengaluru, India

However, the real estate sales/marketing staff are not providing the customers with a proper visualization of the villa's look and feel (Figure 12.1).

(a) (b)

Figure 12.1 *(a) 3D virtual office house roof. (b) Businessman thinking seriously about his house.*

When the customer sees the property ad on the property portals, the real estate salesmen will provide details over the phone and try to persuade the customer to come to the site to view their model villa. However, most customers do not come to the site due to time constraints or they may be in another city or country.

Furthermore, even if the customer does come to the site, the real estate company may not have a model of the villa to show the customer. As a result, the customer may not want to purchase the property.

Metaverse Realestate app solves all these issues (Figure 12.2).

Figure 12.2 *Man with glasses of virtual reality future technology*

The entire residential township can be replicated along the villas, the clubhouse, the roads, etc. with metaverse. You need to be able to see the residential township and the villas from your mobile phone. Metaverse allows you to create a digital twin of your property with both the inside and the outside details. You can enter the Realestate metaverse app with your avatar and explore your property virtually. Metaverse also allows you to see your property from the comfort of your home. You can get virtual tours and virtual experiences that allow you to explore your property without getting out of your home. This not only increases convenience but also increases the reach of your property listings to global audiences. Metaverse brings properties to life with 3D modeling, virtual staging, and virtual tours.

This allows you to see the properties and spaces more vividly and realistically (Figure 12.3).

Figure 12.3 *Man wearing a VR headset and seeing real estate projects in the world*

12.1.1 Process of creating realestate in metaverse

Step 1: Initially floor plan for the villas and township has to be prepared.

Step 2: 3D artists have to create the 3D model of the township along with villas as per the floor plan. Both the interior and exterior of the villas have to be created.

Step 3: Programmers have to do the required programming for navigation all over the township and villas.

Step 4: To give an effective immersive experience, we can create avatars also for the users of the metaverse application (Figure 12.4).

12.1.2 Designing and virtual collaboration

Metaverse collaboration is a new way for real estate developers, designers, and architects to collaborate. Virtual spaces allow teams to collaborate in real time,

Figure 12.4 Metaverse city VR glasses transport business hologram

regardless of physical location or geographical location. Not only does virtual collaboration speed up decision-making, but it also allows for more interactive and creative design exploration. Metaverse virtual collaboration is breaking down traditional boundaries in the design and development stages of real estate projects (Figure 12.5).

Figure 12.5 Avatars in metaverse party, social, and chat VR in the worlds

12.1.3 Metaverse as social and commercial hub

Due to social and commercial integration, metaverse is becoming a social and commercial hub. Many leading companies and brands are establishing virtual storefronts and social interaction within the metaverse creating a sense of community. This has involvements for real estate, as properties within these social hubs gain value based on their location, accessibility, and proximity to popular virtual attractions.

12.1.4 Concerns and considerations

Despite the exciting possibilities, metaverse also has its own challenges. Privacy concerns, security issues, and the need for standardized regulations are among the hurdles that industry stakeholders must address. Questions about the authenticity and permanence of virtual ownership bring about legal as well as ethical considerations that require careful navigation.

12.2 Metaverse in education

In recent years, the metaverse has emerged as a groundbreaking concept with the potential to revolutionize various aspects of our lives, and education is no exception. As technology advances, educators are exploring innovative ways to leverage the metaverse to engage students, enhance learning experiences, and redefine the traditional classroom setting.

12.2.1 Virtual classrooms

Imagine stepping into a virtual classroom where geography is no barrier. The metaverse allows educators to create immersive virtual learning environments, providing students with a sense of presence and interaction that goes beyond conventional online education (Figure 12.6).

Figure 12.6 Metaverse university classroom

12.2.2 Interactive learning spaces

The metaverse enables the creation of dynamic, interactive learning spaces. Students can explore historical events, travel to outer space, or dive into microscopic worlds—all within the virtual realm. This hands-on approach fosters a deeper understanding of subjects through experimental learning.

12.2.3 Virtual laboratories

Science education can be elevated with virtual laboratories in the metaverse. Students can conduct experiments, analyze data, and interact with virtual elements in a safe and controlled environment. This not only expands access to practical learning but also reduces resource limitations (Figures 12.7 and 12.8).

Figure 12.7 Women in chemistry virtual lab

Figure 12.8 Kids with VR headsets

12.2.4 Global collaboration

Collaboration takes on a new dimension in the metaverse. Students from different parts of the world can seamlessly collaborate on projects, share ideas, and learn from diverse perspectives. This global connectivity enhances cross-cultural understanding and prepares students for an interconnected world.

12.2.5 Personalized learning journeys

The metaverse allows for personalized learning experiences tailored to individual needs. Adaptive learning technologies can track students' progress, identify strengths and weaknesses, and adjust the curriculum in real time to optimize each student's learning journey (Figures 12.9 and 12.10).

Figure 12.9 Teacher teaching with VR headset

Figure 12.10 AI-generated group of children sitting in a classroom

12.2.6 Career simulations

Students can explore and stimulate real-world careers in the metaverse. From virtual internships to business simulations. The metaverse provides a platform for students to gain practical insights into various professions, helping them make informed career choices.

12.2.7 Gamified education

Verification in education takes on a new level of engagement in the metaverse. Educational games and simulations can be integrated seamlessly, making learning fun and interactive. This approach not only captures students' interests but also reinforces key concepts through gameplay.

12.2.8 Lifelong learning platforms

The Meta supports lifelong learning by offering continuous access to educational resources. Whether perceiving professional development or exploring new interests, individuals can engage in learning experiences at any stage of life, breaking down traditional barriers to education.

12.2.9 Creative expression and arts

For arts and creative subjects, the metaverse provides a canvas for limitless expression. Students can showcase their artistic creations in virtual galleries, collaborate on multimedia projects and participate in immersive performances, all within the digital realm.

12.2.10 Digital literacy and ethical use

Navigating the metaverse requires digital literacy skills. Educators can incorporate lessons on responsible use, digital etiquette, and online safety to prepare students for a world where virtual and physical spaces intersect (Figure 12.11).

Figure 12.11 Metaverse digital virtual reality technology wears

12.2.11 Professional development and educators

Educators themselves can benefit from the metaverse. Virtual workshops, conferences, and collaborative platforms offer opportunities for professional development, ensuring that teachers stay updated on the latest educational trends and technologies.

As we venture further into the metaverse, the potential for transforming education is vast. The immersive and interactive nature of virtual environments opens new horizons for creativity, collaboration, and learning. While challenges exist, the metaverse offers an exciting frontier for education—one where students can embark on personalized journeys, educators can innovate in teaching approaches, and the traditional boundaries of the classroom are redefined. The metaverse is not just a tool, it is a catalyst for re-imagining the future of education (Figure 12.12).

Figure 12.12 Successful Latin American woman in an office using VR glasses

12.3 Recruitment in metaverse

Imagine a world where it is possible to go to a job interview from the comfort of your own home. Where recruiters and the world's best talent collide in a virtual skyscraper, and the conventional job market is reimagining itself.

In the metaverse—which is essentially a digital world—the way we recruit and hire for jobs is evolving. It is becoming an everyday reality, and let us take a look at how it is shaping the future of recruiting (Figure 12.13).

12.3.1 Global job fair and networking in metaverse

Welcome to the future of job hunting. The metaverse is ushering in the next evolution in the job application process. It is going to be faster, more convenient, and more immersive than ever before (Figure 12.14).

Employers can host a virtual job fair and networking event, connecting with job seekers in a virtual world. Job seekers can explore different companies, learn about

(a) (b)

Figure 12.13 *(a) AI-generated businesswoman wearing a VR headset. (b) Male employee using virtual reality glasses.*

(a) (b)

Figure 12.14 *(a) We are hiring job vacancy posters. (b) Woman scientist experiencing virtual reality using headset.*

different cultures, and improve their interview skills—all from the comforts of their own homes via metaverse. Not only is the metaverse breaking down geographical barriers, but it is also providing employers and candidates with a convenient, immersive way to connect and participate in the ever-changing job market (Figure 12.15).

12.3.1.1 Immersive job interviews and virtual onboarding

The metaverse lets us do job interviews and onboarding in cool virtual places. Imagine having a job interview in a virtual space that feels lively and interactive. When you start a new job, you can learn about it without going to an actual office, thanks to virtual onboarding. It helps you grasp the company's culture and environment online (Figures 12.16 and 12.17).

Figure 12.15 Businessman wearing a VR headset floating in cyberspace

Figure 12.16 Onboarding concept

Figure 12.17 Online business meeting in the metaverse

12.3.1.2 Breaking down geographical barriers: a worldwide talent pool

The metaverse is breaking down distance limits, making a worldwide talent group. Recruiters can talk to job seekers from any place globally, giving them more choices and making sure companies can pick from the top talent. Job fairs and networking events in the metaverse help people worldwide connect with job opportunities. You can explore and talk to potential employers using your virtual character.

12.3.2 Live assessments: showcasing skills in real time

In the metaverse, you can show your skills right away with live assessments. Recruiters can see how good candidates are by making them do practical and interactive tasks, giving a better idea of their skills.

12.3.3 Metaverse jobs: a digital frontier metaverse job market

In conclusion, the metaverse is not a pipe dream, it is a reality that is rapidly transforming the way we find and hire talent. Virtual interviews, global talent sourcing, and innovative job fairs are only the beginning. In this new era of digital transformation, adaptability, and innovation will be key. Leveraging the potential of the metaverse will open up the job market for everyone. Prepare yourself for a digital job search journey.

12.4 Tourism in metaverse

12.4.1 Changing the definition of tourism

The metaverse is the space where through virtual reality users can interact with each other by a computer-generated ecosystem. This method is revolutionizing the tourism industry. Due to the advancement of technology union of the metaverse into tourism is flourishing and because of this countless opportunities for travelers and businesses are being generated (Figure 12.18).

Figure 12.18 Guy with VR glasses is going into space

12.4.1.1 Enhanced virtual travel experiences

While traveling in the metaverse, tourists can travel beyond the boundaries of their home world and explore many places without leaving their homes. They can visit iconic places such as monuments, museums, and religious sites, and they can experience the local culture through virtual travel experiences within the metaverse. This field will provide a glimpse and an idea for potential travelers, but it will also allow tourists who face physical or financial limitations to experience the thrill of exploration (Figure 12.19).

Figure 12.19 Joyful girl, having fun with VR headset

12.4.1.2 Virtual tourism platform

Innumerable platforms are coming out for smoother experiences in virtual tourism. This field uses Augmented reality (AR) and Virtual reality (VR) to create real-life experiences. One can make their own character, communicate with others, and even join guided tours. This transformation of travel experience will open new opportunities for engagement and collaboration as well as connectivity (Figure 12.20).

12.4.1.3 Business opportunities

Within the tourism industry, the metaverse offers a productive place for business. There are good opportunities for virtual travel agencies, virtual tour guides, and creators who

Figure 12.20 Young woman wearing VR glasses doing a game simulation

create immersive experiences. They will get good benefits from the increased interest in metaverse tourism. By all these methods tourism in the metaverse can reach the audiences far away from the traditional geographical boundaries (Figure 12.21).

Figure 12.21 Metaverse city, VR glasses transport business hologram

12.4.1.4 Sustainable tourism

Nowadays the environmental impact happening because of traditional tourism is a huge concern. However, metaverse tourism can provide a good alternative because it provides sustainable tourism by reducing carbon emissions by reducing carbon footprints which are associated with physical traveling and uses of natural fuels. Due to the increasing demand for virtual exploration, the negative impact on fragile ecosystems decreases, which promotes eco-friendly tourism methods (Figure 12.22).

Figure 12.22 Man travels wearing futuristic virtual reality glasses

12.4.1.5 Challenges and considerations

Metaverse has great potential but it also faces challenges. There are many issues that must be handled carefully. Issues like data privacy, security, and digital divergence need careful consideration. It is also important to make sure everyone feels welcome when enjoying metaverse tourism and inscribing worries about shifting it to business-focused is vital for the accurate and unbiased development of tourism in the metaverse (Figure 12.23).

Figure 12.23 Portrayal of AI robot hacker surrounded by a network

12.4.1.6 Cultural preservation

One of the crucial goals of metaverse tourism is to preserve the genuineness of cultural experiences. It is very important to get a good mix of cool digital experiences and show some respect for local cultures to avoid losing the uniqueness of traditional practices. Working together with technology experts, tourist guides, and local people can make sure that the virtual world keeps the essence of different cultures intact.

The metaverse is changing how we travel by giving new and cool ways to see the world more interestingly and differently. It also makes travel better with cool virtual experiences, creating new jobs, and helping the environment. It is making tourism easier for everyone.

12.5 Metaverse gaming

Metaverse is reshaping the Gaming Landscape.

The emergence of the metaverse is revolutionizing the gaming industry, transforming the way players engage with virtual worlds. This digital frontier, interconnected environments, and persistent virtual spaces are altering the very fabric of gaming, creating a dynamic and interconnected ecosystem (Figure 12.24).

Figure 12.24 People using metaverse

12.5.1 Immersive gaming experience

The metaverse introduces a new era of immersive gaming experiences. Players are no longer confined to traditional gaming setups; instead, they can enter expansive virtual worlds where the boundaries between reality and the game blur. Virtual Reality (VR) and Augmented Reality (AR) technologies are key enablers, providing a level of immersion that transcends conventional gaming.

12.5.2 Interconnected gaming realms

In the metaverse, gaming transcends individual titles. Virtual environments seamlessly blend different games, allowing players to navigate interconnected realms. This interconnectedness fosters a sense of continuity, enabling players to carry their avatars, achievements, and possessions across diverse gaming experiences.

12.5.3 Player-owned assets and economies

A notable aspect of the metaverse is the concept of player-owned assets. Virtual items, characters, and even land within these digital realms can be owned, traded, and monetized. Blockchain technology facilitates secure ownership and transactions, creating a player-driven economy where in-game assets hold real-world value.

12.5.4 Decentralized gaming platforms

The metaverse challenges the centralized nature of traditional gaming platforms. Decentralized platforms, powered by blockchain technology, offer players greater control over their gaming experience. This shift empowers players to have a say in the development of games, participate in governance, and shape the virtual worlds they inhabit.

12.5.5 Social interaction and community building

Gaming in the metaverse transcends mere entertainment; it becomes a social experience. Virtual spaces serve as hubs for social interaction, enabling players to connect, communicate, and collaborate in real time. This social dimension enhances the multiplayer experience, fostering friendships and communities that extend beyond individual games.

12.5.6 Virtual events and experiences

The metaverse redefines live events in gaming. Virtual concerts, conferences, and in-game events are becoming increasingly common, drawing players into dynamic and interactive experiences. These events transcend the limitations of physical venues, reaching a global audience and blurring the lines between gaming, entertainment, and real-world experiences.

12.5.7 Accessibility and inclusivity

The metaverse democratizes access to gaming. Virtual reality headsets, augmented reality devices, and even traditional screens become gateways to immersive gaming experiences. This increased accessibility fosters inclusivity, allowing a broader audience to engage with drivers' gaming worlds.

12.5.8 Emergence of metaverse-specific games

Developers are now divining games specifically for the metaverse. These games leverage the interconnected nature of virtual spaces, offering unique and expansive narratives that unfold across different gaming realms. Players can seamlessly transition between games within the metaverse, contributing to a cohesive gaming experience.

12.5.9 Challenges and considerations

The metaverse brings unprecedented opportunities and challenges. Issues related to privacy, security, and ethical concerns must be addressed. Balancing the player-driven economy with fair and sustainable practices is crucial for the long-term success of the metaverse gaming ecosystem.

12.5.10 Future of metaverse in gaming

The metaverse represents a paradigm shift in gaming, offering a glimpse into the future of interactive entertainment. As technology continues to advance, the metaverse will evolve, creating richer, more immersive, and interconnected gaming experiences. The boundary between the physical and virtual worlds is blurring, and the metaverse is at the forefront of this transformative journey.

In conclusion, the metaverse is a game-changer for the gaming industry, redefining how players interact with virtual worlds. This dynamic shift towards immersion, interconnectedness, and player ownership, heralds a new era where gaming transcends traditional boundaries, opening exciting possibilities for both developer and player alive (Figure 12.25).

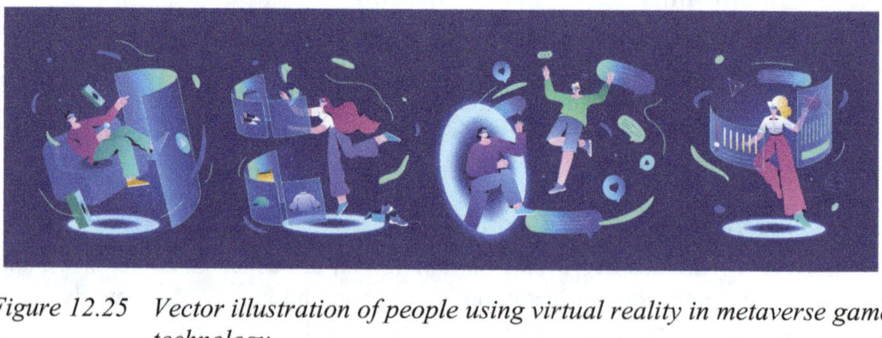

Figure 12.25 Vector illustration of people using virtual reality in metaverse game technology

12.6 Remote work in metaverse

Remote work has changed a lot lately. It is not just about using online tools anymore. Now, we have the metaverse—a virtual reality space where you can chat and work with computer-made worlds and other people. This article looks at how remote work and the metaverse come together, talking about the good things and the problems it might bring.

12.6.1 The metaverse as a workplace

The metaverse is like a digital environment in this world where people can work together as if they are in the same place. It creates virtual offices where colleagues can talk, share ideas, and do team-building activities, making remote work more interactive and engaging (Figure 12.26).

Figure 12.26 Futuristic women engineer wearing virtual reality enhanced collaboration and communication

12.6.2 Enhanced collaboration and communication

Using the metaverse for remote work is better because it makes collaborating and talking with colleagues feel more like being in the same room. Unlike regular video calls, the metaverse lets avatars of people interact in a shared virtual space, making it feel more real and closer, even if team members are far away (Figure 12.27).

Figure 12.27 Metaverse meeting room

12.6.3 Overcoming geographical barriers

Working in the metaverse from anywhere means teams can easily work together worldwide. People can join virtual meetings and collaborate without worrying about time zones or travel. This flexibility helps organizations find talent globally and encourages diverse collaboration among people from different cultural backgrounds (Figure 12.28).

Figure 12.28 Metaverse classroom online school VR camera avatars

12.6.4 Productivity and focus in the virtual realm

Working in the metaverse has challenges. Staying focused needs a well-designed virtual office. It should be immersive but not too distracting. Customizable workplaces, spatial audio, and virtual tools help create a good environment for remote work. Balancing an engaging experience with minimal distractions is crucial for productivity in the metaverse (Figure 12.29).

Figure 12.29 Metaverse office cubicle space with employee avatars

12.6.5 Addressing technological barriers

Lots of companies are using metaverse for remote work. As companies use the metaverse for remote work, it is important to tackle technological challenges. Employees need good devices and fast internet. Need of Wi-Fi technology is a must for conducting things smoothly. Organizations must invest in cybersecurity to protect data and virtual spaces from potential threats in the metaverse.

12.6.6 The future of remote work

Remote work and metaverse coming together show exciting possibilities for the future of how we work. As technology gets better, virtual, and augmented reality will likely become even more important in shaping our work lives. The metaverse gives us a sneak peek into a future where traditional offices do not limit us, and work becomes a lively, interactive, and immersive adventure.

12.7 Events in metaverse

The metaverse is like a big digital playground where people can use virtual reality to play and talk with each other. It is a fast-changing world where cool things happen, like concerts, parties, and business meetings, all in a computer-made space, it is a mix of fun, socializing, and serious stuff, making it a virtual world full of different experiences.

12.7.1 Virtual concerts: a sonic revolution

In the metaverse, musicians and artists are doing virtual concerts. They use this digital space to connect with fans, making it feel like you are at a concert from home. They create realistic avatars and nice realistic visuals, making the concert experience even better and letting them be more creative in the music world.

12.7.2 Socializing in the digital realm

The metaverse is like a lively online place where people can have parties and hang out. You can do things like attend virtual weddings, celebrate birthdays, and casually chat with friends. It makes socializing online feel real, connecting people from different places and time zones, and giving a new way to have fun together.

12.7.3 Business conference and trade shows: a virtual revolution

Companies are using the metaverse for online meetings and shows. It is a cheaper and effective way for them to talk to people worldwide. In this digital space, attendees can explore online exhibition areas, and connect with professionals globally. This change shows that businesses are using more digital ways to do things (Figure 12.30).

Figure 12.30 Business conference room

12.7.4 Niche interest and hobbies: exploring digital realm

In the metaverse, there are places for specific interests like art. Artists can show their work to people worldwide in virtual galleries and museums. You can explore digital art in unique ways, different from visiting a regular gallery. This makes art more accessible to artists and people who love art.

12.7.5 Education in the metaverse: an immersive learning journey

In the metaverse, education is getting more exciting. Students can attend classes in a virtual space, do interactive activities, work with classmates online, and listen to experts from anywhere in the world. The metaverse is changing education to be more interesting and accessible, giving a lively way to learn.

12.7.6 Gaming: driving the evolution of the metaverse

Games are a big reason the metaverse is growing. Virtual reality and augmented reality make games more exciting with cool worlds and stories. Virtual sports and eSPORTS tournaments, where people play games professionally, are getting popular, showing that digital entertainment is changing and becoming more than just regular gaming.

12.7.7 Considerations and challenges: privacy, security, and ethics

As more people use the metaverse, we need to think about keeping things private and secure. Spending a lot of time and virtual spaces makes us worry about protecting our information and who we are online. It is important to find a good balance between new ideas and using the metaverse responsibly so that everyone can enjoy it safely.

12.8 Banking in metaverse

As technology advances, banking continues to evolve. One of these innovations is called metaverse banking. A metaverse bank is a virtual world where users can interact with each other as avatars. It will revolutionize the way banking works in unprecedented ways. Let us explore the potential benefits of metaverse banking, the challenges we may face, and what the future holds (Figure 12.31).

Figure 12.31 Businessman touches online banking and network connection

12.8.1 Enhanced customer engagement

The metaverse gives banks a fantastic chance to make customers more involved and interested. Banks can use cool virtual platforms to make special and personal experiences just for their customers. Picture going into a make-believe bank online. You can interact with a computer character who works at the bank, try out different money stuff like games, and can also learn about financial literacy programs.

12.8.2 Virtual banking services

In the metaverse, regular bank stuff can easily be a part of the online world. In the easier metaverse world, you can check your money, send it to others, and even ask for a loan—all without leaving the virtual space. Imagine virtual ATMs in the online world where you can take out money easily. And there are smart computer advisors that can give you personalized financial advice instantly. These online banking services make it easy for people to do their banking stuff no matter where they are.

12.8.3 Financial education and literacy

The metaverse is a great place for learning about money and how it works. Banks can use simple virtual reality to make fun lessons, games, and pretend situations to teach people about money stuff like budgeting, saving, and investing. Using virtual reality makes learning about money (financial learning) more fun and easier, especially for younger people who like using computers and digital stuff (Figure 12.32).

Figure 12.32 Virtual reality glasses

12.8.4 Security and privacy considerations

In the metaverse banking world, keeping things safe and private is super important. Banks need strong security like locks on a door to protect your information. They use fancy technology like fingerprint scans and face detection tools, and special codes to make sure only the right person can access your money stuff.

12.8.5 Regulatory compliance

For banks in the metaverse, following rules must be very important. They must understand and follow the laws about protecting you, keeping your data private, and handling money. Banks, rule-makers, and technology experts must work together to make sure virtual banking allows all the important rules and standards (Figure 12.33).

12.8.6 Ethical and social implications

Bringing banking into the metaverse makes us think about what is right and fair. We need to make sure everyone, including people with disabilities, can use it easily. Also, we should be careful about spending too much time online. Banks must be responsible and make sure everyone can use virtual banking fairly and safely.

The metaverse can totally change how banks work. It can make customers happier, give easy virtual services, and teach about money in new ways. But banks need to be careful about keeping things safe, following rules, and doing what is

Figure 12.33 Regulation compliance financial control internet technology

right. If they use the good things about the metaverse and solve problems wisely, banks can be leaders in the digital world, giving customers awesome experiences in the virtual space.

12.9 Medical training with metaverse

The use of cutting-edge technology was originally designed for video games to revolutionize healthcare.

Case Western Reserve University's Professor Mark Griswold is highlighted for using 3D anatomical images in a virtual environment with top surgeons' avatars. Powered by Microsoft's HoloLens, this technology enables collaborative surgical planning in multiple locations at once, cutting down on consultation time.

HoloLens makes healthcare discussions faster. Unlike the old way with days of video calls, now it might take just an hour. The virtual room it creates lets doctors talk deeply and analyze better, making healthcare teamwork more efficient and accessible than ever before (Figure 12.34).

Figure 12.34 Illustration of a person wearing a virtual reality VR

In this virtual environment, medical professionals can visualize and discuss complex surgeries, such as brain surgeries, with exceptional detail. The text emphasizes the efficiency and accessibility of this technology, indicating a shift from lengthy video calls to possibly just an hour for a comprehensive consultation.

Furthermore, the technology is not limited to surgical planning; it also offers a new method for teaching anatomy. Studies have shown that virtual models help students learn twice as fast and retain knowledge longer. The immersive experience allows users to explore and understand anatomical structures in ways that traditional methods cannot replicate.

As this technology becomes more accessible, the passage suggests that high school students, as well as those in community college or nursing programs, could benefit from a more advanced understanding of anatomy, previously only available to medical students. The potential impact of this technological integration in healthcare and education is highlighted, demonstrating a significant shift in how medical professionals approach surgeries and anatomy education (Figure 12.35).

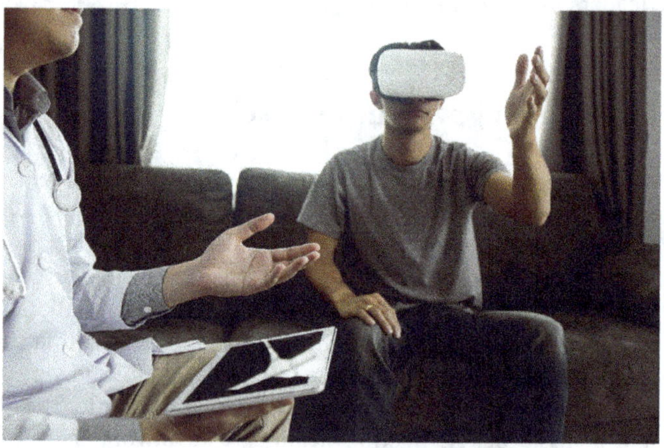

Figure 12.35 Doctor is using the tablet to send the data to the virtual world

12.10 Metaverse shopping

Metaverse shopping is the practice of buying products and services in virtual environments that exist within the metaverse. The metaverse is a collective virtual space formed by the convergence of VR, AR, and the Internet (Figure 12.36).

In a metaverse shopping experience, users use avatars to explore virtual environments that represent products and storefronts. They browse, order, and purchase items in an immersive virtual environment.

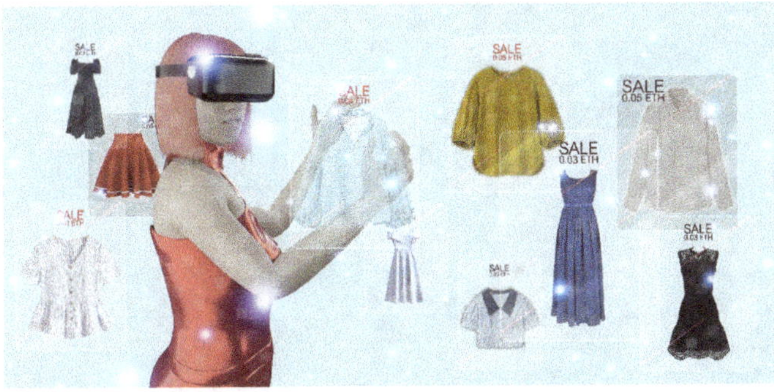

Figure 12.36 Online shopping and VR headset metaverse women clothing

Metaverse shopping combines elements of online shopping with the immersion of virtual reality. It allows users to shop, chat, and interact with brands and others in a dynamic digital space.

Metaverse shopping worlds often feature one-of-a-kind shopping experiences, virtual tries, and product customization options (Figure 12.37).

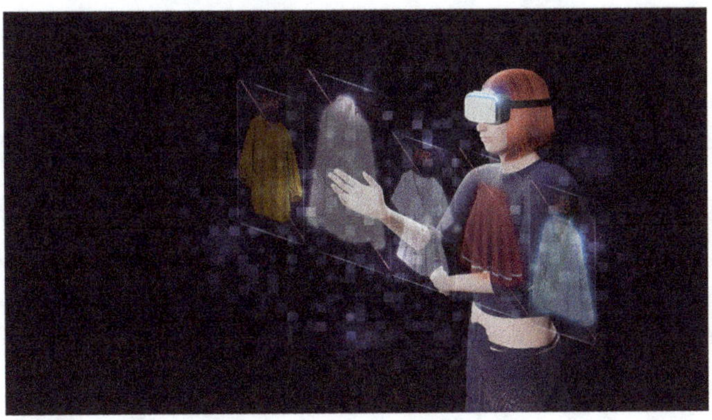

Figure 12.37 Online shopping and VR goggles metaverse women clothing

Chapter 13
Application domains for the metaverse

Prasanna Kumar[1]

Abstract

Several domains such as education, entertainment, real estate, manufacturing, and healthcare are experimenting with the metaverse. As the paradigm is maturing, other industries will jump on the bandwagon. This chapter will explain how various domains can be empowered significantly with the metaverse. With a deeper understanding of the power of metaverse environments, industry verticals explore, experiment, and embrace state-of-the-art applications of metaverse.

Keywords: Platform Applications; Metaverse Finance; Talent Transformation; Metaverse Medicine; Defense; Application Trends; Interplay; Harmonization

13.1 Metaverse application experiments

Metaverse application experiments are spread across multiple domains. Most notably in the fields of Immersive Gaming, eLearning, Defense Training, Flight Simulations, and Augmented Surgical Training. Metaverse applications have traditionally been used in Crypto Commerce, Smart Contracts, and Metaverse models of the Economics and Finance domain. In addition, other applications such as metaverse art galleries and metaverse clubhouses offer rich alternate life experiences in social interaction domains and are also emerging as strong growth categories. However, in order to understand metaverse applications and its domain better it is important to analyze the progression of the technology building blocks, the multitude of inherent drivers, the short-lived demand hype cycles as well as the long-term trends. A longitudinal view of these metaverse applications, from the past to the present, holds the key to their future.

Here are some key events in the metaverse application progression. The historical origins of metaverse applications take us back to 1962 when Morton Heilig built the Sensorama, a machine to simulate riding a motorcycle and watching a 3D movie while sitting in a vibrating chair with a running fan and perfumed air dispenser to simulate smells. The conceptual origin of metaverse applications started much earlier, in 1938, with Antonin Artaud, a playwright, with the use of the term "Virtual Reality," in his

[1]Business Optima, Fairfield, CA, USA

collection of essays "The Theater and Its Double." However, it was not until 1992, when Neal Stephenson coined the term metaverse in his book Snow Crash. It depicts a future world where wealthy people venture into a 3D-connected virtual reality. There are many important inventions, innovations, and events that have propelled the growth of the metaverse application. Let us take a look at some of the key events. In the 1960s, the Department of Defence (ARPANET) established partnership networks with a network of external researchers, universities, and nongovernment institutions that work together to deliver the internet. ARPANET was decommissioned in the 1980s, leading to the establishment of the Internet Engineering Task Force (IETF) to promulgate the technical evolution of the Internet protocol suite. Another key event that further propelled is the emergence of hyperlinking of resources. Most notably web documents, Tim Berners Lee's creation of HTML and hyperlinks, in 1989, became the building blocks for the World Wide Web and accelerated metaverse progression. In 2003, Linden Lab unveiled Second Life which allows users to build things and exchange virtual goods. Linden Lab launches Second Life, a shared 3D virtual space. Experiencing the world outside the realm of current reality. In 2006, Roblox allowed users to create and play massively multiplayer games developed by users. In 2007, Google launched augmented maps with a street view for a virtual at-scale representation of the real world. In 2009, Satoshi Nakamoto (pseudonym) minted the first bitcoin and launched the first blockchain leveraging the proof of work algorithm. Blockchain ledger, connected via hash tables. The trust is managed by blockchain verification based on pathways with the highest computation effort.

In 2010, a game launched games delivering specific VR experiences e.g., the gacha video game (toy vending). This game entices players to spend in-game currency to receive in-game items. In-game currency can be gained through gameplay or by purchasing it from the game publisher using physical world currencies. In 2011, the Futuristic novel Ready Player One. In 2012, Yoni Assia introduced colored coins and coined it bitcoin 2.x. Ethereum was introduced by Vitalik Buterin. Google augments maps with street view, which allows the exportation of virtual representations of real-world objects at scale. Several VR games have been introduced in the decades.

Oculus was launched on Kickstarter as a low-cost VR hardware. In 2014, Oculus was acquired by Facebook in 2014 for $2 billion as part of its hugely expensive and near decade-long pursuit of virtual reality technology assets. The acquisition of Oculus was primarily to help Facebook scale 3D infrastructure. On the digital currency front, Kevin Mccoy and Anil Dash create a non-fungible token (NFT), a unique cryptographically secure virtual asset. In 2015, Vitalik Buterin and Gavin Wood launched Ethereum to build decentralized apps on blockchain. In 2016, DAO raised VC funds and launched the Ethereum blockchain. Pokémon Go introduced augmented reality games to the real world. In 2018, the video play-to-earn game Axie Infinity, developed by studio Sky Mavis, popularized the uses of NFRs integrated into the Ethereum blockchain. In 2019, Epic Games's Fortnite became the most popular virtual world game with 250 million active users—2021 is the year it all came together.

In 2021, Facebook's parent company rebrands itself as Meta, outlining the vision for the metaverse. In 2021, Nvidia announced that the metaverse economy will be larger than the physical world economy and Nvidia's platforms and processors would be at the heart of it. Microsoft also launched Mesh as a synchronized virtual collaboration platform. The same year saw two of the largest initial public offerings (IPO) in the gaming industry with Roblox Corporation and Unity Technologies. In 2022, Siemens and Nvidia partner for industrial applications in metaverse. In 2023, Elon Musk's brain–machine interface, Neuralink, received FDA approval for human trials. With these events, funding patterns and technology building blocks, metaverse applications are now equipped for a transformative roadmap.

The future of metaverse is all set for bending our imaginations with generational evolution. Metaverse platforms have the potential to transform how, when, and where companies interact with their customers, as extended reality platforms enable businesses to deliver new experiences and provide information in new ways. For example, tour companies could provide a persistent immersive experience in the virtual realm overlaid onto the physical world to inform tourists as they move through new destinations, for instance, bringing historical events to life in old cities. Imagine you are trekking, and a virtual guide for trekkers appears and helps you navigate the terrain, delivering personalized information in real time to enhance the experience. Companies could also offer potential customers alternative buying experiences. For example, automakers could offer test drives in an extended reality setting. Imagine the number of test drives and the related metaverse marketing and outreach that can happen because of the economics of scale at low outreach cost—that is the power of the appropriate use case of metaverse applications.

13.2 Metaverse gaming applications

Gaming applications developed for children and young adults have historically seen the highest adoption in recent times. Many of these gaming companies no longer position themselves as gaming companies but as creators of experiences. More precisely, technology platforms allow people of all ages to create and develop experiences, publish to platforms, and share with each other. Virtual world platforms such as Roblox, Minecraft, Fortnite, Farmville, etc. offer world-building capabilities in urban areas and rural settings. The city building process has generated millions of square miles of built-up area. Gaming has gone through a tremendous transformation from traditional fixed location computer terminal-based gaming to tablet and mobile-based Augmented Gaming using PUBG (Player Unknown's Battlegrounds), and further pushing the envelope of experience onto the mixed reality and finally on to the fully virtualized reality with oculus headsets. In addition, a set of smart wearables is incorporated into the gaming domain delivering 12 degrees of freedom. Dungeon & Dragons gaming domain is set in a medieval fantasy world. Players create characters and describe their actions and thoughts as they play. One player referred to as the dungeon master (DM) assumes the role of a storyteller. The DM creates a unique gaming experience for all participants and leads the players through the game. Gamers follow the DM's narrative and events in different ways. Gamers can select character features and skills, and earn points to move up. Demeo, a virtual reality clone of Dungeons & Dragons, is a crawler that users can select a dungeon class and prowl with a crew. These VR scenarios are randomly generated. Users no longer need to be in the same room as another player to kick things off. This game can be played on the following platforms: Valve Index, Oculus Rift, Meta Quest 2, HTC Vive, PS VR, and PS VR2. Other popular VR games include Superhot VR, Beat Saber, Tetris Effect, Connected, Batman, Arkham VR, Elite: Dangerous VR, The Elder Scrolls V, Skyrim VR, No Man's Sky VR, Blade and Sorcery VR, Resident Evil 4 (Remake), Alyx (Half-Life). Here is a detailed list of gaming application platforms (Table 13.1) and their operating domains.

Table 13.1 Platform applications

Platform applications	Description
Axie Infinity	Set in an expanding metaverse-type universe, Axie Infinity helps battle, build, and hunt for treasure. This online video game is NFT-based and features digital pets (Axies).
Decentraland	3D virtual world where users can buy, create, and explore NFT-based plots of land using Ethereum-based cryptocurrency.
Fortnite	Fortnite video games are from Epic Games. These gaming applications offer an immersive digital gaming and social space with a realistic environment.
Horizon Worlds	VR-based game that allows users to socialize with one another in various ways for hosting events and games. Horizon Worlds was formerly Facebook Horizon and it is published by Meta Platforms.
Illuvium	Illuvium is a fantasy role-playing game with a graphic and rich immersive experience built on the Ethereum blockchain.
IMVU	In this online metaverse and social network, users create 3D avatars, connect, and 3D chat.
Nvidia Omniverse	Nvidia offers development toolkits and processor platforms for creating and operating metaverse applications.
Otherside	Otherside is a virtual world and multiplayer game. Gamers can design and develop NFT-based land and interact in a number of ways. This is quite similar to Sandbox and Decentraland.
Pokémon Go	Pokémon Go blends VR and AR settings with virtual characters and images. Players can play the game in the real world.
Roblox	Roblox offers users immersive spaces and a virtual world in which to engage. This is both an online game as well a game-creation platform. Similar to Fortnite, the Roblox game is popular with younger users.
Ready Player One	Ready Player One is framed in a dystopian world in a futuristic time (2040s). It is crafted around a teenager's quest in a popular virtual reality environment—OASIS. OASIS is an immersive and interactive digital space that mirrors their vision of the metaverse.
Sandbox	Sandbox is an Ethereum-based virtual world. The gaming application allows users to build, share, and monetize their creations.
Voxels	Voxels is a user-owned virtual world. Players can buy land, build on it and customize their avatar. This was formerly called Cryptovoxels.

Application in the Metaverse Gaming Industry has seen the osmosis of several technologies through the process of acquisition. One of the biggest acquisitions in 2022 is from Microsoft acquiring gaming company Activision Blizzard, for 69 billion dollars. It is estimated that in the H1 of 2022 alone, Venture Capitalists invested 120 billion dollars in metaverse. Metaverse components extend beyond reality headsets into VR rooms supported by blockchain and NFTs, IoT, and next-gen cloud technologies as a way to deliver novel experiences, entertainment, and offer new sources of revenue. The following section elaborates on metaverse applications in the finance domain and their economic influence.

13.3 Metaverse application in finance and economics

Economics is the art of managing unlimited needs with limited supply. The metaverse economics of matching demand for products and services with the supply requires equilibrium in the minting of the currency for metaverse transactions. Digital currency management and monetary flow require the Metaverse Federal Reserve, which is referred to as the Metaverse Exchange. The policies established by these exchanges control currency valuation, inflation and deflation management. Various metaverse applications allow NFTs, that uniquely identify an asset purchased on the metaverse. This underpinning technology verification not only allows attestation of value but also provides power and transferability to the physical world. The net value of the metaverse assets has been growing, primarily because the metaverse currencies provide the necessary privacy and secrecy of wealth management. In future care cases of digital riots, heists, anarchists and hackers, frauds in metaverse, and helplessness to recover could be cause for concern. Enforcement of restoration of order and providing remedy and delivering metaverse justice could be tough and chaotic. Applications are being developed in the metaverse for capital market products, Metaverse Currency Exchanges, Position management, Call and Put options, forward contracts, and other post trade processing including clearing and settlement. Currently, Bitcoin, Ethereum, Ripple, Litecoin, Monero, Zcash, Dash, Beo, Cardano, and Stellar are some of the well-recognized currencies trading with their unique metaverse symbols. The future of the metaverse is borderless control of humans, humanoids, robots, and AI infrastructure, all requiring currencies.

The value of these metaverse digital assets will far exceed that of physical assets. The application also requires multiverse infrastructure automation, data pipelining, AI (Artificial Intelligence) and MLOps (Machine Learning Operations) integration, universe2universe integration (U2U), user pool, digital identities, user non-repudiation, digital negotiation and arbitration capabilities, prompt engineering, and capabilities to plug and plug into multiverse mode. The entire infrastructure needs to be built on powerful zero-trust architecture while leveraging public key cryptography, message digest, hashing algorithms, and blockchains. Let us see this action.

With multi-domain metaverse integrations, we would be able to book a car on metaverse, pick it up in the real world, refill gas at regular gas stations or charge our EV vehicles and pay with metaverse currencies and drop the vehicle in real world and get billing and refunds processed in metaverse. Credit card usage will disappear from the map of the earth, metaverse QR code and NFT, a unified payment gateway that combines the digital currency of the real world and the virtual currency of the metaverse will take over. Applications that make this integration a center stage will have trillions of dollars, worth of monetary pipelines and assets under management. Creating an abundance of demand and scarcity of supply, modeling instruments of monetary flow and positioning it in between transactions.

Metaverse Digital Locations and Service endpoints can replace existing internet domain names and search engines. Early investors can buy digital representations of real estate, snapping up concert venues, shopping malls, and other properties in the metaverse. This virtual real estate is speculative, but it is drawing interest from several tech-savvy investor groups. What makes it more attractive is the interplay between virtual world and physical world realities. A restaurant creates a presence in a metaverse so customers who are working, playing or exploring in that digital space can easily and quickly order real world pickup or delivery. A restaurant could create a seamless experience on metaverse earnings, wherein the user can virtually enter the restaurant and place an order using or earning loyalty points that the company digitally tracks. Finding customers, booking tables, and realizing and reconciling payments are cost-efficient by moving operations into the metaverse. Few companies in the farmers' market domain are moving their presence into the metaverse. Internet publishing companies have started listing metaverse as their headquarters. The virtual market onboards customers as digital avatars, who can reach vendors, negotiate rates and buy products. Farmers in MetaMarket move local food into virtual markets with a focus on becoming one of the bellwether vendors selling plant-based food within MetaMarket.

Key indicators of the metaverse's economic viability are the successes in revenue cycle management. The sale of digital assets does offer huge opportunities for many companies. Many companies are selling goods and services that only exist in the digital world. That big-name brand companies in the fashion industry are selling digital-only clothing and accessories, following in the footsteps of gaming platforms that have sold similar items for many years, may point the way to opportunities for the broader business landscape. Ralph Lauren is selling clothing for avatars, and Nike is creating an NFT that links to its real-world counterpart. Gucci has teamed up with product and entertainment company Superplastic to create a limited series of collectible NFTs. The next biggest economic crash may originate not in the physical world but on the metaverse affecting the physical world ledger entries resulting in the freezing of accounts and transactions. Metaverse offers infinite spacing and unlimited real estate and the ability to store digital assets and even store a portion of money away from safekeeping, away from the influences of inflation, deflation, and other real-world market dynamics. Considering all things, the Nvidia CEO's prediction might not be too far from the possibility of what he outlined that the metaverse could save companies billions of dollars in the real world.

13.4 Metaverse in training and talent transformation

In the age of information exchange, restrictions on in-person gatherings during the global epidemic and the adoption of work from home had compelled institutions to leverage online meetings, zoom calls, Google Meets, learning tools and platforms, and immersive methodology of communication. Along with augmented reality, organizations are also exploring training in fully virtualized metaverse environments. Organizations across various industries could harness the metaverse to provide enhanced training to their workforce through simulation of the problem domain. So that they can solve the issue in the VR environment and apply the learning into the real-world environment. Mentors, trainers, and learners across the globe can virtually meet in the metaverse world and work through real-life scenarios together while using data and experience from both worlds to propel forward the learning journey. Metaverse applications for learning are available, especially for learning through visualization of simple to complex topics. Learners can learn astrophysics through visualization and bringing far-off planets much closer to the viewer on the metaverse.

Companies have established their presence in VR settings. Hyundai Motor Company established Hyundai Mobility Adventure, a metaverse experience on the gaming platform Roblox. Gamers' avatars can experience Hyundai's future mobility projects and current products. Warner Bros. Pictures hosted a virtual party on Roblox to market its movie *In the Heights*. Still others are branding their own metaverse projects. Walt Disney Co., a leader in Theme parks and movies, offering an imaginative escape from the real world, is actively pursuing the metaverse. Disney's theme park metaverse initiative converges physical and digital worlds, with wearables, smartphones, and digital access points immersing the guests in the metaverse experiences. Digital twins will play a major role in metaverse development, particularly when it comes to industrial uses. For example, German engineering firm Siemens intends to claim its share of the metaverse. The company is focused on transport, infrastructure, and energy verticals, where it already has a strong presence. Siemens is combining its Xcelerator open digital business platform and partner ecosystem with Nvidia's Omniverse, with the goal of driving the use of digital twins to deliver process improvements. Nvidia's GPU chipsets (Graphical Processing Units) are well attuned for processing underpinning technologies such as computer vision, natural language understanding, AR, AI, IoT, and mining cryptocurrencies.

Let us look at another application of the metaverse in hiring and job training: conducting job interviews in metaverse environments, presenting quizzes, and delivering job training. Candidates who pass the metaverse test which simulates the actual work environment: for example, asking candidates to work in the metaverse restaurant to see if the candidates can deliver on the job requirement and verify whether or not the candidates are a good fit with the right work culture before making hiring decisions. Industry Light and Magic (ILM) has created a walled LED metaverse environment that is leveraged by Hollywood moviemakers for production-grade filming. Such a metaverse environment not only helps visualize or train the production crew but also uses Stagecraft as a production environment to create not just camera-ready copy but can in fact produce very high-quality post-production quality content. Unreal engine powers many of the 3D movie product efforts. This computer graphics engine was created by Epic Games. ILM subsequently built their own engine, Helios. Helios is centered around key requirements for a real-time cinematic render engine and quicker turnaround and streamlined for efficient post-production.

13.5 Metaverse application in medicine

Hospitals are leveraging VR technology for patients' bedside assistance. The usage of smart handheld devices for faster recuperation is a clear winner, especially in postoperative care. Studies have revealed higher patient engagement and endorphin-assisted recuperation with the adoption of VR HMD and handhelds. Several of these applications have been adopted on an experimental basis. Patients can also take Virtual Reality vacations using Head Mounted Display from the hospital bedside. There are several theme-based VR vacations and eVisits to theme parks, including popular rides of the gondola canals of Venice. These metaverse experiences along with smart wearables can deliver therapeutic experiences to help alleviate pain experienced by amputees in their phantom limb.

Integrated CT scans and real-time feedback led to corrective surgical operative procedures and technologies that have VR roots, especially Augmented Reality and Robotic Assisted Surgeries. Surgeons can now operate on their patients from the other side of the planet. This is not science fiction. In large hospitals and tertiary care centers, nearly 10% of elective surgeries are now robotic surgeries. DaVinci Surgery system has pioneered Robotic Surgery arms that have low tremors compared to surgeon's arms. The system also delivers high-order field view and magnification, minimum cuts, less blood loss, and avoid needless cuts resulting in quicker recovery. Oculus and HoloLens are used in key medical technology applications, from the design of medical devices to surgical procedures. Johns Hopkins Neurosurgery Spinal Fusion Laboratory has conducted augmented reality surgery. Augmented Reality guides surgeons in surgical navigation points and pathways to ascertain which direction the incision should proceed for precision cuts and guides with real-time inputs for the best surgical success rate.

Mayo Clinic has also applied metaverse building blocks for surgical interventions. Robotic surgery delivers minimally invasive surgery with a clean clear field of view. These procedures are performed through tiny incisions, often referred to as Keyhole surgery because of the smaller size of these incision entry points. It is also sometimes used in certain traditional open surgical procedures. The most widely used clinical robotic surgical system includes a camera arm and mechanical arms with surgical instruments. Ortho Field Fitted Actuators and Metaverse Arm and remotely operated by Surgeons are common. Apollo Hospitals in India has deployed several Robotic Surgery equipment across its vast hospital networks delivering excellent surgical health outcomes. Robotic Surgery offers a clear field of view, less hand tremor, more than 100× magnification, minimum cuts and blood loss, resulting in quicker recovery time.

Plugging Machine Brain Interfaces, Oculus VR headsets, Smart Glasses can vlog the activity by recording and archiving it to be passed on to future generations. These recordings can help alter not only the individual's relationships with society in the present era but also for the times to come. Users can persist their ailing parents and children's activities of daily living in the metaverse. People can relive their memories long after they are gone or no longer available, by bringing them back to life for a lived experience, which can help in curing depression. In a world that is becoming increasingly lonely, the metaverse offers an escape from reality, providing access to the most pleasurable experiences, promoting health, and enhancing well-being.

13.6 Metaverse meetings and service coordination

Organizations across industries already use augmented reality to improve operations. A fully realized metaverse will support a more collaborative environment where data will be ubiquitous and always present. Companies on metaverse development are stepping into the next version of virtual meetings. Since the pandemic era, remote working, zoom meetings, screen sharing, green screening, whiteboard, and 3D avatar enablement have been mainstreamed.

Customers can reach out to the VR-enabled customer care center using their VR headsets. They can talk to CSRs and avatars to resolve issues, create orders, and check the status of their tickets. We will be able to use avatars to meet with people in a virtual space that replicates the feeling of being in an actual room with them. This will require virtual reality (VR) goggles and motion capture gloves to render expressions, body language, and the quality of others' voices. Such tools may extend the reach of workers, enabling them to execute tasks virtually. The technology will be able to transport them to other work locations while also letting them interact with others in both virtual and physical worlds. Through a remote immersive digital twin, one worker might be able to manage multiple retail stores.

Organizations can use metaverse applications for "Zero-Wait" customer support. Instead of getting through the call center, customers can now self-navigate to issue resolution, generate support tickets, check status, connect with previously provided resolutions, persistent workflow, conduct data verification, explore other remedies and escalate if required while avoiding wait queues. Business-focused metaverse uses case-centers on extended reality to help workers do their jobs better, particularly through the use of augmented reality. The fully realized metaverse should be able to stream information in ways that make workers more efficient and productive. Metaverse can be used for citizen engagement: especially citizen reporting town hall discussions and grievance management. Civic workers can check properties across the different parts of the city zones with the use of metaverse overlaying digital information onto the real-world crime watch, riot management, and maintaining law and order. In addition, metaverse platforms could inform community members about their real-world equipment conditions, all from within that platform. Elevator manufacturers have adopted metaverse in combination with Industry Automation 4.0 for training their staff for MRO (Maintenance and Repair Operations).

13.7 Metaverse application in defense

Key applications in the defense sector include flight simulators and zero-visibility landing solutions, especially in foggy weather conditions, through the integration of aircraft radar, ground-based radar, and GPS data. These technologies are used by the military, air force, HUD, and drones, as well as in advanced systems like those developed by Boston Dynamics. These solutions are essential in dangerous or inaccessible environments, aiding in terrain mapping, terrain hugging, and operations across air, water, and land. Underwater, they help hunt submarines and deploy water drones, while in outer space, they enable cost-effective simulations and missions, including landing craft on the far side of the moon.

Although these technologies present an easy entry point, they often require large initial orders and must meet high military standards, which include over-engineering requirements and strict exclusion criteria. Price points are frequently prohibitive due to technical specifications, accumulated tech debt, and high unit material costs, making products and vendors less viable, and resulting in long development cycles.

In terms of training, flight simulators are used to train air force pilots, while special forces train in jungle and urban warfare scenarios. These simulators can adjust settings to provide realistic, risk-free, and cost-effective training experiences, enhancing skills in complex environments.

However, commercialization of intellectual property (IP) in defense is challenging, with many projects unable to complete the maturation cycle due to contractual obligations and regulations like the Official Secrets Act. The transition from lab to market in defense takes much longer compared to non-defense projects. To speed up the maturation cycle, public-private partnerships are necessary, with open-source methodologies offering one of the best approaches to engaging diverse talent, aligning use cases, and accelerating demand cycles.

Additional use cases include VR-enabled airline safety, which provides zero-visibility landing solutions for commercial aircraft through classified Category IIIc landing systems, allowing for safer landings in foggy conditions. For the commercial sector, the metaverse is used for pilot training and licensing, with many airlines adopting virtual reality simulators to improve air safety training and enhance real-world outcomes.

13.8 Metaverse applications' interplay

Digital autonomous vehicles will make an interplay of physical world mobility and digital world mobility. Your physical presence in a location will have value in the virtual world because you can make a virtual world commitment transferable to the real world and vice versa. For the virtual world promises in a VR room can be transferred to the real world into actions depending on courier and execution contracts and to send or receive physical objects and packages. Similarly, your connections in the virtual world and influence and experience can interplay and transfer to the real world. Metaverse concept evolves and matures, people will be able to more easily and seamlessly engage with objects and each other in ways that blur the digital and real worlds. Individuals will be able to use avatars to try on digital versions of actual clothes and receive training for performing complex work tasks such as high-risk surgeries or flying and landing aircraft. Engage in simulated experiences like skydiving while feeling the actual physical sensations. Uber, Lyft, and other rideshare operations and their drivers' physical presence at a geo-location can be interplayed to move, people, products, and goods. Achieve enforcement capability for smart contracts negotiated in the metaverse discussion room, transfer to the physical world for getting injunctions and jurisdictional harmonization. The payment made in VR bank can be fully convertible to physical banking withdrawals and even mortgage micropayments or making mega purchases e.g., paying for your yacht. This interplay of physical geo-location with the metaverse location and decisions requires innovative metaverse applications. Capital will graduate from being just global to meta-global capital.

13.9 Other metaverse application trends

Metaverse applications clearly focus on their target segments, demonstrating initial appeal, sustained engagement, and effective hooks that encourage users to return for more. According to a 2021 global survey by Statista, a consumer data company, metaverse enables users to overcome obstacles, in particular physical disability, that prevent them from engaging in activities in real life. The other benefits are creativity and imagination enhancement and the ability to travel the world without moving. Entertainment in the metaverse is garnering a lot of interest, particularly from younger consumers who are likely to drive metaverse growth. Pop superstar music concert series are streamed within the Fortnite gaming universe delivering novelty in the metaverse with far greater immersive entertainment experiences than the concert itself—with the ability to freely talk and make connections with other concertgoers without fear or inhibitions. Big-name brands and artists have also explored metaverse entertainment and leveraged them in specific industrial micro-vertical experiments.

VR headsets will become prevalent, smart wearables will make our muscles twitch, ingestible will make healthcare interplay, smart sleeves, flexible displays, virtual touch buttons that are haptic, and even enable us to read thoughts and intentions. Neural Link will make these experiences real. It may not be far in the future wherein we can have applications to upload pain-relieving thoughts to neural uplink systems. Let us look at one such application in the experiment stage. Sensory decoding of motor intent is a path-breaking tech innovation. Metaverse applications can now leverage interface devices for the human nervous system using wrist wearable 16-channel electromyography. The output of the motor cortex en route to the hand can now have a representational state for interactions with computers e.g., typing keyboard with the keyboard using just the electromyography device. The potential use cases coming out of the full representation of the user's hand in VR space along with predictive AI to decode motor intent without the user moving at all or with just limited subtle movement has limitless application possibilities. One of the significant events in this space is Facebook acquiring neural interface startup CTRL-Labs for its mind-reading wristband. In the future, we can expect metaverse applications with the capability of neural interface interactions.

Early adopters of metaverse clubhouse applications are primarily younger generations seeking love and acceptance. They are creating virtual communities featuring empty towns with various amenities, such as VR bank, VR Dollar Tree, bowling alley, basketball court, senior centers, book clubs, pool parties, virtual restaurants, music venues, and dance bars equipped with crowd control measures. There are also meditation rooms designed as tranquil islands with shrines at the center, as well as yoga rooms. Additionally, the metaverse includes a simulated criminal justice system through a feature called Meta Court. Users can engage in audio spots to listen in on conversations; however, when a user speaks, other members and visitors in the room can hear them. If any visitor becomes disruptive, room members can vote to remove them.

Future applications will include the ability to build a VR asset including a home in the metaverse and bring it to the physical world, and have the option to pay for it in VR, or the real world. Even if a person lives in a shanti real-world housing, users can put on their headset, build and live in a luxurious villa with digital walls and ambient lighting controlled using a Crestron-like AV automation for mood-setting lighting and music. Experience, light, sound, water, and touch even get food and material items delivered to their physical world. These applications along with the interconnection of real-world supply chain operations and metaverse operations will completely blur the differentials of the metaverse physical world possibilities. A similar experience is delivered in the VR world that is very affordable. Individuals can use avatars on augmented mirrors to try out eDressing. What is potential is to deliver a similar experience without the burden of wearable gadgets. Projection technology and audio spots can be game changers. Spotlight by Holosonic offers a focused narrow beam of spot audio and music transforming retail experience. These technologies have already been experimented with by system integrators in the banking sector to deliver specific products to targeted customers visiting banks. They could be in the queues and the lobby area yet receive audio messages that others nearby cannot hear. This provides both privacy and relevance in information dissemination without burdensome gadgets. Metaverse applications can leverage this technology to combine location-specific services delivered without the burden of carrying gadgets in public areas. It is a mixed reality that can operate in the public space.

Persistent and interconnected network of 3D virtual worlds that will eventually serve as the gateway to most online experiences, and also underpin much of the activities in the physical world. For decades, these ideas have been limited to science fiction and video games, but they are now poised to revolutionize every industry such as finance, healthcare, education, city planning, dating, and others. The metaverse offers trillions of dollars in new value while significantly reshaping our society, lives, labor, and activities of daily living.

13.10 Summary

Metaverse applications need to cycle through the change management process of framing, norming, and conforming in the target domain. Currently, there are pipelines of application use cases that are at different stages of metaverse maturation cycle ranging from early-day experimental proof of concept for metaverse second life to time-tested applications in the medical and military domains. While the use cases are shaped by the utility value and experiences delivered, the creative ideation process does offer compelling value propositions when combined with cutting-edge R&D experiments. These experiments require product governance to manage the technology hype cycle, in order for the application to have a roadmap that is necessary for long-term success.

Further reading

[1] Matthew Ball (2022). *The Metaverse*. New York: Liveright

[2] Neal Stephenson (1992). *Snow Crash*. New York: Bantam Books

[3] Samuel Greengard (2019). *Virtual Reality*. Cambridge, MA: MIT Press

[4] Cornell Hillmann (2021). *UX for XR: User Experience Design and Strategies for Immersive Technologies (Design Thinking)*. New York: Apress

[5] M. Pell (2017). *Envisioning Holograms—Design Breakthrough Experiences for Mixed Reality*. New York: Apress

[6] Erin Pangilinan, Steve Lukas, and Vasanth Mohan (2019). *Creating Augmented and Virtual Realities: Theory and Practice for Next-Generation Spatial Computing*. Sebastopol, *CA*: O'Reilly Media

[7] Marcus Magnor, Alexander Sorkine-Hornung (2020). *Real VR—Immersive Digital Reality: How to Import the Real World into Head-Mounted Immersive Displays (Lecture Notes in Computer Science Book 11900)*. Berlin: Springer

[8] Amit Johri and Kalpesh Parikh (2023). *Revolutionizing Metaverse: Delve Into the Building Blocks of Metaverse Commerce*. New Delhi: BPB Publications

[9] Suchismit Mahapatra, Vladimir Blagojevic, Pablo Bertorello, and Prasanna Kumar (2021). New methods and metrics. Suitable for evaluating LFQA tasks. *arXiv*:2112.13432 [Preprint]

Chapter 14

Illustrating metaverse-driven smart manufacturing

Pethuru Raj[1]

Abstract

The metaverse phenomenon is on the fast track. With the solidity of metaverse technologies, hitherto unheard and unknown use cases are being conceptualized and delivered to ordinary people and end users. The metaverse represents the next evolution of the Internet. Academic researchers and industry professionals are striving hard and stretching further to articulate and accentuate the unique competencies of the metaverse. Pundits and proponents say the metaverse can open new capabilities and opportunities. Metaverse aids in the modeling and simulation of complex products and processes. The unprecedented improvisations smoothen the path towards the metaverse era. Immersive technologies are emerging and evolving to reap all the initially expressed benefits of the metaverse.

Businesses across the globe are keen on leveraging the growing power of the metaverse to conceive and concretize powerful applications and advancements for industry professionals. This chapter is to dig deeper and deal with the industrial metaverse. The readers can learn a lot about the ground-breaking technologies and tools and how they are assisting in building and deploying metaverse systems.

Keywords: Haptic Feedback; Teleporting; Digital Holograms; Telepresence; Hyperconnectivity; Spatial Computing

14.1 Introduction

The manufacturing industry is sincerely adopting distinct advancements unveiled in the domain of the industrial metaverse to be correct and relevant to their partners, customers, and consumers. With the faster maturity and stability of digital transformation technologies and tools, the establishment and sustainment of intelligent manufacturing are progressing steadily. The manufacturing industry is ceaselessly going through a series of technology-inspired innovations and disruptions. Every tangible thing on manufacturing floors is meticulously digitized and connected with

[1]Edge AI Division, Reliance Jio Platforms Ltd., Bangalore, India

other digitized entities in the vicinity, as well as remotely held and cloud-hosted software services and applications through one or other network infrastructures. That is, every physical, mechanical, and electrical system in industrial environments gets digitized and integrated locally with one another and remotely with cloud-based systems. The key contributor to this transition is the suite of digitization technologies. The Internet of Things (IoT) and edge technologies such as tiny sensors, actuators, stickers, RFID tags, barcodes, chips, microcontrollers, etc., in conjunction with wired/wireless communication technologies, facilitate the transition of ordinary and dumb objects into extraordinary and active artifacts. Such digitized elements join and contribute to mainstream computing. Market analysts and researchers forecast that there will be trillions of digitized entities in the years to unfold.

On the other hand, the device ecosystem is growing fast these days. Purpose-specific and agnostic devices are evolving in everyday environments (living, working, relaxing, walking, etc.). With short and long-range network technologies and topologies, devices are deeply and decisively networked to form device clusters that can handle complex tasks elegantly. Devices are increasingly computational, communicative, collaborative, perceptive, and responsive. We have a variety of resource-intensive devices such as appliances, instruments, equipment, machinery, robots, drones, kitchen utensils, and electronics (consumer, medical, automotive, avionics, etc.). Market watchers forecast that billions of connected and cognitive devices will be on planet Earth. Manufacturing industries are benefitting immensely through the accumulation of sophisticated devices. This phenomenon is being termed the Internet of Devices (IoD). That means different and distributed devices find one another purposefully and work together to achieve something useful for businesses and people.

Further on, we have proven and potential software engineering processes, practices, platforms, and patterns to simplify and speed up producing, deploying, and improving software products, solutions, and services. There are many architectural styles, enabling technologies, automated tools, infrastructure optimization methods, etc., for building competent software solutions for personal, professional, and social problems. With the overwhelming support for microservices and event-driven architectural styles, all kinds of software are being constructed as a collection of portable, interoperable, horizontally scalable, publicly discoverable, network-accessible, and easily deployable and observable microservices. Typically, microservices are small in size and fulfill only one business functionality. Microservices, which are customizable, configurable, and composable, emerge as the flexible and futuristic building block for enterprise-scale, mission-critical, event-driven, service-oriented, cloud-hosted, and process-aware software systems. Microservices are being built, tested, curated, improved, and stocked in software repositories (private and public). Software developers, programmers, and engineers can check and use the correct and relevant microservices to construct helpful software applications. Thus, microservices are being dispersed across web servers. This aspect is touted as the Internet of Services (IoS).

With the emergence of an enormous number of digitized artifacts, connected devices, and software services, the amount of digital data generated is enormous.

Terabytes and petabytes of digital data are being produced. The next step is cleaning the captured data to crunch it and derive actionable insights. There are many digitalization technologies, such as artificial intelligence, helping to extract hidden patterns and valuable associations from digital datasets. The knowledge discovered gets disseminated to concerned systems and people so they can embark on countermeasures in time with all the clarity and alacrity. AI-powered data analytics emit helpful information out of digital data. Digitalization technologies and tools enable the transition of data to information and knowledge. Other vital enablers include cloud-native computing, cybersecurity, edge computing, batch and real-time data analytics, 5G communication, digital twins, high-performing processing units, etc.

Thus, digital technologies (digitization and digitalization technologies) come in handy for making sense of digital data. Any industry would immensely benefit from digital technologies for strategizing, planning, prioritizing, and steering in the right direction toward the identified destination.

The manufacturing industry is also getting empowered through the methodical usage of breakthrough digital technologies. The end-to-end manufacturing lifecycle can be accelerated, augmented, and automated. Energy-efficient manufacturing sees the reality with the heightened usage of digital technologies. The mantra of more with less is accomplished with digital transformation technologies' power. Manufacturing becomes versatile, resilient, and intelligent.

As discussed above, factories are purposefully empowered by path-breaking digital transformation technologies to be competent in their manufacturing operations. Automation is peaking in manufacturing. Manufacturing companies could collect massive quantities of multi-structured data from their processes, products, assets, assembly lines, and operators and perform advanced analytics to emit valuable insights. The knowledge produced augments machines to be intelligent in their operations, offerings, and outputs. The efficiency of machinery, equipment, and assets goes up significantly. The resulting products are of high quality. The assets' safety and sustainability are fully guaranteed. Manufacturing costs will come down sharply. Premium and people-centric products can be designed, developed, and taken to markets.

14.1.1 Describing the industrial metaverse

The industrial metaverse combines physical and digital paradigms. Humans are augmented to experience next-generation industrial applications (Industry 4.0 and 5.0 systems). In the metaverse era, humans will have digital representations (typically termed as avatars). Further on, digital representations are being prepared and expounded for manufacturing floors and facilities, industrial assets, production processes, etc. The idea is to empower people to control, communicate, and work with them. For industrial metaverse applications, there is a need for low-latency and highly reliable communication infrastructure capable of accommodating several thousands of IoT edge devices. The phenomenon of edge computing is getting the attention of many these days as it has the power to guarantee real-time communication. Artificial intelligence is another paradigm for achieving the intended goals of the industrial metaverse. Decentralized architecture and federated learning are essential ingredients for envisaging multifaceted metaverse systems. Cybersecurity is another critical area that must be vigorously and rigorously looked into to attain the intended success of the metaverse paradigm.

Cloud-native computing is gaining momentum nowadays. Cloud infrastructures and platforms must be adaptive to play a vital role in shaping the metaverse mission and vision. Simulation is an essential requirement for visualizing metaverse services. Digital twins, as described in detail below, are paramount to a blend or journey toward the worlds and aims.

> The industrial metaverse enables substantial acceleration of engineering efficiency. The industrial metaverse enables real-time collaboration, connectivity, and spatially-aware context within industrial environments.

14.2 Demystifying the metaverse technologies

The brewing idea of the metaverse is gathering momentum. With the implementation technologies accelerating at astronomical speed, the metaverse is flourishing. Nowadays, terms such as virtual games, economy, avatars, and spaces are buzzing. Product and tool vendors, IT software organizations, and cloud and communication service providers are working in unison to smoothen the road toward the metaverse era. Manufacturers are excited to be productive at the intersection of the digital and physical worlds. Precisely speaking, the highly enigmatic metaverse is being realized.

Metaverse is a set of technologies that allows for digital representations of the real world's various aspects (people, properties, and places). The metaverse typically represents the next generation of the social web. There are social networking and professional networking applications. We tell Alexa to turn up our home's thermostat. The metaverse brings in additional layers to immerse us in virtual environments.

We can add information that overlays the real world with the metaverse. For example, smart glasses might remind you about a friend's birthday when you run across him in the park. On the other hand, it is to recreate the physical world in a virtual setting. Walking around at the top of the Eiffel Tower virtually while standing in your living room is possible. It is possible to create entirely new environments, such as previewing your new house before you build it. VR gloves might allow you to feel an object hundreds of kilometers away.

Today, online games create virtual worlds. Avatars/characters are limited to a single game. However, a single avatar representing a physical person can travel and interact in multiple universes in the metaverse. Employees deployed in different parts of the world can collaborate in a virtual room to complete a product design and implementation.

We discussed the evolution of digital transformation technologies. A few more technologies exist for building and experiencing next-generation metaverse systems.

- **Web 3.0**—The web paradigm is steadily evolving from Web 1.0 (the simple web) to Web 2.0 (the social web). The next-generation Web (Web 3.0) was initially called semantic web. However, there is a twist. With the surging popularity of decentralization technologies such as blockchain, Web 3.0 is termed the decentralized web, which serves as the foundation for the fast-emerging and evolving precept of the metaverse.
- **Blockchain**—As mentioned above, there is a massive rush towards decentralized architecture and systems, which contrasts with the hugely popular centralized database systems. Data gets replicated in multiple places. The decentralization happens to solve several limitations of the centralization. Blockchain systems are based on this robust decentralization architecture. Blockchain is famous for ensuring the tightest data security by leveraging encryption. With the broader adoption of cryptocurrencies, product and service purchases, trading, and selling in the ensuing era of the metaverse are being democratized.
- **AR/VR hardware**—To access metaverse systems, specialized devices with stereo sound, gyroscopes, accelerometers, magnetometers, and structured light systems are insisted on. These augmented devices provide an immersive experience for users and act as an interface between the real and virtual worlds.
- **5G/6G communication and edge computing**—Ambient and adaptive communication network topologies and technologies are vital for accessing metaverse systems remotely. Real-time access is being facilitated by 5G communication infrastructure. Edge computing is to take the computing activity to the location wherein data originates. Real-time data capture, preprocessing, and analytics for emitting real-time insights are enabled through edge device clusters/clouds.

In other chapters in this book, the chapter authors have detailed much about immersive technologies. The IoT sensors and devices are the data generators, AI models deployed in cloud servers, and edge devices contribute as data crunchers. Blockchain-enabled data storage is the new arrival.

14.3 Powering manufacturing with the metaverse paradigm

The industrial metaverse is about applying metaverse technologies to build industry automation applications. In the standard metaverse environment, a person may play a game. However, in an industrial metaverse setting, a car manufacturing company employee can use the industrial metaverse to learn how to assemble a car virtually. Digital technologies are considered foundational and fundamental technologies of the industrial metaverse era. Web 3.0, blockchain, edge computing, 3D modeling and simulation, digital twins, and immersive technologies take the metaverse to the industry metaverse. Simulating industry machines, manufacturing floors, assembly lines, and transportation systems has led to the adoption of the industrial metaverse.

We discussed the mainstream digital transformation technologies at the beginning of this chapter. With a greater understanding of metaverse power, adopting and adapting metaverse technologies and platforms are gaining speed these days. Product and tool vendors, software organizations, and manufacturing industries collaborate on intelligent manufacturing. Technological innovations such as 3D modeling and scanning, blockchain, digital twins, immersive technologies (virtual, augmented, mixed, and extended realities), Web 3.0, cybersecurity, edge computing, and artificial intelligence have laid down a stimulating and sparkling foundation to envisage next-generation immersive environments to simplify, speed and do manufacturing activities sagaciously. The metaverse technologies have the innate strength to realize industrial metaverse applications.

Formally speaking, the industrial metaverse is the convergence of digital and immersive technologies to create and sustain immersive 3D virtual environments or the combination of immersive virtual and physical environments. The concept of the industrial metaverse will flourish as these immersive 3D environments can be accessed using any Web-enabled devices such as laptops, smartphones, tablets, and VR and AR devices. With fast and reliable connectivity infrastructure, accessing data-rich and immersive 3D environments from anywhere using any input/output (I/O) device can lead to envisaging and building newer industrial use cases. Thus, the idea of the industrial metaverse is slowly yet steadily capturing the attention and attraction of business executives.

14.4 Exploring the industrial metaverse

The metaverse is three-dimensional, using the metaverse's transformative capabilities and representations of real-world items and scenarios. The metaverse concept is fast evolving to be pervasive and persuasive. Enterprises and manufacturing industries are increasingly making use of the transformative capabilities of the metaverse. With the industrial metaverse, manufacturing industries are generating business value.

The industrial metaverse creates a virtual environment where skilled workers, assistants, and authorities can work together in real time. They can be employed in different manufacturing plants. Users can access virtual representations of products, machinery, and entire manufacturing facilities in the industrial metaverse and simulate different scenarios to optimize designs, identify potential issues, and make informed decisions. This has the potential to significantly improve efficiency, lower costs, and reduce the environmental impact of industrial processes.

Business experts and technology leaders believe that the industrial metaverse offers novel ways to solve many current problems and to envisage newer use cases for factory automation. Production assembly lines and supply chains, the complicated processes in any manufacturing floor, must be succulently enabled through the industrial metaverse. An article published on the Deloitte website indicates that the metaverse helps recruit and retain top talent. Experts have suggested that the industrial metaverse will bring in many turnarounds and twists for the manufacturing industry in the years to unfold. Enterprises keenly strategize and plan to make higher investments to reap all the initially expressed benefits of the metaverse. In a nutshell, the industrial metaverse paradigm has become a buzzword in industry circles. The metaverse can unleash new competencies for the modeling and simulation of production processes and systems. Virtual product prototyping, facility design, employee training, and collaboration with employees, partners, and end customers across the globe are being visibly facilitated through the industrial metaverse. Field workers can get expert training through the metaverse, which enables machinery and facility maintenance. With VR headsets and AR software in digital assistants, the adoption of the industrial metaverse (IMV) is picking up fast. IMV helps create a virtual layout for any factory.

14.5 Industrial metaverse use cases

The concept of simulation can enable industries to improve processes substantially. Real-world simulation simplifies new product designs, development, and distribution to retailers and end users. The distinct advancements in the industrial metaverse can empower manufacturing.

- **Facility design and engineering**—Designing a new manufacturing building can be hugely simplified through the intelligent use of the industrial metaverse. The metaverse comes in handy when creating a virtual building structure design. Such a virtual facility aids in identifying any potential problems before building it physically. Facilities and floors and designing manufacturing equipment, instruments, toolkits, appliances, etc., can be intelligently developed and deployed.
- **Process planning and redesign**—Not only machinery, assets, products, and toolsets but also manufacturing processes can be optimized to be efficient through simulation. The goal of process excellence is achieved through simulation. For example, assembly line performance engineering and enhancement can be guaranteed through simulation.
- **Predictive maintenance**—Every factory piece of equipment must be meticulously maintained to elongate its life. AI-powered predictive maintenance is one of the widely supported activities. Experts say that IMV technology can enable users to view data for not only one machine but for all the processes and systems impacted by that machine undergoing maintenance. With this information, the concerned people can make correct decisions about maintenance timing.
- **Faster virtual product prototyping and testing**—Experts point out that the industrial metaverse helps make virtual prototyping and testing any product fast, easy, and affordable. Potential investors and customers can experience their products and suggest modifications if necessary. People can experience virtual prototypes from many angles.

- **Machinery and product training**—Field workers, sales executives, troubleshooters, and newly joined employees can get detailed training for expertly using complicated and catastrophic machinery situated on manufacturing floors. Any mishap or misstep can result in irreparable loss to people and properties, and hence, the metaverse-inspired training is a huge boost for product makers, managers, marketers, and maintainers.
- **Collaboration and guided work**—Today, we have company offices being set up in multiple locations across the world. Present-day collaboration among professionals dispersed across the company offices is found to be insufficient. Industrial metaverse technology can elegantly enable hands-on employee collaboration. A skilled employee can use the metaverse to handhold a junior employee through a complex operation.

With a greater understanding of the unique power of the metaverse, which can do wonderful things in any industrial environment, newer business and use cases are explored, experimented with, and expounded upon.

The metaverse contributes as a platform for communication and collaboration among distributed teams. Team members could assemble on a virtual factory floor to articulate the nitty-gritty of a vital project regardless of their physical locations. Metaverse application development companies can empower manufacturing industries to elevate their virtual presence to provide immersive and insightful experiences to their employees and customers. In short, the metaverse is to spur innovations toward more profound and decisive automation for industry verticals.

14.6 Digital twins for smart manufacturing

Digital twins are gaining popularity as they have the innate power to bridge the physical-digital divide. Digital twins are virtual replicas of physical assets or processes. They facilitate real-time monitoring, analysis, and optimization of the corresponding physical twins.

Digital twins can manage complex systems and simulate operations successfully. Digital twins have long been pulsating and popular in the industrial sector. Digital twins are virtual copies of industrial machinery and processes. Large-scale structures such as manufacturing facilities and cities are encoded as digital twins. Digital twins can provide a lot of structural and behavioral knowledge of machines. Digital twins can simulate alternative situations to give a detailed comparison (functional and non-functional capabilities) between the solution and its competing solutions. Digital twins help understand multiple aspects such as productivity, safety, and other things without halting production or jeopardizing worker safety. Process and manufacturing industries are training their staff on how to use and maintain equipment efficiently using VR headsets safely and securely. Therefore, there is no need to practice using real equipment.

The physical twins are integrated with digital twins over one or other networking options. That is, both physical and digital twins are constantly interacting. Sensors and actuators attached to physical assets at the ground continuously transmit operational, event, health condition, performance, security, and log data to the digital twins. That is, real-time data capture, transmission, and analytics to evaluate and extract valuable insights in time are made possible with the initiation and integration of digital twins. The complete plant operations are being minutely monitored, measured, and managed insightfully through the leverage of digital twins. The goals of business process optimization and automation are being accomplished through digital twins, which is a critical technological paradigm for the industrial metaverse. There is an integration of AI-backed real-time data analytics with digital twins. Digital twins become cognitive as they collect and analyze data from ground-level entities. New business models can be tested in a low-risk environment. This enables businesses to be innovative and inventive. The metaverse empowers learners to be skilled in newer business and technological initiatives. Employees and operators can practice heavy and high-end machinery through the metaverse capability. Similarly, blockchain ensures the impenetrable and unbreakable security of digital twins and the data stored and used by digital twins.

Digital twins help compare a product's design to the physical version produced. If there is any visible deviation or defect in the final product, corrective actions can be initiated and implemented immediately without any loss of face and brand value. As inscribed above, car manufacturers leverage the distinct advantages of simulation to produce high-quality products.

As explained in another chapter, immersive commerce is emerging with the metaverse. Today, electronic commerce is pervasive and popular. With so many incredible improvisations in the metaverse space, the new and reverberating concept of immersive commerce is taking a central place. Thus, it is not an exaggeration to state that digital twins open fresh possibilities and opportunities for industrial houses and business behemoths.

14.7 The potential of the metaverse in manufacturing

The industrial metaverse is to bring in a suite of technology-inspired automation for different industry verticals. By combining physical spaces with digital counterparts, the metaverse concept is seen as a game-changer. This digital and physical world convergence enables the manufacturing industry to create seamless and spontaneous value chains. Therefore, manufacturing operations are optimized, whereas manufacturing productivity increases drastically. Industries are enthusiastically watching the emergence and evolution of digital twins, 3D modeling, digital representations such as avatars, wearable devices such as VR headgear, on-device data processing, 5G communication, Web 3.0 infrastructure, etc. The immersive technologies (VR, AR, MR, and XR) guarantee holistic power and potential for the beneficial disruption of the manufacturing sector.

These solutions increase industrial efficiency, resilience, and risk-free operations. The long-pending goal of achieving more with less can be elegantly fulfilled. With AI, predictive and prescriptive insights will allow manufacturing to function in autopilot mode.

- **Empowering customers**—Businesses extensively use the metaverse to enable and excite their customers. Furniture manufacturers provide several unique and empowering capabilities to their customers. Prospective customers can design furniture requirements for their homes, hospitals, hotels, and companies through company websites and express their mind-boggling preferences to furniture manufacturers. Similarly, home buyers can interact with the design and layout of interiors before making their final buying decisions. Companies can get an accurate 3D virtual representation of the manufacturing floors, facilities, and production lines for manufacturing different products.
- Further, progress at construction sites can be verified remotely. Thus, clients and consumers can design anything they like and visualize it from different angles. Such a metaverse-powered facility goes a long way in enthralling customers. The design decision lies with end users.
- With haptics and 3D technologies, outside-in and inside-out thinking and sharing will flourish. The metaverse can especially facilitate product design and engineering sessions between customers and businesses. Teams dispersed in geographically distributed places can collaborate to arrive at innovative designs and functionality. Realtors, hotels, and offices can create realistic tours of their properties to enable remote views and decisions. The industrial metaverse is transformative for many industrial domains.
- **Enabling employees**—The industrial metaverse aims to empower employees. Collaboration, skill training, and learning will help employees be productive in their assignments and engagements. Recruitment and retention of skilled workers will become easy and fast. Companies provide VR headsets to their workers to be safe, as training on physical equipment is unnecessary.
- Immersive technologies come in handy in monitoring production equipment, server farms, processes, and machinery. Employees need not physically go into risky work locations. With digital twins, workers can remotely handle and troubleshoot equipment. The metaverse can ensure the required product quality.
- **Improving decision-making**—Artificial intelligence (AI)-backed digital twins are secured by blockchain. Digital twins are being increasingly deployed in cloud environments, which are highly optimized and organized IT environments. With the integration of AI, digital twins turn out to be analytical tools. Digital twins use mathematical models to simulate any mission-critical plant or product. Several multifaceted sensors are being deployed in and around the plant.
- Similarly, multiple sensors are attached to any physical product. Such a setup collects and transmits multi-structured data to remotely held/cloud-hosted digital twins to be processed. The knowledge discovered gets passed on to the concerned people and system to ponder the following action. Thus, AI-powered digital twins improve decision-making for people at work.
- Manufacturers can empower consumers to make decisions. For example, automotive manufacturers use the metaverse to enable prospective buyers to configure cars to their tastes. This empowerment can be a game-changer for car makers and buyers.

The idea of the metaverse is steadily and steadfastly growing. One promising growth area for the metaverse is none other than the industrial world. Factories, supply chains, and industrial assets are being systematically digitized and readied to be viewed, used, and managed remotely. Factory floors can be minutely monitored, and all problems can be addressed through the metaverse.

14.8 The industrial metaverse and generative AI

The metaverse is a virtual representation of the physical world. The industrial metaverse is gaining the attention of manufacturers these days. Industrial assets are methodically digitized and connected, and the integration of digital and physical systems is being facilitated. It is pointed out that with the fusion of generative AI and the industrial metaverse, the manufacturing industry will be transformed. Industry 4.0 and 5.0 applications will be the new normal, with greater robustness, resilience, and versatility. The manufacturing industry will become the new breeding ground for innovations and disruptions.

Generative AI is emerging as a powerful tool for manufacturers because it enables the generation of new product and process designs. The traditional methods do not help here. The power of generative AI penetrates every noteworthy domain. Industry stalwarts indicate that generative AI will simplify and speed up industry and business process optimization. With optimized processes in place, many business advantages can be acquired and used. Business productivity is bound to go up remarkably through waste reduction, less carbon dioxide emission, less power energy consumption, less heat dissipation, etc. Above all, consumers get premium and preferred products, solutions, and services.

Generative AI is being tested across multiple industry verticals. It has proven an effective tool for improving communications and enhancing customer service experiences within the aviation industry. Besides inventory management, the aircraft industry uses generative AI to manufacture aircraft parts and manufacturing process excellence with the direct assistance of digital twins.

Similarly, the automotive industry consciously leverages AI's generative power to create fresh vehicle designs. Generative AI empowers manufacturers to analyze vehicle, sensor, and production line data to analyze various aspects of vehicle systems. Such data-driven insights and decisions go a long way in manufacturing and delivering high-quality vehicles and post-purchase services.

Thus, generative AI penetrates every tangible domain with its untapped and enormous potential. As widely accepted, the business transformation journey is being sagaciously spearheaded by digital technologies and tools. Generative AI is one of the most promising digital technologies. As discussed above, the industrial metaverse is another powerful technological paradigm capable of bringing in a dazzling array of breakthroughs for the manufacturing sector. The enigmatic paradigm of digital twins is critical to the abounding success of the industrial metaverse. Manufacturers can achieve higher levels of disruption, innovation, and transformation by combining the power of generative AI with the industrial metaverse. This combination can result in virtual factories and virtual collaboration workspaces.

With enabling technologies maturing and stabilizing fast, the trendsetting concept of the industrial metaverse is getting many minds and market shares. Business houses and start-ups are seeking ways and means of achieving process excellence. The industrial metaverse is a simulated and 3D environment where business people, employees, partners, and consumers collaboratively design, develop, and verify products and processes. Technology pioneers and pundits envisage an excellent future for the industry metaverse, which has the strength to improve productivity, sustainability, and collaboration.

14.9 Conclusion

Metaverse describes a shared and simulated space (a computer-generated environment) where users represented as avatars can interact with other users. This unique interaction intersects the physical and virtual worlds. This transition represents the next generation of the Internet. People can have an immersive experience while gaming, shopping, socializing, and working. The metaverse will change how we consume and reciprocate content from the Internet.

The metaverse will drastically transform how people interact with each other and with data. The metaverse technologies, such as immersive technologies (VR, AR, MR, and XR), 3D modeling and simulation, AI, blockchain, the IoT, edge computing, 5G communication, etc., will lead to an innovative and immersive Internet and intranets (widely termed as Web 3.0). Engineers, employees, and end users can get immersive and enthralling experiences while they design, work, and use Web 3.0. This chapter focused on the industrial metaverse and its pioneering use cases for manufacturing.

Chapter 15

The metaverse as an educational tool: enhancing learning with blockchain technology

B. Narendra Kumar Rao[1] *and Shaik Shameen Taz*[2]

Abstract

Recently, the meta-world has received the most attention due to its potential for the internet of the future. However, to fully exploit these potential uses of the meta-world, several challenges must be addressed, including resource-intensive issues, application interoperability, and security and privacy hazards. We are starting to see the future of meta-worlds as a way to bring people together. The term "meta world" refers to potential future iterations of the internet and other digital experiences in blockchain, cloud computing, and artificial intelligence (AI) environments as well as virtual reality (VR), augmented reality (AR), and VR environments. Through the use of sophisticated haptic feedback and motion detection, these technologies improve user experiences by allowing users to create digital assets, interact with virtual environments, and access virtual worlds. By discussing the beginnings, definitions, and commonalities of the metaverse, this study aims to close the gap between blockchain technology and metaverse technology. A decentralized meta version that uses blockchain technology can have various advantages, including improved security, transparency, and ownership. It defines the educational meta-version as well as a synthesis and in-depth study of its features.

Keywords: Blockchain Technology; Meta-world; Immersive Learning; Augmented Reality

15.1 Introduction

In this study, we explore the concept of the meta-world by examining the integration between blockchain and artificial intelligence (AI). To do this, we analyze the latest developments in various aspects of the meta-world, including its components, digital currencies, applications of artificial intelligence in virtual environments, or technologies based on the blockchain. The success of interdisciplinary research

[1]School of Computing, Mohan Babu University, India
[2]Department of Computer Science and Engineering, Mohan Babu University, India

and studies on the convergence of AI and blockchain in the metauniverse will inevitably depend on the collaboration between institutions and academic branches. We intend that this study will become a valuable resource for researchers, engineers, and educators and contribute to the development of inclusive, equitable, and logical meta-worlds of the future. Metaverse Uni has developed connected training represented by e-learning. Metaverse technology is currently being developed in four categories: augmented authenticity, accurate worlds, reflect worlds, and virtual worlds. As a teaching tool, the metaverse aims to provide more engaging and interactive learning. While current research suggests that the potential of the meta-world in education is not small, blockchain technology can also be used to ensure user security and privacy in the meta-world. By decentralizing the infrastructure of the meta-world, blockchain can help prevent cyberattacks and other forms of malicious activity. The term meta-world refers to a virtual universe that is an extension of the physical world in which we live (Figure 15.1).

We will examine how the metaverse can be used as a teaching tool and how blockchain technology can enhance this learning experience. Instead of just reading about a topic, students can experience it themselves in a virtual environment. Explore the human body or travel to different parts of the world without leaving the classroom. An engaging experience can help students retain information better and engage more deeply with the material. this research will ultimately help expand the scope and depth of future research and provide foundational data that paves the way for future world-class research. With the rapid development of blockchain technology, the metaverse is becoming ever more accessible and poised to revolutionize the way we learn and educate. Another benefit of this meta-world is to provide better visualization that enables collaboration and social learning. Students can work together on projects in a virtual environment, exchange ideas, and learn from each other. Students can gain crucial social and communication skills through this collaborative learning, which are necessary in today's employment market. Learn how blockchain technology can improve education in the meta-world. Blockchain

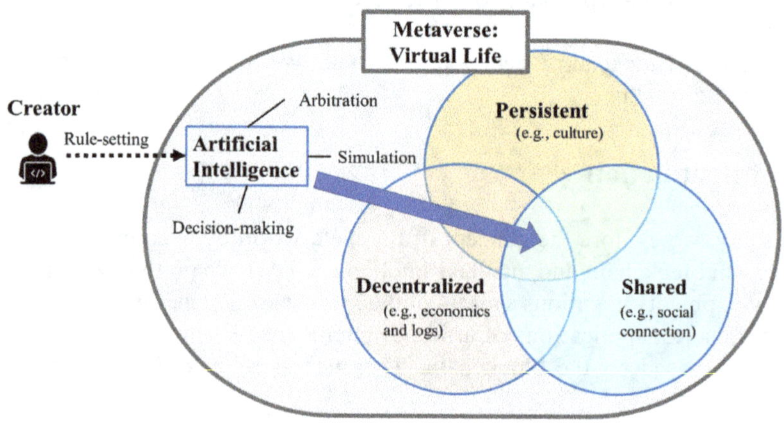

Figure 15.1 Definition, roles, and potential issues of metaverse in education

technology provides a secure and transparent trading platform that is essential to the metaverse. For example, blockchain technology can be used for the authentication of digital identities, tracking virtual asset ownership, and secure meta-global transactions. In addition, blockchain technology can be used to create a decentralized education system in the meta-world. This system allows users to create and share educational content and earn tokens or other rewards for their contributions. This decentralized system would provide people with more learning and educational opportunities while creating a fairer and more accessible education system. Blockchain technology can enhance this science by providing security and transparency and the creation of a decentralized meta-world learning system. As the meta-world grows, it is exciting to see how it can be used to enhance education and provide new opportunities for learning and personal growth. Another potential application for blockchain technology in the metaverse is the establishment of a network of digital credentials and certificates that are maintained on the blockchain and are easily verifiable by anyone. This would allow students to showcase their skills and achievements safely and transparently, and allow employers and educational institutions to verify their qualifications more credibly. This technology can also be used in the meta version for creation With the rapid development of blockchain technology, the metaverse is becoming ever more accessible and poised to revolutionize the way we learn and educate. Decentralized Autonomous Organizations (DAOs) can facilitate collaborative learning and research. These DAOs allow people from all over the world to come together and work on common goals and projects, sharing resources and knowledge in a more decentralized and democratic way. Using blockchain technology, we can create a safer, more decentralized, and collaborative learning environment that benefits both students and teachers. We discuss the technical analysis of data collecting, storage, sharing, interoperability, and data protection for blockchain-based metaverse approaches. Let us first talk about the meta-world's technological difficulties from each standpoint, and then we will show how blockchain might be useful. We are also investigating the effects of the metauniverse's core technologies, such as the Internet of Things, digital twins, multisensory and immersive applications, artificial intelligence, and big data. We will look at how blockchain technology can improve this educational process and how the metaverse can be used as a teaching tool. Instead of just reading about a topic, students can experience it themselves in a virtual environment: explore the human body or travel to different parts of the world without leaving the classroom. Students can learn more effectively and more fully interact with the topic with the aid of an engaging experience. Collaboration and social learning are made possible by the meta-world, which is another advantage. In a virtual setting, students can collaborate on projects, share ideas, and pick each other's brains for new insights. The social and communication skills that are so crucial in today's job market can be developed by students through collaborative learning: explore how blockchain technology might improve education in the meta-world. The metaverse depends on blockchain technology because it offers a safe and transparent trade environment. For example, blockchain technology can be used for the authentication of digital identities, tracking virtual asset ownership, and secure meta-global transactions. In addition, blockchain technology can be used to create a decentralized education system in the meta-world. This system allows users to create and share educational content and earn tokens or other rewards for their contributions. This decentralized system would provide people with more learning and educational opportunities while creating a fairer and more accessible education system. Blockchain technology can enhance this science by providing security and transparency and the creation of a decentralized meta-world learning system. As the meta-world grows, it is exciting to see how it can be used to enhance education and provide new opportunities for learning and personal growth. Another possible use of blockchain technology in the metaverse is to create a system of digital credentials and certificates that are stored on the blockchain and can be easily verified by anyone. This would allow students to showcase their skills and achievements safely and transparently. Finally, we present potential developments that can inspire future innovation and research advancements in the use of blockchain.

The justification for integrating the blockchain into the meta-world is presented after a quick explanation of the blockchain and the meta-world. Second, we go over how blockchain can be used to solve problems with data gathering, storage, sharing, interoperability, and privacy that are related to the many technical components of meta-worlds. Third, we talk about how blockchain affects some of the most significant meta-world technologies, including big data, artificial intelligence, IoT, digital twins, holographic telepresence, and XR multi-sensor technology. Let us discuss how blockchain is used in the metaverse through intriguing projects like Decentraland, Sandbox, Axie Infinity, and Illuvium. They appear to be discussing the potential applications of blockchain technology. In order to evaluate the advantages, possibilities, and hazards of meta-worlds for interesting and creative learning experiences, researchers in the field of education used the PRISMA procedure and the educational meta-world. Reviewing these concepts now, the science fiction book "Snow Crash" by American writer Neal Stephenson, published in 1992, was the first to mention a meta-universe. Characters from Snow Crash can change into avatars and interact with the meta world, a virtual environment in three dimensions (3D). Another world known as the "metaverse" is referred to as a virtual reality. The words "meta" and "universe," which denote transcendence and virtuality respectively, are its roots. "Digital earth" refers to a brand-new reality that is expressed through digital media like cell phones and the internet. Making the meta-world a reality requires a lot of effort and investigation. An example of a meta-world research organization is the Accelerated Studies Foundation (ASF). The idea of the meta-world, defining it as the meeting point of the real world and the virtual world, and presenting four of its categories. "A 3D-based virtual reality in which your daily activities and other activities take place" is how the meta-world is characterized. The term "metaverse" can also refer to the universe where daily life and business operations are coordinated. Some applications of the meta-world have already been used in education as the meta-world has been rapidly integrated into modern life. Blended learning has become increasingly popular after the COVID-19 pandemic and many innovations have been introduced around the

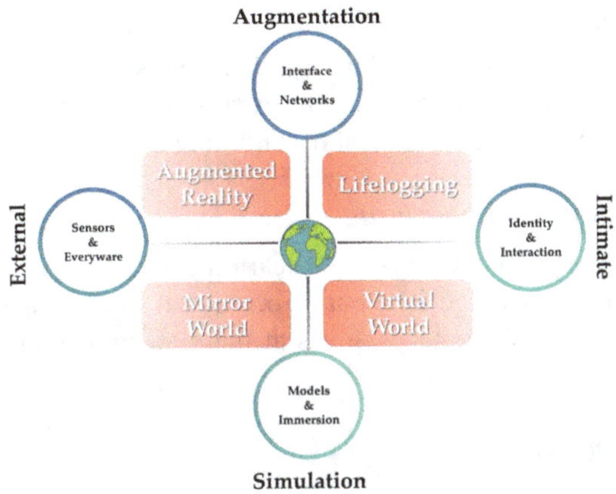

Figure 15.2 Kinds of metaverse

world. One of the greatest advances in education is the use of the meta-world to represent teachers, students, and visitors. Metaverse provides students with a safe environment in which to improve their soft skills. Students can practice their VR skills without feeling nervous or overwhelmed. It can also help people with limited mobility live happier lives. Organizations can gain insight into student performance in the meta-world to improve the quality of their learning. This information can then be used to identify areas of their business that need improvement. The phrase "life after the internet" refers to the meta-world. Initial applications include gamification, 3D simulations, and virtual campus simulations. Many other technologies can be used to transform education, so this technology is just the beginning. Avatars that solely depict real persons. In this instance, the real world and the virtual world collide, as real life intrudes into the virtual world through routine activities and business. In other words, he connects with his avatar in the metauniverse as being who he really is. The avatar engages in social, economic, and cultural activities in the metaverse realm. The meta-world is a sphere where the virtual and real worlds coexist, a place where social, economic, and cultural activities take place whose purpose is the creation of value and common development. The world and virtual reality are not only connected but also interact (Figure 15.2).

15.2 Probable applications of the metaverse in education

15.2.1 Blended learning

Combining online learning and traditional classroom instruction is made easier by the metaverse. It can offer a virtual setting where teachers and students can interact, work together, and take part in different learning activities, bridging the gap between traditional and digital learning.

15.2.2 Language learning

Language learning can be enhanced through an immersive experience in the metaworld. Students can practice languages in virtual environments that simulate real-world scenarios, using their language skills in a practical context.

15.2.3 Competency-based education

Metaverse can support competency-based learning by allowing students to showcase their skills and knowledge in a hands-on virtual environment. This personalized approach allows students to progress at their own pace and receive targeted feedback.

15.2.4 Inclusive education

Metaverse can provide a more inclusive learning environment for students of all ability levels. Virtual spaces can be adapted to different learning needs and offer opportunities for engagement and participation that may be difficult in traditional settings.

15.3 Applying the PRISMA protocol

The Preferred Reporting Items for Systematic Reviews and Meta-analyses (PRISMA) procedure is a structured method for carrying out these studies. PRISMA enables a systematic review of existing literature to gain a comprehensive understanding of the implications of meta-words for education and to identify potential benefits, challenges, and risks associated with their implementation. Blended learning, language learning, skills-based education, and inclusive education are just a few of the exciting revolutionary prospects that the marriage of blockchain and metaverse technologies offers. Assessment of the potential and hazards connected to these developments in engaged and innovative learning can be done rigorously and systematically by using the PRISMA procedure. In this context, the PRISMA protocol can be used to collect and analyze relevant research, analysis, and data to better understand the benefits, opportunities, and risks of meta versions for engaging and innovative learning experiences. The protocol includes several phases that include the definition of the research questions, the search and selection of the relevant literature, the assessment of the quality of the selected studies, the collection and synthesis of the data, and the final communication of the results (Figure 15.3).

15.4 Applying the PRISMA protocol to find the potential risk of metaverse as a tool for immersive and innovative learning experience

15.4.1 Objectives

The purpose of this objective is to provide general information about the possible existence of the metaverse a concept that can be applied to education and the

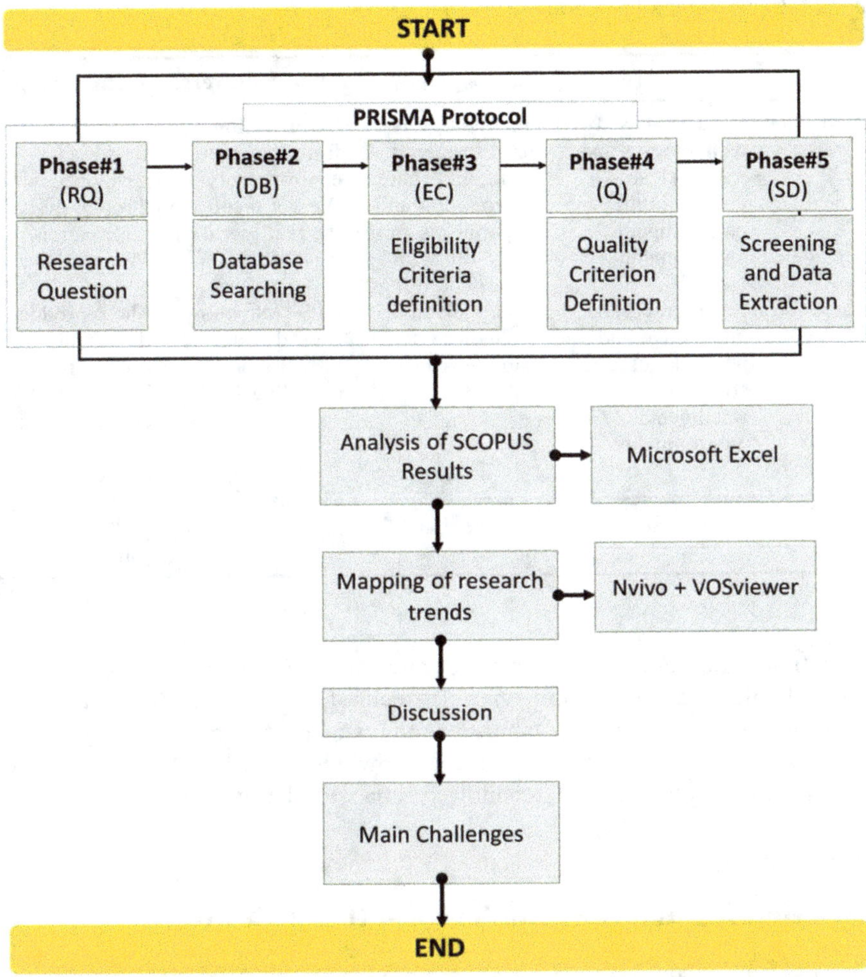

Figure 15.3 Stages of PRISMA protocol

purpose describe four classifications of the meta-world and to explain their possibilities and limitations in educational applications. In particular, the attributes of each meta-word type are explained using case studies. It also highlights the benefits of using meta-world in education and explores in depth its limitations and shortcomings.

15.4.2 Kinds of metaverse

Hyperverse Extension—When we talk about technology, we are talking about a technology that gives an actual system in the world new capabilities. Assistive technologies alter the physical world in a way that we cannot sense, adding more

Table 15.1 Distinct simulation technologies

	Artificial reality	Lifelogging	Mirror universe	Virtual world
Classification	Location-based technologies and networks are used to build an intelligent environment	Technology is used to record, store, and share information and experiences from daily life with others via things	By providing data from the external environments. We get a copy of the real world as it is	The virtual world is developed through digital information
Features	Location-based knowledge and networks used to structure an intelligent environment	Using advanced technology to capture data	GPS technology is used to develop virtual maps and modeling	The reproduction of the user's character is through the communication activities between avatars
Advantages	Smartphones, vehicle HUDs	Wearable devices, black boxes	Map-based services	Online multiplayer games

information than we can see. A distinct environment is created through simulation technology, as opposed to synthesis technology. To make the meta-world simulation a real environment where people can interact, many different strategies are used. According to whether the knowledge is utilized in the virtual or physical world, sophisticated technology and simulation can be categorized (Table 15.1).

15.5 Merging and the complexity of the meta world

Each of the four categories of meta-worlds has been examined in terms of its traits and illustrations. One way to describe the meta-world is as a place where the real world and virtual reality coexist. Real-world phenomena are replicated in virtual reality, merged with it, or create new worlds in virtual reality. Information retrieval, social networking, and gaming components are all combined functionally in the meta world. The meta-world portrays an expanding and evolving universe as a result of the COVID-19 pandemic and, from an evolutionary perspective, combines the internet with 5G. Technically speaking, the meta-world is a collection of virtual reality tools. The social dimension is a place where members of the digital generation leave traces of their everyday and professional lives in the online world and its many manifestations (characters, avatars). This is made possible by 3D technology. Each form of meta world outlined above is summarized in Table 15.2 along with its characteristics and pedagogical implications.

Table 15.2 Basic metaverse technological features and their educational consequences

Type	Technology-related traits	Potential effects on education
Artificial reality	• Add virtual elements to real objects to make them appear three-dimensional and authentic (paper greeting cards, for instance, might be improved to resemble 3D graphic cards). • Include fancy yarn (such as Pokémon Go on the street and Zepeto, which recognizes faces and creates 3D avatars).	• Quickly solve difficulties by using computer simulation to learn the invisible elements graphically and in 3D. • Reading, writing, and speaking are available interactive activities when within a learning setting.
Lifelogging	You can use social media and social networks to capture and share your daily life and your thoughts, such as blogs, YouTube, wikis, and other online communities. • To provide value, wearable technology and various IoT sensors are used to gather and analyze data on users' everyday activities (for instance, health tracking with Nike Plus).	Taking stock of your day and commenting on it can help you present and use information more effectively, and comments made by others on social networking sites can inspire and motivate you. • Monitor science and improve it based on analysis (e.g., using a dashboard).
Mirror world	• GPS and network technology that goes beyond what is physically possible, such as Google Earth and other map-based apps. • Adding real-world components to the virtual environment for a specific purpose, such as Airbnb, Minerva School, food ordering apps, taxi calls, bus schedules, parking finding apps, etc. • In actuality, though, it does not include everything. By encouraging happiness and enjoyment, organizational and operational flexibility, and collective intelligence (as seen in games like Minecraft, Upland, Digital Lab, etc.), it essentially broadens the actual world.	• Learning transcends the boundaries of space and physicality by occurring in the meta-world of the mirror world. • Use video conferencing and collaboration tools that act as dynamic mirror worlds, including Zoom, WebEx, Google Meet, and Teams, and deliver live online courses on these tools. • With the aid of the mirror world, students can more effectively engage in "learning by creating" (for instance, in the game Minecraft, students construct iconic buildings like the Taj Mahal, the Eiffel Tower, Gyeongbokgung, Bulguksa, etc.).
Virtual reality	Users can enjoy a range of games through a fully integrated user interface thanks to computer graphics' exceptional performance, especially in a virtual setting using 3D technology (for example: various 3D games, such as Roblox). • Users can engage with AI characters and other users in virtual reality through chat and communication tools (for example, in online multiplayer games).	• The exercise can be completed through virtual simulation in situations that are costly and dangerous to produce, such as fire scenes, aircraft controls, hazardous procedures, etc. Playing 3D games based on virtual environments can help users obtain practical skills needed in the real world, as well as the ability to think strategically and globally.

15.6 A setting for modern social interaction

It is difficult to plan private meetings with multiple individuals or to have a group meal in a restaurant because of the current COVID-19 occurrence. But in the meta-world, tens of millions or even hundreds of thousands of individuals might band together to organize a festival or go to a concert by a beloved artist. With the introduction of a new common area in VR metaverses like Roblox and Zepeto, those COVID-19-restricted individuals can now socialize and unwind without having to leave their houses. The Zepeto 3D map titled Classroom Map was the most popular when schools were shut down because of COVID-19 and students were unable to attend class. The students entered Zepeto's class, not the actual classroom.

15.7 A greater degree of creativity and freedom

Contrary to what some people may think, the metaverse is a lot more than just a virtual game. Online game players are required to perform certain tasks to complete the goals defined by the platform provider. But the meta-world eventually permits users to achieve whatever they choose, in the absence of a predetermined goal. Users have a wide range of real-world activities they can partake in, such as studying, shopping, performing, exhibiting, and traveling, depending on their optimum amount of freedom. Furthermore, people can take advantage of experiences that are difficult to have in the actual world, like flying and space travel, because of physical limitations. Through the use of virtualization, consumers can take a break from their busy schedules and enjoy new experiences with a high degree of immersion. Through the precise integration of many technologies, a unique value of feelings related to the modern internet era can be offered. The meta-world allows you to create an experience that defies both space and time. The metaverse class has the advantage of allowing interaction similar to face-to-face learning and allowing the usage of infinite space and data.

15.8 Limitations of the metaverse in the field of education

The meta-world has made it possible for users to have a "social connection" by providing them with a venue to meet and engage with people who have similar interests despite restrictions placed on them by the real world, such as "social distancing." However, compared to the bonds created through encounters in the real world, the social relationships in the meta-world are weaker. Information that one does not want to reveal is suppressed to create the "I that I want to show" rather than the "I as I am" in the real world. The invasion of privacy is another issue to consider when participating in social interactions in the meta-world because a range of data that is not generated during actual interactions is captured and processed in real time. Users of the meta-world are more dangerous than those who use other online games and services because of the meta-world's great degree of freedom as it offers such a wide range of options. Due to the great level of user freedom, the administrator is unable to predict each user's performance. Because the virtual world's essential components of anonymity and virtual space exist, people feel less guilty about their transgressions. High-tech crimes that are brand-new and far worse are reportedly becoming more prevalent. The "I" that interacts in the virtual world might seem to be a continuation of reality and have a similar sense of self, but it could also interact as a new self with a distinct appearance and point of view. It is conceivable for users to be unclear of who the "real me" is because the line separating the real and virtual worlds is blurring more and more. They might struggle to adapt to virtual reality healthily. There is a danger that neglecting real-world connections can exacerbate circumstances or prevent partnerships from forming if you become overly engrossed in or comfortable with interpersonal relationships in VR.

15.9 Challenges of the metaverse in education

Even though the meta-world offers us fresh learning opportunities, we must use caution while using it for education or other purposes. This section's primary discussion points will be the four difficulties of the meta-world in education.

15.10 Knowledge and equipment

It is crucial to have a well-designed, reasonably priced smart wearable device so that instructors and students can teleport to the meta-world. Hardware still has to be perfected, even though it is advancing quickly with technology (such as HMDs). For instance, it has been proposed that long-term wearers of wearable electronics may experience specific symptoms (such as computer sickness, blurred vision, or dizziness) or even lose their balance and fall to the ground. In actuality, a security issue can be present. Hardware costs are still out of reach for the majority of people in today's society, but price is still a significant consideration. Consideration should be given to how to satisfy the demands for open access, high fidelity, and user interface availability. For broad usage of the meta-world in education, the gear and software that is currently on the market fall well short of the technical requirements. From the standpoint of evolution, the quick growth of virtual reality, digital twins, and 5G networks offers optimism for the meta-world. So, to exploit the meta-world in education more effectively, technological businesses and relevant departments must create more advanced methods.

15.11 Privacy and data security

Regardless of whether the environment is a virtual 3D environment or a 2D internet, user privacy and data security present significant issues. Data is the fundamental unit of management for the meta-world, allowing you to gather more specific data from users, such as B. A few examples of data are face photographs, physical condition (heart rate, blood pressure, disease, etc.), transactions, consumption data, etc. Students who lack social skills may find it easier to be exposed to illegal activities (including fraud, espionage, and leaks) because of the increased online anonymity in the meta-world. Students' privacy is at risk, which might potentially have a negative effect on how they live their daily lives. Moreover, both teachers' and students' creative work may be in danger. One of those regulations that must be put into place is genuine name authentication, and regulators must act with the urgency of traditional law enforcement agencies. To enable the tracking of works and works in the metaverse, it is also important to make use of technologies like cryptocurrencies, NFT, and blockchain. If not, the virtual world of the meta devolves into a lawless one.

15.12 Integrity and principles

Users can access the meta-world from anywhere in the world because of the vast freedom. The emergence of the virtual self raises new concerns that may result in international, inter-racial, inter-religious, inter-gender, and other conflicts (for instance, various ideas and worldviews, simulated experiences, data theft, ethnic concerns, religious disputes, bullying, violence, etc.). A functioning meta-world with rules and ecosystems is also essential. It will be crucial to simultaneously teach ethics and the law while also fostering civic engagement among meta-global students.

15.13 Compulsion

Students' learning is facilitated by the richness of the environments and objects that are present in the meta-world but not in the real world, as well as by the high degree of immersion and presence provided by sensory and virtual technology. Young pupils who lack discipline and self-control, however, always run the risk of developing addictions that significantly harm their physical and mental health. If students wish to avoid the illusory spiritual fulfillment of technology, they must balance the amount of time they spend in and out of the metaverse and avoid wandering around too much.

15.14 Uniqueness and social interaction

Digital identities can serve as a direct representation of users' egos and give them access to a variety of meta-world activities. When the line separating the real and virtual worlds blurs, users risk losing sight of who they are as "real me" and "virtual me." Additionally, over time, students who rely too much on the social connections formed between their avatars and non-player characters (NPCs) in the virtual world

Table 15.3 Features of the metaverse and the profits and restrictions of its educational uses

Metaverse characteristics	Merits	Shortcomings
New social media platform	Even when their schools are closed due to the 2019 coronavirus outbreak, students can communicate on a virtual level.	Playful interactions with others lead to the development of weaker bonds than those that result from face-to-face encounters, and the gathering and processing of various personal data poses privacy issues.
The high degree of freedom	By sharing experiences between content producers and consumers, you can increase the subjectivity of learning for students.	Due to the great level of freedom and the anonymity and virtual character of the meta-world, platform managers may not be able to predict each user's conduct and may be vulnerable to a variety of crimes.
Through virtualization high immersion	By offering students one-of-a-kind experiences that transcend time and space, educators may increase student interest and immersion and increase their active engagement in the learning process.	This can result in identity uncertainty, escapism, and a lack of ability to adjust to the outside world for students whose identities are still being formed.

may build emotional and social barriers that make it difficult to maintain relationships in both the virtual and real worlds. NPC instructors might jeopardize instructors' jobs in the real world (Table 15.3).

15.15 Conclusion

The potential for educational applications, the convergence, and complexity of types, as well as the potential and constraints of the meta-world for such applications, are four different forms of meta-world functionality that are discussed. The meta-world ought to affect not just games and entertainment, but also the economy and the way we conduct our daily lives. Additionally, the new platform will house all of the social, cultural, and commercial activities of the meta-world. This chapter introduces Meta Chain, a revolutionary blockchain platform, to deal with new problems in the development of metaverse applications. The internet, virtual worlds, augmented reality, and other digital experiences are idealized versions of the meta-world that effortlessly meld into our daily lives. The 3D virtual world, where reality and virtuality coexist, represents a promising future development in education. The origins, definitions, and common characteristics of the meta-world are first described in this chapter in order to close this gap. With the help of blockchain technology, which has several advantages including improved security, transparency, and individual accountability, a decentralized meta world may be established. He then establishes a precise framework for the meta-world of education and provides an in-depth examination of each of its component sections. Four possible uses of the meta world in education are also looked at, in addition to the justification and supporting information. These programs include competency-based education, blended learning, language learning, and inclusive education. The difficulties the meta-world presents in the classroom are also highlighted. To encourage further research, we discuss several meta-related study concepts, a thorough appreciation of the meta-world's educational potential, and support for further research on the topic. In an ever-expanding meta-world, it is anticipated that blockchain and artificial intelligence technologies will be crucial. In order to fully utilize the meta-world and transdisciplinary research and work toward an open, just, and rational future, collaboration between scientists and businesses is necessary. The use of the latest blockchain and artificial intelligence technologies is also accelerated by using the metaverse. Let us take a look at the most relevant research on digital currency, AI, metaverse components, and blockchain. To fully capitalize on the meta-world and transdisciplinary research, scientists and businesses must work together to advance the cause of an open, just, and rational future.

Further reading

[1] Almahasees, Z., Mohsen, K., and Amin, M. O. (2021). Faculty's and students' perceptions of online learning during COVID-19. *Front. Educ.* 6:638470. doi:10.3389/feduc.2021.638470.

[2] Anderson, L. W., Krathwohl, D. R., Airasian, P. W., Cruikshank, K. A., and Wittrock, M. C. (2001). *A taxonomy for Learning, Teaching, and Assessing: A Revision of Bloom's Taxonomy of Educational Objectives*. New York, NY: Longman.

[3] Antonietti, C., Cattaneo, A., and Amenduni, F. (2022). Can teachers' digital competence influence technology acceptance in vocational education? *Comput. Hum. Behav.* 132:107266. doi:10.1016/j.chb.2022.107266.

[4] Bloom, B. S., Engelhart, M. D., Furst, E. J., Hill, W. H., and Krathwohl, D. R. (1956). *Taxonomy of Educational Objectives, HandbookI: The Cognitive Domain*. New York, NY: David McKay Co, Inc.

[5] Bobrowski, M. (2021). *Mark Zuckerberg Sets Facebook on Long, Costly Path to Metaverse Reality*. Available at: https://www.wsj.com/articles/mark-zuckerberg-sets-facebook-on-long-costly-path-to-metaverse-reality-11635252726?mod=article_inline (Accessed July 22, 2022).

[6] Bork-Hüffer, T., Kulcar, V., Brielmair, F., *et al.* (2021). University students' perception, evaluation, and spaces of distance learning during the COVID-19 pandemic in Austria: what can we learn for post-pandemic educational futures? *Sustainability* 13:7595. doi:10.3390/su13147595.

[7] Bourlakis, M., Papagiannidis, S., and Li, F. (2009). Retail spatial evolution: paving the way from traditional to metaverse retailing. *Electron. Commer. Res.* 9:135–148. doi:10.1007/s10660-009-9030-8.

[8] Center for Journalism Studies of Tsinghua University. (2021). *Report on Development Research of the Metaverse (2020-2021)*. Available at: https://sjc.bnu.edu.cn/sywdlm/zkfb/xwdt2/121319.html (Accessed July 18, 2022).

[9] Chen, C.-Y., Chang, S.-C., Hwang, G.-J., and Zou, D. (2021). Facilitating EFL learners' active behaviors in speaking: a progressive question prompt-based peer-tutoring approach with VR contexts. *Interact. Learn. Environ.* 30:1–20. doi:10.1080/10494820.2021.1878232.

[10] Chen, Y.-C., Chi, H.-L., Hung, W.-H., and Kang, S.-C. (2011). Use of tangible and augmented reality models in engineering graphics courses. *J. Prof. Issues Eng. Educ. Pract.* 137:267–276. doi:10.1061/(asce)ei.1943-5541.0000078.

[11] Duan, H., Li, J., Fan, S., Lin, Z., Wu, X., and Cai, W. (2021). Metaverse for social good: a university campus prototype. *Proceedings of the 29th ACM International Conference on Multimedia*. doi:10.1145/3474085.3479238.

[12] Dwivedi, Y.K., Hughes, L., Baabdullah, A.M., *et al.* (2022). Metaverse beyond the hype: multidisciplinary perspectives on emerging challenges, opportunities, and agenda for research, practice and policy. *Int. J. Inf. Manag.* 66:102542. doi: 10.1016/j.ijinfomgt.2022.102542.

[13] Gamage, K. A. A., Wijesuriya, D. I., Ekanayake, S. Y., Rennie, A. E. W., Lambert, C. G., and Gunawardhana, N. (2020). Online delivery of teaching and laboratory practices: continuity of university programmes during COVID-19 pandemic. *Educ. sci.* 10:291. doi:10.3390/educsci10100291.

[14] Gartner (2022). *Predicts 2022: 4 Technology Bets for Building the Digital Future*. https://www.businesswire.com/news/home/20220207005085/en. (Accessed August 06, 2022).

[15] Genay, A.C.S., Lecuyer, A., and Hachet, M. (2021). Being an avatar "for real": a survey on virtual embodiment in augmented reality. *IEEE Trans. Vis. Comput. Graph.* 1–2. doi:10.1109/tvcg.2021.3099290.

[16] Guo, H., and Gao, W. (2022). Metaverse-powered experiential situational English-teaching design: an emotion-based analysis method. *Front. Psychol.* 13:859159. doi:10.3389/fpsyg.2022.859159.

[17] Huang, H., Hwang, G.-J., and Chang, S.-C. (2021). Facilitating decision making in authentic contexts: an SVVR-based experiential flipped learning approach for professional training. *Interact. Learn. Environ.* 1–17. doi:10.1080/10494820.2021.2000435.

[18] Hwang, G.-J., and Chien, S.-Y. (2022). Definition, roles, and potential research issues of the metaverse in education: an artificial intelligence perspective. *Comput. Educ. Artif. Intell.* 3:100082. doi:10.1016/j.caeai.2022.100082.

[19] Jeon, J. H. (2021). A study on the principle of Metaverse composition with a focus on Roblox. *Korean Assoc. Vis. Cult.* 38:257–279. doi:10.21299/jovc.2021.38.10.

[20] Jovanović, A., and Milosavljević, A. (2022). VoRtex metaverse platform for gamified collaborative learning. *Electronics* 11(3):317. doi:10.3390/electronics11030317.

[21] Kang, Y. (2021). Metaverse framework and building block. *J. Korea Inst. Inf. Commun. Eng.* 25:1263–1266. doi:10.6109/JKIICE.2021.25.9.1263.

[22] Kim, J.H., Lee, B.S., and Choi, S.J. (2022). A study on metaverse construction and use cases for non-face-to-face education. *J. Converg. Cult. Technol.* 8:483–497. doi:10.17703/JCCT.2022.8.1.483.

[23] Ko, H., Jeon, J., and Yoo, I. (2022). Metaverse platform-based flipped learning framework development and application. *J. Korean Assoc. Inf. Educ.* 26:129–140. doi:10.14352/jkaie.2022.26.2.129.

[24] Kocur, M., Graf, S., and Schwind, V. (2020). The impact of missing fingers in virtual reality. *26th ACM Symposium on Virtual Reality Software and Technology*. doi:10.1145/3385956.3418973.

Chapter 16

IoT, AI, and metaverse in smart healthcare systems: a review of recent advances and future trends

B. Narendra Kumar Rao[1], N. Bala Krishna[1] and Chinthapatla Pranay Varna[2]

Abstract

The combination of AI and IoT has great potential to revolutionize healthcare, particularly in managing chronic diseases. Electronic and software-enabled IoT devices and facilities can gather, organize, and transfer data that is subsequently analyzed by artificial intelligence (AI) algorithms to improve the health of patients. Computerized eye examination, medical guidance, population's vulnerability, and patient self-monitoring devices are the primary fields where AI developments might be helpful in the diabetes care sector. Additionally, AI and IoT can alleviate the difficulties faced by medical professionals with electronic health records (EHRs), storage, security, and access. AI may assist doctors in recognizing and treating patients with greater precision and efficiency by reviewing their prior medical data to identify developments and evaluate their risk for contracting certain diseases. Healthcare delivery might undergo a revolution as a result of AI and IoT, becoming more effective, precise, and available.

Keywords: Electronic Health Records; Supervised Learning Algorithms; Disease Diagnosis; Digital Twin Models

16.1 Introduction

The healthcare sector might be completely transformed by the integration of IoT (Internet of Things) and AI. The distance between patients and doctors can be greatly shortened through the use of IoT and portable monitoring devices, enabling doctors to monitor the health of patients instantaneously. However, there are still certain challenges in creating suitable online applications for conventional medicine. The gathering, analysis, and interpretation of big data may be sped up and made easier with the widespread adoption of digital healthcare records and an increasing volume

[1]School of Computing, Mohan Babu University, India
[2]Department of Computer Science and Engineering, Sree Vidyanikethan Engineering College, India

of digitalized medical data. AI, on the other hand, can help with the analysis and treatment of patients, identifying diseases faster and with greater accuracy through the historical record of a patient's EHRs (electronic health records). Through predictive analysis, AI can identify patterns that suggest a patient is at risk for a particular disease, enabling doctors to take appropriate action. Healthcare administration may be improved by skillfully fusing the potential of modern screening, gathering, and evaluating tools with the opportunities for actual human interaction.

These technological advancements in healthcare will alleviate many of the headaches that healthcare professionals face today, including the storage, safety, and access of EHRs. AI can assist doctors in making intelligent and individualized judgments by analyzing enormous volumes of data. The capacity to gather and analyze massive volumes of data in real time represents one of the main advantages of combining IoT with AI in medical treatment. This allows for the early detection of diseases and the identification of patterns that may not be immediately apparent to a human doctor. Wearable health monitoring devices equipped with IoT sensors can track a patient's vital signs and activity levels continuously. This data can be analyzed using AI algorithms to detect any changes in the patient's condition that may be indicative of an impending health problem. Another important use case for IoT and AI in healthcare is personalized treatment. The combination of IoT sensors and AI algorithms can provide doctors with a detailed understanding of each patient's health status and medical history. The medical records of a person may be examined by artificial intelligence (AI) techniques, which can then suggest therapies depending on the patient's unique circumstances. IoT and AI fusion might also save healthcare expenses while improving the lives of patients. Doctors may track patients using IoT sensors and machine learning algorithms, which eliminates the requirement for physical visits and being hospitalized. Giving patients more prompt and precise care can save costs for patients as well as medical professionals while also improving the clinical results.

To better assist patients and simplify healthcare administration, this chapter will examine the possible advantages of IoT and AI in medical treatment. The primary objective of this study is to supply a comprehensive analysis of the role that IoT and AI will play in the future of healthcare and to shed light on how these technologies can be used to improve patient outcomes and transform healthcare management.

16.2 Applications of AI

AI technologies are getting better at communicating with people due to developments in natural language processing (NLP) and AI frameworks. As a result, scientists are creating AI tools like robots that can do preliminary diagnostic evaluations. These technologies are a component of the idea of healthcare and are frequently accessed through computer or smartphone interfaces. The applications of artificial intelligence are illustrated below.

16.2.1 Role of AI in diabetes

An estimated 420 million people globally are believed to be affected by diabetes, an alarming global health problem. Uncontrolled diabetes affects approximately one out of two of those with diabetes, which is tragic. Artificial intelligence (AI) and neural networks provide fresh approaches to improving the treatment of diabetes. Computerized vision tests, health choice assistance, population vulnerability, and self-monitoring by patients' equipment—the investigations reflect novel techniques that seek to revolutionize diabetes treatment. Eye scanning devices, simulation software, sugar monitors, insulin dispensers, mobile devices, and other decision-making aids are presently available which are based on AI. Applications of AI have the potential to enhance blood glucose regulation, lessen hypoglycemic episodes, and lessen the consequences and comorbidities of diabetes. For those with disabilities, they provide increased accuracy, efficiency, convenience, and satisfaction.

The successful reductions in the range of individual postprandial and post-action glucose results were a significant finding, suggesting that AI-powered systems like Sugar-IQ may offer an efficient, affordable method for improving individual patient management through tailored insights and prompts for engagement. The Sugar-IQ app offers personalized insights that show the times and days of activities associated with glucose levels, motivational signals to promote positive behavior, glucose prompts based on patterns, and a smart food log to make recording meals and snacks simple and reliable.

When exposed to the device feedback over time, participants' full acceptance of the prompts rose, finally reaching 100% by day 18. According to iQ, initially, 80%–85% of participants enjoyed the prompts. The most important conclusion was that there was less variation in each person's postprandial and post-action glucose values, indicating that the Sugar.IQ aide's personalized insights and engagement prompts were a successful strategy for enhancing patient management on an individual basis.

Type 1, Type 2, prediabetes, and pregnancy-related diabetes are among the several forms of diabetes. The body's defense system targets and kills cells in the digestive tract that make glucose in type 1 diabetes, which is an autoimmune disorder. Diabetes of type 2 arises whenever the human system becomes less responsive to the hormone insulin and glucose levels rise. Prediabetes is the term for glucose levels in the blood that are higher than usual but not high enough to be categorized as diabetes of the type 2 variety. A kind of diabetes called gestational diabetes appears during pregnancy.

The diabetes crisis in the United States is alarming, with millions of Americans diagnosed with diabetes and millions more at risk for developing the disease. Diabetes is a leading cause of death and has a significant impact on healthcare costs in the United States. AI can help healthcare providers monitor and manage blood glucose levels, prevent dangerous drops in blood sugar, and reduce hospitalization rates. Healthcare practitioners may improve clinical results by implementing artificial intelligence-powered systems like Rhythm, which regulates the amount of glucose in the blood using simple sensor technology and AI. The ability of AI to enhance medical results has already been shown by the Diabetes Centre in the Netherlands. In an observational experiment, seven out of eight diabetic patients who used the Rhythm device alone had a 20%

improvement in time within the range and a 9% decrease in severe blood sugar. Doctors can cut the number of hospitalizations connected to diabetes and save billions of dollars in medical expenditures if AI-based solutions like Rhythm can be implemented on a broader scale. AI can completely change how we detect, track, and treat diabetes.

16.2.2 Role of AI in cardiology

In India, cardiovascular disorders are the leading cause of mortality, especially in those aged 35 to 70 who have dangerous conditions like as obesity, high blood pressure, and smoking. Lowering costs, efficient therapy, successful treatment for patients, and high rehabilitation and low mortality rates are some of the challenges being addressed in cardiovascular clinical care. Artificial intelligence (AI) networks, particularly those that employ gadget training and conceptual reasoning, may be crucial for the creation of cardiac medicine. With the help of AI, massive, complicated datasets may be analyzed and new genetic variations in illnesses that already exist can be found. Additionally, it can aid in raising affordability, decrease recurrence and mortality rates, and raise treatment quality.

The use of AI techniques in cardiovascular disease diagnosis and prediction has been increasing over the last decade. However, the challenges of implementing such systems include the complexity and heterogeneity of data, which are too vast to be analyzed manually, as well as the need for specialized knowledge of cardiovascular medicine and statistics. Despite these challenges, AI has the potential to revolutionize cardiovascular medicine and shift the focus toward more accurate and personalized medicine. Therefore, there is a need for collaborations between medical professionals and data analysts to develop clinically relevant AI models. Artificial Intelligence (AI) can have a significant impact on predicting and diagnosing cardiovascular disease by developing algorithms that can efficiently analyze and represent data. To predict patient readmission with congestive heart failure, clinicians now have to dig through a sizable, unorganized EHR database that contains diverse characteristics including clinical codes, medications, lab results, scans, and comments. This dataset makes it difficult to determine which factors to include in a predictive model and what kind of techniques to use.

Using supervised training algorithms, which need a set of records with indicator elements and labeled results, AI may aid in the generation of prediction models. For instance, a spot-tracking echocardiographic dataset was combined with an AI system to discern between problematic and normal growth patterns. Unsupervised learning algorithms are a different class of algorithms that look at the interactions between factors to uncover hidden patterns in a dataset. Algorithms for reinforcement learning may be utilized to create customized therapies, such as ones for controlling resuscitation rates and tracking metabolic stability in critical care units. Less underlying data implications are made while using AI algorithms, which produce more precise predictions and classifications.

The implementation of AI in cardiac treatment can be very advantageous, as traditional statistical methods have limitations in terms of accuracy and efficiency.

By using AI algorithms, doctors can more quickly and accurately predict and identify cardiovascular disorders, which will eventually improve the results for patients.

Artificial Intelligence (AI), and specifically, deep learning, is a relatively new field in healthcare, and its use in cardiology is still limited. The earliest applications of AI in healthcare were in image processing, where Convolutional Neural Networks (CNNs) were used to analyze large databases of medical images. One research obtained high precision equivalent to that of human eye doctors by using a CNN to recognize diabetic retinal damage from an inventory of eye pictures. Similarly, another study used a CNN to classify dermatological lesions, achieving accuracy comparable to a group of board-certified dermatologists.

The application of deep learning in cardiology shows great potential. Data analysts without medical training developed a model that accurately assesses end-systolic and end-diastolic volumes in cardiac magnetic resonance imaging (MRI) images for a Kaggle database Data Science Bowl assignment. In a further study, blood vessel optical coherence tomography (OCT) pictures of patients with Kawasaki illness were automatically classified using a CNN.

16.2.3 Role of AI in Parkinson's disease

Artificial intelligence looks to be heavily utilized in the early diagnosis and treatment of Parkinson's illness. Parkinson's disease is a neurodegenerative ailment brought on by the loss of dopamine, a chemical messenger used by neurons to send signals to other nerve cells. It causes a range of symptoms, including tremors, rigidity, and slow movement, which can take years to develop, and by the time a patient presents at a clinic, the disease has usually progressed to the point where the symptoms can only be managed, rather than the underlying cause addressed.

One of the most significant challenges for clinicians is diagnosing Parkinson's disease early enough to provide patients with effective treatment. To solve this problem, AI has shown a lot of potential. Large datasets may be analyzed by algorithms employing machine learning, which can then identify trends that would be challenging or unattainable for people to observe. Diagnostic testing, genetic information, and medical files are just a few of the several kinds of data that may be utilized in refining these mathematical models.

Rapid Eye Movements Sleep Behavior Disorder (RBD) and Parkinson's disease are being investigated by researchers. RBD is a condition in which the mechanism that typically inhibits movement during sleep is broken, causing individuals to move or shout while asleep. Because sleep disorders can be an early indicator of problems with the nervous system, researchers are exploring whether RBD could serve as a biomarker for Parkinson's disease. By examining sleep study data to find trends and signs that predict the possibility of acquiring Parkinson's disease, AI might aid in this study. Early illness identification and management may result from this, which could boost the treatment of patients. AI may be beneficial in the creation of individualized treatment programs for people with Parkinson's disease. Clinical professionals may customize medications to meet the needs of every patient by using algorithms that employ machine learning to analyze clinical data and find tendencies that indicate the success rate of various therapies.

AI can significantly advance the Parkinson's disease research field. AI can assist in the early identification of diseases by processing enormous quantities of information and uncovering patterns that would be tough for people to detect. AI may help in early illness diagnosis, the discovery of disease-related biomarkers as well and the creation of individualized treatment regimens by analyzing vast volumes of data and spotting trends that would be challenging for humans to notice. AI has the potential to assist millions of individuals who have Parkinson's disease throughout the world to live better lives with additional research and advancement.

16.2.4 Role of AI in dementia

Dementia is the sixth biggest cause of mortality in the United States and a condition that affects approximately a hundred thousand Americans, dementia is becoming a significant worry for healthcare professionals throughout the world. These startling numbers have compelled scientists to investigate the possibility of artificial intelligence to enhance the standards of life for those suffering from dementia and lessen the monetary expense of this illness. One area of AI research in dementia is speech monitoring. Companies are using AI to analyze speech patterns to identify and monitor the progression of dementia. Speech is a useful tool for detecting dementia because changes in language and communication are often among the first signs of the disease. By analyzing speech patterns, AI algorithms can detect changes in tone, pace, and other characteristics that may indicate cognitive decline.

Another area of AI research is medical image analysis. Companies are developing software that uses AI to analyze brain scans and predict the onset of dementia. Medical imaging is a valuable tool for detecting dementia because it can reveal structural changes in the brain that may be indicative of cognitive decline. By using AI algorithms to analyze brain scans, researchers hope to detect dementia in its early stages and intervene with treatment before the disease progresses too far.

Visual indicators are another area of AI research in dementia. Companies are developing algorithms to assess eye movement patterns to track cognitive function and brain activity. Eye movement patterns are useful indicators of cognitive function because they are associated with attention, memory, and other cognitive processes. By analyzing eye movement patterns, AI algorithms can track changes in cognitive function and predict the onset of dementia. In the field of AI research on dementia, genetic analysis is expanding. Companies are using AI to analyze genetic data to predict the onset of dementia. Genetic analysis is useful for predicting dementia because it can reveal genetic risk factors that may predispose individuals to cognitive decline. By using AI algorithms to analyze genetic data, researchers hope to identify individuals who are at risk for dementia and intervene with preventative measures before the disease develops. In radiology, researchers combined neuroimaging with AI to predict whether a patient with memory impairment would develop Alzheimer's disease. The study used PET scans to measure glucose levels in the brain, which have been linked to Alzheimer's disease. However, because changes in glucose levels are subtle and difficult to detect with the naked eye, researchers used an AI algorithm to analyze the scans and predict the onset of the disease more reliably. By combining medical imaging with AI algorithms, researchers can detect subtle changes in the brain that may indicate cognitive decline. These changes can be difficult to detect with traditional diagnostic methods, making AI a valuable tool for predicting the onset of dementia and intervening with treatment before the disease progresses too far. AI can completely transform how we identify and treat dementia. By analyzing speech patterns, medical images, eye movement patterns, and genetic data, AI algorithms can detect the early signs of dementia and predict the onset of the disease. These predictive tools can be invaluable for healthcare providers and patients alike, as they can allow for earlier intervention and treatment before the disease progresses too far. We could be expecting even more advanced technology developments in the area of dementia research and therapy as AI technology develops.

16.3 Applications of IoT

16.3.1 Role of IoT in enhancing diagnosis

The administration of patients, clinical practice, and research may all significantly benefit from the usage of IoT devices in healthcare. In the financial and manufacturing industries, it is also used. Collecting information, data transformation, storing it, and data interpretation are the four fundamental tenets of IoT in healthcare. Interconnected devices including receptors, tracks, sensors, equators, and recording devices provide evidence for these ideas. For patients, wearable technology is a critical component of the IoT network. Wearables can offer specialized care in the event of sudden illnesses or slow decline. If they are linked to time management software, calorie counting software, or workout applications, they can also serve as alerts.

IoT technology allows for continuous data flow, providing users with instant feedback and decision-making support. IoT in healthcare can also improve clinical workflows and operations, such as inventory management, staff scheduling, and equipment maintenance. By using connected devices, hospitals and clinics can monitor the availability and usage of medical equipment, track staff productivity, and optimize workflows to improve efficiency and reduce costs.

Remote surveillance of patients, which enables medical professionals to keep an eye on their physical and mental well-being, is a significant use of IoT in healthcare. Patients who reside in rural or isolated places, have chronic illnesses or are old and have trouble walking will find this to be very helpful. Real-time data on health conditions, activity levels, and medication adherence may be collected by IoT-enabled devices, such as detectors, wearables, and home surveillance structures, and transferred to healthcare practitioners for analysis.

In addition, IoT can also improve the efficiency and safety of healthcare facilities by automating various processes and reducing the risk of errors. For example, IoT-enabled devices can help healthcare providers manage inventory, track equipment and supplies, and monitor environmental factors such as temperature and humidity in hospital rooms and storage areas. By making sure the correct antibiotic is given to the appropriate patient at the appropriate time and in the appropriate amount, IoT can additionally be used to reduce mistakes when taking medication. IoT in healthcare can also improve public health by enabling early detection and prevention of disease outbreaks. Connected devices can collect data on environmental factors, such as air quality and temperature, as well as on the health status of individuals and communities. This information can be used to identify and respond to outbreaks of infectious diseases, as well as to develop targeted public health interventions.

IoT can play a crucial role in healthcare research by providing access to large amounts of real-world data. By collecting and analyzing data from a variety of sources, including wearables, EHRs, and clinical trials, researchers can gain new insights into disease prevention, treatment, and management, and develop more personalized and effective healthcare solutions.

16.3.2 Metaverse

Through the use of medical-related artificial intelligence technologies, the metaverse a virtual collaborative environment that combines physical and digital realities is achieving substantial progress in the medical field. When used in the medical sector, digital twins' virtual versions of practical structures, procedures, or objects create significant prospects for individualized treatment for patients and technological breakthroughs.

Healthcare professionals can develop virtual replicas for individuals in the metaverse, recording their biometric data and medical background in real time. With the help of these electronic clones, professionals can keep an eye on clients from a distance, improving managing illnesses, early identification of illnesses, and the effectiveness of therapy strategies. The metaverse enables medical practitioners to practice difficult operations like surgery on virtual patients before performing them on humans.

16.3.2.1 Digital twin models in healthcare

In the framework of the IoT, the idea of digital twins has grown in acceptance. Virtual representations of real-world systems or objects are known as "digital twins," and they may be used to imitate their operations and behavior in real time. Integrating detectors as well as additional IoT gadgets to such digital representations enables real-time data monitoring and analysis, which may be utilized to improve the functionality and upkeep of real-life infrastructure.

Digital twin technologies have the power to completely change how patients are treated and managed in the field of healthcare. Doctors can mimic the impacts of various therapies and drugs, for instance, by building virtual simulations of their patients. This can assist in optimizing dosages and enhance results. Real-time tracking of patients using digital twin replicas is another way to spot possible problems beforehand they get worse.

The use of digital twin models has been growing rapidly in various industries, including manufacturing, aerospace, and automotive, to improve operational efficiency, reduce costs, and enhance product performance.

The possible uses of digital twin systems for medical care are listed below:

1. **Patient-specific diagnosis and treatment**
   Digital twin models can be used to create patient-specific models that replicate the physiological characteristics of individual patients. These models can be used to predict how a patient's body will respond to certain treatments and interventions. By using digital twin models, healthcare providers can optimize treatment plans and reduce the risk of complications. For example, digital twin models can be used to simulate the effects of different dosages of medications on a patient's body and help healthcare providers determine the optimal dosage.
2. **Surgical planning and training**
   Digital twin models can also be used to create virtual replicas of organs or body parts, which can be used for surgical planning and training. By simulating surgeries in a digital twin environment, surgeons can practice and refine their techniques before performing the actual surgery on the patient. This can reduce the risk of complications during the surgery and improve patient outcomes. In addition, digital twin models can be used to train medical students and residents, allowing them to gain experience in a safe and controlled environment.
3. **Predictive maintenance and asset management**
   In addition to patient care, digital twin models can be used to optimize hospital operations and asset management. By creating digital twin models of hospital equipment, healthcare providers can monitor equipment performance in real time, predict failures before they occur, and perform preventive maintenance. This can reduce equipment downtime, increase operational efficiency, and reduce maintenance costs.
4. **Patient monitoring and management**
   Digital twin models can also be used to monitor patients in real time and provide personalized care. Wearable gadgets may gather information on the health of a person, degree of action, and sleeping routine, which can be utilized in creating a digital twin representation of the patient. Healthcare professionals can track the progress of digital twins to identify modifications to the state of the patient's health and initiate early treatments as needed.
5. **Clinical research and development**
   Medical science and technology can also benefit from the usage of digital twin models. By creating digital twin models of diseases, researchers can simulate disease progression and test new treatments in a virtual environment. Clinical tests can be conducted faster and for less money if this is done, and novel therapies can be developed more quickly. The ability to provide personalized treatment, improve the functioning of hospitals, and accelerate advancements in technology are just a few of the ways that digital twin systems can revolutionize healthcare.

16.3.2.2 Metaverse in healthcare

The concept of a metaverse based on IoT refers to a virtual world created by the convergence of physical and digital reality. In healthcare, the potential of a metaverse based on IoT is enormous. It can enable healthcare professionals to provide better care to their patients and also help patients take control of their health. One way a metaverse based on IoT can help in healthcare is by providing a platform for remote consultations. With a metaverse based on IoT, doctors and patients can interact in a virtual environment that simulates the real world. This could render it more practical and efficient for medical professionals to recognize and treat illnesses remotely. A metaverse based on IoT can also help in medical training. Medical students and healthcare professionals can practice procedures in a virtual environment that is realistic and safe. This would allow them to learn and perfect their skills without putting patients at risk. Another way a metaverse based on IoT can help in healthcare is by providing personalized treatment plans. With the help of IoT devices, patients can monitor their health in real time and share that data with their doctors. This data can be used to create personalized treatment plans that take into account the patient's specific needs and conditions.

A metaverse based on IoT can help in clinical trials. Clinical trials are a vital part of the drug development process, but they can be expensive and time-consuming. With a metaverse based on IoT, researchers can conduct trials in a virtual environment that simulates the real world. This would allow them to collect data more efficiently and at a lower cost. The use of a metaverse based on IoT can also help in disease prevention. IoT devices can be used to monitor environmental factors that can impact public health, such as air quality, water quality, and weather conditions.

This data can be used to identify potential health risks and take preventive measures to reduce the risk of disease outbreaks. A metaverse based on IoT can help in emergency response. In the event of a natural disaster or public health emergency, a metaverse based on IoT can be used to coordinate emergency response efforts. Emergency responders can use real-time data to make informed decisions and deploy resources more efficiently.

The capacity to mimic actual medical conditions in a secure and regulated setting is one of the many important benefits of a metaverse built on IoT. Medical professionals and researchers can use digital twin models of patients and medical equipment to run simulations of complex procedures and analyze the outcomes in a virtual setting.

Without entering the surgical area, a surgeon might design and practice a difficult procedure using a digital twin of someone's heart and connected blood veins. The metaverse could be used to train medical professionals in a virtual environment, allowing them to practice and refine their skills in realistic scenarios without putting real patients at risk. This could be especially useful for rare or complicated procedures that are difficult to replicate in traditional training environments.

Another potential benefit of a metaverse based on IoT is the ability to remotely monitor patients in real time. Patients' data might be continually gathered by wearable gadgets and sensed and integrated into a virtual representation of the patient. Then, healthcare practitioners might keep an eye on the patient's health and modify their medical regimen as necessary, thereby lowering the number of stays in hospitals and ambulance trips.

Additionally, the metaverse could enhance patient participation and learning. To learn more about their ailment, treatment options, and likely results, patients might view their digital twin model. They could interact with various patients and medical experts through the metaverse, perhaps enhancing their medical results.

By offering a secure and regulated environment for medical practitioners and academics to mimic complicated scenarios, an IoT-based metaverse has the capacity to completely transform the healthcare sector.

16.4 Trends of AI and IoT in healthcare

Healthcare has been significantly impacted by both artificial intelligence and the IoT. Together, these two technologies have the potential to transform healthcare in many ways. We will discuss some of the latest trends of AI and IoT in healthcare.

16.4.1 Predictive analytics

Analyzing information to find habits, patterns, and knowledge that may be used to forecast upcoming results is known as predictive analytics. Predictive data analysis may be employed in medical settings to pinpoint patients who are at an increased risk of contracting specific illnesses, project results for patients, and refine approaches to treatment. The capacity of predictive analytics for medical purposes has been significantly improved by combining network gadgets with the latest artificial intelligence technologies. The following are some of the trends of AI and IoT in predictive analytics in healthcare:

1. **Early disease detection and prevention**: AI and IoT can be used to monitor patients remotely, collect data on their vital signs, and identify any abnormalities or changes that may indicate the onset of a disease. By analyzing this data using predictive analytics algorithms, healthcare professionals can detect and diagnose diseases at an early stage, before they become more severe. This early detection and prevention can save lives, reduce healthcare costs, and improve patient outcomes.
2. **Personalized treatment plans**: Large volumes of individual patient data, including health records, genetic data, dietary preferences, and medication reactions, may be gathered using AI and IoT. This data can then be analyzed using predictive analytics to develop custom regimens for therapy for every client according to their unique requirements and desires. This method of providing medical assistance can boost patient happiness, enhance the satisfaction of patients, and lower healthcare expenditures.
3. **Real-time monitoring and alerts**: Instantaneous medical surveillance may be done using AI and IoT, providing healthcare professionals with continuous

updates on their condition. By analyzing this data using predictive analytics, healthcare professionals can identify any changes or abnormalities that may require immediate attention, and respond accordingly. This real-time monitoring and alert system can improve patient safety, reduce hospital readmissions, and prevent complications.

4. **Drug discovery and development**: AI and IoT can be used to analyze large datasets related to drug discovery and development. By using predictive analytics algorithms to analyze this data, researchers can determine possible medication targets, estimate drug effectiveness, and optimize dosing strategies. This approach can significantly reduce the time and cost required for drug discovery and development, and improve the chances of success.
5. **Telemedicine**: Telemedicine, which includes using technology to deliver medical attention remotely, may be made easier with the help of AI and IoT. By using predictive analytics algorithms to analyze patient data collected through IoT devices, healthcare professionals can provide virtual consultations, diagnose conditions, and prescribe treatments remotely. The integration of AI and IoT technologies has greatly enhanced the capabilities of predictive analytics in healthcare. From early disease detection and prevention to personalized treatment plans, real-time monitoring and alerts, drug discovery and development, and telemedicine, AI and IoT are transforming the way healthcare is delivered. AI and IoT might facilitate telemedicine, which involves utilizing computers to provide healthcare distantly.

16.4.2 Remote patient monitoring

The term "remote patient monitoring" (RPM) describes the process of keeping track of the wellness of an individual outside of a conventional medical facility using digital technologies like gadgets, detectors, and IoT devices. RPM has been increasingly popular over the past decade as IoT and AI technology are being used more often in the medical sector. The integration of AI and IoT in RPM has enabled healthcare providers to offer personalized care to patients, enhance their clinical outcomes, and reduce healthcare costs.

The usage of IoT tools and sensors to remotely track patients' health conditions serves as one of the key developments in RPM. A variety of health factors, including cardiovascular activity, blood pressure, sugar levels, oxygen intake, and others, may be tracked and monitored by such gadgets. Medical personnel can track patients' illnesses and take appropriate action using the data obtained by these gadgets, which can be relayed to them in real time.

Utilizing machine learning techniques to examine patient records and spot possible illnesses is another development in RPM. Large medical record sets may be processed by neural networks, which can then spot sequences of events that human physicians would miss. This can assist physicians in the early identification of possible health hazards and the adoption of strategies to lower the probability of negative health outcomes. The latest development in RPM is the use of robots and automated systems that are driven by AI. These robots and chat machines may communicate with patients and offer them individualized assistance, guidance, and treatment. Additionally, they let healthcare professionals track patients' health problems online by gathering patient data and analyzing it immediately.

Utilizing telehealth to offer patients online counseling and assistance is a further important development in RPM. Technology like webinars and texting are used in eHealth to link patients and medical professionals. This eliminates the requirement for personal discussions and hospital trips by allowing people to obtain medical guidance and help from the convenience of their own residences.

The creation of forecasting algorithms that may recognize individuals who have a danger of contracting specific medical illnesses is also made possible by the insertion of machine learning and IoT technology into RPM. By analyzing patient data and identifying risk variables including gender, age, lifestyle choices, and medical records, these models are able to forecast the possibility of particular health issues occurring. This can assist medical professionals in creating individualized therapies and measures to lower the probability of unfavorable health outcomes.

The capability of RPM to increase the quality of life for patients while lowering healthcare expenditures is one of its main advantages. Medical professionals can respond quickly if patients' illnesses worsen by employing digital technology to track patients. This lowers the likelihood of hospitalizations and emergency room (ER) visits. This can enhance the quality of life while lowering healthcare expenses.

The integration of AI and IoT technologies in RPM is transforming the way healthcare is delivered. The ability to monitor patients remotely and analyze their data in real time is enabling healthcare providers to offer personalized care to patients, improve their clinical outcomes, and reduce healthcare costs. As these technologies continue to advance, it is expected that RPM will become increasingly prevalent, allowing people to obtain top-notch care in the convenience of their residences.

16.4.3 Chatbots and virtual assistants

Chatbots and virtual assistants have been increasingly adopted in the healthcare industry due to their ability to enhance patient engagement and experience, provide personalized healthcare services, and streamline healthcare operations. The functions of chatbots and artificially intelligent agents for medical use have substantially expanded with the development of computational intelligence (also known as AI and the advent of the IoT). The developments of artificial intelligence and the IoT in chatbots and AI-powered assistants in healthcare will be covered in this chapter.

1. **Personalized healthcare services**: The potential of chatbots and artificial intelligence (AI) to give personalized medical care constitutes one of the biggest advantages of these technologies in medicine. AI-powered chatbots can analyze patients' health data and provide customized health advice and

recommendations. This can be quite beneficial for individuals who are suffering from chronic conditions including diabetes, high blood pressure, and cardiovascular disorders. Virtual assistants can also be used to personalize patients' treatment plans, schedule appointments, and remind them to take medication.

2. **Enhanced patient engagement and experience**: Chatbots and virtual assistants can enhance patient engagement and experience by providing 24/7 access to healthcare services, reducing waiting times, and answering patients' questions in real time. Patients can also interact with chatbots and virtual assistants through NLP technology, which makes the experience more conversational and human-like.
3. **Streamlined healthcare operations**: By streamlining managerial tasks like arranging appointments, prescription notifications, and invoicing questions, chatbots and AI-powered assistants can significantly streamline the daily tasks of the healthcare industry. It may save the working hours of healthcare professionals and enable them to concentrate on other important responsibilities, including handling patients.
4. **Integration with IoT devices**: The integration of chatbots and virtual assistants with IoT devices such as wearables and sensors can provide real-time health monitoring and analytics. This can help healthcare providers detect and prevent health issues before they become severe, as well as track patients' progress over time.
5. **Improved diagnostic accuracy**: AI-powered chatbots and virtual assistants can analyze patient data and provide accurate diagnoses. This can aid healthcare professionals in making knowledgeable judgments regarding the treatment of patients. This may result in lower medical expenses and better health results.
6. **Integration with electronic health records (EHRs):** Healthcare practitioners may access patients' health information and prescribe medications by integrating chatbots and virtual assistants with EHRs. It can boost the security of patients, decrease mistakes, and strengthen communication between healthcare providers.
7. **Telemedicine and remote patient monitoring**: Chatbots can aid with healthcare and monitoring patients remotely. Virtual assistants may be used by patients to set up virtual consultations, ask them concerns regarding their wellness, and get remote treatment. Patients with mobility challenges or who reside in distant places may find this to be very beneficial. Medical chatbots and automated assistants are quickly advancing thanks to IoT and AI technologies. By offering personalized healthcare services, these advancements have the ability to completely change how healthcare is provided. It enhances patient engagement and experience, streamlining healthcare operations, improving diagnostic accuracy, and supporting telemedicine and RPM. As healthcare providers continue to adopt these technologies, we can expect to see significant improvements in healthcare outcomes and patient satisfaction.

16.4.4 Personalized medicine

Individualized medical treatment is one of the many ways that AI and the IoT have reshaped the medical profession. Precision health care, another name for personalized medicine, includes creating specialized therapies based on an individual's particular traits. This method of providing treatment has the ability to boost the standard of care while also reducing costs and improving the experiences of patients. The potential to gather and examine massive volumes of medical information constitutes one of the greatest important developments in AI and IoT in personalized medical care. IoT devices such as wearables, smart sensors, and medical equipment are now capable of collecting real-time data on a patient's health status. This data is then transmitted to an AI-powered system that can analyze the data and provide healthcare providers with insights into a patient's health.

With advancements in genetic testing technology, it is now possible to sequence a patient's entire genome. AI algorithms can then analyze this data to identify genetic markers associated with certain diseases, as well as to predict how a patient will respond to certain treatments. Personalized medicine has several advantages, one of which is that it can result in more precise diagnoses and more efficient treatments. Healthcare professionals may create personalized therapies that are suited to the specific client's requirements by analyzing a patient's unique features, such as their genetic structure, history of illness, environmental variables, and actual time clinical information.

This is particularly useful for patients with chronic conditions, as it allows healthcare providers to monitor their condition in real-time and intervene if necessary. IoT devices such as wearables and smart sensors can collect data on a patient's health status, which is then transmitted to healthcare providers. Following this information analysis, AI systems can offer medical experts conclusions about the condition of a patient. The requirement for patient confidentiality and the safety of data constitutes a few personalized medical problems. Medical professionals must make sure that client information is secure and that only those with permission may access it. By offering safe and secured data transfer and combining blockchain systems to make medical information impenetrable, IoT and artificial intelligence might address these issues. The use of artificial intelligence algorithms to analyze data on genes, the ability to track patients remotely, and the collection and analysis of massive volumes of medical data are the main themes of IoT and AI in personalized medicine. These developments have the ability to transform healthcare by giving professionals the resources they require to create personalized treatment regimens that cater to the specific requirements of each patient. Such innovations will become more crucial in the execution of personalized medicine as they constantly advance.

16.4.5 Robotics

The use of robots, AI, and IoT technology has had a tremendous impact on the medical field. These technologies are transforming various aspects of healthcare, including surgeries, diagnostics, patient monitoring, and drug delivery. The convergence of these advancements has provided healthcare professionals with new options to improve patient treatment outcomes, enhance productivity, and lower healthcare costs.

We will explore the trends of AI and IoT in robotics in healthcare and their potential impact on the industry.

16.4.5.1 Robotic-assisted surgery

With the advancement of surgical techniques, robotic surgery has grown in popularity recently. Patients' recuperation times have been greatly shortened because of these techniques, which also lessen the possibility of problems. With the use of robotic equipment, surgeons can now carry out intricate operations with more efficiency and precision. Robotic surgery has evolved much further with the use of AI and IoT technology. To assist the surgeon in making wise judgments during the operation, AI systems can analyze the client's information. IoT devices can track the health of a patient and give the surgeon advice. The surgeon can alter their strategy throughout the surgery with the use of this actual time input, lowering the chance of problems.

16.4.5.2 Rehabilitation robotics

Rehabilitation robotics is another area that is witnessing significant growth with the integration of AI and IoT. These technologies are being used to create new assistive devices for patients with mobility impairments. AI algorithms can analyze the patient's movements and provide real-time feedback to help the patient improve their mobility. IoT sensors can monitor the patient's progress and provide feedback to the healthcare provider.

16.4.5.3 AI-enabled diagnostics

AI-enabled diagnostics is another area that is seeing significant growth in the healthcare industry. Massive amounts of data may be analyzed by neural networks to find trends that might not be evident to the human retina. These algorithms can be used to diagnose diseases and identify potential risk factors. With the integration of IoT, these algorithms can be fed with real-time data from sensors and wearables, providing a more comprehensive picture of the patient's health.

16.4.5.4 Drug delivery

Drug delivery is another area where robotics and AI technologies are being used to improve patient outcomes. With the development of nanorobotics, drugs can be delivered to targeted areas of the body with greater precision. Machine learning algorithms may review the client's data and give the healthcare professional suggestions, enabling them to modify the drug's dose and periodicity. IoT sensors can monitor the patient's response to the medication and provide real-time feedback to the healthcare provider.

16.4.5.5 Robotic process automation

Another field that is expanding significantly in the medical field is robotic process automation (RPA). The goal of RPA is to simplify monotonous operations like data input and record maintenance. The daily tasks of healthcare professionals may be greatly reduced by this technology, freeing them up to concentrate on caring for patients. RPA may be used to build smarter processes, increasing productivity and lowering costs, by integrating AI and IoT. Medical professionals may now deliver more individualized treatment and enhance the results for patients because of the confluence of AI, IoT, and robotics technology. Healthcare professionals may analyze massive volumes of information and make better judgments regarding the treatment of patients with the combination of these tools. These innovations have immense prospective benefits, and in the upcoming years, we should continue to witness progress in this sector. As the healthcare industry advances, the employment of robotics, neural networks, and the internet will become increasingly crucial to offer patients affordable, excellent treatment.

16.5 Discussion on the latest platforms based on cloud, AI, and IoT

One of the most complicated and data-driven businesses is the medical field. Systems powered by the cloud, IoT, and AI are becoming more and more crucial in the healthcare industry. By enhancing patient satisfaction, lowering medical expenses, and allowing novel approaches to treatment, a number of recent technologies built around cloud, IoT, and AI are revolutionizing healthcare.

16.5.1 Philips digital health platform

The cloud-based Philips HealthSuite Online Platform uses IoT and artificial intelligence to enhance the health of patients and offer a more individualized method of treatment. The system combines information from numerous sources, such as gadgets that are worn on medical equipment, and EHRs, to create a thorough picture of a person's medical state.

The content layer, foundation layer, and software layer are the three levels that make up the tool's architecture. The data layer consists of various sources of healthcare data, including EHRs, medical devices, and wearables. The platform layer provides the infrastructure and tools to store, manage, and process this data. Finally, the application layer includes various applications that utilize the platform's capabilities to provide personalized care to patients.

The platform uses AI algorithms to analyze healthcare data from various sources and provide insights into patient health. The software can analyze information about patients using artificial intelligence algorithms to spot movements and trends that might point to a possible health problem. The platform can also use NLP algorithms to analyze unstructured data, such as physician notes and patient-generated data from wearables.

The platform's IoT capabilities allow it to connect to various medical devices and wearables, providing real-time data on patient health. With less need for appointments in person and improved care for patients, this data may be utilized to track the health of patients. The software may also utilize IoT data to offer information on human behavior, such as physical activity levels, sleep patterns, and diet, which can be used to develop more personalized treatment plans.

The platform's telemedicine capabilities enable healthcare providers to provide remote care to patients. The system has a video conferencing feature that enables healthcare professionals to speak with patients and eliminate the need for face-to-face encounters. This platform features a patient interface that enables users to view their medical records, get in touch with their doctors, and make appointments.

One of the key benefits of the Philips HealthSuite Digital Platform is its ability to provide a more personalized approach to healthcare. By integrating data from various sources and using AI algorithms to analyze this data, the platform can provide insights into patient health that can be used to develop more personalized treatment plans.

The Philips HealthSuite Digital Platform is a powerful tool that leverages cloud, AI, and IoT technologies to transform healthcare. By integrating data from various sources and using AI algorithms to analyze this data, the platform provides a more personalized approach to healthcare.

16.5.2 Microsoft Azure for healthcare

Microsoft Azure is a cloud-based platform that utilizes AI and IoT technologies to transform the healthcare industry. The platform provides a secure, scalable, and flexible infrastructure that enables healthcare providers to store, manage, and analyze healthcare data from various sources.

Microsoft Azure's architecture consists of various services that can be used to build customized healthcare solutions. The platform provides tools for data analytics, machine learning, and IoT, among others. These services can be combined to create healthcare solutions that meet the unique needs of healthcare providers.

Medical specialists can analyze a lot of clinical information from multiple sources, including EHRs, medical equipment, and wearables, because of Microsoft Azure's statistical capabilities.

Doctors may get involved before a situation worsens by using this information to spot developments and patterns that could point to a possible health problem.

Through the use of Microsoft Azure's machine learning software, doctors may develop methods of prediction that can be used to identify individuals who are more likely than not to have chronic diseases. The artificial intelligence algorithms in Azure can identify patients with a serious risk of developing hyperglycemia by examining medical records. Then, medical professionals can offer focused therapies to delay the illness's emergence.

With the help of Azure's internet capacities, medical professionals can pair with a range of healthcare goods and gadgets to get immediate health information on patients. Microsoft Azure's security features ensure that healthcare data is protected from unauthorized access. The platform provides various security controls, such as role-based access control, encryption, and identity management, to ensure that healthcare data is secure. Azure's compliance certifications, such as HIPAA and HITRUST, ensure that healthcare providers are meeting regulatory requirements.

Microsoft Azure's AI capabilities enable healthcare providers to develop intelligent healthcare solutions.

Microsoft Azure is a powerful tool that uses cloud, AI, and IoT technologies to transform healthcare. By providing a secure, scalable, and flexible infrastructure, healthcare providers can store, manage, and analyze healthcare data from various sources. With a decrease in the need for personal interactions and improved patient results, the resulting information may be utilized to remotely track patient health.

16.5.3 Google cloud healthcare API

A cloud-based system called Google Cloud Service Healthcare API uses machine learning, the IoT, and cloud computing to enhance medical results. One of the key benefits of the Google Cloud Healthcare API is its ability to support interoperability across different healthcare systems.

The platform provides a set of standards-based APIs that enable healthcare providers to securely exchange healthcare data across different systems, with the use of this technology, doctors may identify individuals at an elevated risk of developing a chronic illness and offer them specific therapies to prevent it, using medical imaging systems.

A key feature of the Google Cloud Healthcare API is its support for machine learning and AI. The system offers a collection of ready-to-use mathematical models of machine learning that can be utilized to analyze healthcare information and produce ideas that may be applied to enhance the treatment of patients. These models include NLP models for analyzing clinical notes and medical imaging models for analyzing radiology images. The Google Cloud Healthcare API supports IoT technologies. The platform provides a set of APIs that enable healthcare providers to securely collect and transmit data from IoT devices, such as wearables and sensors. This information may be used to continuously monitor patient health, giving medical professionals immediate information about patients' situations and allowing them to take action before a significant issue arises.

The Google Cloud Healthcare API is being used in healthcare through its partnership with Mayo Clinic. The Mayo Clinic is using the platform to develop a set of AI-powered tools that can be used to analyze medical imaging data and detect early signs of cancer. The platform analyzes large volumes of medical imaging data to identify subtle changes in tissue that may be indicative of early-stage cancer.

The Google Cloud Healthcare API in action is through its partnership with Biogen. The system is being utilized by Biogen to create a collection of tools that may be used to analyze genetic information from individuals with neurological illnesses including Parkinson's and Alzheimer's. To find possible drug targets and create individualized therapies for individuals, the channel analyses massive amounts of genetic data.

The platform provides healthcare providers with tools to manage, analyze, and derive insights from healthcare data, enabling them to deliver personalized care to patients. The Google Cloud Healthcare API is being used in a range of applications, from cancer detection to personalized treatment plans for neurological diseases.

16.5.4 IBM Watson Health

A cloud-based tool called IBM Watson Health makes use of AI and IoT to enhance medical results. The platform provides healthcare providers with tools to manage, analyze, and derive insights from healthcare data.

Watson Health's architecture consists of various services, including data analytics, machine learning, and IoT, among others. Combining these resources would enable the development of innovative medical services that correspond to the specific requirements of medical professionals.

With the aid of Watson Health's data analysis solutions, clinicians can now analyze substantial amounts of patient information. The platform employs algorithms that use machine learning to find habits and patterns in the data, allowing for the development of knowledge regarding the physical and mental well-being of the patients.

IBM Watson Health also provides healthcare providers with a range of tools to improve clinical decision-making. The platform's clinical decision support tools can be used to identify the most effective treatments for specific patient populations, based on their clinical data. With the use of the platform's data analytics capabilities, medical professionals may act quickly and offer tailored therapies to avoid the emergence of chronic illnesses in individuals who are in high danger of getting them.

By analyzing medical records, Watson Health's predictive algorithms may spot patients who are at a greater risk of contracting diseases like cardiovascular disease. This makes it possible for medical professionals to act quickly and offer tailored therapies that reduce the emergence of certain illnesses.

Watson Health's IoT capabilities can provide insights into patient behavior, such as physical activity levels which can be used to develop more personalized treatment plans.

Watson Health's security features ensure that healthcare data is protected from unauthorized access. The platform provides various security controls, such as identity management, encryption, and data access controls, to ensure that healthcare data is secure.

16.5.5 Applications of the latest trends of Cloud, IoT, and AI in healthcare

16.5.5.1 Personalized medicine

One field where AI-based technologies, the IoT, and cloud services are now having a significant impact on health services is the improvement of tailored therapies. In the application of customized medicine, the medical treatment of a patient is modified to take into account their particular DNA characteristics, style of life, and environment. This method can improve medicinal efficacy while reducing side effects.

Large volumes of DNA information may be stored and analyzed on systems hosted on the cloud, allowing medical professionals to pinpoint specific genes linked to particular diseases. IoT gadgets may be used to track patients' medical conditions and collect information on behavioral and environmental variables that may affect illness risk.

These data may be analyzed using AI algorithms to create predictions that may recognize patients in danger of contracting specific illnesses.

16.5.5.2 Decision-making

Additionally employed to enhance medical decision-making are technologies built on the cloud, IoT, and AI. Large volumes of medical data may be used to train artificial intelligence algorithms to find trends and create prediction models that will aid healthcare professionals in making better decisions.

Algorithms based on AI may be utilized to analyze clinical photos and spot early illness indications. As a result, patients' outcomes may be improved and healthcare expenses may be decreased.

AI algorithms could be used to analyze patient information and create individualized treatment regimens that cater to a person's unique requirements.

Doctors can utilize medical information from everywhere, at any moment, by using cloud-based technologies to store and distribute it securely. This might enhance medical staff coordination.

16.5.5.3 Drug discovery

Drug research and discovery is another field that is using cloud, IoT, and AI-based technologies. Large-scale clinical trial data analysis and the identification of prospective therapeutic targets may be done using AI systems.

This can reduce the time and cost of drug development, enabling new treatments to be brought to market more quickly. Cloud-based platforms can be used to store and analyze this data, enabling researchers to collaborate more effectively and share data securely.

IoT devices can also be used to monitor patient outcomes during clinical trials, providing real-time data on treatment efficacy and side effects.

16.5.5.4 Telemedicine

Telemedicine is one sector of medicine that is being transformed by platforms built on the cloud, IoT, and AI. By using the internet, telemedicine enables people to obtain treatment without visiting a doctor. Patients who reside outdoors or in isolated places, have mobility problems or are not able to get to a doctor will find this to be extremely helpful.

Doctors may access information about patients from any place by using cloud-based technologies to put and handle patient data. This is crucial in telemedicine, as it may be necessary for healthcare professionals to access patient information from a distance to give medical treatment. IoT devices may be utilized for monitoring patients as well as delivering healthcare.

This can be especially useful in telemedicine, where healthcare providers may not have access to medical imaging equipment.

Cloud, IoT, and AI-based platforms are transforming healthcare by providing personalized medicine, improving patient engagement and education, improving healthcare management and operations, improving healthcare in underserved areas, transforming telemedicine, and enabling precision medicine. These platforms offer tremendous potential for improving healthcare outcomes and reducing healthcare costs.

16.6 Conclusion

In conclusion, the combination of AI and IoT has immense potential to revolutionize healthcare. Large volumes of data may be collected, analyzed, and interpreted in real time by these technologies, resulting in more quick and precise recommendations, individualized therapies, and monitoring of patients at home. They can also provide personalized treatment plans and enable early detection of diseases. The trends in AI and IoT in healthcare are constantly evolving, with new applications and technologies being developed regularly. The ongoing pandemic has also highlighted the importance of these technologies in addressing healthcare challenges and has accelerated their adoption.

In summary, AI and IoT have the potential to drastically alter how healthcare is delivered and patient outcomes. Healthcare organizations need to continue exploring and adopting these technologies to stay ahead in an ever-changing healthcare landscape.

Further reading

[1] Paranjape, K., Schinkel, M., Nanayakkara, P.: Short keynote paper: mainstreaming personalized healthcare-transforming healthcare through new era of artificial intelligence. *IEEE J. Biomed. Health Inform.* 1 (2020).

[2] Ergen, O., Belcastro, K.D.: AI-driven advanced Internet of Things (Iotx2): the future seems irreversibly connected in medicine. *Anatol. J. Cardiol.* 22, 15–17 (2019).

[3] Sadoughi, F., Behmanesh, A., Sayfouri, N.: Internet of Things in medicine: a systematic mapping study. *J. Biomed. Inform.* 103, 103383 (2020).

[4] Tyagi, S., Agarwal, A., Maheshwari, P.: A conceptual framework for IoT-based healthcare system using cloud computing. In: 2016 6th International Conference—Cloud System and Big Data Engineering, Conflu (2016).

[5] Ahirwal, M.K., Londhe, N.D., and Kumar, A. (2022). *Artificial Intelligence Applications for Healthcare*. Boca Raton, FL: CRC Press.

[6] Baker, S.E., Xiang, W., Atkinson, I.M.: Internet of Things for smart healthcare: technologies, challenges, and opportunities. *IEEE Access* (2017).

[7] Ayiter, E.: Further dimensions: Text, typography, and play in the Metaverse. In *2012 International Conference on Cyberworlds* (pp. 296–303). Piscataway, NJ: IEEE; 2012.

[8] Al-Fuqaha, A., Guizani, M., Mohammadi, M., Aledhari, M., and Ayyash, M.: Internet of things: A survey on enabling technologies, protocols, and applications. *IEEE Commun. Surv. Tutor.*, 17(4),2347–2376 (2015).

[9] Barbiero, P., Torñe, R.V., and Lío P.: Graph representation forecasting of patient's medical conditions: Toward a digital twin. *Front. Genet.*, 2021; 1289.

[10] Chukwu, E., Garg, L.: A systematic review of blockchain in healthcare: frameworks, prototypes, and implementations. *IEEE Access*. 8,21196–21214 (2020).

[11] Masoni, M., Guelfi, M.R., Gensini, G.F.: Darknet and bitcoin, the obscure and anonymous side of the internet in healthcare. *Technol Health Care*. 24 (6),969–972 (2016).

[12] Li, M., Yu, S., Zheng, Y., Ren, K., Lou. W.: Scalable and secure sharing of personal health records in cloud computing using attribute-based encryption. *IEEE Trans. Parall. Distrib. Syst*. 24(1),131–143 (2012).

[13] Abugabah, A., Nizam, N., Alzubi, A.A.: Decentralized telemedicine framework for a smart healthcare ecosystem. *IEEE Access*. 8,166575–166588 (2020).

[14] Udgata, S.K., Suryadevara, N.K.: COVID-19, sensors, and Internet of Medical Things (IoMT). *Internet of Things and Sensor Network for COVID-19*. New York: Springer; 2021:pp 39–53.

[15] Gopal, G., Suter-Crazzolara, C., Toldo, L., Eberhardt, W.: Digital transformation in healthcare—architectures of present and future information technologies. *Clin. Chem. Lab. Med.* 57, 328–335 (2019).

Chapter 17

Application of metaverse in regenerative medicine: applications and challenges

R. Ranjana[1], R.K. Sahana[2] and B. Narendra Kumar Rao[3]

Abstract

The convergence of regenerative medicine and the metaverse represents a groundbreaking synergy between advanced healthcare technologies and immersive virtual environments. Regenerative medicine, driven by innovations such as stem cell therapy, tissue engineering, and gene editing, aims to restore or replace damaged tissues and organs, offering new avenues for treating injuries, diseases, and age-related conditions. Meanwhile, the metaverse is a digital realm where users interact with computer-generated environments and other users through virtual reality (VR), augmented reality (AR), and other immersive technologies. In this virtual space, individuals can explore, create, and socialize in ways previously unimaginable. The integration of regenerative medicine into the metaverse opens up a myriad of possibilities. Virtual reality simulations could be used to visualize complex biological processes, aiding researchers in understanding and developing novel regenerative therapies. Patients could undergo immersive VR experiences to better comprehend their conditions and potential treatment options. Surgeons might practice intricate procedures in virtual environments before performing them on real patients, enhancing precision and reducing risks.

Moreover, the metaverse could serve as a platform for personalized healthcare experiences. Patients could create digital avatars representing their physiological data and treatment progress, fostering greater engagement and empowerment in their healthcare journeys. Virtual support groups and communities within the metaverse could offer invaluable emotional and social support to individuals undergoing regenerative treatments. However, challenges such as data privacy, regulatory considerations, and equitable access to virtual healthcare services must be addressed to fully realize the potential of this integration. Despite these challenges, the fusion of regenerative medicine and the metaverse holds immense

[1]Department of Artificial Intelligence and Data Science, Dr. Mahalingam College of Engineering and Technology, India
[2]Department of Bio-Technology, SRM Institute of Science and Technology, India
[3]School of Computing, Mohan Babu University, India

promise for revolutionizing healthcare delivery, enhancing patient outcomes, and shaping the future of medicine in the digital age.

Keywords: Metaverse Applications; Regenerative Medicine; Artificial Intelligence; Digital Healthcare; Stem Cell Therapy

17.1 Introduction

Metaverse in its simplest terms can be defined as a collective shared space that is created virtually by converging virtually augmented physically real elements and virtual elements that are persistent [1]. Access to this space is through the internet browser and the environment is normally immersive and three-dimensional in nature. The concept integrates a wide range of digital environments that can interact and collaborate with each other in the digital world performing varied activities like humans. This chapter aims to give a basic introduction to metaverse and its application in healthcare with an emphasis on regenerative medicine. A case study is also discussed in this context.

17.1.1 The major characteristics of metaverse

Interactivity: Users can interact with the environment and with other users in real time.

Persistence: The metaverse continues to exist and evolve even when individual users are not logged in.

Interoperability: Users can move and interact across different virtual spaces, often retaining their digital identity and assets.

Immersive experiences: Use of technologies such as virtual reality (VR), augmented reality (AR), and extended reality (XR) to create more engaging and lifelike experiences.

Social presence: Strong emphasis on social interactions and community-building within the virtual space [2].

The metaverse is often depicted in science fiction but is becoming increasingly relevant with advancements in VR, AR, blockchain, and other digital technologies, pointing towards a future where virtual and physical realities are deeply interconnected.

17.1.2 Applications of metaverse

The metaverse has a wide range of applications across various fields, leveraging its immersive and interactive nature to enhance user experiences and create new opportunities [3]. Some key applications of the metaverse include:

17.1.2.1 Gaming

- Immersive Games: Games that offer deeply immersive experiences, allowing players to explore vast virtual worlds and interact with them in real time.
- Social gaming: Multiplayer games that emphasize social interaction, such as virtual worlds and online role-playing games.

17.1.2.2 Social interaction

- Virtual social spaces: Platforms like VRChat and Second Life where users can meet, socialize, and interact through avatars.
- Virtual events: Hosting events such as concerts, conferences, and parties in virtual spaces, providing interactive and engaging experiences.

17.1.2.3 Work and collaboration

- Virtual offices: Environments like Spatial and Horizon Workrooms where remote teams can collaborate in a shared virtual space.
- Collaboration tools: Applications that allow for virtual meetings, brainstorming sessions, and project management in immersive settings.

17.1.2.4 Education and training

- Virtual classrooms: Platforms that offer immersive educational experiences, enabling students to attend classes, interact with peers, and engage with interactive content.
- Simulations: Training simulations for fields like medicine, aviation, and military, providing realistic and risk-free environments for practice.

17.1.2.5 Commerce

- Virtual marketplaces: Online spaces where users can buy, sell, and trade virtual goods and services, often using cryptocurrencies and NFTs.
- Virtual showrooms: Retail environments where customers can explore products in 3D before making a purchase.

17.1.2.6 Healthcare

- Telemedicine: Virtual consultations and medical examinations conducted in immersive environments.
- Therapeutic applications: Using VR for treatments such as exposure therapy, physical rehabilitation, and mental health therapy.

17.1.2.7 Entertainment and media

- Virtual performances: Concerts, theater performances, and other entertainment events hosted in virtual venues.
- Interactive media: Immersive storytelling experiences and interactive films.

17.1.2.8 Real estate

- Virtual property tours: Allowing potential buyers to explore properties in a virtual space.
- Virtual real estate: Buying, selling, and developing virtual land within the metaverse.

17.1.2.9 Travel and tourism

- Virtual tours: Enabling users to visit and explore destinations around the world virtually.
- Cultural experiences: Accessing historical and cultural sites in an immersive manner.

17.1.2.10 Personal development

- Skill training: Learning new skills through interactive and immersive simulations.
- Fitness and wellness: Virtual fitness classes and wellness experiences.

The metaverse's applications are continually expanding as technology evolves, creating new possibilities and transforming how we interact with digital spaces and each other.

17.2 Use of digital technologies in healthcare

Digital technologies are transforming healthcare by improving patient care, enhancing operational efficiency, and enabling new treatment possibilities. Here are key areas where digital technologies are being utilized in healthcare:

- **Electronic Health Records (EHRs)**
- Data management: EHRs provide a digital version of patients' paper charts, offering real time, patient-centered records that are accessible to authorized users.
- Interoperability: EHRs enable seamless sharing of patient data across different healthcare providers and systems, improving coordination and continuity of care.
- **Telemedicine**
- Remote consultations: Telemedicine platforms allow patients to consult with healthcare providers remotely via video calls, reducing the need for in-person visits and expanding access to care.
- Remote monitoring: Wearable devices and home monitoring systems can track patients' vital signs and other health metrics, enabling continuous monitoring and timely interventions.
- **Mobile health (mHealth)**
- Health apps: Mobile applications offer various health-related services, such as appointment scheduling, medication reminders, fitness tracking, and chronic disease management.
- Patient engagement: mHealth apps empower patients to take an active role in their health management by providing educational resources and self-monitoring tools.
- **Artificial Intelligence (AI) and Machine Learning**
- Diagnostics: AI algorithms can analyze medical images and other diagnostic data to detect diseases with high accuracy.

- Predictive analytics: AI can predict patient outcomes and disease progression, helping to tailor personalized treatment plans and improve preventative care.
- **Blockchain technology**
- Secure data sharing: Blockchain provides a secure and transparent method for sharing patient data, ensuring privacy and data integrity.
- Supply chain management: Blockchain can track pharmaceuticals and medical supplies, reducing fraud and ensuring the authenticity of products.
- **Internet of Things (IoT)**
- Connected devices: IoT devices, such as smart sensors and wearables, can monitor patients' health metrics in real time and send data to healthcare providers.
- Home automation: IoT technology can support elderly and disabled individuals by automating home functions and providing alerts in case of emergencies.
- Virtual Reality (VR) and Augmented Reality (AR)
- Medical training: VR and AR provide immersive training environments for medical students and professionals to practice procedures and surgeries.
- Patient treatment: VR is used in pain management, physical therapy, and mental health treatment, offering therapeutic experiences and simulations.
- **Robotics**
- Surgical robots: Robotic systems assist surgeons in performing precise and minimally invasive procedures, improving outcomes and reducing recovery times.
- Rehabilitation robots: Robots help patients with physical therapy and rehabilitation exercises, enhancing recovery.
- **3D printing**
- Custom prosthetics and implants: 3D printing enables the creation of personalized prosthetics, implants, and medical devices tailored to individual patients' needs.
- Surgical models: Surgeons use 3D-printed models of patients' anatomy for preoperative planning and simulation.
- **Big data and analytics**
- Population health management: Analyzing large datasets helps identify health trends, track disease outbreaks, and inform public health strategies.
- Clinical research: Big data analytics accelerates medical research by uncovering patterns and insights from extensive datasets, leading to new treatments and discoveries.
- **Wearable technology**
- Fitness trackers: Devices that monitor physical activity, sleep patterns, and other health metrics, encouraging healthier lifestyles.
- Medical wearables: Devices that track specific health conditions, such as glucose monitors for diabetes patients, providing real-time data and alerts.
- **Health Information Exchange (HIE)**
- Data integration: HIE platforms enable the secure sharing of health information across different healthcare organizations, improving care coordination and reducing duplication of tests and procedures.

These digital technologies are driving significant advancements in healthcare, making it more efficient, accessible, and personalized. As technology continues to evolve, its impact on healthcare is expected to grow, further transforming the landscape of medical practice and patient care.

17.3 Use of AI in healthcare

The scope for AI use in healthcare is vast and continuously expanding, driven by advancements in machine learning, data analytics, and computational power. Here are some key areas where AI is making a significant impact in healthcare:

17.3.1 Medical imaging and diagnostics

Image analysis: AI algorithms can analyze medical images (X-rays, MRIs, CT scans) to detect abnormalities such as tumors, fractures, and other conditions with high accuracy.

Early detection: AI can identify early signs of diseases such as cancer, often before they become detectable by human experts [4].

17.3.2 Predictive analytics

Disease prediction: AI models can predict the likelihood of developing certain conditions based on genetic, lifestyle, and environmental factors.

Patient outcomes: Predictive analytics can forecast patient outcomes, helping in creating personalized treatment plans and managing chronic diseases more effectively.

17.3.3 Personalized medicine

Treatment plans: AI can analyze a patient's genetic makeup, lifestyle, and medical history to recommend personalized treatment plans.

Drug development: AI can accelerate the discovery and development of new drugs by predicting how different compounds will interact with targets in the body.

17.3.4 Clinical decision support

Assisting clinicians: AI systems can provide real-time support to clinicians by offering evidence-based recommendations, reducing diagnostic errors, and improving treatment accuracy.

Workflow optimization: AI can streamline administrative and clinical workflows, allowing healthcare providers to focus more on patient care [5].

17.3.5 Robotic surgery

Precision and minimally invasive procedures: AI-powered robots can assist surgeons in performing precise and minimally invasive procedures, enhancing surgical outcomes and reducing recovery times.

17.3.6 Telemedicine and virtual health assistants

Remote consultations: AI can enable more effective telemedicine services by providing virtual health assistants who can conduct preliminary assessments and triage.

Patient monitoring: AI-powered devices can monitor patients remotely, collecting data on vital signs and alerting healthcare providers to potential issues.

17.3.7 Natural Language Processing (NLP)

Electronic Health Records (EHR): NLP can analyze and extract relevant information from EHRs, making it easier for clinicians to access patient data and improving the efficiency of documentation.

Clinical documentation: AI can assist in creating and managing clinical documentation, reducing the burden on healthcare providers.

17.3.8 Drug interaction and safety

Adverse drug reaction detection: AI can analyze patient data and medical literature to detect and predict adverse drug reactions.

Medication management: AI systems can help in optimizing medication regimens and ensuring patient adherence to prescribed treatments.

17.3.9 Population health management

Public health surveillance: AI can track and predict the spread of infectious diseases, helping public health officials to respond more effectively.

Health trend analysis: AI can analyze large datasets to identify health trends and inform policy decisions.

17.3.10 Mental health

Chatbots and virtual therapists: AI-powered chatbots can provide mental health support and preliminary counseling, making mental health services more accessible.

Behavioral analysis: AI can analyze speech and behavior patterns to detect early signs of mental health conditions such as depression and anxiety.

The integration of AI in healthcare is revolutionizing how medical services are delivered, improving patient outcomes, enhancing efficiency, and reducing costs. As technology continues to evolve, the potential applications of AI in healthcare are expected to grow, offering even more innovative solutions to complex medical challenges.

17.4 Regenerative medicine

Regenerative medicine is a rapidly advancing field that focuses on repairing, replacing, regenerating, or enhancing the function of damaged tissues and organs through innovative approaches [6]. It harnesses the body's natural healing processes, using a combination of biology, engineering, and clinical techniques to restore normal function. Here are the key components and applications of regenerative medicine:

17.4.1 Stem cell therapy

Embryonic Stem Cells (ESCs): Derived from early-stage embryos, these cells have the potential to differentiate into any cell type in the body.

Adult Stem Cells: Found in various tissues like bone marrow and fat, these cells can differentiate into a limited range of cell types and are used for specific tissue repair [7].

Induced Pluripotent Stem Cells (iPSCs): Adult cells reprogrammed to an embryonic-like state, offering the potential to generate any cell type without the ethical concerns associated with ESCs.

17.4.2 Tissue engineering

Scaffolds: Three-dimensional structures that provide support for cell attachment and tissue development. Scaffolds can be made from natural or synthetic materials.

Biomaterials: Materials that interact with biological systems to support tissue regeneration. These include hydrogels, biocompatible polymers, and decellularized matrices.

17.4.3 Cellular therapies

Chondrocyte Implantation: Repair of cartilage using cultured chondrocytes (cartilage cells).

Myoblast therapy: Use of muscle cells to repair damaged heart tissue after a heart attack.

17.4.4 Gene therapy

Gene editing: Techniques like CRISPR/Cas9 allow for precise modifications of genes to correct genetic disorders or enhance regenerative capabilities.

Gene transfer: Introducing new or modified genes into cells to promote healing and regeneration.

17.4.5 Bioprinting

3D Bioprinting: Layer-by-layer construction of tissues and organs using bioinks composed of cells and biomaterials, creating structures that mimic natural tissue architecture.

Bone regeneration: Use of scaffolds, stem cells, and growth factors to heal bone fractures and defects.

Cartilage repair: Techniques like autologous chondrocyte implantation (ACI) to treat joint cartilage damage.

17.4.6 Cardiology

Heart repair: Stem cell therapy to regenerate damaged heart tissue following myocardial infarction (heart attack).

Vascular tissue engineering: Creation of blood vessels using stem cells and scaffolds for bypass surgery and vascular repair.

17.4.7 Neurology

Spinal cord injury: Stem cell therapies and biomaterials to promote regeneration of spinal cord tissue and restore function.

Neurodegenerative diseases: Research into stem cell treatments for conditions like Parkinson's disease and Alzheimer's disease to replace lost or damaged neurons [8,9].

17.4.8 Ophthalmology

Corneal regeneration: Use of stem cells and tissue-engineered constructs to repair damaged corneas.

Retinal repair: Stem cell therapy to treat retinal diseases such as macular degeneration.

17.4.9 Dermatology

Wound healing: Application of stem cells, growth factors, and biomaterials to accelerate the healing of chronic wounds and burns.

Skin grafting: Tissue-engineered skin substitutes for severe burns and other extensive skin injuries.

17.4.10 Hematology

Bone marrow transplants: Use of hematopoietic stem cells to treat blood disorders such as leukemia and lymphoma.

Gene therapy for blood diseases: Correction of genetic defects in blood cells using gene editing techniques.

17.4.11 Hepatology

Liver regeneration: Use of stem cells and bioengineered tissues to treat liver diseases and promote liver regeneration.

17.4.12 Urology

Bladder reconstruction: Tissue-engineered bladders using patients' own cells to treat bladder dysfunction and disease [4].

Kidney repair: Research into regenerating kidney tissue for chronic kidney disease.

17.4.13 Challenges and future directions

Immune rejection: Overcoming immune responses to transplanted cells and tissues.

Scalability: Developing methods to produce tissues and organs at a scale suitable for widespread clinical use.

17.4.14 Ethical and regulatory issues

Addressing the ethical considerations and establishing clear regulatory pathways for new therapies.

Integration and functionality: Ensuring that engineered tissues integrate properly with the host's body and function as intended.

Regenerative medicine holds immense promise for revolutionizing healthcare by providing solutions to conditions that currently have limited treatment options. As research progresses, it is expected to lead to groundbreaking therapies that improve quality of life and extend human healthspan.

17.5 Use of metaverse in healthcare

The metaverse in healthcare refers to the use of immersive virtual environments to enhance various aspects of medical practice, patient care, and healthcare management. By integrating technologies such as virtual reality (VR), augmented reality (AR), artificial intelligence (AI), and blockchain, the metaverse offers innovative solutions that can transform the healthcare landscape [10]. Here are some key applications of the metaverse in healthcare:

17.5.1 Medical training and education

Virtual simulations: Medical students and professionals can practice surgical procedures and other medical techniques in a risk-free virtual environment. VR and AR simulations provide realistic scenarios for hands-on learning.

Interactive learning: Virtual classrooms and 3D anatomical models enable interactive and engaging learning experiences, improving the understanding of complex medical concepts.

17.5.2 Telemedicine and remote consultations

Virtual clinics: Patients can visit virtual clinics for consultations with healthcare providers, reducing the need for physical travel and increasing access to care, especially for those in remote areas.

Remote monitoring: Wearable devices and IoT technology can monitor patients' health metrics in real time, with data integrated into the metaverse for continuous tracking and remote intervention.

17.5.3 Patient rehabilitation and therapy

Physical therapy: VR environments can be used for physical rehabilitation exercises, making the process more engaging and motivating for patients. Therapists can monitor progress and adjust treatments remotely.

Mental health therapy: Virtual reality can provide immersive environments for treating mental health conditions such as PTSD, anxiety, and phobias. Virtual therapy sessions and mindfulness exercises can be conducted within the metaverse [11].

17.5.4 Surgery and preoperative planning

Surgical training: Surgeons can use VR to plan and rehearse complex surgeries. Detailed 3D models of a patient's anatomy can be created from medical imaging data, allowing for precise preoperative planning.

Remote assistance: Experienced surgeons can provide guidance and assistance to colleagues performing surgeries in different locations through virtual collaboration platforms.

17.5.5 Collaborative research and development

Virtual research labs: Scientists and researchers can collaborate in virtual laboratories, sharing data and conducting experiments in a shared virtual space, facilitating global collaboration.

Clinical trials: The metaverse can streamline the process of conducting clinical trials by creating virtual environments for patient recruitment, monitoring, and data collection [12].

17.5.6 Health education and patient engagement

Patient education: Interactive 3D models and virtual simulations can help patients understand their conditions and treatments better, improving patient engagement and adherence to treatment plans.

17.5.7 Health awareness campaigns

Public health initiatives can leverage the metaverse to create engaging and informative campaigns to raise awareness about various health issues and promote healthy behaviors.

17.5.8 Virtual health communities

Support groups: Patients with similar conditions can connect in virtual support groups, sharing experiences and providing emotional support in a safe, immersive environment.

Fitness and wellness: Virtual fitness classes, wellness programs, and guided meditation sessions can be conducted within the metaverse, promoting overall health and well-being.

17.5.9 Healthcare administration and management

Virtual hospitals: Entire hospital infrastructures can be managed in the metaverse, allowing for virtual walkthroughs, equipment management, and facility planning.

Data security and privacy: Blockchain technology can be integrated to ensure secure and transparent management of patient data and medical records in the virtual environment.

17.5.10 Benefits and challenges

17.5.10.1 Benefits

Accessibility: Increased access to healthcare services for patients in remote or underserved areas.

Efficiency: Streamlined processes and reduced costs through virtual consultations and remote monitoring [13].

Engagement: Enhanced patient and provider engagement through interactive and immersive experiences.

Collaboration: Improved collaboration among healthcare professionals and researchers globally.

17.5.10.2 Challenges

Technology integration: Ensuring compatibility and seamless integration of various technologies within the metaverse [14].

Privacy and security: Protecting patient data and ensuring privacy in virtual environments.

Regulatory compliance: Adhering to healthcare regulations and standards in a virtual context.

Accessibility and equity: Ensuring that all patients have access to the necessary technology and internet connectivity to benefit from metaverse applications.

The metaverse has the potential to revolutionize healthcare by providing innovative solutions that enhance medical education, patient care, and healthcare management. As technology continues to evolve, the integration of the metaverse into healthcare is likely to expand, offering new opportunities for improving health outcomes and transforming the patient experience [15].

17.6 Metaverse in regenerative medicine

The integration of the metaverse into regenerative medicine holds transformative potential, combining immersive virtual environments with cutting-edge medical technologies to enhance research, treatment, and patient care [16,17]. Here are several key applications and benefits of using the metaverse in regenerative medicine:

1. Enhanced research and collaboration
    - Virtual research labs: Researchers from around the world can collaborate in virtual laboratories, sharing data and conducting experiments in real time. This can accelerate the development of regenerative therapies.
    - Simulated environments: Scientists can create and manipulate virtual models of tissues and organs to study disease mechanisms and the effects

of potential treatments, allowing for rapid hypothesis testing and iterative research.

2. Advanced medical training and education
   - Virtual simulations: Medical students and professionals can practice regenerative medicine techniques, such as stem cell transplantation and tissue engineering, in a virtual environment without the risk of harming patients.
   - 3D anatomical models: Interactive 3D models of human anatomy, including detailed representations of tissues and organs, help learners understand complex regenerative processes and procedures.
3. Patient-specific treatment planning
   - Personalized virtual models: Using patient-specific data, such as MRI and CT scans, doctors can create detailed virtual models of a patient's anatomy to plan and visualize regenerative treatments.
   - Preoperative simulations: Surgeons can rehearse complex procedures in a virtual environment, improving precision and outcomes for regenerative surgeries.
4. Telemedicine and remote consultations
   - Virtual consultations: Patients can consult with specialists in regenerative medicine from anywhere in the world, receiving expert advice and treatment plans tailored to their specific conditions.
   - Remote monitoring: Virtual environments can integrate data from wearable devices and biosensors to monitor patients' progress and adjust treatments in real time.
5. Patient rehabilitation and therapy
   - Virtual physical therapy: Customized rehabilitation programs can be delivered through VR, guiding patients through exercises designed to enhance tissue regeneration and recovery.
   - Mental health support: Immersive environments can provide therapeutic experiences for patients undergoing regenerative treatments, addressing mental health aspects such as anxiety and depression [18].
6. Development of biomaterials and scaffolds
   - Virtual testing: Engineers and material scientists can use the metaverse to design and test new biomaterials and scaffolds in a simulated environment, optimizing their properties for tissue engineering before creating physical prototypes.
   - Collaborative design: Multidisciplinary teams can work together in virtual spaces to develop innovative scaffolds that support cell growth and tissue regeneration.
7. Clinical trials and patient recruitment
   - Virtual clinical trials: The metaverse can facilitate decentralized clinical trials by creating virtual environments for patient recruitment, monitoring, and data collection, making trials more efficient and accessible.
   - Patient education: Virtual platforms can educate potential participants about clinical trials, explaining procedures and benefits in an engaging and comprehensible manner.

8. Public health and education
    - Awareness campaigns: The metaverse can host interactive campaigns to educate the public about regenerative medicine, its potential benefits, and ongoing research [19].
    - Virtual support groups: Patients undergoing regenerative treatments can connect in virtual support groups, sharing experiences and providing mutual support in an immersive environment.

17.6.1 Benefits and challenges

Benefits:

- Enhanced accessibility: Patients and professionals can access cutting-edge regenerative medicine resources and expertise regardless of their geographical location.
- Improved collaboration: Virtual environments enable seamless collaboration between researchers, clinicians, and patients, fostering innovation and accelerating progress.
- Personalized care: The ability to create and manipulate virtual models of individual patients enhances the personalization and precision of regenerative treatments.

Challenges:

- Technical integration: Ensuring the compatibility of different technologies and maintaining a seamless user experience in the metaverse.
- Data privacy and security: Protecting sensitive patient data within virtual environments and ensuring compliance with healthcare regulations.
- Cost and accessibility: Addressing the cost of advanced technologies and ensuring equitable access for all patients and healthcare providers.

17.7 Case study: Metaverse in healthcare

The MeTAI ecosystem is an innovative integration of the metaverse and artificial intelligence (AI) designed to revolutionize healthcare delivery and management. This ecosystem leverages immersive virtual environments and advanced AI technologies to create a comprehensive platform for various healthcare applications. Below is a case study of the MeTAI ecosystem, highlighting four major healthcare applications [20].

17.7.1 Case study: MeTAI ecosystem in healthcare

17.7.1.1 Overview

The MeTAI ecosystem combines the metaverse's immersive capabilities with AI's analytical power to create a unified platform that addresses key challenges in healthcare. By providing a virtual environment for medical professionals, patients, and researchers to interact, MeTAI aims to enhance medical training, patient care, research collaboration, and health management.

17.7.1.2 Application 1: medical training and education

Implementation

Virtual simulations: MeTAI provides a virtual simulation platform where medical students and professionals can practice surgical procedures, diagnostics, and patient interactions. These simulations use AI to adapt to the learner's level, providing personalized feedback and scenarios.

3D anatomical models: The ecosystem offers detailed 3D models of human anatomy that can be manipulated and studied in a virtual space, enhancing the understanding of complex structures and procedures.

Benefits

Risk-free learning: Medical professionals can hone their skills without the risk of harming actual patients.

Enhanced retention: Interactive and immersive learning experiences improve knowledge retention and understanding.

Case example

A group of surgical residents uses MeTAI's VR simulation to practice complex heart surgery. The AI component provides real-time feedback on their performance, highlighting areas for improvement and suggesting best practices.

17.7.1.3 Application 2: telemedicine and remote consultations

Implementation

Virtual clinics: MeTAI enables the creation of virtual clinics where patients can have consultations with healthcare providers from the comfort of their homes. These clinics are equipped with AI tools for preliminary assessments and data analysis.

Remote monitoring: Integrating IoT devices with the MeTAI platform allows for continuous monitoring of patients' vital signs and health metrics, with AI algorithms alerting providers to any anomalies.

Benefits

Increased access: Patients in remote or underserved areas can access specialist care without the need to travel.

Continuous care: Real-time monitoring and consultations ensure that patients receive timely interventions.

Case example

An elderly patient with chronic heart disease uses a wearable device linked to the MeTAI ecosystem. The device continuously monitors their heart rate and blood pressure, sending data to their cardiologist who reviews the information in the virtual clinic and adjusts the treatment plan as necessary.

17.7.1.4 Application 3: patient rehabilitation and therapy

Implementation

Virtual physical therapy: MeTAI offers virtual physical therapy sessions guided by AI, which tailors exercises to each patient's needs and tracks progress.

Mental health support: Patients can participate in virtual therapy sessions for mental health support, using immersive environments to enhance the therapeutic experience.

Benefits

Personalized rehabilitation: AI-driven customization of therapy sessions ensures that exercises are suited to individual patient needs.

Improved engagement: Virtual environments make rehabilitation exercises more engaging and motivating for patients.

Case example

A stroke patient undergoes virtual physical therapy in the MeTAI ecosystem. The AI adjusts the difficulty of exercises based on the patient's progress, providing encouragement and feedback to maximize recovery.

17.7.1.5 Application 4: collaborative research and development

Implementation

Virtual research labs: MeTAI facilitates virtual research labs where scientists can collaborate on regenerative medicine projects, share data, and conduct experiments in a simulated environment.

Clinical trials: The platform supports virtual clinical trials, allowing for efficient patient recruitment, data collection, and monitoring.

Benefits

Global collaboration: Researchers from different parts of the world can work together seamlessly, accelerating the pace of innovation.

Efficient trials: Virtual trials reduce logistical challenges and improve patient participation rates.

Case example

A multinational team of researchers uses MeTAI's virtual lab to develop a new stem cell therapy for spinal cord injuries. They conduct virtual experiments, share results in real time, and use AI to analyze data and predict outcomes, significantly speeding up the research process.

17.8 Conclusion

The MeTAI ecosystem represents a significant advancement in healthcare, leveraging the strengths of the metaverse and AI to improve medical training, patient care, rehabilitation, and research collaboration. By providing immersive and interactive virtual environments, MeTAI enhances the capabilities of healthcare professionals and improves patient outcomes, demonstrating the transformative potential of digital technologies in healthcare.

17.8.1 Case study: metaverse usage in regenerative medicine

The integration of the metaverse into regenerative medicine combines immersive virtual environments with advanced technologies to enhance research, treatment, patient education, and collaboration. This case study explores how a fictional hospital, MetaHealth Institute, utilizes the metaverse in regenerative medicine to improve outcomes and advance the field.

Hospital: MetaHealth Institute.

17.8.1.1 Application 1: enhanced research and collaboration

Virtual research labs: MetaHealth Institute sets up virtual research labs within the metaverse where scientists from around the world can collaborate in real time. These labs feature 3D models of tissues and organs, enabling researchers to visualize and manipulate biological structures.

AI-driven simulations: AI algorithms within the metaverse simulate the behavior of stem cells and tissue growth under various conditions, allowing researchers to test hypotheses and refine techniques before applying them in the real world.

Benefits

Global collaboration: Researchers from different geographical locations can work together seamlessly, sharing data and insights without physical constraints.

Accelerated innovation: Virtual simulations and AI analytics speed up the research process, enabling rapid iteration and refinement of regenerative techniques.

Case example

A team of researchers at MetaHealth Institute collaborates with scientists in Japan and Germany to develop a new method for regenerating cardiac tissue. Using the virtual research lab, they conduct joint experiments, share findings in real-time, and use AI simulations to predict the outcomes of different approaches, leading to a breakthrough in treatment within months instead of years.

17.8.1.2 Application 2: patient-specific treatment planning

Implementation

Personalized virtual models: Patients undergoing regenerative treatments at MetaHealth Institute have detailed 3D models of their affected tissues or organs created from MRI and CT scan data. These models are used to plan and visualize regenerative procedures in the metaverse.

Preoperative rehearsals: Surgeons use the metaverse to rehearse complex regenerative surgeries. They can manipulate virtual models of the patient's anatomy, practice the procedure multiple times, and adjust their approach based on AI feedback.

Benefits

Precision and personalization: Surgeons can tailor treatments to the unique anatomical features of each patient, improving the precision and success rates of regenerative procedures.

Enhanced preparation: Preoperative rehearsals in the metaverse increase surgeon confidence and reduce the risk of complications during actual surgeries.

Case example

A patient with severe liver damage is scheduled for a regenerative treatment involving stem cell implantation. Surgeons at MetaHealth Institute use a personalized virtual model of the patient's liver to plan the procedure. They rehearse the implantation in the metaverse, identifying potential challenges and refining their technique, resulting in a successful real-world surgery with minimal complications.

17.8.1.3 Application 3: patient rehabilitation and therapy

Implementation

Virtual physical therapy: Patients recovering from regenerative treatments participate in virtual physical therapy sessions guided by AI. These sessions are conducted in immersive environments that simulate real-world scenarios, making rehabilitation exercises more engaging.

Progress monitoring: AI algorithms track patients' progress in real-time, adjusting therapy exercises based on individual performance and providing feedback to both patients and therapists.

Benefits

Personalized rehabilitation: AI-driven customization ensures that therapy exercises are tailored to each patient's recovery needs and capabilities.

Increased engagement: Immersive virtual environments make rehabilitation more enjoyable, improving patient adherence to prescribed exercises.

Case example

A patient recovering from a knee regeneration procedure at MetaHealth Institute uses the metaverse for physical therapy. The AI customizes exercises to strengthen the regenerated tissue and monitors the patient's progress, providing feedback and encouragement. As a result, the patient experiences a faster and more effective recovery.

17.8.1.4 Application 4: patient education and support

Implementation

Interactive education: Patients at MetaHealth Institute receive detailed explanations of their regenerative treatments through interactive 3D models and simulations in the metaverse. These educational sessions help patients understand the procedures, expected outcomes, and recovery processes.

Virtual support groups: Patients can join virtual support groups within the metaverse, connecting with others undergoing similar treatments. These groups provide emotional support, share experiences, and foster a sense of community.

Benefits

Informed patients: Enhanced understanding of treatments and procedures empowers patients, reducing anxiety and improving compliance with medical advice.

Emotional support: Virtual support groups provide a platform for patients to share experiences and support each other, improving overall well-being.

Case example

A patient scheduled for a spinal cord regeneration procedure participates in an educational session in the metaverse, where a virtual model of the spine is used to explain the surgery and recovery process. The patient also joins a virtual support group of others who have undergone similar procedures, gaining insights and emotional support that aid in their recovery journey.

The MetaHealth Institute's integration of the metaverse into regenerative medicine demonstrates the transformative potential of immersive virtual environments combined with advanced technologies. By enhancing research collaboration, personalizing treatment plans, improving rehabilitation, and supporting patient education and community, the metaverse significantly advances the field of regenerative medicine, leading to better patient outcomes and accelerated medical innovation.

Future directions

The integration of the metaverse in regenerative medicine is poised to revolutionize the field by offering new ways to visualize, plan, and execute treatments. Future advancements might include:

AI-driven insights: Leveraging AI within the metaverse to provide real-time insights and predictive analytics for regenerative therapies.

Global research networks: Expanding virtual research networks to include more diverse and inclusive collaborations.

Enhanced patient experiences: Continuously improving the patient experience through more intuitive and immersive virtual environments.

By bridging the gap between virtual and physical worlds, the metaverse can significantly enhance the capabilities of regenerative medicine, leading to better outcomes and more efficient treatments.

References

[1] Lee, Lik-Hang, Dimitris Chatzopoulos, Pengyuan Zhou, and Tristan Braud. "Metaverse: An introduction." *Metaverse Communication and Computing Networks: Applications, Technologies, and Approaches*, (2023): 1–16.

[2] Wang, Hang, Huansheng Ning, Yujia Lin, *et al.* "A survey on the metaverse: The state-of-the-art, technologies, applications, and challenges." *IEEE Internet of Things Journal*, vol. 10, no. 16 (2023): 14671–14688.

[3] Park, Sang-Min, and Young-Gab Kim. "A metaverse: Taxonomy, components, applications, and open challenges." *IEEE Access*, vol. 10 (2022): 4209–4251.

[4] Kim, Eun Joung, and Jung Yoon Kim. "The metaverse for healthcare: trends, applications, and future directions of digital therapeutics for urology." *International Neurourology Journal*, vol. 27, no. Suppl 1 (2023): S3–12.

[5] Riva, Giuseppe, Daniele Di Lernia, Elena Sajno, *et al.* "Virtual reality therapy in the metaverse: Merging VR for the outside with VR for the inside." *Annual Review of Cybertherapy & Telemedicine*, vol. 19 (2021): 3–8.

[6] Andersson, Elisabeth R., and Urban Lendahl. "Regenerative medicine: a 2009 overview." *Journal of Internal Medicine*, vol. 266, no. 4 (2009): 303–310.

[7] Kolios, George, and Yuben Moodley. "Introduction to stem cells and regenerative medicine." *Respiration*, vol. 85, no. 1 (2012): 3–10.

[8] Ilic, Dusko, and Julia M. Polak. "Stem cells in regenerative medicine: introduction." *British Medical Bulletin*, vol. 98, no. 1 (2011): 117–126.

[9] Bajada, Stefan, Irena Mazakova, James B. Richardson, and Nureddin Ashammakhi. "Updates on stem cells and their applications in regenerative medicine." *Journal of Tissue Engineering and Regenerative Medicine*, vol. 2, no. 4 (2008): 169–183.

[10] Yang, Eunsil. "Implications of immersive technologies in healthcare sector and its built environment." *Frontiers in Medical Technology*, vol. 5 (2023): 1184925.

[11] Cerasa, Antonio, Andrea Gaggioli, Flavia Marino, Giuseppe Riva, and Giovanni Pioggia. "The promise of the metaverse in mental health: the new era of MEDverse." *Heliyon*, vol. 8, no. 11 (2022): e11762.

[12] Rane, Nitin, Saurabh Choudhary, and Jayesh Rane. "Healthcare metaverse: Applications, challenges, and future development." (2023) http://dx.doi.org/10.2139/ssrn.4637901.

[13] Petrigna, Luca, and Giuseppe Musumeci. "The metaverse: A new challenge for the healthcare system: A scoping review." *Journal of Functional Morphology and Kinesiology*, vol. 7, no. 3 (2022): 63.

[14] Usmani, Sadia S., Medha Sharath, and Meghana Mehendale, "Future of mental health in the metaverse." *General Psychiatry*, vol. 35, no. 4 (2022): e100825.

[15] Liu, Zhen, Lingfeng Ren, Chang, Xiao, Ke Zhang, and Peter Demian. "Virtual reality aided therapy towards Health 4.0: A two-decade bibliometric analysis." *International Journal of Environmental Research and Public Health*, vol. 19, no. 3 (2022): 1525.

[16] Wang, Ge, Andreu Badal, Xun Jia, *et al.* "Development of metaverse for intelligent healthcare." *Nature Machine Intelligence*, vol. 4, no. 11 (2022): 922–929.

[17] Zhou, Yihao, Xiao Xiao, Guorui Chen, Xun Zhao, and Jun Chen. "Self-powered sensing technologies for human Metaverse interfacing." *Joule*, vol. 6, no. 7 (2022): 1381–1389.

[18] Chengoden, Rajeswari, Nancy Victor, Thien Huynh-The, *et al.* "Metaverse for healthcare: A survey on potential applications, challenges and future directions." *IEEE Access*, vol. 11 (2023): 12765–12795.

[19] Román-Belmonte, Juan M., E. Carlos Rodríguez-Merchán, and Hortensia de la Corte-Rodríguez. "Metaverse applied to musculoskeletal pathology: Orthoverse and rehabverse." *Postgraduate Medicine*, vol. 135, no. 5 (2023): 440–448.

[20] Wang, Ge, Andreu Badal, Xun Jia, *et al.* "Development of metaverse for intelligent healthcare." *Nature Machine Intelligence*, vol. 4, no. 11 (2022): 922–929.

Chapter 18

Metaverse for heart illness prediction and analysis

Bollapalli Althaph[1], Nagendra Panini Challa[1], Narendra Kumar Rao[2], Kamepalli SL Prasanna[3], Nagaraju Jajam[4], Venkata Sasi Deepthi Ch[5] and Beebi Naseeba[1]

Abstract

Heart illness risk level forecast has been a challenge for the metaverse environment which requires a wide range of technical data collection to build a comprehensive profile of users' health and risk factors. Demographic information, such as age and gender, is recorded together with lifestyle choices like smoking and amount of physical activity. This information can be shown either numerically or categorically. In addition to dietary preferences and nutrient intake, users' eating behaviors provide further insight into their nutritional patterns. The virtual environment provides insight into various human factors such as blood pressure, heart rate, and body mass index that are meticulously documented to assess cardiovascular health concerns. All the medical history information, such as present medical issues and a family history of heart illness, is necessary to comprehend genetic predispositions and pre-existing health disorders. Pollution levels and air quality are two examples of environmental factors that are examined in order to evaluate external influences on cardiovascular health. Diagnostic information for acute heart issues can be obtained from reports of symptoms like dyspnea and chest pain. Information on medication adherence, including what medications are taken, how much is taken, and how often, can provide insight into patients' treatment regimens and compliance. Metaverse serves as a promising platform that helps users analyze the human body to provide an in-depth analysis of various heart disease-causing factors. Other layers of information include stress levels, coping strategies, social support networks, and mental health markers in addition to the assessment of heart

[1]School of Computer Science and Engineering (SCOPE), VIT-AP University, India
[2]School of Computing, Mohan Babu University, India
[3]School of Computing, Amrita Vishwa Vidyapeetham, India
[4]Department of Information Technology, Tirumala Engineering College, India
[5]Department of Computer Science and Engineering, Shri Vishnu Engineering College for Women, India

illness risk. Furthermore, in order to determine health literacy levels and knowledge gaps, users' comprehension of heart disease risk factors is assessed. This multi-dimensional dataset, which was painstakingly gathered within the metaverse environment, provides the basis for the creation of sophisticated deep-learning models that precisely estimate the risk of heart illness.

Keywords: Hear Rate; Heart Illness Prediction and Analysis; Machine Learning; Deep Learning

18.1 Introduction

In recent years, the intersection of healthcare and metaverse technology has emerged as a promising frontier for revolutionizing healthcare delivery and improving patient outcomes. Within this dynamic landscape, several persistent challenges have come to the forefront, including limited access to healthcare facilities, data privacy and security concerns, and user engagement and adherence. Limited access to healthcare facilities, particularly in remote or underserved areas, presents a significant barrier to individuals seeking essential medical care, including screenings for assessing heart disease risk. Furthermore, the proliferation of virtual platforms raises legitimate concerns about the privacy and security of sensitive health data shared within these digital ecosystems. Collecting and managing health data in virtual environments introduces inherent risks, such as data breaches and unauthorized access, which can compromise patient confidentiality and trust. Additionally, maintaining user engagement and adherence to health assessments and interventions in virtual environments presents unique challenges, given the abundance of distractions and the lack of physical presence and direct supervision. However, amidst these challenges lie transformative opportunities to leverage metaverse technology as a catalyst for positive change in healthcare delivery. By establishing virtual health clinics, implementing telemedicine capabilities, and leveraging advanced encryption techniques, healthcare providers can extend healthcare services to remote populations while safeguarding patient privacy. Moreover, integrating gamification elements, virtual support communities, and personalized coaching services within virtual platforms can enhance user engagement and promote adherence to health goals. This chapter explores the multifaceted landscape of healthcare in the metaverse, highlighting key challenges and proposing innovative solutions to address them, ultimately paving the way for a future where equitable access to quality healthcare is a reality for all, irrespective of geographical location or socioeconomic status.

18.2 Literature survey

Wang *et al.*'s [1], with an emphasis on healthcare applications, study explores how physical and virtual realities can coexist in the metaverse. It draws attention to the necessity of industry-academia cooperation in creating data-sharing guidelines and the need for standardization in the correction of raw imaging data. Applications of the MeTAI ecosystem are outlined, including "metaversed" medical intervention, virtual comparative scanning, augmented regulatory science, and raw data sharing.

Kulkarni *et al.*'s [2] research introduces a hybrid illness prediction model named DAE-BLS, which combines a Denoising Auto Encoder (DAE) with a Broad Learning System (BLS) to deliver trustworthy feature extraction from medical data. The BLS incremental learning technique is used in the study to train the DAE-BLS model. If the target accuracy is not reached, the addition of improved nodes is advised.

In Ali *et al.*'s [3] study, the use of blockchain, artificial intelligence, and the metaverse in healthcare is examined. It talks about the potential benefits of using the metaverse in healthcare and emphasizes the usage of explainable AI and blockchain technology. Previous research has shown that metaverse technology can be used to treat diseases like cancer and Parkinson's, as well as to educate patients and provide them with personalized care.

In Kumar *et al.*'s [4] study, the application of multimodal medical picture fusion is critical to raising the caliber of diagnosis and therapy outcomes. The fusion technique merges images from different modalities, such as CT and MRI, to improve image quality. Deep learning and transform domain approaches are used for image fusion, with a focus on improving picture quality measures such as MSE, PSNR, and SSIM.

In Waris *et al.*'s [5] study, the primary focus is on using magnetocardiograms (MCG) to identify cardiac electrical activity. Ischemia is predicted using fractal analysis, statistical analysis, and machine learning techniques like Support Vector Machine (SVM) and Probabilistic Neural Network (PNN) based on ECG recordings. Multi fractal Detrended Fluctuation Analysis (MFDFA) and Spearman's rank order correlation are used to extract important fractal properties from ECG data.

Xiao-Yan Gao *et al.* [6] conducted tests using NB, DT, KNN, SVM, random forest, and ensemble techniques. Attributes were chosen utilizing linear discriminant analysis and principal component analysis methodologies. The ensemble method, when combined with decision trees, achieved a maximum precision of 98.6%. Gárate-Escamila *et al.* [7] implemented an RF method that utilized chi-square and principal component analysis to identify the most effective set of characteristics. On the Hungarian dataset, the system produced a 99% accuracy rate; on the Cleveland dataset, it was 98.7%; and on the Cleveland-Hungarian dataset, it was 99.4%.

Vardhan Shorewala [8] constructed a stacked model utilizing RF, KNN, and SVM algorithms to detect cardiac illness. The LASSO method was employed for the resolution of feature selection. The method was assessed using a dataset on cardiovascular illness, which included data from a total of 70,000 patients. The evaluation demonstrated an accuracy rate of 75.1%. Constructed an enhanced model utilizing Random Forest. A genetic algorithm selected the features. The model achieved a 90.7% precision rate when evaluated using the Z-Alizadeh dataset.

Patro *et al.* [9] implemented an SVM model that was tuned using a Bayesian approach. On the Cleveland dataset, this model achieved a 93.3% accuracy rate.

Almustafa *et al.* [10] utilized the MICE, mean, K-nearest neighbor, and mode techniques to calculate the missing data. The dataset was also subjected to class balancing. The stacking algorithm obtained an accuracy of 95.83%.

Louridi *et al.* [11] utilized many classifiers to forecast the occurrence of heart illness. The estimate was made using KNN, the DT-J48, SVM, JRip, NB, SGD, decision tables, and Ada-Boost classifiers. The researchers employed a mutual dataset from Hungary, Cleveland, Long Beach, and Switzerland, which existed on the Kaggle internet platform, to conduct the investigations. Out of the 76 available features, a subset of 14 was utilized. The classifier-subset evaluator method was used to choose the related attributes out of the 14 available. The algorithms DT, KNN, and JRIP had the highest precision rates of 98.04%, 99.70%, and 97.26%, respectively. In addition, the novelist conducted compassion analyses on both DT and NB classifiers. The decision tree's sensitivity analysis was conducted by varying the pruning assurance issue as a parameter. Similarly, the sensitivity examination of the NB classifier was performed by varying the exercise scope as a restriction. The DT was selected for sensitivity analysis due to its high accuracy, while the NB was picked for its low precision.

Youness Khourdifi *et al.* [12] implemented a system utilizing NB, MLP, KNN, RF, and SVM classifiers. The rapid correlation-based feature selection technique was employed to identify pertinent characteristics for classification based on the association among the attributes. The chosen collection of characteristics was additionally refined using Ant Colony Optimization (ACO) and particle swarm optimization techniques. Within the framework of PSO, a population of particles collaborates to collectively search for an optimal solution that is globally optimal. The ACO method improves the attribute set by choosing characteristics that exhibit lower similarity to other features, thereby minimizing redundancy in the particular attributes. The system underwent validation using the Cleveland dataset. The KNN method achieved the highest precision of 99.65% in the system.

Luxmi Verma *et al.* [13] developed Naïve Bayes, C4.5, and multilayer perceptron algorithms for CAD analysis. The researchers gathered data from 335 people at IGMC, Shimla, India. The detection of illness severity achieved a precision of 77.6% using the C4.5 algorithm, 73.73% using the NB algorithm, and 71.94% using the MLP algorithm.

Udhaya Kumar *et al.* [14] identified a heart illness using electrocardiogram (ECG) signals. The authors learned the ECG signal records from the MIT-BIH Arrhythmia database. To remove background noise and extract features from ECG data, the discrete wavelet transform was employed. The novelists suggested using the NRSC for the purpose of diagnosis. In order to find out how close the neighborhood was, the metric used was the Euclidean distance. The classification of the indicator as a regular or irregular heartbeat by the system determined the condition. The system attained a precision rate of 99.32%.

Vijayashree *et al.* [15] employed SVM to accurately classify heart disease. Feature selection was conducted with an enhanced PSO algorithm. The performance of PSO was enhanced through the selection of appropriate weights. The utilization of an SVM facilitated the optimization of a fitness function, resulting in the identification of the most advantageous weights. The method attained a precision of 84.36% on the Cleveland dataset. K. S. Archana *et al.* [16] formed a hybrid approach by combining the NB and RF methods. The relief algorithm was used to choose the features. A precision of 92% was achieved on the Cleveland dataset.

Williams Samuel *et al.* [17] constructed an artificial neural network (ANN) model that precisely forecasts the likelihood of cardiac failure. The network weight was enhanced using the fuzzy method. A precision of 91.10% was attained. Jae Kwon Kim *et al.* [18] created an ANN-based method for accurately forecasting the risk level of heart illness. The selection of relevant features for analysis was achieved by doing a correlation analysis of the attributes. Establishing connections to the neural network's hidden layer connected the correlated features. Only pertinent attributes were utilized as efforts for the neural network for illness prediction. The studies were conducted using the data composed in the KNHANES-VI (6th Korea National Health and Nutrition Check Review). The system attained a precision rate of 82.51%. Srinivas Koppu *et al.* [19] presented a methodology that initially employed spline interpolation for data imputation and entropy correlation for outlier detection. The fitness-oriented dragonfly optimization method was utilized to find the most optimal attributes. The DBF (deep belief network) was utilized with specific features, resulting in a precision of 84.44%.

Renji P. Cherian *et al.* [20] presented a traditional ANN model to predict the occurrence of cardiac illness. PCA was employed to diminish the feature set. An optimization method that blended lion progression and particle swarm optimization in a mixed way discovered the best weights for a neural network. The precision of the results was verified using the Statlog dataset, and a precision of 87.09% was attained. Malav *et al.* [21] utilized ANNs and the K-means method to forecast the occurrence of heart illness. The writers made use of the Cleveland data collection. The dataset underwent clustering using the K-means algorithm, and the resulting clusters were then used as input for the ANN to perform the arrangement. K-means decreased the convergence time of ANN. The system attained a sensitivity of 89.53% and a precision of 93.52%. Giovanni Paragliola *et al.* [22] advanced a technique for detecting the likelihood of cardiovascular events caused by hypertension. The system was constructed utilizing LSTM and CNN architectures, with signals serving as inputs. The system attained a precision rate of 98%. Caliskan and Yuksel [23] have developed a DNN model for computer-aided diagnosis (CAD) that integrates a soft-max function and two auto-encoders. The authors verified the accuracy of the model using four distinct datasets. In four different datasets—Cleveland, Long Beach, Switzerland, and Hungary—the system achieved a precision of 85.2%, 84%, 92.2%, and 83.5%, respectively.

Ashir Javeed *et al.* [24] advanced two hybrid classifications, namely the FWAFE-deep neural network and the FWAFE-ANN, specifically designed for diagnosing heart illness. The novelists presented the floating window of adjustable size for the feature elimination technique as a technique for feature selection, which was utilized in the two classifications. This feature selection technique utilizes a floating space to eliminate attributes. The space size was adjusted from 1 to n-1, and the characteristics contained within the window were removed.

Feature selection was conducted by assessing the system's presentation using various subsets of attributes. After choosing the features, the classification task was done with an ANN configured in an FWAFE-ANN mix way and a DNN configured in the same hybrid way. The novelists employed the Cleveland data collection and utilized the hold-out authentication technique, allocating 70% of the data for training and 30% for challenging. The FWAFE-ANN model reached a precision of 91.11%, whereas the FWAFE-ANN model achieved a precision of 93.33%.

Murugesan *et al.* [25] created an advanced learning system by integrating three bio-inspired algorithms with an ANN. Three sets of characteristics were chosen by cat swarm optimization, bacterial searching optimization, and Krill herd measures. Each algorithm's chosen features served as the basis for training a back-propagation neural network (BPNN). A precision of 85.0% was attained on the Statlog dataset, while a precision of 83.9% was attained on the Cleveland dataset.

Poornima and Gladis [26] advanced a hybrid classifier to forecast heart illness. The attributes were selected using the orthogonal local preservation forecast method. ANN carried out the categorization. There were four neurons in the input layer, one hundred in the hidden layer, and five in the output layer of the NN. Neuronal connection weights varied from −10 to 10. To fine-tune the network, the weights were determined using the Group Search Optimization (GSO) algorithm and the Levenberg–Marquardt (LM) algorithm. The optimal weights from the two sets acquired from the LM and GSO algorithms were selected for use in the network. By utilizing three datasets—one each from Cleveland, Hungary, and Switzerland—the authors were able to verify the precision of the results. On the Hungarian dataset, the structure achieved a precision rate of 98%, and on the Switzerland dataset, it reached 87%. On the Cleveland dataset, it reached 94%.

Pan *et al.* [27] created a heart illness forecast system with an advanced DL-assisted convolutional NN. The data collection underwent pre-processing by eliminating missing values and implementing scaling techniques. Feature selection was performed using deep learning. The classification was conducted utilizing Multilayer Perceptron (MLP) and Bayesian Network (BN) techniques. The system attained a precision of 94.9%.

18.3 Navigating the complexity: heart disease risk level prediction unveiled

18.3.1 Limited access to healthcare facilities

Limited access to healthcare facilities poses a significant challenge, particularly in remote or underserved areas where individuals face barriers such as geographical distance, transportation limitations, and socioeconomic disparities. This lack of access can result in delays in receiving essential medical care, including routine check-ups and screenings for assessing heart disease risk. However, leveraging metaverse technology offers innovative solutions to overcome these challenges. By establishing virtual health clinics and implementing telemedicine capabilities within the metaverse, individuals can access healthcare services remotely, regardless of their physical location. Additionally, deploying mobile health units equipped with telehealth technologies enables healthcare outreach directly to underserved communities, bridging the gap in access to care. Through virtual platforms, individuals can also receive remote monitoring and home-based care, empowering them to manage their heart health from the comfort of their homes. Furthermore, virtual health navigation tools and community partnerships facilitate the identification of nearby healthcare resources and promote health equity by addressing the unique healthcare needs of underserved populations. By harnessing the power of the metaverse, we can ensure that everyone has equitable access to essential healthcare services for heart disease risk assessment and prevention.

18.3.2 Data privacy and security concerns

Collecting sensitive health data in the metaverse introduces significant privacy and security concerns. Health data, such as medical history, diagnostic tests, and treatment plans, contain highly personal and confidential information that must be safeguarded against unauthorized access and misuse. In virtual platforms, where users interact and share information remotely, there is an inherent risk of data breaches, cyberattacks, and privacy violations. Malicious actors may exploit vulnerabilities in virtual environments to intercept, manipulate, or steal health data, leading to identity theft, financial fraud, or reputational damage for individuals. Moreover, the seamless integration of virtual platforms with other digital systems and devices amplifies the complexity of data privacy management, as data flows between different platforms and across diverse networks, increasing the potential for data leaks or breaches. Ensuring the privacy and security of health data in the metaverse requires robust encryption protocols, stringent access controls, and comprehensive compliance frameworks to mitigate risks and protect individuals' privacy rights.

18.3.3 User engagement and adherence

Maintaining user engagement and adherence to health assessments and interventions presents a multifaceted challenge, especially within virtual environments where distractions abound. In virtual settings, individuals are often surrounded by numerous stimuli competing for their attention, ranging from social interactions and entertainment options to work-related tasks and notifications. These distractions can easily divert individuals' focus away from health-related activities, making it challenging to sustain their engagement over time. Moreover, the absence of physical presence and direct supervision in virtual environments may lead to a diminished sense of accountability and motivation among users. Without the immediate oversight of healthcare professionals or peers, individuals may feel less compelled to actively participate in health assessments or adhere to recommended interventions. Furthermore, the lack of tangible consequences or immediate rewards for engaging in health-related behaviors within virtual platforms can further undermine users' motivation to stay committed to their health goals. As a result, ensuring sustained user engagement and adherence to health assessments and interventions in virtual environments necessitates the development of innovative strategies that address these inherent challenges while leveraging the unique opportunities afforded by virtual platforms.

18.4 Metaverse innovations: revolutionizing heart disease risk prediction

18.4.1 Limited access to healthcare facilities via the metaverse

As healthcare accessibility continues to be a challenge for remote and underserved communities, metaverse technology emerges as a groundbreaking tool to bridge these gaps by offering accessible and innovative healthcare solutions. By establishing virtual health clinics within the metaverse, individuals in isolated or rural areas gain direct access to essential healthcare services without the burden of traveling long distances. These virtual clinics not only offer convenient appointments but also enable real-time consultations with healthcare providers, making healthcare more accessible and personalized. Furthermore, telemedicine integration within the metaverse allows individuals to connect with specialists and healthcare professionals from any location, creating a new paradigm for delivering healthcare across vast geographical divides.

In addition to virtual clinics, mobile health units equipped with telehealth capabilities enhance outreach by bringing healthcare services directly to communities in need. By leveraging telemedicine technology in these mobile units, healthcare providers can conduct virtual consultations, deliver medications, and monitor patient progress remotely. This hybrid approach overcomes geographical barriers and provides a flexible solution that meets patients where they are, promoting equitable access to healthcare services for underserved populations.

Moreover, remote monitoring systems, facilitated by wearable devices and virtual platforms, empower individuals to manage their health from the comfort of their homes. For instance, patients with heart conditions can use wearable technology to track vital signs like heart rate and blood pressure, which healthcare providers can monitor remotely to identify any risks or changes in health. These home-based care solutions not only reduce the burden of travel but also improve patient engagement by enabling continuous monitoring and real-time feedback, fostering a proactive approach to heart health.

To support these initiatives, virtual health navigation tools within the metaverse play a crucial role in empowering individuals to navigate the complex healthcare landscape. Through these tools, patients can identify nearby healthcare facilities, connect with support groups, and receive guidance on health resources available to them. Additionally, partnerships with local communities and health organizations within the metaverse help ensure that the most relevant resources are accessible, promoting health equity and catering to diverse populations' needs.

By harnessing the immersive and inclusive capabilities of the metaverse, these initiatives not only provide comprehensive solutions to the challenge of limited access to healthcare but also cultivate a culture of proactive healthcare management. Through community-driven support systems, individuals are encouraged to take an active role in managing their health, contributing to heart disease prevention and fostering an environment of accessible and collaborative healthcare.

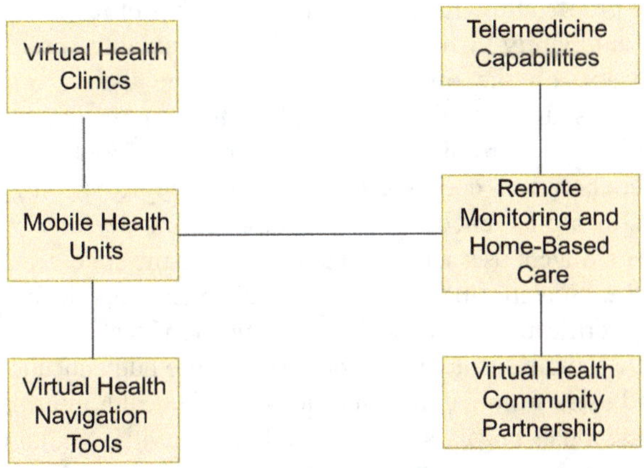

Figure 18.1 Proposed architecture for limited access to healthcare facilities

Figure 18.1 shows a diagram of components within a virtual healthcare system, including virtual health clinics, mobile health units, and telemedicine Ccapabilities. It illustrates connections between elements like remote monitoring, virtual health navigation tools, and community partnerships to support remote and accessible care. This setup highlights the integration of virtual services aimed at enhancing healthcare reach and continuity.

18.4.2 Data privacy and security concerns in the metaverse

The increasing integration of health applications within the metaverse introduces a novel yet complex environment where users can engage in virtual spaces for healthcare consultations, fitness tracking, and wellness activities. However, this digital ecosystem also raises critical concerns about the privacy and security of sensitive health data. In the metaverse, user health data is not only shared and stored but may also be transmitted across virtual environments in real time, exposing it to potential privacy breaches and unauthorized access. Addressing these challenges requires implementing robust data protection measures to ensure the confidentiality, integrity, and security of health information within the virtual landscape.

To safeguard user health data in the metaverse, advanced encryption techniques play a crucial role by ensuring that data remains confidential both in transit and at rest. These encryption protocols, tailored to the unique requirements of virtual environments, help prevent unauthorized access to health information, making it accessible only to verified parties. Additionally, decentralized storage mechanisms such as blockchain technology, add an extra layer of security by distributing health data across a network of nodes, thus reducing the likelihood of centralized data breaches. This decentralized approach ensures that no single point of vulnerability can compromise the entire data system, enhancing security and reliability.

Beyond encryption and storage strategies, the metaverse benefits from privacy-preserving technologies like zero-knowledge proofs and differential privacy.

Zero-knowledge proofs allow for data verification without revealing the data itself, ensuring user anonymity while still enabling valuable predictive analysis. Differential privacy, on the other hand, enables the use of anonymized data, allowing researchers and healthcare providers to gain insights into population health trends without compromising individual privacy. Together, these techniques enable a balance between data security and meaningful health data analytics, empowering healthcare advancements without exposing personal information.

Furthermore, stringent user authentication mechanisms are essential to controlling access to virtual health platforms. Multi-factor authentication, which requires multiple forms of identity verification, and biometric verification, such as fingerprint or facial recognition, create a more secure access protocol. These authentication measures prevent unauthorized users from gaining entry to sensitive health information, protecting the privacy of individuals engaging in health-related activities within the metaverse.

By integrating these comprehensive privacy and security solutions, the metaverse can serve as a secure platform for health data exchange, allowing individuals to confidently participate in virtual health activities. This trust in data security fosters collaborative health initiatives, such as heart disease risk assessment and preventive care, where users can safely share their health data. As the metaverse continues to evolve, prioritizing privacy and security will be critical to maintaining user trust and promoting meaningful health engagements in virtual spaces.

Figure 18.2 represents a flow of components in a secure virtual healthcare framework within the metaverse. It begins with "Metaverse Infrastructure," which uses encryption, decentralized storage, zero-knowledge proof, multi-factor authentication, and biometric verification to protect data. This infrastructure supports addressing "Virtual Health Problems" and securely managing "Healthcare Data (Sensitive Health Information)".

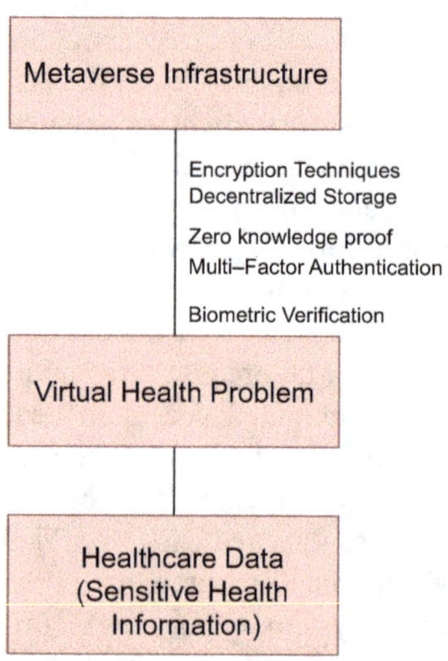

Figure 18.2 Proposed architecture for data privacy and security concerns

18.4.3 Enhancing user engagement and adherence through the metaverse

As the metaverse evolves, creating engaging and sustainable health experiences becomes essential to encourage users' ongoing participation in health assessments and interventions. One effective strategy is to embed gamification elements and interactive challenges within virtual health platforms. By incorporating features like progress tracking, achievements, leaderboards, and reward systems, users are incentivized to participate actively and stay committed to their health goals. Additionally, establishing virtual support communities within the metaverse provides users with valuable social support and motivation. These communities foster peer connections, enabling individuals to share experiences, provide encouragement, and hold each other accountable.

Moreover, personalized coaching services and feedback mechanisms can be tailored to users' unique health profiles and progress, offering guidance and motivation. AI-driven virtual assistants and chatbots can deliver real-time feedback, reminders, and advice to help users adhere to their health routines. To further engage users, immersive health education modules leverage virtual reality (VR) and augmented reality (AR) technologies to offer interactive simulations, educational games, and virtual tours. Integrating virtual health platforms with wearable devices and fitness trackers enables users to monitor health metrics and activities in real time, empowering them with actionable insights to make informed wellness choices.

These solutions within the metaverse not only enhance user engagement but also create immersive, empowering experiences that inspire individuals to prioritize their health and make proactive steps toward achieving wellness goals.

Figure 18.3 presents a framework in which metaverse infrastructure is leveraged to address virtual health problems for users. This infrastructure includes

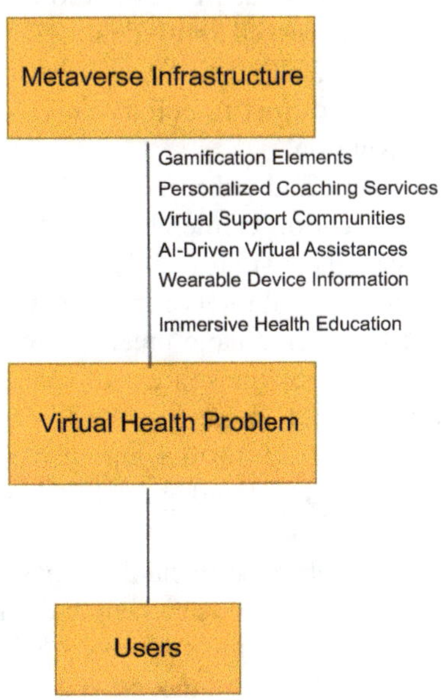

Figure 18.3 Proposed architecture for user engagement and adherence

elements like gamification, personalized coaching, virtual support communities, AI-driven assistants, integration with wearable devices, and immersive health education. These resources collectively aim to provide personalized support and enhance user engagement, ultimately helping users manage or improve their health outcomes within a digital environment.

18.5 Results

The integration of metaverse technology has yielded transformative outcomes in addressing critical challenges in healthcare delivery. In response to limited access to healthcare facilities, virtual health clinics and telemedicine capabilities within the metaverse have provided individuals in remote or underserved areas with convenient access to essential healthcare services. Mobile health units equipped with telehealth technologies have extended healthcare outreach directly to communities in need, overcoming geographical barriers and ensuring equitable access to care. Furthermore, the implementation of remote monitoring systems and home-based care services facilitated by wearable devices and virtual platforms has empowered individuals to manage their heart health from the comfort of their homes, reducing the burden of travel and enhancing patient engagement. Virtual health navigation tools and community partnerships have further empowered individuals to navigate the healthcare landscape effectively, facilitating the identification of nearby healthcare resources and promoting health equity among diverse populations.

Addressing data privacy and security concerns, robust solutions within the metaverse infrastructure, such as advanced encryption techniques and decentralized storage mechanisms, have safeguarded the confidentiality and integrity of health data shared over virtual platforms. Measures like zero-knowledge proof and stringent user authentication have preserved individual privacy, instilling confidence among individuals to share their health data over virtual platforms. These privacy-preserving measures have fostered trust in collaborative efforts towards heart disease risk assessment and prevention.

In terms of user engagement and adherence, tailored solutions within virtual environments, including gamification elements, virtual support communities, and personalized coaching services, have significantly enhanced user participation and commitment to health assessments and interventions. Gamification features such as progress tracking and rewards systems have incentivized users, while virtual support communities have provided valuable sources of social support and motivation. Personalized coaching services and immersive health education modules leveraging virtual reality technologies have further enriched user engagement by delivering interactive experiences and tailored guidance based on individual health profiles and progress.

Overall, the integration of metaverse technology has revolutionized healthcare delivery, fostering proactive healthcare management and empowerment among individuals. These outcomes signify a paradigm shift towards improved health outcomes and enhanced well-being facilitated by the innovative capabilities of the metaverse.

References

[1] Wang, G., Badal, A., Jia, X., *et al.* (2022). Development of metaverse for intelligent healthcare. *Nature Machine Intelligence*, 4(11), 922–929.

[2] Kulkarni, C., Quraishi, A., Raparthi, M., *et al.* (2024). Hybrid disease prediction approach leveraging digital twin and metaverse technologies for health consumer. *BMC Medical Informatics and Decision Making*, 24(1), 92.

[3] Ali, S., Abdullah, Armand, T. P. T., *et al.* (2023). Metaverse in healthcare integrated with explainable AI and blockchain: Enabling immersiveness, ensuring trust, and providing patient data security. *Sensors*, 23(2), 565.

[4] Kumar, V., Joshi, K., Kumar, R., Anandaram, H., Bhagat, V. K., and Baloni, D. (2023). Multi Modalities Medical Image Fusion Using Deep Learning and Metaverse Technology: Healthcare 4.0 A Futuristic Approach. *Biomedical and Pharmacology Journal*, 16(4), 1949–1959.

[5] Waris, S. F. (2024). Analysis of ECG Signals to Prediction of Ischemic Heart Disease Using Hybrid Neuro-fractal Analysis. *International Journal of Intelligent Systems and Applications in Engineering*, 12(5s), 78–90.

[6] Gao, X. Y., Amin Ali, A., Shaban Hassan, H., and Anwar, E. M. (2021). Improving the accuracy for analyzing heart diseases prediction based on the ensemble method. *Complexity*, 2021, 1–10.

[7] Gárate-Escamila, A. K., El Hassani, A. H., and Andrès, E. (2020). Classification models for heart disease prediction using feature selection and PCA. *Informatics in Medicine Unlocked*, 19, 100330.

[8] Shorewala, V. (2021). Early detection of coronary heart disease using ensemble techniques. *Informatics in Medicine Unlocked*, 26, 100655.

[9] Patro, S. P., Nayak, G. S., and Padhy, N. (2021). Heart disease prediction by using novel optimization algorithm: A supervised learning prospective. *Informatics in Medicine Unlocked*, 26, 100696.

[10] Almustafa, K. M. (2020). Prediction of heart disease and classifiers' sensitivity analysis. *BMC Bioinformatics*, 21, 1–18.

[11] Louridi, N., Douzi, S., and El Ouahidi, B. (2021). Machine learning-based identification of patients with a cardiovascular defect. *Journal of Big Data*, 8(1), 133.

[12] Khourdifi, Y., and Baha, M. (2019). Heart disease prediction and classification using machine learning algorithms optimized by particle swarm optimization and ant colony optimization. *International Journal of Intelligent Engineering & Systems*, 12(1), 242–252.

[13] Verma, L., Srivastava, S., and Negi, P. C. (2018). An intelligent noninvasive model for coronary artery disease detection. *Complex & Intelligent Systems*, 4, 11–18.

[14] Kumar, S. U., and Inbarani, H. H. (2017). Neighborhood rough set based ECG signal classification for diagnosis of cardiac diseases. *Soft Computing*, 21, 4721–4733.

[15] Vijayashree, J., and Sultana, H. P. (2018). A machine learning framework for feature selection in heart disease classification using improved particle swarm optimization with support vector machine classifier. *Programming and Computer Software*, 44, 388–397.
[16] Archana, K. S., Sivakumar, B., Kuppusamy, R., Teekaraman, Y., and Radhakrishnan, A. (2022). Automated cardioailment identification and prevention by hybrid machine learning models. *Computational and Mathematical Methods in Medicine*, 2022.
[17] Samuel, O. W., Asogbon, G. M., Sangaiah, A. K., Fang, P., and Li, G. (2017). An integrated decision support system based on ANN and Fuzzy_AHP for heart failure risk prediction. *Expert Systems with Applications*, 68, 163–172.
[18] Kim, J. K., and Kang, S. (2017). Neural network-based coronary heart disease risk prediction using feature correlation analysis. *Journal of Healthcare Engineering*, 2017.
[19] Koppu, S., Maddikunta, P. K. R., and Srivastava, G. (2020). Deep learning disease prediction model for use with intelligent robots. *Computers & Electrical Engineering*, 87, 106765.
[20] Cherian, R. P., Thomas, N., and Venkitachalam, S. (2020). Weight optimized neural network for heart disease prediction using hybrid lion plus particle swarm algorithm. *Journal of Biomedical Informatics*, 110, 103543.
[21] Malav, A., and Kadam, K. (2018). A hybrid approach for heart disease prediction using artificial neural network and K-means. *International Journal of Pure and Applied Mathematics*, 118(8), 103–110.
[22] Paragliola, G., and Coronato, A. (2021). An hybrid ECG-based deep network for the early identification of high-risk to major cardiovascular events for hypertension patients. *Journal of Biomedical Informatics*, 113, 103648.
[23] Caliskan, A., and Yuksel, M. E. (2017). Classification of coronary artery disease data sets by using a deep neural network. *The EuroBiotech Journal*, 1(4), 271–277.
[24] Javeed, A., Rizvi, S. S., Zhou, S., Riaz, R., Khan, S. U., and Kwon, S. J. (2020). Heart risk failure prediction using a novel feature selection method for feature refinement and neural network for classification. *Mobile Information Systems*, 2020, 1–11.
[25] Murugesan, S., Bhuvaneswaran, R. S., Khanna Nehemiah, H., Keerthana Sankari, S., and Nancy Jane, Y. (2021). Feature selection and classification of clinical datasets using bioinspired algorithms and super learner. *Computational and Mathematical Methods in Medicine*, 2021, 1–18.
[26] Poornima, V., and Gladis, D. (2018). A novel approach for diagnosing heart disease with hybrid classifier. *Biomedical Research*, 29(11), 2274–2280.
[27] Pan, Y., Fu, M., Cheng, B., Tao, X., and Guo, J. (2020). Enhanced deep learning assisted convolutional neural network for heart disease prediction on the internet of medical things platform. *IEEE Access*, 8, 189503–189512.

Chapter 19

Metaverse for Indian palm leaf manuscripts

Basaraboyina Yohoshiva[1], Nagendra Panini Challa[1], Narendra Kumar Rao[2], Beebi Naseeba[1] and Venkata Sasi Deepthi Ch[3]

Abstract

The metaverse stands as a transformative realm where the convergence of virtual reality and digital connectivity unlocks the treasures concealed within ancient Indic manuscripts. These manuscripts, repositories of cultural and historical richness, have long posed formidable challenges to scholars and enthusiasts alike. In this chapter, we embark on a journey to dissect the myriad complexities inherent in the study, preservation, and interpretation of Indic manuscripts. From the delicate task of preservation to the daunting hurdles of accessibility, language diversity, and contextual understanding, we delve into the multifaceted obstacles that have historically hindered widespread engagement with these invaluable artifacts. However, the advent of the metaverse heralds a new era of exploration and enlightenment, offering innovative solutions to age-old dilemmas. Through virtual libraries that transcend geographical boundaries, remote collaboration platforms that foster global scholarly exchange, and sophisticated technologies like deep learning and augmented reality, the metaverse empowers users to navigate the intricate tapestry of Indic manuscripts with unprecedented ease and depth. It serves as a digital sanctuary where ancient wisdom is not only preserved but also brought to life, inviting users to embark on a voyage of discovery that transcends physical limitations. In this chapter, we unravel the transformative potential of the metaverse in revolutionizing the study of Indic manuscripts, ushering in an era of accessibility, engagement, and enlightenment for generations to come.

Keywords: Metaverse Technology; Virtual Reality; Augmented Reality; Deep Learning; Artificial Intelligence

[1]School of Computer Science and Engineering (SCOPE), VIT-AP University, India
[2]School of Computing, Mohan Babu University, India
[3]Department of Computer Science and Engineering, Shri Vishnu Engineering College for Women, India

19.1 Introduction

The metaverse is a captivating fusion of virtual reality and the internet, akin to stepping into a fantastical realm where possibilities are endless. For enthusiasts of Indic manuscripts, this digital landscape resembles a treasure trove, offering novel avenues to explore, safeguard, and glean insights from these ancient texts. Utilizing cutting-edge technologies like virtual reality and online collaboration, the metaverse empowers users to unravel the mysteries of Indic manuscripts from any corner of the globe. It transforms the experience of delving into these historical writings into a seamless journey, akin to immersing oneself in a boundless digital library where the profound narratives, wisdom, and allure of ancient India are brought to life within the comforts of home.

In this captivating realm, users can traverse through virtual archives and repositories, seamlessly navigating through centuries of preserved knowledge and cultural heritage. They can engage with digitized manuscripts in ways previously unimaginable, utilizing interactive features and immersive environments to deepen their understanding and appreciation. Through the metaverse, geographical barriers dissolve, allowing scholars, researchers, and enthusiasts alike to connect, collaborate, and exchange insights in real time, fostering a vibrant global community dedicated to the preservation and exploration of Indic manuscripts. It heralds a new era of accessibility and discovery, where the rich tapestry of India's past is not just preserved but actively celebrated and shared with the world.

19.2 Literature review

Al-Ghaili *et al.* [1] provide insights into the development, definitions, architecture, applications, challenges, and future trends of the metaverse, offering valuable information for researchers and designers. It discusses the productivity and period calculation of papers, highlighting the importance of including new publications in the analysis for future researchers. Trends in Web 3.0 and metaverse are highlighted, emphasizing the importance for businesses to engage in the metaverse for marketing, branding, and customer interactions. A comparison between selected papers is made, analyzing issues addressed, objectives, methods used, advantages, and weaknesses, which can guide future research in the field.

Muhammad Shoaib Farooq *et al.* [2] provide an overview of metaverse technologies, including core components, potential applications in various domains, challenges, and opportunities. The study focuses on recognizing high technologies, tools, and algorithms used in creating the metaverse, developing applications in different domains, and identifying gaps and challenges in the domain. Metaverse technologies have the potential to revolutionize various domains such as gaming, social networking, training, education, healthcare, and marketing. The development of the metaverse must prioritize ethical considerations and ensure accessibility for all individuals. Research is needed to understand the impact of the metaverse on data ownership, privacy, digital identity, social and economic aspects, education, and underlying technologies for seamless integration.

Stylianos Mystakidis [3] explains that the metaverse can bridge social media with VR and AR technologies, transforming industries like online education. Virtual environments with avatars allow for identity construction and influence behavior and learning, impacting education and social connection. Limitations of 2D learning environments can be overcome by immersive technologies like VR, enhancing user interaction and engagement in education.

Kùrtùnlùoğlu *et al.*'s [4] study compares the security of authentication methods in virtual reality environments, highlighting the importance of securing biometric data. Multi-model authentication is identified as the most reliable method, emphasizing the need for further research on integrating authentication processes into VR environments. The combination of eye-gaze knowledge and information-based authentication shows promise for the future, suggesting the use of blockchain and smart contracts for data integrity enhancement.

Jungho Kim *et al.* [5] explain that decreased blink rate in VR HMD and AR glasses environments may lead to ocular issues, emphasizing the need for safety guidelines. Users should be aware of the physiological role of blinking to prevent dryness and eye discomfort when using immersive technologies. Excessive screen time in metaverse environments could potentially cause a decrease in blink rate, leading to ocular dryness and discomfort. Recommendations include taking breaks from HMD usage to rest the eyes, especially for adults experiencing dryness, and providing guidance to children using such devices.

Yihao Zhou *et al.* [6] propose that self-powered sensing technologies are crucial for building high-fidelity human metaverse interfaces. These technologies can aid in the early detection of diseases like cancer and adaptively regulate human physiological states. Multi-modal operation of self-powered sensors can create a realistic metaverse with avatars and virtual environments. Efficient energy management systems are essential to maximize the utilization of harvested ambient energy in self-powered sensor networks. Near-sensor computing architecture can improve energy efficiency and data latency in self-powered sensors.

Yang *et al.* [7] in their paper discuss the establishment of a new teaching and learning environment in medical education, integrating the real and virtual worlds to cater to the needs of both teachers and students. It highlights the significance of digital human anatomy systems in addressing limitations in traditional experimental teaching, such as scarcity of cadaveric specimens and lack of three-dimensional depth in anatomical diagrams.

Jovanović and Milosavljević [8] in their paper review related work on collaboration and education in Virtual Worlds (VWs). It introduces the concept and purpose of VW platforms and describes the VoRtex software architecture for collaborative learning in VWs. A comparative analysis is conducted between VW platforms Vircadia, Sansar, and the VoRtex prototype using Mannien's matrix. The VoRtex prototype was tested on users with engineering backgrounds, focusing on e-learning and gamification processes. The prototype demonstrated a MicroLesson on VR and 3D technologies in a computer-generated classroom setting.

Duan *et al.* [9] discuss the potential of the metaverse for social good and propose a three-layer metaverse architecture. It highlights the importance of human-centered computing and its positive impact on accessibility, diversity, equality, and humanity. The three-layer architecture includes infrastructure, interaction, and ecosystem, with detailed discussions on key components and open research questions. The development of the metaverse is described, including historical and novel examples, along with a blockchain-driven university campus prototype.

Tlili *et al.* [10] conducted a mixed-methods systematic review, combining bibliometric analysis and content analysis, to identify the knowledge base and evolution of the metaverse in education. Three thematic waves of research trends in metaverse education were identified: social aspects, technology-mediated presence, and AI-powered virtual learning ecologies. The research methods used in metaverse education studies included literature reviews, theory expounding, mixed methods, as well as quantitative and qualitative approaches.

Lee *et al.* [11] conducted a literature review from 2012 to 2021 focusing on primary sources like ACM, CHI, and IEEE conferences to understand the landscape of studies related to the metaverse. The review identified various system solutions and architectures addressing scalability issues in the metaverse. Additionally, the survey highlighted research articles proposing user interaction techniques across physical and virtual environments.

Wua *et al.* [12] conducted a scoping review to understand the current development and application of the metaverse in emergency medicine. The review included data charting on study types, published time, technology types, and applications in emergency medicine. Eligibility criteria for the review included papers reporting on metaverse technology in acute medicine fields, irrespective of maturity levels, and excluded papers not directly related to healthcare applications. A total of 628 articles were identified and categorized into AR, VR, lifelogging, and mirror world, with VR being the most common type in emergency medicine applications.

Ji-Eun Yu [13] classified metaverse technology into four categories: augmented reality, lifelogging, mirror worlds, and virtual worlds. Augmented reality technology, such as "Ghostpacer," is used in physical education classes to enhance exercise experiences. Instructors in the metaverse should facilitate active user engagement, professional content production, content development, user interaction, and link establishment with learners. The metaverse offers practical classes in physical education through augmented reality, enhancing interaction with virtual information in real time and space.

Selcen Ozturkcan [14] launched the IKEA Place app in September 2017, utilizing augmented reality to visualize furniture in users' homes. The app aimed to address practical issues in furniture shopping, showcasing IKEA's service-centered value and commitment to technology-based customer support. Updates to the app included features like multi-placement options and wish lists for improved virtual room furnishing experiences. The app exemplifies service innovation based on the

Service-Dominant logic, focusing on co-created value through knowledge and skills in service interactions.

In Pooyandeh *et al.*'s [15] work, the metaverse combines physical and digital reality, with cybersecurity becoming crucial due to increasing cybercrime. Biometric methods are commonly used for user identification in the metaverse, but they can be susceptible to misuse. AI plays a significant role in enhancing cybersecurity in the metaverse, with neural network algorithms improving attack detection accuracy. Researchers face challenges in accessing specific metaverse data, and AI can be used by hackers to develop mutating malware to evade detection. Comprehensive research is needed to identify vulnerabilities and weaknesses in metaverse security based on artificial intelligence.

In Chow *et al.*'s [16] work, various surveys have reviewed research efforts on different facets of the metaverse, focusing on cybersecurity threats faced by visualization technologies in virtual worlds. Recent surveys have discussed security and privacy threats in the metaverse, along with existing research on countermeasures and future research directions. Surveys have also explored the integration of blockchain, AI technologies, and building information modeling with the metaverse. Specific surveys have classified cybersecurity challenges in VR environments, discussed AR and digital twin technology benefits for cybersecurity, and reviewed protection methods for user and data security in mixed reality.

In Sun *et al.*'s [17] work, the metaverse aims to build a virtual shared digital space, closely related to extended reality, digital twin, and blockchain technologies. Existing surveys cover definitions, frameworks, applications, security, and privacy issues of the metaverse, highlighting research gaps. Surveys discuss the need for powerful computing in the metaverse and its impact on real-world accessibility, diversity, equality, and humanity. Various surveys focus on different aspects such as AI, blockchain, security, privacy, and the overall development of the metaverse.

Yun-Cheng Tsai [18]—The concept of the metaverse has been widely used in classroom teaching since 2022 and integrated into teaching activities. The paper redefines the value chain and characteristics of the "Education Metaverse," emphasizing the integration of VR, AR, and MR into teaching and transforming into a learner-centered learning model. The future teaching model may shift towards an experiential learning model based on the metaverse, allowing anyone to learn anytime, anywhere, not just in the classroom.

Lin *et al.* [19]—The paper provides a systematic literature review of the metaverse in education, focusing on current technologies, challenges, opportunities, and future directions. It introduces key characteristics of the metaverse and traditional education, discussing how the metaverse will change education. The review includes state-of-the-art industry case applications and comprehensive challenges and issues for evaluating the metaverse in education.

Jagatheesaperumal *et al.* [20]—The paper provides a comprehensive review of educational use cases in metaverses, focusing on XR and IoE technologies. Previous works have extensively researched XR and IoE, with some focusing on their convergence for metaverse applications in education. It compares its review paper with related metaverse survey papers, emphasizing the application, XR, and IoE aspects in education.

Petrigna and Giuseppe [21]—The study aimed to review literature connecting the metaverse with prevention, treatment, education, and research in healthcare. Only 21 articles were included in the review, mainly comprising literature reviews or editorials. The metaverse was highlighted as a potential tool for health promotion, requiring further studies and investments for developing effective health programs in this virtual environment. Various studies discussed the benefits and threats of blockchain technology, Health 4.0 applications, and the application of the metaverse for medical-educational purposes in healthcare.

Ahmad *et al.* [22]—Most literature on MOOCs after 2014 focused on Artificial Intelligence/Machine Learning, Big Data, and Gamification Technologies. The study did not consider non-peer-reviewed research publications or postgraduate and graduation theses and dissertations. The proposed MOOC 5.0 integrates Industry 4.0 technologies and emphasizes improved universal access, higher learner engagement, adaptive learning, increased collaboration, security, and curiosity.

Zallio and Clarkson [23]—The metaverse is a digital immersive environment shaping new interactions, with a forecasted significant increase in user engagement by 2026. Research explores the ethical and social impact of the metaverse, emphasizing inclusion, diversity, equity, accessibility, and safety interviews with industry experts focused on understanding the metaverse, safety, personalization, data impact, accessibility, and social equity. The study raises questions and proposes principles for designing a safe, accessible, and inclusive metaverse, stressing the importance of inclusion, diversity, equity, accessibility, and safety. Disorientation in the metaverse compared to physical environments may lead to user confusion.

Fara *et al.* [24]—NFTs have rapidly become popular in industry and academic research, with various applications reviewed in the study. The paper outlines the organization, preliminaries, applications of NFTs, and future directions in the metaverse. Blockchain technology, proposed by S. Nakamoto in 2008, is transparent and distributed, recording immutable strings and codes.

Lv *et al.* [25]—The paper discusses the evolution of technology from early graphics to the metaverse, passing through visualization, HCI, virtual reality, and Digital Twins. It emphasizes the importance of multidomain cutting-edge knowledge, real-time information transfer, model building, and versatility in the development of Digital Twins and the metaverse. The integration of various technologies like IoT, virtual reality, blockchain, artificial intelligence, and big data is highlighted for the creation of a mature research and development system. The metaverse is described as a more complex system than Digital Twins, focusing on human–human interactions and moving towards urbanization and industrialization.

Mehta and Challa [26]—Customized grammar in speech recognition leads to accurate word recognition at 73%. Dictation grammar provides predefined speech models for applications, reducing error rates in speech recognition. Combining different grammars can improve speech recognition performance, especially in noisy environments. Speech recognition allows for natural interaction without the need for keyboards or remote controls, benefiting users. Grammars help customize vocabulary for specific applications and filter recognition results, enhancing the overall speech recognition process.

Challa and Mehta [27]—India has a rich heritage of palm-leaf manuscripts covering various subjects, with efforts like the National Mission for Manuscripts digitizing over a crore pages. Challenges exist in cataloging these manuscripts, with text-mining algorithms proposed for better access and categorization. The focus is on enhancing different stages of the digitization process, with scope for further research and development.

Deepthi and Seenu [28]—Metadata schemas play a crucial role in efficient data retrieval from databases. Following metadata standards is essential for easy management of digitized data, especially for preserving valuable heritage documents like palm leaf manuscripts. Metadata classification into descriptive, administrative, and structural types offers advantages such as increased accessibility and preservation of context.

19.3 Understanding the complexities of Indic manuscript challenges

Indic manuscripts stand as invaluable repositories of cultural heritage, providing a tangible link to the past and offering profound insights into the diverse civilizations of ancient India. These manuscripts encompass a wide array of subjects, including literature, philosophy, religion, science, and history, reflecting the intellectual richness and cultural diversity of the Indian subcontinent. They serve as windows through which we can glimpse the beliefs, traditions, and aspirations of bygone eras, offering a unique perspective on the evolution of human thought and society.

However, despite their significance, the journey of exploring and preserving these manuscripts is fraught with challenges. One such challenge lies in the physical fragility of these ancient documents. Many manuscripts are centuries old and are susceptible to damage from factors such as exposure to light, humidity, pests, and mishandling. Preserving them requires meticulous care, specialized techniques, and adequate resources to ensure their longevity for future generations.

Moreover, accessing and deciphering the content of Indic manuscripts presents hurdles for scholars and enthusiasts alike. These manuscripts are often written in ancient languages such as Sanskrit, Pali, Prakrit, and others, using scripts like Devanagari, Grantha, and Brahmi, which may be unfamiliar to modern readers. Deciphering these scripts and languages requires expertise and specialized training, posing a barrier to accessing the wealth of knowledge contained within the manuscripts.

Additionally, the contextual understanding of Indic manuscripts can be challenging due to their complex historical and cultural references. Many manuscripts contain allegorical narratives, symbolic imagery, and philosophical concepts that may be obscure or ambiguous to contemporary readers. Interpreting these nuances requires not only linguistic proficiency but also a deep understanding of the cultural, religious, and philosophical frameworks of the time in which they were written.

In this chapter, we will delve into these multifaceted challenges faced by scholars, researchers, and custodians of Indic manuscripts. By exploring the intricacies of manuscript preservation, accessibility, language diversity, and contextual analysis, we aim to shed light on the complexities of engaging with these invaluable artifacts and highlight the innovative solutions offered by emerging technologies in the digital age.

19.3.1 Preservation concerns

Preserving the integrity of Indic manuscripts stands as an arduous yet essential endeavor, given their profound historical and cultural significance. These ancient texts serve as invaluable repositories of knowledge, offering insights into the beliefs, practices, and traditions of past civilizations. However, the passage of time inevitably takes its toll on these delicate artifacts, posing a constant threat to their longevity and accessibility.

Traditional preservation methods, while effective to a certain extent, often prove inadequate in safeguarding Indic manuscripts against the ravages of time. Factors such as exposure to light, fluctuations in humidity and temperature, and the natural degradation of materials present formidable challenges to preservation efforts. Moreover, the fragility of the manuscripts themselves, often composed of materials like parchment or palm leaves, further complicates preservation endeavors.

End users tasked with the stewardship of these invaluable documents find themselves grappling with the ongoing challenge of ensuring their long-term survival. Preservation initiatives must encompass a multifaceted approach, integrating advanced conservation techniques with meticulous care and attention to detail. This may involve measures such as digitization to create archival-quality facsimiles, controlled storage environments to mitigate environmental hazards, and specialized treatment to repair damage and prevent further deterioration.

Despite the complexities involved, the imperative to preserve Indic manuscripts remains steadfast. These texts not only serve as windows into the past but also as bridges connecting contemporary society with its cultural heritage. By confronting the challenges of preservation head-on and adopting innovative strategies informed by best practices and technological advancements, end users can safeguard these invaluable artifacts for future generations to study, cherish, and learn from.

19.3.2 Accessibility issues

Accessing Indic manuscripts presents a formidable challenge, primarily due to their restricted availability in specialized repositories such as libraries, archives, and private collections. These manuscripts are often scattered across various institutions, making it difficult for researchers, scholars, and enthusiasts to locate and access them. Moreover, the geographical dispersion of these collections adds another layer of complexity, requiring individuals to travel extensively to access disparate sources of information.

In addition to geographical barriers, institutional restrictions compound the accessibility issues surrounding Indic manuscripts. Many repositories impose stringent regulations on access, requiring individuals to navigate bureaucratic processes and obtain permissions before they can study or examine the manuscripts. These institutional hurdles can significantly impede the research process, deterring potential scholars and enthusiasts from pursuing inquiries into these valuable artifacts.

The overarching challenge lies in bridging the gap between the rich cultural heritage encapsulated within Indic manuscripts and the individuals eager to explore and learn from them. Addressing these accessibility issues requires concerted efforts to enhance collaboration and resource-sharing among institutions, streamline access procedures, and promote digital initiatives aimed at democratizing access to manuscript collections. By breaking down barriers and fostering greater inclusivity in the dissemination of knowledge, stakeholders can ensure that Indic manuscripts remain accessible and relevant to a diverse global audience.

19.3.3 Language and script diversity

Indic manuscripts encompass a wide spectrum of languages and scripts, reflecting the linguistic diversity of the Indian subcontinent. These manuscripts are written in languages such as Sanskrit, Pali, Prakrit, Tamil, Telugu, and others, each with its own unique script and orthographic conventions. The variety of scripts used in these manuscripts includes Devanagari, Grantha, Tamil script, Telugu script, and more, further adding to the complexity of deciphering and understanding them.

For end users encountering these manuscripts, especially those lacking proficiency in the relevant languages, deciphering their contents can be a daunting task. The intricate linguistic nuances and script variations pose significant challenges, requiring a deep understanding of the language and script in which the manuscript is written. Moreover, the evolution of scripts over time and regional variations further complicates the interpretation process, making it essential for scholars and enthusiasts to possess specialized knowledge and training in paleography, linguistics, and textual analysis.

To overcome these challenges, efforts are underway to develop resources and tools that facilitate the study and interpretation of Indic manuscripts. Digital repositories and online databases provide access to digitized manuscripts accompanied by transliterations, translations, and annotations to aid comprehension. Additionally, initiatives focused on education and capacity-building aim to equip scholars and researchers with the necessary skills to navigate the linguistic and scriptural complexities of these invaluable artifacts. Through collaborative endeavors and technological innovations, the barriers to understanding Indic manuscripts are gradually being dismantled, enabling broader access and appreciation of their cultural and historical significance.

19.3.4 Contextual understanding

Indic manuscripts are rich repositories of historical, religious, cultural, and philosophical knowledge, providing insights into ancient civilizations and traditions. However, these texts frequently reference events, beliefs, practices, and concepts that are unfamiliar to modern readers. Without specialized knowledge or guidance, end users may struggle to interpret and contextualize the content, thus hindering their ability to grasp the full significance of the manuscripts.

These challenges arise due to the vast temporal and cultural distances separating modern readers from the contexts in which the manuscripts were produced. Historical events, religious rituals, cultural practices, and philosophical ideas may have evolved or become obsolete over time, making them difficult to interpret without proper background knowledge. Moreover, the symbolism, metaphorical language, and allegorical narratives commonly employed in these texts further complicate the interpretation process.

To address these challenges, interdisciplinary approaches are required, drawing upon expertise from fields such as history, religious studies, anthropology, linguistics, and philosophy. Scholars and researchers collaborate to unravel the layers of meaning embedded within the manuscripts, employing comparative analyses, historical contextualization, and linguistic interpretation to elucidate their significance. Additionally, digital humanities initiatives leverage technology to enhance accessibility and understanding, providing annotated translations, multimedia resources, and interactive platforms that facilitate engagement with the content.

By bridging the gap between past and present, these efforts enable modern readers to appreciate the richness and complexity of Indic manuscripts, fostering a deeper understanding of their cultural heritage and intellectual legacy. Through scholarly inquiry and interdisciplinary dialogue, the significance of these texts is illuminated, ensuring that their wisdom continues to inspire and enlighten generations to come.

19.3.5 Limited interactivity

Traditional methods of accessing manuscripts, whether through physical copies or digital scans, often lack the interactivity and engagement desired by end users. While these methods provide access to the content, they offer limited opportunities for deeper exploration and interaction. As a result, users may seek more immersive experiences that enable them to engage with the manuscripts in meaningful ways, delving into their intricacies and uncovering hidden insights.

In contrast to static formats, immersive technologies such as virtual reality (VR) and augmented reality (AR) offer transformative possibilities for manuscript exploration. Through VR environments, users can step into digital replicas of historical libraries or archives, where they can virtually handle manuscripts, turn pages, and examine details up close. AR overlays contextual information and interactive elements onto physical manuscripts, enriching the reading experience with multimedia content, annotations, and supplementary materials.

Moreover, interactive features such as clickable annotations, audiovisual presentations, and gamified learning experiences enhance user engagement and comprehension. By providing dynamic and multi-sensory interactions, these immersive technologies transform the way users interact with manuscripts, fostering deeper understanding, appreciation, and connection with the material. As technology continues to advance, the potential for immersive and interactive manuscript exploration will only grow, offering new avenues for scholarship, education, and cultural enrichment.

19.4 Solutions with metaverse for manuscripts

19.4.1 Virtual libraries and archives

Metaverse platforms have transformed the landscape of manuscript preservation by providing a digital sanctuary for Indic manuscripts. These platforms digitize and consolidate collections, ensuring that these invaluable artifacts are safeguarded for future generations. By transcending geographical boundaries and institutional limitations, virtual libraries and archives hosted on metaverse platforms grant unparalleled access to users worldwide. Through intuitive interfaces and advanced search functionalities, users can seamlessly navigate through vast repositories of digitized manuscripts, exploring the richness of ancient texts with unprecedented ease and convenience.

The architectural framework depicted in Figure 19.1 illustrates the sophisticated infrastructure that underpins these virtual libraries and archives. This framework encompasses robust storage systems, efficient indexing algorithms, and seamless user interfaces designed to optimize the exploration and retrieval of

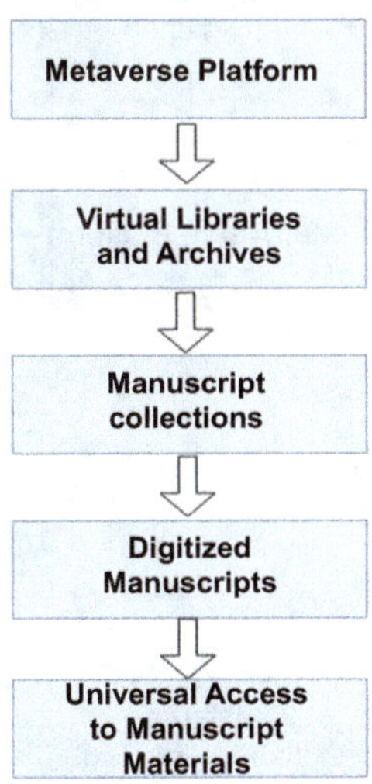

Figure 19.1 Proposed architecture for virtual libraries and archives

manuscript content. By leveraging cutting-edge technologies within the metaverse, such as deep learning and natural language processing (NLP), these platforms ensure that users can delve into the depths of Indic manuscripts with enhanced clarity and comprehension. Furthermore, collaborative features enable scholars, researchers, and enthusiasts to engage in collective efforts toward manuscript preservation and scholarly inquiry, fostering a vibrant ecosystem of knowledge exchange and collaboration within the digital realm.

19.4.2 Remote access and remote collaboration

Metaverse platforms serve as dynamic hubs for scholarly collaboration and engagement with Indic manuscripts, fostering a vibrant community of researchers, scholars, and enthusiasts worldwide. Through remote access features, users gain unprecedented flexibility to explore manuscript collections at their convenience, transcending barriers of time and space. The collaborative environment facilitated by metaverse platforms encourages interdisciplinary dialogue and knowledge sharing, enriching the study of Indic manuscripts with diverse perspectives and insights. Additionally, the integration of advanced technologies such as artificial intelligence and machine learning further enhances the analytical capabilities of these platforms, enabling users to conduct in-depth textual analysis, linguistic research, and contextual interpretation with unprecedented accuracy and efficiency. As a result, metaverse platforms represent a paradigm shift in the study and preservation of Indic manuscripts, democratizing access to cultural heritage and fostering a global community dedicated to unraveling the mysteries of ancient texts. Figure 19.2 depicts the metaverse platform for remote access and collaboration in manuscript collections.

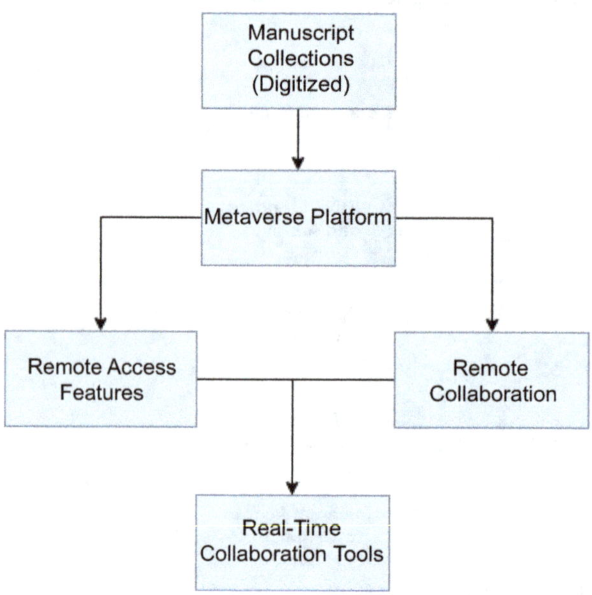

Figure 19.2 Proposed architecture for remote access and remote collaboration

19.4.3 Script recognition and transliteration

In the realm of metaverse platforms, cutting-edge technologies like deep learning are leveraged to tackle the intricate task of script recognition and transliteration in Indic manuscripts. These platforms deploy advanced algorithms, such as convolutional neural networks (CNNs) and recurrent neural networks (RNNs), to discern and interpret the diverse array of scripts found in manuscripts, ranging from Devanagari to Grantha and Bengali [29]. Once identified, NLP techniques are employed to seamlessly convert the script into English or other desired languages, ensuring accessibility for a wider audience.

Furthermore, metaverse platforms enhance user engagement and understanding through immersive visual narration features. These features enable users to explore transliterated manuscripts alongside visual annotations and explanations, providing a multi-dimensional understanding of the content. By integrating deep learning technologies, metaverse platforms bridge language barriers and democratize access to manuscript content, enriching the study and appreciation of ancient texts. Figure 19.3 illustrates the intricate process of script recognition and transliteration within the dynamic landscape of the metaverse, showcasing its transformative impact on manuscript exploration and interpretation.

19.4.4 Contextual analysis with Natural Language Processing (NLP)

Certainly, let us delve deeper into the significance of contextual analysis with NLP in the context of Indic manuscripts within the metaverse. The utilization of advanced NLP techniques within metaverse platforms signifies a profound shift in the way scholars and enthusiasts interact with ancient texts. By employing deep learning algorithms, these platforms can discern subtle linguistic nuances and historical references that might evade traditional modes of analysis. This process not only enhances comprehension but also opens avenues for new discoveries and interpretations.

Moreover, the integration of NLP-driven contextual analysis enhances the accessibility of Indic manuscripts to a wider audience. By extracting key information such as names, dates, and events, these platforms bridge the gap between modern readers and the intricate narratives of ancient texts. Users, regardless of their familiarity with the historical and cultural context, can now engage with Indic manuscripts in a more meaningful and enriching manner.

Furthermore, the insights gained from contextual analysis contribute to ongoing scholarly debates and research endeavors surrounding Indic manuscripts. By uncovering hidden connections and shedding light on obscure references, NLP-driven analysis fosters interdisciplinary collaboration and encourages deeper exploration into the diverse facets of ancient Indian civilization.

In summary, the incorporation of advanced NLP techniques within the metaverse represents a groundbreaking advancement in the study of Indic manuscripts. It not only democratizes access to ancient wisdom but also revitalizes scholarly

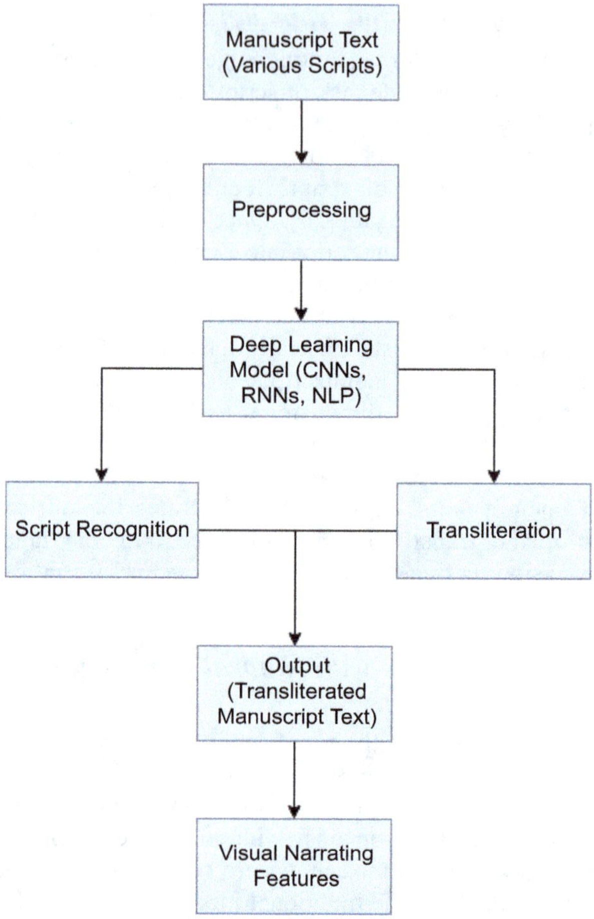

Figure 19.3 Proposed architecture for script recognition and transliteration

inquiry, paving the way for a more comprehensive understanding of India's rich cultural heritage. Figure 19.4 illustrates contextual analysis with natural language processing using the metaverse.

19.4.5 Augmented Reality (AR) interpretation guides

Metaverse platforms integrate AR interpretation guides that overlay contextual information and historical references directly onto the manuscript pages in real time. Deep learning algorithms recognize key entities and events mentioned in the manuscript and display contextual information, explanatory notes, and multimedia content as augmented overlays. Users can interact with these AR guides to access additional insights, explanations, and interpretations, enhancing their understanding of the manuscript's context.

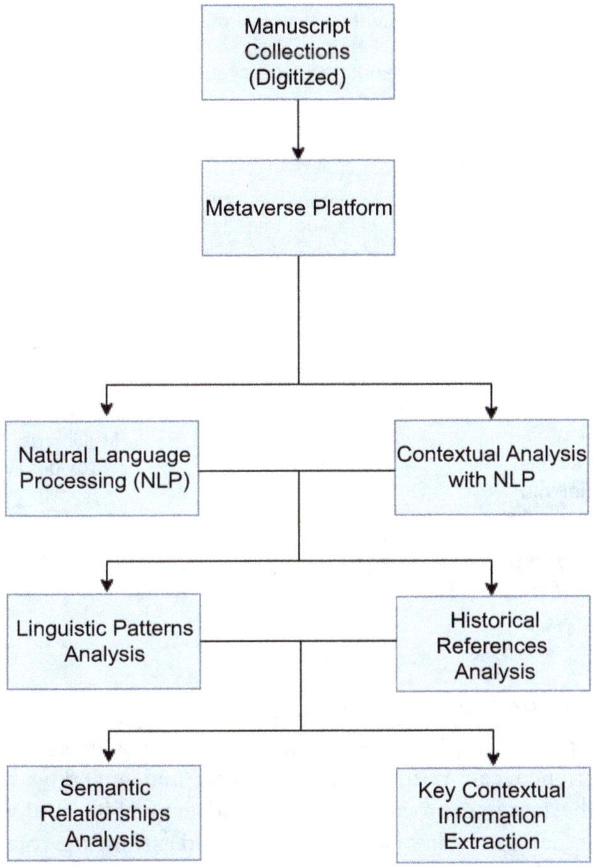

Figure 19.4 Proposed architecture for contextual analysis with Natural Language Processing (NLP)

Imagine being immersed in a virtual library where an AR avatar, resembling a scholarly sage, accompanies users on a journey through the intricacies of Sanskrit manuscripts. As users engage with the manuscript's pages, the avatar provides insightful commentary and explanations, enriched by AR visualizations. For example, while exploring a Sanskrit scripture describing a mythological tale, the avatar conjures lifelike depictions of celestial beings and divine realms, overlaid onto the manuscript's illustrations. Through interactive gestures, users can delve deeper into the narrative, zooming in on details or triggering supplementary AR annotations that elucidate cultural nuances and historical contexts. This immersive experience transcends traditional manuscript study, offering a dynamic and enlightening exploration of Indic heritage [30] within the digital realm of the metaverse. Figure 19.5 showcases the Augmented Reality (AR) interpretation guides, illustrating how contextual information and historical references are overlaid onto manuscript pages in real time.

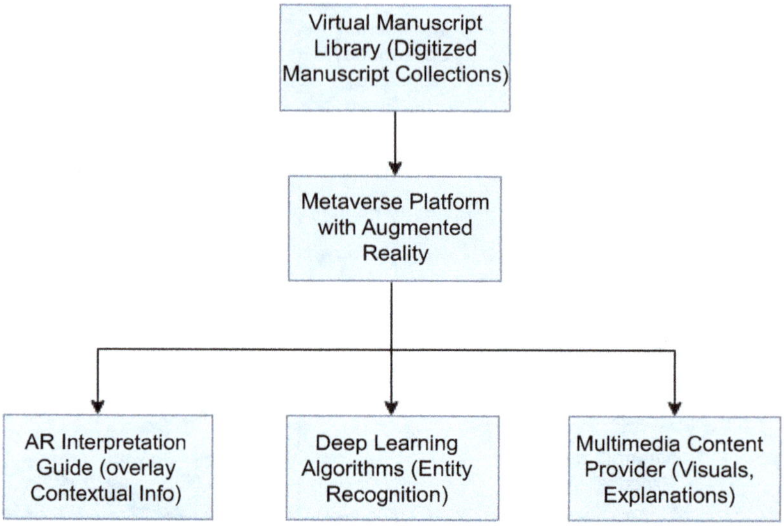

Figure 19.5 Proposed architecture for Augmented Reality (AR) interpretation guides

19.4.6 Historical role-play games

Integrating interactive games like historical Role-Play Games (RPGs) into the metaverse experience can further enhance users' understanding of manuscripts while making the learning process engaging and enjoyable. Within these RPGs, players immerse themselves in historical settings and assume the roles of characters from different epochs. As they navigate through virtual environments inspired by manuscript contents, they encounter challenges and puzzles that require them to apply their knowledge of the manuscripts.

For example, players may come across a virtual library within the metaverse where they must search for specific manuscripts. To progress in the game, they must correctly identify the author of a particular script, determine the timeline in which it was written, and recognize the script and language used in the manuscript. By answering these questions correctly, players unlock new clues, artifacts, or paths within the game, encouraging them to explore further and deepen their understanding of manuscript history. Through historical RPGs in the metaverse, users not only test their knowledge but also actively participate in the learning process, fostering a deeper connection with the material and promoting a sense of discovery and achievement. This gamified approach to manuscript exploration offers an innovative and immersive way to engage users of all ages in the rich cultural heritage preserved within these ancient texts. Figure 19.6 depicts the Historical Role-Play Games (RPGs), showcasing how users immerse themselves in historical settings and navigate through virtual environments inspired by manuscript contents.

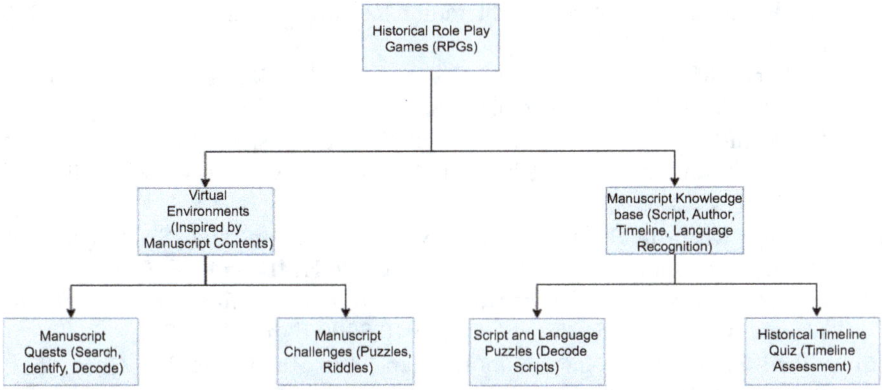

Figure 19.6 Proposed architecture for Historical Role-Play Games

19.5 Results

The integration of metaverse technology with advanced deep learning and AI techniques has revolutionized the study of ancient Indic manuscripts, offering innovative solutions to longstanding challenges. Through virtual libraries and archives, users now have unparalleled access to digitized manuscript collections, overcoming geographical barriers and institutional restrictions. Remote collaboration tools facilitate real-time interaction among scholars worldwide, fostering a vibrant community of manuscript enthusiasts.

Deep learning algorithms enable accurate script recognition and transliteration, making manuscript content comprehensible to a wider audience. NLP techniques extract key contextual information, providing deeper insights into the historical and cultural significance of the manuscripts. Augmented reality interpretation guides bring manuscript narratives to life, enhancing user engagement and understanding. Historical role-play games offer a gamified approach to manuscript exploration, encouraging active participation and deepening users' appreciation of manuscript history. Together, these innovations ensure that the rich cultural heritage preserved within Indic manuscripts remains accessible and cherished in the digital age.

References

[1] Abbas M. Al-Ghaili, Hairoladenan Kasim, Naif Mohammed Al-Hada, *et al.* "A Review of Metaverse's Definitions, Architecture, Applications, Challenges, Issues, Solutions, and Future Trends" *IEEE Access.* 2022, 10, 125835–125866.

[2] Muhammad Shoaib Farooq, Kashif Ishaq, Mahdia Shoaib, Adel Khelifi, and Zabihullah Atal "The Potential of Metaverse Fundamentals, Technologies, and

Applications: A Systematic Literature Review" *IEEE Access* doi:10.1109/ Access.2023.3338627.

[3] Stylianos Mystakidis "Metaverse" *Encyclopedia* 2022, 2, 486–497. https:// doi.org/10.3390/Encyclopedia2010031.

[4] Pınar Kurtunluoglu, Beste Akdik, and Enis Karaarslan, "Security of Virtual Reality Authentication Methods in Metaverse: An Overview" *arxiv*:2209. 06447v1.

[5] Jungho Kim, Leehwan Hwang, Soonchul Kwon and Seunghyun Lee "Change in Blink Rate in the Metaverse VR HMD and AR Glasses Environment" *International Journal of Environmental Research and Public Health* 2022, 19, 8551. https://doi.org/10.3390/ijerph19148551.

[6] Yihao Zhou, Xiao Xiao, Guorui Chen, Xun Zhao, and Jun Chen "Self-Powered Sensing Technologies for Human Metaverse Interfacing" *Joule* 2022, 6, 1368–1389.

[7] Dawei Yang, Mengting Sun, Jian Zhou, *et al.* "Expert Consensus on the 'Digital Human' of Metaverse in Medicine" 2588-9141/ 2023 The Authors. Publishing Services By Elsevier B.V. On Behalf of Keai Communications Co., Ltd. This Is an Open Access Article Under the Cc By-Nc-Nd License (http://Creativecommons.Org/Licenses/By-Nc-Nd/4.0/).

[8] Jovanović Aleksandar, and Aleksandar Milosavljević "Vortex Metaverse Platform for Gamified Collaborative Learning" *Electronics* 2022, 11, 317. https://doi.org/10.3390/Electronics11030317.

[9] Haihan Duan, Jiaye Li, Sizheng Fan, Zhonghao Lin, Xiao Wu, and Wei Cai "Metaverse for Social Good: A University Campus Prototype" *arxiv*:2108. 08985v1 [Cs.Mm] 20 Aug 2021.

[10] Ahmed Tlili, Ronghuai Huang, Boulus Shehata, *et al.* "Is Metaverse in Education a Blessing or a Curse: A Combined Content and Bibliometric Analysis" *Springer Open*. https://slejournal.springeropen.com/articles/10. 1186/S40561-022-00205-X.

[11] Lik-Hang Lee, Tristan Braud, Pengyuan Zhou, *et al.* "All One Needs to Know about Metaverse: A Complete Survey on Technological Singularity, Virtual Ecosystem, and Research Agenda" *arxiv:2110.05352v3* [Cs.Cy] 3 Nov 2021.

[12] Tzu-Chi Wua, B, Chien-Ta Bruce Ho "A Scoping Review of Metaverse in Emergency Medicine" *Australasian Emergency Care* 2023, 26(1), 75–83, https://doi.org/10.1016/J.Auec.2022.08.002.

[13] Ji-Eun Yu "Exploration of Educational Possibilities by Four Metaverse Types in Physical Education" *Technologies* 2022, 10(5), 104. https://doi.org/ 10.3390/technologies10050104.

[14] Selcen Ozturkcan "Service Innovation: Using Augmented Reality in the IKEA Place App" *Journal of Information Technology Teaching Cases* 2021, 11(1), 8–13.

[15] Mitra Pooyandeh, Ki-Jin Han, and Insoo Sohn "Cybersecurity in the AI-Based Metaverse: A Survey" Applied *Science* 2022, 12, 12993. https://doi. org/10.3390/App122412993.

[16] Yang-Wai Chow, Willy Susilo, Yannan Li, Nan Li, and Chau Nguyen "Visualization and Cybersecurity in the Metaverse: A Survey" *Journal of Imaging* 2023, 9, 11. https://doi.org/10.3390/Jimaging9010011.

[17] Jiayi Sun, Wensheng Gan, Han-Chieh Chao, Philip S. Yu "Metaverse: Survey, Applications, Security, and Opportunities" *arxiv*:2210.07990v1 [Cs.Db] 14 2022.

[18] Yun-Cheng Tsai "The Value Chain of Education Metaverse" *arxiv*:2211.05833v2 [Cs.Cy] 14 2022.

[19] Hong Lin, Shicheng Wan, Wensheng Gan, Jiahui Chen, and Han-Chieh Chao "Metaverse in Education: Vision, Opportunities, and Challenges" *arxiv*:2211.14951v1 [Cs.Cy] 27 2022.

[20] Senthil Kumar Jagatheesaperumala, Kashif Ahmadb, Ala Al-Fuqahac, and Junaid Qadir "Advancing Education Through Extended Reality and Internet of Everything Enabled Metaverses: Applications, Challenges, and Open Issues" *arxiv*:2207.01512v1 [Cs.Cy] 27 2022.

[21] Luca Petrigna, and Giuseppe Musumeci "The Metaverse: A New Challenge for the Healthcare System: A Scoping Review" *Journal of Functional Morphology and Kinesiology* 2022, 7, 63. https://doi.org/10.3390/Jfmk7030063

[22] Ishteyaaq Ahmad, Sonal Sharma, Rajesh Singh, Anita Gehlot, Neeraj Priyadarshi, and Bhekisipho Twala "MOOC 5.0: A Roadmap to the Future of Learning" *Sustainability* 2022, 14, 11199. https://doi.org/10.3390/Su141811199.

[23] Matteo Zallio, and P. John Clarkson "Designing the Metaverse: A Study on Inclusion, Diversity, Equity, Accessibility and Safety for Digital Immersive Environments" *Telematics and Informatics* 2022, 75, 101909, https://doi.org/10.1016/J.Tele.2022.101909.

[24] Saeed Banaeian Fara, Seyed Mojtaba Hosseini Bamakanb, Qiang Quc, and Qingshan Jiang "A Review of Non-Fungible Tokens Applications in the Real-World and Metaverse" *Procedia Computer Science* 2022, 214, 755–762, https://www.sciencedirect.com/science/article/pii/s1877050922019482.

[25] Zhihan Lv, Shuxuan Xie, Yuxi Li, M. Shamim Hossain, and Abdulmotaleb El Saddik "Building the Metaverse Using Digital Twins at All Scales, States, and Relations" *Virtual Reality & Intelligent Hardware* 2022, 4(6), 459–470, https://www.sciencedirect.com/science/article/pii/s2096579622000602.

[26] R. V. K. Mehta, and N. P. Challa, "Facilitating Enhanced User Access Through Palm-Leaf Manuscript Digitization — Challenges and Solutions," *2017 Second International Conference on Electrical, Computer and Communication Technologies (ICECCT)*, Coimbatore, India, 2017, pp. 1–4, doi:10.1109/ICECCT.2017.8117838.

[27] N. P. Challa, and R. V. K. Mehta, "Automatic Data Acquisition — A Major Challenge," *2017 Second International Conference on Electrical, Computer and Communication Technologies (ICECCT)*, Coimbatore, India, 2017, pp. 1–5, doi:10.1109/ICECCT.2017.8117839.

[28] C. V. S. Deepthi, and A. Seenu, "A Systematic Review on OCRs for Indic Documents & Manuscripts," *2022 International Conference on Data*

Science, Agents & Artificial Intelligence (ICDSAAI), Chennai, India, 2022, pp. 1–4, doi: 10.1109/ICDSAAI55433.2022.10028802.

[29] Duddela Sai Prashanth, R Vasanth Kumar Mehta, and Nagendra Panini Challa, "A Multi-purpose Dataset of Devanagari Script Comprising of Isolated Numerals and Vowels", *Data in Brief*, 2022, 40, 107723, https://doi.org/10.1016/j.dib.2021.107723.

[30] Nagendra Panini Challa, and R.Vasanth Kumar Mehta "Applications of Image Processing Techniques on Palm Leaf Manuscripts – A Survey", *Helix* 2017, 7(5), 2013–2017, doi:10.29042/2017-2013-2017.

The conclusion and the future of the metaverse

A metaverse environment typically represents a digital space populated by virtual representations of people, places, and things. The metaverse is a vast and interconnected universe of virtual worlds. The metaverse implications are tremendous. That is, the metaverse is not just for distributed gaming. It is much more than that. It empowers social interaction, B2B and B2C e-commerce, entertainment, education, and even how employees work. It represents the next generation of the internet. Today, social platforms are pervasive. Experts point out that the metaverse is the next version of present-day social platforms. The metaverse has the power to contribute to real-world business transformation immeasurably. In the future, many aspects of our lives may occur within the metaverse (An immersive, fully digital world accessed using headsets).

The enabling technologies of the metaverse

Digitization and digitalization technologies are enabling the journey towards metaverse system engineering. The Internet of Things (IoT) technologies (infinitesimal sensors and actuators, microcontrollers, stickers, RFID tags, bar codes, etc.) digitize every tangible object in our environments. With 5G, the next generation of cellular communication, and other communication technologies, all digitized entities become connected. These technologies enable high-speed, low-latency communication, allowing connected edge sensors and devices to find one another in the vicinity and with remote systems through direct or indirect networking. Edge devices generate massive multi-structured data when they interact and collaborate purposefully. Edge and cloud-native computing platforms are bound to play a stellar role. Microservices and event-driven architectures (MSA and EDA) in conjunction with DevOps practices and products, site reliability engineering (SRE), value stream management (VS), and platform engineering solutions are being pitched as the correct and relevant.

The most relevant technology for the metaverse's colossal success is artificial intelligence (AI). Web 3.0 (the decentralized web) is the most appropriate infrastructure for hosting and managing metaverse applications and services. Upended with cryptography algorithms, blockchain technology guarantees the tightest security for metaverse interaction and transaction data.

The role and responsibility of immersive technologies (virtual, augmented, mixed, and extended realities (VR/AR/MR/XR) are rising in the metaverse era. Digital twins are powerful approaches to simplify and speed up metaverse systems' setting up and sustenance. Advanced and artistic 3D modeling techniques and tools come in handy in establishing and evolving path-breaking metaverse systems.

The idea of generative AI is progressing fast and has laid down a stimulating foundation for envisaging sophisticated metaverse applications. Language models (large, small, and visual) are the most sought-after innovations for decisively empowering metaverse systems and environments. Thus, multimodal generative AI is a pivotal concept that ensures the desired success and unprecedented adoption of the metaverse paradigm. Precisely speaking, all the distinct improvisations being unearthed in the generative and creative AI space are to succulently and smartly impact the phenomenon of the metaverse.

Finally, the slow yet steady improvements in the quantum computing landscape are taking the metaverse to the next level. The forthcoming cellular communication (6G) is powering up the phenomenon of the metaverse significantly. Undoubtedly, the simulation and 3D modeling technologies and tools have laid down a pulsating platform for envisioning and engineering sophisticated metaverse systems across industry verticals. Multiple technologies are fusing well to set the path smooth towards the metaverse.

The metaverse use cases

The metaverse is rapidly evolving into a captivating world brimming with possibilities. Every object, character, and environment within the metaverse is constructed from 3D models. These models breathe life into the virtual world, allowing us to explore, interact, and build. The metaverse idea is penetrative and pervasive. Most industrial verticals are keenly exploring, experimenting, and expounding the breakthrough metaverse applications that are multi-faceted, resilient, business-critical, people-centric, user-friendly, and insights-driven.

Tending towards the industrial metaverse

With the implementation technologies continuously maturing and stabilizing, there will be a noteworthy movement from personal to industrial metaverse. One domain that started fully embracing the metaverse is engineering and manufacturing. There will be more talk on the industrial metaverse in the coming days. The metaverse is not just about technology, it is about people. It is about collaboration and community. For different industries, there may be different metaverse systems. A pundit and proponent in the metaverse field says that he envisions the industrial metaverse as a virtual world that is nearly indistinguishable from reality. The industrial metaverse can enable people to collaborate to address real-world challenges in real time.

The metaverse has the potential to revolutionize our everyday lives. It will empower customers to accelerate innovation, enhance sustainability, and adopt new technologies faster and at scale, leading to a profound transformation of entire industries and our everyday lives.

Generative AI in medical simulation and training creates lifelike virtual patients, facilitates communication practice, introduces dynamic scenarios, and offers real-time performance assessments—the widespread leverage of 3D technologies in medical applications, including therapy, training, and rehabilitation. Disruptive and transformative AR and VR technologies are critical in shaping versatile and robust medical systems. One famous use case is surgical guidance, where generative AI delivers real-time, data-driven support to surgeons, enhancing precision and reducing procedural errors. Additionally, it contributes to anatomical visualization within AR settings by generating intricate 3D models of organs and tissues, which can be overlaid onto a patient's body.

In VR, generative AI models contribute significantly to medical simulations, creating intricate 3D anatomical models vital for surgical training, anatomical exploration, and a comprehensive understanding of human anatomy. VR has been used recently in amputee rehabilitation, particularly for prosthetic hand training.

In summary, with the futuristic advancements being unveiled in computing, communication, perception, knowledge discovery and dissemination, and actuation fields, trendsetting metaverse systems will be designed, developed, deployed, and maintained.

Pethuru Raj PhD, SMIEEE
Vice President and Chief Architect
Edge AI Division, Reliance Jio Platforms Ltd.
Bangalore, India
https://peterindia.vercel.app/books
https://scholar.google.com/citations?user=MgMlqAwAAAAJ&hl=en&oi=ao

Index

www.ingramcontent.com/pod-product-compliance
Lightning Source LLC
LaVergne TN
LVHW011559200926
848484LV00001B/334
9781839538803